Rhetorical Delivery and Digita Technologies

"Like delivery itself, Sean Morey's book offers more than it suggests at first glance. Beneath its insightful readings of delivery/hyprokrisis in the classical tradition and its examinations of delivery's many meanings and possibilities in new media contexts, it delivers something else as well: a new style of reading and writing—indeed, a new method for rhetorical inquiry—specifically attuned to the medial logics of the digital age."

—Scot Barnett, Indiana University, USA

This book theorizes digital logics and applications for the rhetorical canon of delivery. Digital writing technologies invite a re-evaluation about what delivery can offer to rhetorical studies and writing practices. Sean Morey argues that what delivery provides is access to the unspeakable, unconscious elements of rhetoric, not primarily through emotion or feeling as is usually offered by previous studies, but affect, a domain of sensation implicit in the (overlooked) original Greek term for delivery, *hypokrisis*. Moreover, the primary means for delivering affect is both the logic and technology of a network, construed as modern, digital networks, but also networks of associations between humans and nonhuman objects. Casting delivery in this light offers new rhetorical trajectories that promote its incorporation into digital networked-bodies. Given its provocative and broad reframing of delivery, this book provides original, robust ways to understand rhetorical delivery not only through a lens of digital writing technologies, but all historical means of enacting delivery, offering implications that will ultimately affect how scholars of rhetoric will come to view not only the other canons of rhetoric, but rhetoric as a whole.

Sean Morey is an Assistant Professor of English at Clemson University where he teaches writing and digital media in the department of English. He is the author of *The New Media Writer* (Fountainhead Press, 2014) and co-edited the collection *Ecosee: Image, Rhetoric, Nature* (SUNY Press, 2009).

Routledge Studies in Rhetoric and Communication

Rhetorical Delivery and Digital Technologies

Networks, Affect, Electracy

Sean Morey

Routledge
Taylor & Francis Group

LONDON AND NEW YORK

First published 2016
by Routledge

2 Park Square, Milton Park, Abingdon, Oxfordshire OX14 4RN
711 Third Avenue, New York, NY 10017

Routledge is an imprint of the Taylor & Francis Group, an informa business

First issued in paperback 2017

Library of Congress Cataloging-in-Publication Data

Morey, Sean, 1979- author.
Rhetorical delivery and digital technologies: networks, affect, electracy / By Sean Morey.
  pages cm. — (Routledge Studies in Rhetoric and Communication; 27)
Includes bibliographical references and index. (alk. paper)
  1. Rhetoric—Data processing. 2. Rhetoric—Study and teaching.
  3. Literacy—Study and teaching. 4. Computers and literacy. I. Title.
P301.5.D37M67 2015
808.00285—dc23   2015030073

ISBN: 978-1-138-92544-1 (hbk)
ISBN: 978-0-8153-9636-9 (pbk)

Typeset in Sabon
by codeMantra

This one's for Aubrey, Sofia, and Fisher

Contents

Acknowledgements

This book was a product of seen and unseen relationships, too numerous and complex to fully acknowledge. These networks provided many types of feedback, motivation, and support; without which, this book would not have been conceived, or, at least not as it is here. To all of you within those networks, whether you realize your participation or not, my deepest thanks.

Of my local network, I'm grateful to my incredible current and former colleagues at Clemson University, who offer me a vibrant and forefront department in which to work. I'm lucky to be in the company of such colleagues, all of whom have helped make me a better scholar, and I hope, a better colleague. I want to acknowledge and thank Susanna Ashton, Amanda Booher, Cameron Bushnell, David Coombs, Jonathan Beecher Field, Gabriel Hankins, Cynthia Haynes, Susan Hilligoss, Jan Holmevik, Tharon Howard, Walt Hunter, Martin Jacobi, Steven Katz, Michael LeMahieu, Lee Morrissey, Angela Naimou, Barbara Ramirez, Elizabeth Rivlin, Lindsay Thomas, and Victor Vitanza. I'm especially grateful to Scot Barnett, David Blakesley, Erin Goss, Steve Holmes, Kimberly Manganelli, Brian McGrath, Aga Skrodzka-Bates, and Glen Southergill for, in different measures, your wisdom, partnerships, mentorships, and friendships.

I'm also grateful to the many students I've had the privilege of teaching at Clemson. Their willingness to experiment along with me in classes, testing pedagogies and technologies, has greatly informed many of the ideas in this book, even if the connections between their classroom experience and this research do not seem explicit to them (or sometimes myself).

I must also acknowledge Collin Brooke and Jeff Rice, whose works and suggestions have greatly impacted the nature and direction of this book.

I thank the Routledge Press reviewers who provided insightful feedback on the manuscript for this book. I also thank the entire editorial and production team at Routledge, with my sincerest appreciation to Felisa Salvago-Keyes and Andrew Weckenmann for their interest and dedication toward this project, and for helping usher it to publication.

Thanks to David Blakesley for granting permission to reprint my article "Becoming T@iled" in chapter 6 (From *Writing Posthumanism, Posthuman Writing* (c) 2015 by Parlor Press. Used by permission.), and to Sarah Hartwell for granting permission to print her illustration, also in chapter 6 (Sarah Hartwell/Messybeast.com).

Most of all, this book demands a debt of gratitude for two interrelated and inseparable networks of intellectual and personal support. To those who were there from the beginning of this project—Sid Dobrin, Raúl Sánchez, and Greg Ulmer—my sincerest thanks for your continued support, feedback, and enthusiasm. This book would not exist without you all. It would also not exist without John Tinnell, who taught me everything I know about augmented reality. I'm lucky to count this network as friends, and to extend this list to include Judd and Penny Wise, Nic Guest-Jelley, Aaron Beveridge, Nicholas Van Horn, Laurie Gries, Julie Drew, Joe Hardin, and Cathy Bester.

Finally, I thank all of my family in the Morey clan (especially Frank and Susan) and the Zaffke household (especially Karen and Matias) for their unconditional support, and Brittany Ubaldini and Danielle Tatro for their endless hours of dedication to both these families. Of nonhumans, there are also many, but I'll limit thanks to Dusty, Skye, Toss, Kip, and Milo. But I'm most grateful for the unwavering support (and prodding) from Aubrey, Sofia, and Fisher. Two of you were not here when this started, but I'm sure glad all of you are here now.

Introduction
The Rebirth of Delivery

Don't kill the messenger.

—Sophocles *et al.*[1]

This introduction's title is really a question, for I'm not convinced that delivery needs to be reborn, or should be reborn. The title suggests that I argue for a new age of delivery, a recovery of delivery from its ashes out of orality and literacy. I'm not sure that I do. The language apparatus of orality may be the only time delivery has really been born, as Aristotle attempted to kill a literate delivery before it had a chance to develop. Each subsequent millennium either continued traditions of oral delivery, tweaking them when necessary, or else changed the notion of delivery from one of bodily performance to a transitive exchange of objects. At best, then, delivery has had a series of stillbirths. In many ways, I'm calling for a death of delivery, a death of delivery tied to the separation of rhetorical canons, and a death of delivery tied to literate logic. That is, if there is a possibility for a rebirth of delivery, it is because conditions have changed, that an electrate apparatus has made delivery possible again.

As a concept originally born in classical Greece, delivery—in both orality and literacy—has traditionally received inadequate theoretical attention from scholars of rhetoric, beginning with Aristotle's reticence for the practice of delivery as a whole. Delivery fell out of prominent use as communication shifted from the medium of the body to the medium of writing (and eventually print). However, digital writing technologies—through which the body again becomes visible and telepresent—invite a reevaluation about what delivery can offer to rhetorical studies and writing practices. *Rhetorical Delivery and Digital Technologies: Networks, Affect, Electracy* argues that what delivery provides is access to the unconscious elements of rhetoric, not primarily through emotion or feeling as is usually offered by previous studies, but affect, a domain of sensation implicit in the (overlooked) original Greek term for delivery, *hypokrisis*. Moreover, the primary means for delivering affect is both the logic and technology of a network, construed as modern, digital networks, but also networks of associations between humans and nonhuman objects, what Gilles Deleuze and Félix Guattari might describe as desiring-machines (assemblages), or what Bruno

Latour might identify through actor-network-theory. Casting delivery in this light offers new rhetorical trajectories that promote its incorporation into digital networked-bodies.

As current studies about delivery have argued, most recently Ben McCorkle's *Rhetorical Delivery as Technological Discourse* (2012), such inattention to delivery made practical sense given that Aristotle was trying to invent rhetorical practices pertinent to the technology of an emerging literacy, foregrounding the features of writing and shifting the focus away from the technologies of the body. Our present situation is analogous to Aristotle's: a new language apparatus, electracy (as developed by Gregory L. Ulmer) is emerging, and new practices, or at least theories, should also emerge to make use of digital technologies. Ulmer defines electracy as being "to digital media what literacy is to print," the skill set necessary to use all of the communicative technologies of digital writing and media.[2] Metaphorically, electracy breaks from "digital literacy," as the latter term retrofits a prior logic (literacy) onto a new technology, a logic that was designed for an older technology (alphabetic writing). Thus, a concept of digital literacy closes off possible lines of inquiry that a new, native term and concept would allow to emerge. Likewise, with delivery, many scholars in rhetoric and composition studies—or even writing studies in general—attempt to fit digital technologies into the existing logic of literacy and rhetoric. However, Ulmer notes that because each language technology works within a unique language apparatus, many scholars of digital literacy are looking in the wrong places, from the wrong perspective, trying to retrofit the logics developed specifically for alphabetic writing toward a technology that uses hypertext, image, video, sound, and telepresence, all driven by the digital Internet. Many approaches to delivery confront the same problem as Aristotle, trying to theorize a delivery of digital technologies at the dead end of literacy instead of the birth of electracy; that is, such approaches look toward understanding how the visual and networked aspects of writing become aspects of existing paradigms of delivery, or how to retrofit new practices to old models rather than asking what new kinds of delivery electracy makes possible.

Thus, delivery keeps reaching dead ends. That is, whenever scholars take up a study of delivery, its intended usefulness is almost surely limited by its potential elsewhere. Aristotle struggled with this when he tried to reconcile the canon of delivery into his treatise on rhetoric; he found that even though delivery proved useful in an oral context, he developed little taste for delivery's practices since they often allowed orators with weaker arguments and faulty logic to win the approval of the audience simply by being better performers with their bodies, with many orators taking acting lessons as part of their training. As a result, Aristotle never did invent literate practices for delivery as he did for invention, style, or arrangement. Subsequently, the technology of literacy provided a different kind of application for delivery, mostly developing into what Collin Gifford Brooke might call a transitive mode of delivery in which delivery simply becomes a conduit for the trans-mission of information and little else.[3] Although scholars and teachers of rhetoric other than Aristotle did develop practices and pedagogies for delivery—most notably Cicero, Quintilian, and the elocutionary movement of the nineteenth century—these practices, again, focused on an oral deliv-ery of speeches, which, although using literacy in their development, did not use a literate-specific mode of delivery.

Delivery, within the context of an orator speaking before an assembly, makes several assumptions about how the technology of speech—and by extension, writing—functions. It often assumes a privileged speaker that has control of both the words and meaning of those words, and again, that those words have a representational element, that the speaker can transmit meaning through language. However, delivery extends and augments this control of meaning by relying on traits of communication that occur in face-to-face utterance. The words themselves are influenced by the body: how the body performs their production, but also the visual aspects that surround the performance of the words themselves, which deliver multiple tracks of "information." This kind of information, often unspeakable, uses an image-based information of the body—but also a body operating within a larger networked environment—becoming unavailable when the words in a speech are abstracted through their appearance on a page, devoid of the speaker's body. Through a network of environment, props, audience, and other elements and apparatuses, the body produces affective traits of a performative language that the technology and logic of literacy alone cannot accommodate, presenting difficulty for Aristotle as he considered a literate rhetoric for delivery.

Although we still have large assembly spaces for physical performances (concerts, sporting events, political speeches, or various ceremonies), most everyday groups gather through online assemblages via a variety of online platforms such as Facebook, Twitter, Second Life, Wikipedia, blogs, cha-trooms, and numerous other ways to join together online. Do to so, we form machinic assemblages and become digital cyborgs, as Donna Haraway and others suggest. As cognitive scientist Anthony Chemero explains, "The per-son and the various parts of their brain and the mouse and the monitor are so tightly intertwined that they're just one thing … The tool isn't separate from you. It's part of you."[4] If we are to deliver online, via the pathways of the Internet and other digital technologies, we need to understand how to construct delivery-machines that will allow us to take advantage of what this technology has to offer. If the tool is a part of us, we might find ways to let it think, or deliver, for us.

What delivery best delivers is not an information of literate logic, but affect produced by a larger network of associations between bodies, objects, and environments. This affect is not the same as feeling or emotion, which are learned responses (though these, too, are at play), but sensation, uncon-scious intensities. As a rhetorical canon, delivery contends with desires, providing an interface for affect to produce a particular kind of communication designed to solve problems. Should the Greeks attack Phillip of Macedonia? Should Socrates be put to death? How should we commemorate the 9/11 attacks? What should we do about climate change? These questions all revolve around desires: the desire for freedom and city-state protection; the desire to "protect our youths"; the desire to reinvent national values in the aftermath of a disaster; the desires around the metaphysics of physics. Most of these are conscious, communal desires. But delivery, in addition to providing a method of group invention toward identifying such desires and their solutions, also works with unconscious, invisible, unspeakable desires. Especially as understood in the Greek term *hypokrisis*, delivery uncovers these desires, revealing the unconscious moods that affect rhetoric. Delivery as a process makes knowledge, but it goes deeper, delivering self-knowledge related to these communal questions.

One of my own desires in this work is to consider delivery within the framework of electracy—a digital delivery that can account for and extend new identity and institutional formations that develop around the emerging technologies of the image and Internet. Although text has become hyper, our logic (at least for delivery) must become *hypo*. Desire works at the level of taste: a craving. Yet, desire often becomes blind to such cravings. It is not always clear what we want, or if what we want is in our best interest—yet this unconscious knowledge influences decision-making. Part of Ulmer's work in electracy tries to create a new kind of public policy formation, one that includes not only expert opinions, but also the state of mind of both individuals and collectives as they make political choices. If we are to overcome the possible general accident that Paul Virilio claims is inevitable,[5] and if we are to maintain a democracy within a society of the spectacle, then new, electrate practices and theories of decision-making are necessary. Because delivery, in myriad manifestations (at least, so it seems), plays such a large part in this spectacle (if the medium, what some reduce delivery to, is the message), then an electrate delivery becomes a crucial practice toward such decision-making. The question this project takes up, then, is to ask how delivery might be invented or useful for electracy, moving along a different path that hopefully does not end before it begins. This project does not necessarily attempt to answer that question outright, undertake the task of creating a set of practices, or even offer an argument of proof. Instead, it speculatively asks questions of delivery and suggests some possibilities that might be useful for others on that path.

With this history in mind, and the potential of an electrate delivery as an agenda, *Rhetorical Delivery and Digital Technologies* does not attempt to recover the canon of delivery as it existed before and during the development of literacy, at another dead end, but at a beginning of digital technologies in order to invent delivery practices specifically for electracy. Toward such invention, *Rhetorical Delivery and Digital Technologies* re-theorizes the very idea of delivery as a rhetorical concept, demonstrating why it necessarily failed to gain traction within literacy in the first place, and using such failure as a navigational aid to avoid further failures within the present situation in which communication happens digitally, in print, images, video, sound, networks, code, and at the speed of light.

As described above, *Rhetorical Delivery and Digital Technologies* enters a conversation about delivery that begins in starts and stops. Most of this punctuation occurs because of changes in technologies that affect conversations about delivery. For instance, in his article "*Actio*: A Rhetoric of Written Delivery," Robert Connors tries to equate only the final written product as the essence of delivery (what Collin Brooke identifies as transitive delivery), and organizational devices such as the use of headers and typeface as tools of delivery. While he is correct in saying that "Contemporary *actio* is concerned with learning to use effectively the instruments that are being put into our hands," his conception of "instruments," and perhaps even "hands," needs broadening.[6] And while John Trimbur, in "Composition and the Circulation of Writing," makes a cogent argument that understands delivery within the Marxist idea of circulation, this "tool" use and circulation operate mainly under literate practices developed out of the invention of the printing press, not the digital Internet.[7]

Recently, several important articles have attempted to re-start conversations about delivery in relation to digital technologies. James Porter, in "Recovering Delivery for Digital Rhetoric," argues for a delivery that accounts for a five-part framework of 1) body/identity; 2) distribution/ circulation; 3) access/accessibility; 4) interaction; and 5) economics, marking a significant contribution in delivery studies.[8] Jim Ridolfo and Dànielle Nicole DeVoss also offer a significant strategy for digital delivery in their concept of "rhetorical velocity ... the strategic theorizing for how a text might be recomposed (and *why* it might be recomposed) by third parties, and how this recomposing may be useful or not to the short- or long-term rhetorical objectives of the rhetorician."[9] This concept starts to push delivery beyond the role of a single actor into a larger acting network. However, despite this uptick in attention to delivery, few full-length monographs have been devoted to it, appearing infrequently every several years and trying to contend with new understandings of delivery as rhetorical technologies and strategies change. Since Kathleen Welch's 1999 work *Electric Rhetoric*, due to the rapid increase of digital technologies such as the World Wide Web, social media platforms, and mobile Internet technologies, new conversations have begun to emerge. However, such conversations are nascent and hardly represent the full scope of theories about delivery that need inventing and exploring.

John Frederick Reynold's 1993 collection *Rhetorical Memory and Delivery* focuses on updating the classical conversations of memory and delivery for current use. This work takes a transhistorical perspective, looking at how classical and contemporary periods might inform each other. Composed of eleven contributions, only four contributions focus directly on delivery, and so delivery receives limited attention even in a collection dedicated to showing the importance of these two canons. Some of the contributors (Winifred Bryan Horner, Kathleen Welch, Jay David Bolter) note the importance that electronic technologies might play in thinking about delivery; however, this book also appears before wide-spread use of the Internet and so misses the opportunity to approach delivery from a digital perspective. Most of the discussion of the "electronic" focuses on Walter Ong's conception of secondary orality and the effect of radio and television on delivery, and so also misses Ulmer's important development of electracy as a more sophisticated theory about electronic communication technologies. However, Reynolds's collection was an important rethinking of delivery for its time, demonstrating the desire to keep delivery in the consciousness of rhetoric and writing studies even if few scholars devote much sustained effort to its theorization.

Kathleen Welch's *Electric Rhetoric* picks up where her article in Reynolds's collection leaves off. However, although her article in *Rhetorical Memory and Delivery* focuses predominantly on delivery, her monograph explores other aspects of rhetoric and so dilutes this initial concentration. Only in her chapter "Technologies of Electric Rhetoric" does she specifically address delivery, framing delivery as it manifests in electronic technologies through new mediums and design elements. In other words, she doesn't attempt to develop a theory of delivery so much as offer some possibilities for investigation and further work. As in Reynolds's collection, Welch still focuses on electric rhetoric through the lens of "secondary orality," but she also mentions Ulmer's work (prior to his invention of electracy), and so begins a conversation of bringing delivery into more complex discussions of digital rhetorics that would develop soon after (and partly from) *Electric Rhetoric*.

More recent books have reaffirmed the field's on-going interest in scholarship about delivery, such as Ben McCorkle's 2012 book *Rhetorical Delivery as Technological Discourse*.[10] This work picks up classical conversations of delivery and updates those begun by John Trimbur and Robert Connors. Other works consider delivery in terms of complex, networked theorizations of delivery, such as Collin Brooke's 2009 *Lingua Fracta*,[11] as well as Lindal Buchanan's 2005 work that investigates gender and delivery in antebellum America.[12] Although none of these works directly reference the work before it, in total these three volumes have begun to renew the conversations about delivery. These books offer evidence of the continuing call for investigation about delivery.

Winner of the 2010 Computers and Composition best book award, Brooke's *Lingua Fracta* is a remarkable study of how we have come to understand new media technologies by way of entrenched rhetorical methods. Ultimately, what Brooke argues is that we cannot rely upon these methods to understand new media technologies. In order to develop a rhetoric of new media, Brooke shows how close attention to "ecologies of practice" and examination of technological interfaces rather than specific texts might lead to developing new media rhetorics.[13] What is fascinating about Brooke's argument is his detailed development of what "ecologies of practices" might look like, showing how rhetoric's *trivium* might be rethought as layered ecologies. Using transdisciplinary media ecology as the foundation for his ecology, Brooke establishes a close connection between media studies and rhetorical studies.

Although limited to one chapter in the book, Brooke's *Lingua Fracta* provides two important points of departure for considering delivery within a new media (or digital media) context: first, it methodically introduces the use and possibility of established media ecology research that undergirds the method of inquiry in *Rhetorical Delivery and Digital Technologies*. Second, it uses this methodology to offer a new understanding of the rhetorical canons, showing how they might be re-theorized individually and collectively within larger ecologies of media. As it revisits ancient rhetorical terms toward new practices, Brooke's work also reestablishes the continued importance and acceptance of these terms to the field of rhetoric, even as the field attempts to refashion them.

Besides *Lingua Fracta* and *Rhetorical Delivery as Technological Discourse*, Lindal Buchanan's work is one of the few monographs devoted exclusively to delivery. In *Regendering Delivery: The Fifth Canon and Antebellum Women Rhetors*, Buchanan looks at the ways that antebellum women rhetors made use of different strategies and techniques to deliver their message on the public stage. In addition to considering the traditional elements of delivery, such as voice and gesture, Buchanan examines the larger social forces that affected how these women effectively delivered speeches as they were often encumbered by social and material limitations, such as their other expected roles as wives and mothers. According to Buchanan, delivery has ignored these larger social questions that affect who has the ability to speak in public settings, and she argues that studies of delivery have been too narrowly restrained by a few false assumptions and oversights: rhetors are mostly male, privileged, and authorized to speak publicly; delivery is chiefly concerned with vocal and physical presentation; delivery is defined according to corporeal terms; social context has little role in understanding delivery.

Although Buchanan looks particularly at antebellum women orators, she makes a few key theoretical insights that help inform *Rhetorical Delivery and Digital Technologies*, which in turn continues her conversation about delivery outside of this historical period. Buchanan shows how women rhetors during this period relied on unseen, backstage networks of support in order to gain entrance to the stage, suggesting that delivery is a more social and collaborative activity than initially perceived. When viewed through this lens, such unseen networks appear in other historical contexts—toward the future in our own digital networks, but also to past networks composed of both humans and machines, such as the many contraptions that the Greek orator Demosthenes assembled for practicing delivery. Blockages to these networks affect the ability of women rhetors to reach the stage at all, and we can see how such network blockages can affect delivery for both digital rhetors as well as ancient orators. *Rhetorical Delivery and Digital Technologies* doesn't directly take up questions of gender, but builds upon *Regendering Delivery* by shifting toward a transhistorical framework of delivery at a more abstract level, hopefully implicitly extending some of Buchanan's theoretical insights to contemporary women rhetors.

The most recent treatment on delivery, Ben McCorkle's book *Rhetorical Delivery as Technological Discourse* makes the argument that rhetorical delivery provides a practice for new technologies to become integrated into a society and become naturalized and comfortable. For example, the use of writing by Plato in his dialogues or the use of writing to craft orally delivered speeches provided a safe place for writing to be used, making it appear that writing was subordinated to traditional oral practices. McCorkle's book posits that such subordination made writing more acceptable and less frightening to those civilizations that encountered it. Or, by reading this transition through Jay David Bolter and Richard Grusin's concept of remediation, such symbiosis between delivery and technology, and the remediation of one form of delivery into another, repeats with each new writing technology, from the printing press to computers. McCorkle's work also renews conversations started by John Trimbur and Robert Connors that have argued that textual features found in print and made more accessible through word processors—typeface, color, layout, graphics, hypertext—also contribute to a written text's delivery.

In many ways, *Rhetorical Delivery as Technological Discourse* mirrors *Rhetorical Delivery and Digital Technologies*. Both employ a transhistorical look at how delivery has been considered, examine the ways that delivery relies on technology, and discuss how delivery fits into rhetorics of digital media. However, while *Rhetorical Delivery as Technological Discourse* mostly focuses on the ways that delivery as a practice has helped to make writing and rhetorical technologies more "natural" to a specific culture or society (writing for the Greeks, the printing press for medieval Europe), *Rhetorical Delivery and Digital Technologies* focuses on the logics of those technologies as used and developed by rhetors as an attempt to theorize delivery more broadly and specifically within current writing technologies.

Although none of his works are on rhetorical delivery as such, the most prolific theorist of a contemporary, electrate delivery has been Marshall McLuhan. While many critics point out the problems of his prognostications, McLuhan offers important insights into how we might consider delivery in digital environments. Although one can certainly make the case that his famous phrase "the medium is the message"[14] can support a particular notion of delivery as embedded in the technologies that make delivery possible (that is, that the medium is the message about how delivery occurs), his more important contribution is situating electronic media as "extensions," theorizing not only a hybrid, cyborg body, but a cybernetic one, offering that one's central nervous system extends across the electronic grid, what we might now identify as the digital network.[15] So although *Rhetorical Delivery and Digital Technologies* is indebted to all of these works, and hopefully builds on them, it most relies on theories and methodologies from media studies in order to explore delivery, and this study grounds its investigation in grammatology and the emergence of electracy.

To make the necessary transdisciplinary moves, building a concept of delivery beyond treatments traditionally made by rhetorical studies, this book investigates delivery not only through the lens of electracy, but also with electrate or networked methodologies, particularly chorography grounded in a grammatological perspective. As an applied methodology developed from Jacques Derrida's theoretical grammatology, this method reads texts against themselves so that new meanings or lines of inquiry might emerge. Partly focused on terminology and metaphors, grammatology allows us to "decompose or unfold and redirect the possibilities of meaning inherent in the material,"[16] whereas chorography requires gathering at the level of repeating signifiers toward "the recognition and formation of a pattern."[17] As I explore delivery, mapping its relationships across identities, classical rhetorical histories, and classical concepts, I do so to expand these traditional ideas about delivery to offer new possibilities. In contrast to *topos*, which "collects entities into universal homogenous sets based on shared essences, necessary attributes,"[18] chora "gathers singular ephemeral sets of heterogeneous items based on associations of accidental details. Yet chora paradoxically becomes categorical (general) through the aesthetic evocation of an atmosphere by means of these details."[19] My approach here also uses Ulmer's conduction—a fourth mode of inference used by grammatology to build concept formation through the homonymic principle (what Ulmer calls the "puncept").[20] This means of networking juxtaposes unrelated topics or concepts such as definitions, anecdotes, sports, media, and theory, organizing their relationships through the connections that emerge between them. Sometimes this is done simply by the shared term "delivery" that stretches across many domains, but sometimes through other concepts related to but little discussed about delivery, such as the tools and logics that drive these different delivery acts. Ultimately, I find that delivery is central to electracy, and that the methods of electrate invention can help develop other theories of delivery within rhetoric (and other disciplines) that have been neglected, abandoned, or overlooked.

Of course, this method and treatment of delivery also overlooks and is filled with blind spots. Since this work isn't significantly tied to any specific digital technology (i.e., particular mobile devices, wearable computing, software, etc.), it takes no in-depth account of how such particular technologies might function as delivery devices, although I do touch on augmented reality in chapter 5, and more work should be done related to individual devices. However, the bigger limitation in this book is how access to delivery changes depending on gender, race, ethnicity, social issues, cultural norms, socioeconomic status, and other factors that, as Buchanan has argued, can philosophically and materially limit who can participate in delivery.

Given that this work asks about the integration of humans with machines to facilitate delivery, a major omission in this study is a critique of the perfectly abled body, one that can interact with people, environments, and technology in traditional, expected ways. Such expectations rely upon an ableist perspective; as Fiona Kumari Campbell argues, ableism "characterises impairment or disability ... as inherently negative."[21] At the risk of applying a modern concept to past culture, this expectation and attitude was surely held by classical orators, for Demosthenes had to overcome his own physical "disabilities" in order to become an effective deliverer for his time. However, a more probing treatment would ask questions of multi-sensory appeals, the extent to which some differently abled bodies can perform necessary gestures, and to what extent a particular body can construct and engage with machines of delivery. For instance, Sushil K. Oswal points out that "From a digital technology viewpoint, ableist assumptions are inherent in all the producer-based accessibility standards,"[22] and argues about interface, the point of contact where delivery occurs, that "In the context of technology and systems, accessibility at the interface level, not as a retrofit or add-on, is true accessibility; all other options are fixes and are intrinsically inferior to the primary access available to the able-bodied because such an access sets the disabled apart in a separate category."[23] It could be that such integration can help differently abled bodies deliver when and where they couldn't before. But, of course, we must also look at the very ideologies of ableness and the impression that differently abled bodies need to be augmented with technologies in the first place. As Amanda K. Booher states, "We expect technology to improve our lives in particular ways; if we assume, consciously or not, that disabled bodies need improvement, technological innovation presents an obvious—and very positive!—answer. But again, technological enthusiasm must be balanced with awareness of our ableist assumptions."[24] Although I try to touch on these issues (and this book, no doubt, makes many ableist assumptions that will need critique), I call on those who are expert in rhetoric and body studies to take a deeper look at these interconnections.

Rhetorical Delivery and Digital Technologies is divided into three major parts. Although the entire book asks the question, "What is Delivery?," Part I focuses more specifically on this question by looking at the cluster of ways that delivery has been explored, considered, and defined, and offers some definitions that have been overlooked in relation to rhetorical delivery. I do not claim that this book presents a resolution to this question, but instead primarily seeks to complicate the traditional questions posed about traditional definitions of delivery. Chapter 1 starts this process by declassifying delivery, mainly by asking this question of "what is," a question that seems hardly to be asked when investigating delivery. Usually a basic assumption is made that links delivery to a classical construction, a definition through which current theorizations are made, attempting to extend the definition into modern writing technologies and practices. Or, this assumption is only briefly investigated or referenced to provide a foundation for considering delivery within a context of current communications technologies. Such posturing then shifts to focus on the technology more than the rhetorical logic of what delivery actually attempts to accomplish with the technology. Thus, a turn toward delivery is usually a cursory move through and beyond delivery aimed at what Raúl Sánchez identifies as a "something else."[25] This "something else" is analyzed through delivery, but it is not delivery, which has never undergone a rigorous investigation into what it is and how it might work. That is, if delivery has an essence, what is it? Although no chapter or book can fully answer such a question, chapter 1 investigates this question through a variety of examples and methods, including historical, philological, and rhetorical analyses, but mostly thorough Ulmer's practice of chorography to see what a sifting of "delivery" can reveal about its use in digital approaches to rhetoric.

The next chapter revisits classical terminology related to delivery and attempts to re-classify how we have come to understand delivery and its historical trajectory. By tracing the threads that link the many ways rhetorical studies have come to practice, teach, and name delivery, a common logic emerges in the original ancient Greek term, *hypokrisis*. While this name for delivery meant "acting" in the vernacular, *hypokrisis* has an etymological depth that reveals a much more sophisticated idea of delivery that is concealed by most translations of the term. Broken down, *hypokrisis* means not just acting, but a judgment (*krinein*) that occurs below (*hypo*). *Hypokrisis* is a mode of rhetoric that occurs beneath judgment, in the unconscious. Defined this way, delivery (as *hypokrisis*) provides a spirit of delivery that allows us to understand "what" delivery "is" across its many iterations and through all of its other names, such as *actio, pronuntiatio*, elocution, performance, and delivery itself. Having gone back to *hypokrisis*, and now carrying the term forward into an electrate moment, I offer that the *hypokritical* logic of delivery persists from classical theories into current delivery practices, building a network of links that connect its traditions. This reclassification doesn't claim that delivery works identically everywhere all the time, either throughout rhetorical history or even currently, but that certain patterns of delivery continue to surface, or rather lurk below, which inform how we might understand what we mean when we write about this canon.

Part II shifts from specific terminology to what a digital deliverer might look like, what kind of logics she might employ in order to deliver. Toward these questions, chapter 3 explores why and how delivery works and posits that delivery requires assemblages to develop affective networks. Most often the praise and blame given to delivery originates from its effect on the audience's emotions; logical arguments being equal, the more impassioned or emotionally attuned delivery will succeed in persuasion, and logical arguments being unequal, the better delivery still often wins out.

However, a reduction of delivery to emotion, or even feeling, misdiagnoses the most powerful register on which delivery works, affect. Delivery works best not when appealing to the conscious, learned phenomena of emotions and feelings, but of the sensations of affect. Or, delivery has to work on these three levels simultaneously. Of course, affect in contemporary contexts is no longer delivered by the speaker alone, but through larger, more complex assemblages of human and machine, whether these machines are older ones (language and writing), or more modern (print, hypertext, video, networks). In *Anti-Oedipus* and *A Thousand Plateaus*, Gilles Deleuze and Félix Guattari provide a model for affective linking via the schizophrenic's logic of coupling desiring-machines (assemblages) to the Body without Organs.[26] Delivery makes connections between desiring-machines by constructing delivery-machines (a specialized form of the desiring-machine) to reveal the collective "dumbness" of the group's body. Moreover, delivery allows the rhetor to deliver this desire, creating intensities in the Body without Organs—making an audience develop the organs it needs to feel the unspeakable effects of the "speaker." Delivery-machines—hybrid/cyborg relationships—create new ways of enframing necessary for an electrate body to deliver. The schizophrenic logic provides a relay for how a digital deliverer might create her or his own desiring-machines in order to reach the level of unconsciousness native to delivery (as *hypokrisis*). If the schizophrenic's goal though desiring-machines is to create desire, then an electrate, digital deliverer uses delivery-machines to deliver desire to the schizophrenic group. Through a logic of affect developed by Deleuze and Guattari and furthered by Brian Massumi and others, chapter 3 offers a logic of sensation through which delivery has primarily functioned, providing a model for how it might work within electracy.

The next chapter continues this discussion, but suggests a different model for who delivers. If the Greek orator Demosthenes is the historical archetype for an oral deliverer, who, or what, is the ideal figure for an electrate deliverer? In other words, how might we envision a digital Demosthenes? This chapter explores this question and offers that instead of the classical orator we might look at another public figure, the shaman. Traditionally, shamans undertake a similar role in the community to that of an orator, but offer a practice of *hypokrisis* more applicable to electracy. Although one myth of delivery often portrays an individual communicating information to another or many others, delivery can be thought of as a larger ecological process whereby a collective group invention is facilitated with the shaman as medium. In this context, the rhetor no longer becomes the originator of the message, but the mediator (as Bruno Latour might describe though actor-network-theory), a node in a network, fulfilling a shamanic function between the unseen affects and desires of a community and their realization. As many media scholars have argued, especially McLuhan and Ulmer, the image-based network society that we inhabit actually inhabits us, and this environment is analogous to the spirit world that the shaman navigated on behalf of a community in many non-Western oral societies. The shaman serves as an intermediary between multiple worlds, providing his or her community with practical reason, making them aware of the intersection of the invisible and visible worlds, where the problems lie, and what solutions may be taken. This function resembles the classical portrayal of the deliverer who must also become an intermediary between two worlds: the possible, deliberative world, and the current contingent world in which he or she makes an argument, all part of a larger process striving toward practical solutions to problems. Moreover, the shaman, like the schizophrenic and often diagnosed as schizophrenic, joins with machines in order to produce her own networked delivery-system; the shaman invents and constructs delivery-machines. This shamanic metaphysics provides a relay for an image-based society where, as W. J. T. Mitchell argues, we grant to images (often unconsciously) similar characteristics to the spirits that shamans had to befriend, confront, attack, and make use of. One of the first steps toward becoming a digital deliverer is becoming a digital shaman, one who can foster an interaction in which the audience and shaman-rhetor co-deliver (invent) a solution to their shared, unconscious problems.

Part III begins to look at digital technologies more specifically, particularly network technologies. A deliverer assembles with objects to become a delivery-machine, but a more accurate description of the kind of machine they produce is a delivery-network. Whereas networks certainly function as a technology of current delivery, chapter 5 explores how delivery often relies not just on technological networks, but other kinds of networks, so that a larger network epistemology becomes inherent and necessary to understanding the functions of delivery no matter the technology. In a larger sense, then, this chapter discusses the role of machines in performing the rhetorical act of delivery, arguing that the most basic technology of delivery has historically been networks. For instance, although existing in different technological formations than contemporary computer-based networks, networks were required of ancient Greeks to successfully enact delivery, and as Buchanan has shown, was required of nineteenth-century women orators to reach the podium at all. Thus, this chapter considers the network in specific ways beyond just a digital technology, relying on Jeff Rice's conception of network as requiring a "very many" that is in motion. Networks are not just flows of digital information, but also connections of associative psychic and affective sensations as he explores in *Digital Detroit*.[27] Moreover, as Steven Jones has argued, digital networks are increasingly everting, moving out of servers and displays into everyday objects and environments, creating new conditions for which to consider delivery. By examining various forms of networks that have historically aided delivery—from ancient Greece to present day—chapter 5 argues that such comparisons can teach us how contemporary networks allow delivery to occur in ways that extend beyond the invisible (and even visible) understandings of "network" that commonly circulate in contemporary rhetorical theory.

Through this integration of deliverer and machine into network, the deliverer is no longer human, but posthuman. For an augmented, enhanced being, traditional aspects of delivery such as tone, gesture, clothing, facial expressions, and the other elements assume new meanings, implications, and positions. Moreover, as McLuhan might argue, these "extensions" expand not our bodies *per se*, but our central nervous system, enhancing both the range of one's abilities to deliver across networks and the audience's ability to participate in the delivery process. One of these extensions is a reintegration of our latent tails, performed through a logic of the @ symbol. A posthuman Demosthenes delivering with a t@il, within an invisible space and with an invisible audience, one that he cannot speak to, complicates how delivery occurs—how affect might be delivered in hyper-complex networks of circulation. Gestures, tonality, and expression can now be made not just with the body alone, not just with machines that are immediately present, but with a range of tele-technologies and tele-media. Moreover, the posthuman must also contend with the nonhuman, such as Web robots and posthuman audiences. Toward such configurations, chapter 6 extends the discussion from chapters 3 and 4 and investigates those who best represent potential models for posthuman delivery, specifically artists such as Eduardo Kac who create artworks through which digital delivery-networks might be designed. As an artist who makes "gestures," Kac constructs delivery-machines, providing new networked relationships that question what a gesture means within delivery. Kac uses digital media installations to gesture toward both the invisible spirits with which he integrates, and an audience who is unconscious to such forces. In this role, Kac serves as a shamanic mediator between the two realms. But just as the deliverer is different, so is the audience, and so this chapter also considers the audience as the target of delivery. While classical notions of delivery involve an orator addressing a crowd, usually arranged in a structure made for such gatherings, an electrate delivery requires not only the audience to gather around the deliverer, but also the deliverer to gather around the audience. The delivery-machine of the deliverer does not just stop with his or her integration with digital technologies, but extends to the audience as well within/throughout a rhizomatic structure. Digital delivery requires not just a performance of the deliverer, but requires the audience to also perform and take a role in the delivery process.

The postscript observes the relationship between delivery and death, which have always gone together, from cradle to grave, but also in pleas of "don't kill the messenger" and in Pheidippides's heroic run from Marathon to Athens to inform the city of a Greek victory over the Persians, a run that ended with him collapsing to his death. Of course, many other examples exist, from Hamlet's trickery to have his deliverers Rosencrantz and Guildenstern put to death instead of himself, to the modern bicycle courier who risks his or her life pedaling through the city. Delivery is dangerous, even for those who do it in a safe environment, for if the wrong tune is struck with an audience, disaster can occur. Thus, failure to deliver has consequences. One of the ways that we deliver acceptable information about death is through the process of monumentality. Monuments provide an official, approved way to consider death, linking death to the values that a society recognizes and shares. Using the work of Ulmer's *Electronic Monuments*, this chapter will propose that Ulmer has already established a model for electrate delivery even though he frames his work in terms of invention and memory. Toward this mixing of canons, this chapter will also theorize the death of delivery and re-question the usefulness of the canons as a whole even though *Rhetorical Delivery and Digital Technologies* seeks to rethink delivery as a canon within a contemporary digital environment. While delivery as the fifth and last canon connotes an end to writing, a telos, the death of a process, this death is merely a transition toward another rhetorical beginning: delivery precedes invention, even if it appears to come last. By offering a death of delivery and a delivery of death, this chapter will suggest further questions about this canon's role in the future (and history) of rhetoric.

Notes

1. Although Sophocles was perhaps the first to express this idea in writing (*Antigone*, 276–277), the theme and plea were most likely prevalent before this work, and continues to be.
2. Gregory L. Ulmer, *Internet Invention: From Literacy to Electracy* (New York: Longman, 2002), xii.
3. See Collin Gifford Brooke, *Lingua Fracta: Towards a Rhetoric of New Media* (Creskill, NJ: Hampton Press, 2009).
4. From an interview with Brandon Keim, "Your Computer is a Part of You," *Wired*, March 9, 2010, accessed July 18, 2015, http://www.wired.com/2010/03/heidegger-tools/; also, see Dobromir G. Dotov, Lin Nie, and Anthony Chemero, "A Demonstration of the Transition from Ready-to-Hand to Unready-to-Hand," *PLoS ONE* 5.3 (2010): doi: 10.1371/journal.pone.0009433.
5. See Paul Virilio, *Politics of the Very Worst* (Cambridge, MA: MIT Press, 1999).
6. Robert J. Connors, "*Actio*: A Rhetoric of Written Delivery (Iteration Two*)," in *Rhetorical Memory and Delivery: Classical Concepts for Contemporary Composition and Communication*, ed. John Frederick Reynolds (Mahwah, NJ: Lawrence Erlbaum, 1993), 66. This article is a revision of his original article "*Actio*: A Rhetoric of Manuscripts," *Rhetoric Review* 2, no. 1 (1983): 64–73.
7. John Trimbur, "Composition and the Circulation of Writing," *CCC* 52, no. 2 (December 2000): 188–219.
8. James E. Porter, "Recovering Delivery for Digital Rhetoric," *Computers and Composition* 26, no. 4 (December 2009): 207–224.
9. Jim Ridolfo and Dànielle Nicole DeVoss, "Composing for Recomposition: Rhetorical Velocity and Delivery," *Kairos: A Journal of Rhetoric, Technology, and Pedagogy* 13, no. 2 (Spring 2009), accessed November 16, 2009, http://kairos.technorhetoric.net/13.2/topoi/ ridolfo_devoss/velocity.html.
10. Ben McCorkle, *Rhetorical Delivery as Technological Discourse: A Cross-Historical Study* (Carbondale, IL: Southern Illinois University Press, 2012).
11. Brooke, *Lingua Fracta: Towards a Rhetoric of New Media*.

12. Lindal Buchanan, *Regendering Delivery: The Fifth Canon and Antebullum Women Rhetors* (Carbondale, IL: Southern Illinois University Press, 2005).
13. Brooke, 47–53.
14. Marshall McLuhan, *Understanding Media* (Cambridge, MA: MIT Press, 1994), 7.
15. Ibid., 3.
16. Gregory L. Ulmer, *Applied Grammatology: Post(e)-Pedagogy from Jacques Derrida to Joseph Beuys* (Baltimore, MD: The Johns Hopkins University Press, 1984), 314.
17. Gregory L. Ulmer, *Electronic Monuments* (Minneapolis, MN: University of Minnesota Press, 2005), 205.
18. Ibid., 120.
19. Ibid.
20. See Gregory L. Ulmer, *Heuretics: The Logic of Invention* (Baltimore, MD: Johns Hopkins University Press, 1994), 228–229.
21. Fiona Kumari Campbell, *Contours of Ableism: The Production of Disability and Abledness* (Basingstoke, UK: Palgrave Macmillan, 2009), 5.
22. See Sushil K. Oswal's contribution "Ableism" in the collaborative article Yergeau et al., "Multimodality in Motion: Disability & Kairotic Spaces," *Kairos: A Journal of Rhetoric, Technology, and Pedagogy* 18, no. 1 (Fall 2013), accessed June 10, 2015, http://kairos.technorhetoric.net/18.1/coverweb/yergeau-et-al/pages/ableism/index.html.
23. See Oswal's contribution "Technologies" in the collaborative article Yergeau et al., "Multimodality in Motion: Disability & Kairotic Spaces," *Kairos: A Journal of Rhetoric, Technology, and Pedagogy* 18, no. 1 (Fall 2013), accessed June 10, 2015, http://kairos.technorhetoric.net/18.1/coverweb/yergeau-et-al/pages/ableism/tech.html.
24. Amanda K. Booher, "Technological Ableism," *Intercom* (April 2014), 37, accessed June 15, 2015. http://intercom.stc.org/.
25. Raúl Sánchez, *The Function of Theory in Composition Studies* (Albany, NY: State University of New York Press, 2005), 4.
26. See Gilles Deleuze and Félix Guattari, *Anti-Oedipus: Capitalism and Schizophrenia*, trans. Robert Hurley, Mark Seem, and Helen R. Lane (Minneapolis, MN: University of Minnesota Press, 1983).
27. See Jeff Rice, *Digital Detroit: Rhetoric and Space in the Age of the Network* (Carbondale, IL: Southern Illinois University Press, 2014).

Bibliography

Booher, Amanda K. "Technological Ableism." *Intercom* (April 2014), 35–37. Accessed June 15, 2015. http://intercom.stc.org/.
Brooke, Collin Gifford. *Lingua Fracta: Towards a Rhetoric of New Media*. Creskill, NJ: Hampton Press, 2009.
Campbell, Fiona Kumari. *Contours of Ableism: The Production of Disability and Abledness*. Basingstoke, UK: Palgrave Macmillan, 2009.
Connors, Robert J. "*Actio*: A Rhetoric of Written Delivery (Iteration Two*)." In *Rhetorical Memory and Delivery: Classical Concepts for Contemporary Composition and Communication*, edited by John Frederick Reynolds, 65–78. Mahwah, NJ: Lawrence Erlbaum, 1993.
Dotov, Dobromir G., Lin Nie, and Anthony Chemero. "A Demonstration of the Transition from Ready-to-Hand to Unready-to-Hand." *PLoS ONE* 5, no. 3 (2010). Accessed March 15, 2010, doi: 10.1371/journal.pone.0009433.

Keim, Brandon. "Your Computer is a Part of You." *Wired*, March 9, 2010. Accessed July 18, 2015. http://www.wired.com/2010/03/heidegger-tools/.

McLuhan, Marshall. *Understanding Media: The Extensions of Man*. Cambridge, MA: MIT Press, 1994.

Ridolfo, Jim and Dànielle Nicole DeVoss. "Composing for Recomposition: Rhetorical Velocity and Delivery." *Kairos: A Journal of Rhetoric, Technology, and Pedagogy* 13, no. 2 (Spring 2009). Accessed November 16, 2009. http://kairos.technorhetoric.net/13.2/topoi/ridolfo_devoss/velocity.html.

Sánchez, Raúl. *The Function of Theory in Composition Studies*. Albany, NY: State University of New York Press, 2005.

Ulmer, Gregory L. *Applied Grammatology: Post(e)-Pedagogy from Jacques Derrida to Joseph Beuys*. Baltimore, MD: The Johns Hopkins University Press, 1984.

———. *Electronic Monuments*. Minneapolis, MN: University of Minnesota Press, 2005.

———. *Heuretics: The Logic of Invention*. Baltimore, MD: Johns Hopkins University Press, 1994.

———. *Internet Invention: From Literacy to Electracy*. New York: Longman, 2002.

Yergeau, Melanie, Elizabeth Brewer, Stephanie L. Kerschbaum, Sushil Oswal, Margaret Price, Michael J. Salvo, Cynthia L. Selfe, and Franny Howes. "Multimodality in Motion: Disability & Kairotic Spaces." *Kairos: A Journal of Rhetoric, Technology, and Pedagogy* 18, no. 1 (Fall 2013). Accessed June 10, 2015. http://kairos.technorhetoric.net/18.1/coverweb/yergeau-et-al/index.html.

Part I

What is Delivery?

I imagine one day viewing a biopic on Demosthenes. His story, at least what we know of it, has all the dramatic elements to make an uplifting story, but also a tragic one. Although born into a fairly wealthy family, Demosthenes loses his parents while he was a young boy and stands helpless as his uncles steal and squander his inheritance (initial obstacle for the hero to overcome). As he grows to young adulthood, he schemes to take his uncles to court and sue them to recoup what they have taken. However, due to his speech impediment, he must work hard to overcome his physical limitations. During his youth, he watches the great orators of his time: Callistratus, Isocrates, and Isaeus, noting their intonations, gestures, facial features, word choices, lines of argument, figures of speech, appeals to emotion, use of clothing. This film might even include a Rockyesque montage: Demosthenes shouting to the surf, speaking with pebbles in his mouth, exercising to increase his endurance, practicing with the various contraptions he builds to improve his posture, and writing and rewriting speeches. Ultimately, Demosthenes wins against his uncles, and the next act begins.

Such a story reveals much about Demosthenes himself, but also the work that goes into delivery before one ever sets foot before the assembly. Delivery requires a materiality, a physicality, a development, a network. This film would show the interplay of actors and audiences in a rhetorical situation, how exigency emerges for a young boy who is treated unfairly, and how rhetorical engagement can be used to solve problems (Demosthenes doesn't seek to revengefully murder his uncles in some Shakespearian fashion; he sues them). This anecdote, of course, only presents the first act of the story, and so this section presents only the first part of a new narrative about delivery, itself only a part of rhetoric as a whole. Given what I write in the introduction, the overall goal of this book is to investigate what an electrate delivery could look like. While Ulmer devotes most of his writing to invention and memory (and to some degree, implicitly, arrangement and style), he never addresses delivery directly (although one could argue, as I will at the end of the book, that his latest projects—*Electronic Monuments* and *Avatar Emergency*—skirt this canon). What, then, are some of the conditions for an electrate delivery that is emerging as we speak, a development that needs some investigation if electracy can (or should) make use of this part of rhetoric.

However, before further exploring some of these implications, we have to ask and attend to a basic question (not that we will answer it fully): What is delivery? We have to start with this question since it's one that is hardly asked when making theoretical claims about delivery. Other arguments about delivery often take as given that delivery has some underlying essence, or make basic assumptions that link delivery to classical constructions, a definition through which current theorizations are made, attempting to extend the definition into modern writing technologies and practices. However, if we ask what delivery is all by itself, outside of any particular writing technology, how might we answer (could we answer)?

If we were to ask a modern-day Demosthenes about the most important aspect of rhetoric—assuming it's still delivery—how would she answer? What would the thrice-spoken term be? To ask these questions also requires that we have some criteria for identifying a digital Demosthenes, which I explore in part II. This section, however, explores "delivery" as a term that needs to be declassified, reclassified, and finally re-Classified. Part I probes this question through several routes. Toward reclassifying, the first chapter offers a chorographic approach to tease out the different ways we understand the term "delivery" and interrogate what those meanings tell us about delivery as a rhetorical or communicative act. As a whole, this section is also conductive, a mode of inference that operates in tandem with chorography. As Ulmer explains, conduction provides a fourth mode of inference to supplement induction, deduction, and abduction. As a particularly electrate logic, conduction will help push the limits of theorizing delivery and open a few new avenues. Even if some of these paths prove to be dead ends, the scenery helps us to think about delivery's potential (and how it can be made kinetic). Chapter 2 then rethinks the classical Greek term *hypokrisis*—which, like delivery, is often oversimplified and without rigorous investigation—and examines its overlooked meanings to reveal what has been missing from many conversations about delivery.

1   Declassifying Delivery

Delivery, also known as *hypokrisis*, *actio*, or elocution, has suffered from a sort of disciplinary schizophrenia over the millennia.

—Ben McCorkle[1]

When you're writing, you are robbed of your delivery.

—Calvin Trillin

In his chapter about delivery in *Lingua Fracta*, Collin Brooke suggests that—due to a keynote address by Andrea Lunsford, Kathleen Blake Yancey's collection *Delivering College Composition: The Fifth Canon*, and articles by James Porter and Dànielle Nicole DeVoss—"we are rapidly approaching a time where we can dispense with prefacing discussions of delivery by bemoaning its neglect."[2] Approaching, perhaps, but we have still not arrived. Proportionally, given the number of books traditionally written about the other canons, delivery is neglected, but I do not bemoan this—there are good grammatological reasons why delivery is (and has been) neglected. However, I do agree with Brooke when he writes, "One of the factors that interferes with our ability to reconceive delivery in light of new media, however, is our tendency to view the canon through the lens of our commonsense definition of the term."[3] Indeed, if we are to take into account Burke's concept of the terministic screen, the term *delivery* limits how we understand the rhetorical action based not only on the commonplace definition, but the very term itself, now bogged down by transitive understandings of delivery even as Brooke attempts to break them out with his treatment of delivery as performance.

Brooke also notes how easy the transitive and intransitive forms of delivery can be conflated; that is, the delivery of an object versus the delivery of an action. Although I'm sensitive to the need for terminological tidiness—to avoid conflating similar terms or misusing terms—my intention is to conflate and deflate all (or many) of the ways that we understand the term delivery and what each of those deliveries might entail for how we could or should understand delivery as a rhetorical act. Working conductively and choragraphically, I examine all these meanings already in the English term delivery and terminologically untidy them for a moment. While the rest of this chapter gets messy, I hope the mess provides necessary muck to fill in some gaps.

Delivery Unleashed

One sense of delivery refers to "the action of setting free," often in the term *deliverance*. One who delivers in this sense is either freeing herself, or perhaps freeing another. The deliverer, then, performs a hero function (assuming that this freeing is a good thing, or perhaps at least from the perspective of the one who is bound). Heracles delivers Prometheus from his suffering of being de-livered, a punishment predicated on another kind of delivery, giving fire (knowledge) to humans. Princess Leia was rescued, and thus delivered from Darth Vader, by Luke, Han, and Chewbacca. The sinner finds deliverance through the grace of his deity or the religious intuition that supports Him or Her. This kind of delivery often occurs in death as the soul finds deliverance from the body and is free to leave. Traditional gospel music, such as the song "Deliverance Will Come" (also called "Palms of Victory" and "The Way-worn Traveler"), frequently employs the figure of Christ as the deliverer of pain and suffering via a passage to heaven after a long life of suffering. The physicality of the body, its ability to be delivered, to be restricted from deliverance, and its ability to suffer, play important roles in the act of delivery. This physical journey may be one reason why James Dickey chose "Deliverance" for the title of his book, for the quartet of men undergoes a variety of physical trials and tribulations.

However, this deliverance also occurs in the middle voice, especially in classical Athens. If accused in a court of law, Athenians could not have lawyers speak for them, but instead had to speak for themselves. Alan Boegehold discusses the need for ordinary citizens taken to court to show at least a cursory understanding of delivery, "to look as well as sound as though they were themselves, i.e., private citizens pushed into court through no fault of their own and certainly not through any specially developed skills."[4] Such citizens needed to act without art, as they would in any public or private space outside of court and not seem like they were keen on delivery. If they were expert, or had some tutelage in delivery, then they needed to hide it, appearing to be absent of delivery while enacting a purposeful craft of delivery. Thus, we might say that delivery happens underneath or behind the curtain—it has to remain hidden. Their speech had to contain an unspoken element of delivery (which is, of course, itself a mode of delivery).

The relationship between the written word and public performance also had to mirror this subterfuge. As Alcidamas notices, "those who write for the lawcourts seek to avoid this pedantic precision [of writing], and imitate the style of extempore speakers; and they make the most favorable impression when their speeches least resemble written discourses. Now, since speeches seem most convincing when they imitate extemporaneous speakers, should we not especially esteem that kind of training which shall readily give us ability in this form of speaking?"[5] Here, we can surmise that Alcidamas prefers the fluid, though sometimes discontinuous delivery of unrehearsed, unprepared speech, or as Boegehold writes, "utterances that are not in tight compliance with the rules of syntax defining formal written prose: it is a medium in which sentences can change subjects in mid-course and where whole clauses can be left to the improvisatory skills of a litigant/performer, to be expressed by gesture, or not."[6] Demosthenes, in *On the Crown*, had to deliver for himself why he was worthy of such an undemocratic gesture by Ctesiphon. However, he could not directly deliver for someone else through his own speech but instead helped others' delivery through his work as a logographer, offering words he could not speak himself, much as Cyrano wrote the words that Christian delivered to Roxane in Edmond Rostand's *Cyrano de Bergerac*.

Delivery as freeing, then, is not transitive in the sense that some "thing" is delivered to someone else, but a condition that makes possible some other action or outcome. Rhetorical delivery is not simply the transmission of information from a rhetor to an audience, but laying out the conditions by which the audience may discover or realize deliverance, whatever this means for their particular situation. Like Prometheus, the deliverer may help spark an insight that frees a blockage toward solving a particular problem. The act of delivery might also unburden the deliverer, allowing her to finally speak her mind, free a weight from her chest, or any other metaphors we use when describing the outpouring of an uncontainable utterance. Of course, we usually don't think of delivery as only such uttering, as only speaking or writing for an audience, but doing so with some technique in mind that goes beyond speaking. Delivery, even in this one way of understanding the term, becomes a more nuanced and multi-stage process than we might initially consider for the rhetorical act, whether live before an audience or through the clicks of a mouse. Or, as Raúl Sánchez suggests about writing, delivery, like writing and bound up in and with writing, is not simply representational of thought, speech, or reality, even though it initially seems to serve a representational function. Instead, Sánchez writes that the "most salient feature of writing is therefore not its representational function but its ability to proceed as if it has a representational function."[7] As I will explore in the last chapter, delivery's chief function may not be to perform a speech or represent an idea through unspoken utterance, but to appear as if it did or must, or to appear as having a beginning and end. If, in a networked world, "the most striking features of writing are its sheer proliferation and its constant, rapid circulation,"[8] we might say the same of delivery, as others such as John Trimbur have suggested. Ultimately, I offer that delivery be unleashed from the same hermeneutic approaches and perspectives that Sánchez associates with the study of writing toward new studies of delivery, which is to say, writing.

Delivery Bound

Just as delivery can be freeing, it can also constrain or put one into difficult positions through the act of delivery. A specific definition of delivery pertains to delivering a prisoner to a jail: binding Prometheus to the rock; delivering Luke to the Emperor; Jean Val Jean delivering himself to Inspector Javert. Perhaps this is delivery at its worst, when it constrains, binds an audience toward particular interpretations, that it becomes the "manipulative" kind of delivery that Aristotle struggles with. Yet, understanding "best" and "worst" delivery depends upon point of view. Aristotle had good reasons for shunning the emotive aspects of delivery; poor decisions made by the citizens, led astray by emotional temptations, might ruin the state. We may sympathize with Val Jean or Skywalker from humanistic perspectives, but they were bread thieves and war prisoners, respectively. Some prisoners are falsely tried and convicted, but many are in prison for a valid reason. Prometheus stole from the gods. Delivery, from this perspective (and, I would argue, from Aristotle's), has deep societal and institutional implications.

The prisoner, in this metaphor, plays the part of the thing delivered, of "information," information that must be properly handled and contained for it has operated outside of the limits of information, of the law. It may seem that this role of the thing delivered occurs in an active construction, and that the thing delivered, the prisoner or information, has agency where it doesn't, or shouldn't have any. After all, isn't the guard or the speaker the deliverer? But perhaps one's surrendering does not usurp institutional power in the way that it may seem, and perhaps the act of delivery is not as active. The meaning of "surrender," an activity that happens in the middle voice when it involves one's own person ("I surrender myself to you" and thus "I deliver myself to you"), informs surrendering one's own words upon delivery, and also an audience's surrender to the impact of those words, or the images of the body or spectacle that appear with such words. One can make conditions and prepare oneself to surrender on either end of this exchange, but the whole exchange is a matrix of active, passive, and middle voices. However, to "deliver a gaol" was also to clear the jail of prisoners, to bring them to trial to either acquit or condemn them. Such sentencing then delivered justice. In contrast and tension with deliverance, delivery offers a duality in which prisoners can be freed, they can be captured, they can be tried, they can be released, and perhaps delivered in the ultimate sense, again a return to delivery as deliverance. In any of these actions, multiple implications of delivery circulate, and when "rhetorical" delivery is considered, it must be done so when saturated with all of these meanings.

We see all of these meanings circulate in the film *Deliverance*.[9] The four men—Lewis, Ed, Bobby, and Drew—try to free themselves from city life by returning to nature. However, this nostalgic, oversimplified understanding of "nature" actually produces an opposite, alternative meaning of deliverance by the end of the narrative, especially in the film adaptation of the novel. Ed, played by Jon Voigt in the film (co-written by director John Boorman and the novel's author James Dickey), "recognizes … a mistaken assumption he had had about where he could find self-renewal. He originally regarded the canoe trip as a chance to escape from the banal quality of ordinary city life. Now he knows that life in the outdoors can be every bit as harsh, impersonal, and oppressive as life in the city."[10] Rather than venturing into some Edenic paradise (an idea fraught with its own implications), the four men commit to a kind of catabasis to a place that prompts Bobby to deduce that "this is where everything winds up."

This place is not the river they seek (the river Lethe? Styx?), but the small town in which they remark upon the inbrededness of the locals, the place of the well-known dueling banjos scene. Here, Drew is able to connect with the young boy, but only through music, for when he speaks, or offers the gesture of a handshake, the boy quickly withdraws. Here, communication can be felt only through unspoken vibrations of sensation, a rhythm bouncing from one banjo to another. As the narrative progresses, the four men delve further into an underworld, encountering the mountain men who rape Bobby and who are both eventually killed by Lewis and Ed (after one kills Drew). We might think that this is where deliverance occurs, in being freed from the pursuit of the men and the ordeals they have undergone. Keen Butterworth offers that these deliverances are cursory compared to the self-knowledge that Ed gains, knowledge that he has what it takes to make it in the woods by the end of the story, a kind of "making it" that Drew feels Lewis lacks. Does Lewis know the woods, Bobby asks? Drew opines: "Not really. He learn 'em. He doesn't feel 'em. That's Lewis's problem. He wants to be one with nature, and he can't hack it." Butterworth feels that such knowledge is what becomes delivered:

> Deliverance. From what? From the murderous mountain men? From the primordial dangers of the river? Certainly these are the most obvious referents of the title. But there is also the implication of a deliverance from the enslaving monotony of modern urban life. And, beyond that, to a deliverance from the parts of ourselves which also hold us in a kind of bondage, which thwart self-knowledge and consequently hinder our pursuit of vitality itself.[11]

As Longen writes, the "deliverance that [Ed] at one time had thought to find in sex, he did in fact find on the trip down the Cahulawassee. But what exactly did he find?"[12] Longen answers this question with a quote from Dickey:

> in this country a man can live his whole life without knowing whether he's a coward or not. And I think it's important to know. And what you're supposed to believe, gradually, and to see about Ed Gentry, is that he ... is really a born killer. He figures it out exactly right as to how to kill this guy, and he does it. He carries it out, and he gets away with it. ... That's all he needs to know, that he's capable of it. And as you see in the last few pages, it's a quietly transfiguring influence on him.[13]

However, in the experience of killing the man who stalks them along the riverbank, Ed finds a second kind of deliverance, not only the one that comes from a self-realization, one that provides a eureka moment of his own nature, but also a realization that entraps him as much as it frees him.

In the film's denouement, we see an Ed who is troubled by this realization. As R. Barton Palmer offers, this very knowledge has placed Ed (at least in the film) into his own kind of prison house, a kind of self-delivery into prison that we must each place ourselves in if we are not to be delivered to the gaol—one that the characters avoid by hiding the bodies beneath the flooding of the river. While this last detail literally and metaphorically suggests that the truth will become suppressed and placed underneath consciousness by water, it also points to the role of the unconscious in delivery— that deliverance plays upon something repressed, either by exposing it or keeping it hidden. As Palmer writes:

> Boorman's Ed is disquieted by his memories, for they represent the fall from an innocent and civilized ignorance into the sinful knowledge of human nature and culture. The journey downriver makes Ed recognize the extent to which everydayness is bought at the price of repression, for this is the price which, in lying to the police and others, he must pay to return to domestic comfort. The film's Ed has internalized the river, but his fear is that what the river covers will be exposed; internalization, in other words, can be achieved only at the cost of continuing surveillance, and it is banal—if still significant—that this frightening image returns to him in his dream, an element of the cultural unconscious that surfaces, unwilled, in his own.[14]

Thus, rather than unbinding Ed, such knowledge ultimately constrains him. As Palmer surmises, "the film undermines the notion of 'deliverance,' suggesting as it does, both the failure of subjectivity to master phenomenal experience and the uneasiness—both Ed's and our own—which necessarily results from the fall into knowledge."[15] One question about delivery that *Deliverance* proposes is the extent to which the deliverer precipitates a fall via knowledge for the audience, one that may be unrecognizable as such when an appeal has been made and is accepted by the audience, when a group knowledge has been created among the crowd. Of course, the fall may be taken by the deliverer should an unwelcome delivery—the content of a performance—be met by a crowd unwilling to face or accept an act of knowledge-making proposed by the deliverer, especially when such delivery reveals the shadowy parts of a society that we would rather remain hidden. In Ed's case, deliverance is doubly unwelcome, causing him to reach deliverance through murder and to fear that he will be delivered to the gaol and be sentenced for his crimes should the facts rise to the surface. His dream reminds us that delivery has no end, for one act of delivery eventually delivers the need for another, and another. Even the deliverance to one's maker creates other exigencies for delivery, and the dream continues.

Of course, this is Ed's dream, and so we assume that deliverance, in whatever form it comes, or doesn't come, refers to him and his crew. However, this is not the dream of the other characters of the film, mainly the local inhabitants that live within the valley to be flooded. While the local community is meant to benefit from the construction of the dam that will create the lake in Ed's dream, their voice, for or against, is never heard, and so deliverance—from poverty toward civilization—is thrust upon them through technological advancement at the cost of the loss of their cultural heritage. In this sense, deliverance might be seen negatively, a delivery not coming at the request of the receiver (like the typical prisoner), but at a cost, like C.O.D. but with no option to return to sender. This deliverance comes from a power structure that allows no say from the audience, like cultural delivery, hegemony, and colonialism. These are deliveries that, once delivered, cannot be accepted or returned. The most the town can do is deliver the "Church of Christ" somewhere else, and request from Ed, the city folk, that "I'd like to see this town die peaceful."

Delivery Rooms

One of the most common uses of the term delivery most likely entails childbirth. This kind of delivery is a hard, physically strenuous and painful process, one that requires months of development to be successful. While not nearly as physically challenging (an extreme understatement), what we identify as rhetorical delivery also requires preparation and labor (as seen through the anecdotes of Demosthenes) and can be physically exhausting (as described by Quintilian). Once a rhetor births his utterance, it's impossible to undeliver, creating a threshold when any semblance of control begins to be lost and the words take a life of their own, breathed into the world and into each audience member's ears, eyes, and body.

But the many ways of delivering an infant also tell us something about delivering messages. Sometimes the mother is only given credit for laboring, and another actor in the process, a doctor, nurse, or midwife, is described as the one that actually "delivers" the child. Or, perhaps we should say that this delivery—while the pain is borne by one individual—occurs within a larger cybernetic network of human actors and electronic and chemical feedback systems. While we can clearly point to the most important actor in this activity, delivery requires a broader understanding of the networks that make delivering anything possible.

These networks and methods of delivery are often hidden, forgotten, or ignored whereas the primary focus of these moments of delivery, biological and rhetorical, is on that which is delivered (after all, the mother is often numbed to reduce the perception of the process). The conjugation that began—if there can be a beginning—the delivery process is usually a private act. Delivery rooms themselves are often created to hide delivery from view so the rest of us don't have to be subject to another's delivery, creating segregate acts of delivery that divide rather than join. Many spaces designed for rhetorical delivery, save the most public spaces such as the Roman Forum, often enclose and envelop, section off delivery from others outside of the space of delivery, yet also keep delivery in, restraining it from overflowing into the streets. At times, however, what one wishes to deliver, when it is indeed a "thing," and if it can be called a "thing," spills out beyond the sanctioned spaces. Occasionally, births happen in public spaces, spaces not designated as delivery spaces. Occasionally, a speaker will attempt to deliver in spaces, or to spaces, not officially sanctioned, or not recognized as sanctioned for the particular speaker, often prompting an unwelcoming audience to deliver the deliverer to jail, or worse. Chelsea (Bradley) Manning was sent to prison and Martin Luther King, Jr. was killed for trespassing the boundaries of delivery.

A delivery room relays the importance of physical space and tools to this network of delivery, as it not only provides a place of relative privacy for the mother—often considered a more ideal environment for this kind of delivery—but also proximity to support networks when necessary. Various machines such as heart, fetal, and contraction monitors all provide delivery feedback to ensure delivery goes smoothly (at least, according to Western medical standards). Environment and feedback become two important features of delivery that continue to persist, and even thrive, in electrate modes of delivery that can distribute information and teleactivity across environments and receive audience responses over space and time.

Delivery also requires preparation, a preparation that can be as shocking as the shock of delivery itself. Many hospitals offer delivery classes to prepare expecting parents for the delivery process, and all the options and necessities of delivery are covered, from the choices that parents can make within the delivery process (natural or with interventions), the tools used in delivery (suction tools, forceps), and the chemicals available so that pain and sensations are diminished. Many parents, upon seeing these tools and their depiction and use in videos, become shocked and have to leave the room, having become emotionally distraught. The delivery of delivery becomes overwhelming, a harbinger of the emotion to come. But this emotion is often constructed here by the mores and beliefs of the particular culture. Some cultures focus on the pain of giving birth, whereas other cultures accept or even embrace it. As Lynn Clark Callister writes, "The perception of pain and behaviors associated with pain are influenced by the sociocultural contexts of the individuals experiencing pain" and that "Pain is a culturally defined physiological and psychological experience."[16] The expectations and acceptable reception of delivery become skewed even before the action of delivery occurs. The response to the tools of delivery is also constructed, as for some women the use of established medical devices might be preferable and seen within a context of safety and sterility.

Such delivery spaces, however, can have the effect of covering up aspects of delivery, smoothing out a process that has historically not been so stripped of environmental variables. As Margaret Mead writes, "In our own society, our images of the carefully guarded rituals of the delivery-room, in which the mind conjures up an even temperature maintained by a thermostat, the most medically perfect oils and unguents, and the softest of appropriate materials in which to wrap the baby, overlay any realisation of what a shock birth is."[17] The delivery room becomes an extension of the mother-infant-family-nurse-doctor-monitor-machine-hospital assemblage, an extension that, as McLuhan would note, numbs one human capacity (the ability to be shocked) while enhancing another (the ability to deliver). Does the narcotic of the delivery room—figuratively in this case—take something from the process? Should one be shocked? Does it constrain like those delivered to a prison, becoming another kind of prison? Does an affective dimension become lost in this delivery, shadowing the affective dimension of rhetorical delivery? Isn't the delivery room, like any environment for rhetorical delivery, itself rhetorical on an unspoken level?

Perhaps, this unspoken-ness is the point, which therefore speaks. For those who design the room, the delivery room should speak, perhaps calmly, but at an unconscious level, or at a background level. Thus, for the tourist population that enters and exits delivery rooms, it is perhaps unspoken just as any tourist can only leave the rhetoric of a space/place unspoken. But what does it mean to be unspoken? If the transient occupant of the room enters the delivery room in anticipation of some form of delivery, thus validating the room as a delivery room, isn't the rhetorical-ness spoken through the situation? That is, what if a patient shows up expecting a delivery and the manager of the room (a doctor or nurse, for example) takes her to the garage? In this case, what would otherwise be unnoticeable presents itself, and the space of the garage speaks in an unpleasant voice. In fact, we might say that the entire delivery room, and the medical complex that houses it, is one of reducing feeling, not just of the mother and infant, but of the supporting network as well. However, does the room simply reduce the feeling, silencing it, or as described above, attempt to substitute one feeling for another? Machines and medical devices designed for the medical industry are much different in style from those designed for manufacturing. The delivery room's rhetoric encourages comfort and confidence; it doesn't eliminate feeling, but injects a particular feeling.

Although delivery has a history of occurring within a network of actors, this network has increasingly grown to include these nonhuman elements, which by definition do not "feel" as humans do. This network resembles the Taylorism of a modern-day factory, as Judith Walzer Leavitt describes:

> In 1938, half of all American babies were born in the hospital; by 1955 it was 95 percent. Yet along with professionalized medical care, an expectant mother now found herself "alone among strangers" on a kind of conveyor belt moving from admissions to a prep room, where she was shaved and given an enema. Then she was moved to the labor

room, where she stayed, mostly alone and sometimes sedated, during the long hours while her body got ready for delivery.[18]

We see Foucault's medical *regard* at work here, separating the body from person, a body that prepares the woman independent of the same woman who will give birth. The attending physician works from behind this medical gaze, one that separates patient from person, mechanics from spirit, reducing the emotional component of the situation. But this view is a bit reductive and creates a subject/object, placing the body outside of the hospital as something to bring in and quickly remove as an abnormality. The body is a technology in the system already integrated within the hospital by its very design. The hospital is a database of technology designed to be selected and integrated with the technology of the body, not simply a space to enter and exit the way Leavitt describes.

Instead, as the mother labors, she is not solely responsible for the whole of "delivery." But what role does she take? Iris Young writes that the woman in the delivery room is placed in a passive position, one often ascribed to the audience in rhetorical delivery, the components assembled along a conveyor system, or the beast delivered to slaughter: "During labor, however, there is no sense of growth and change, but the cessation of time. There is no intention, no activity, only a will to endure."[19] Perhaps this is not a passive position, nor active, but a networked activity of these technologies working together. Yet this interaction still does not address the affective and sensory input experienced by the mother. If the body pains during this cessation of time, it no longer delivers (if it ever did). Perhaps the term itself strips some agency from the mother. While the machines in the delivery room are designed to make sure delivery goes smoothly and enhance the comfort of the body (or bodies), it disturbs the person of the body. In other words, while the pain felt by a mother is real, the delivery room has a tendency to deliver the emotion of fear only to offer its devices to assuage it, the way any product fills the need that its own advertisement delivers in the first place. The delivery room attempts to quiet its own noise.

This question, to feel or not to feel, has received increased attention by the network that surrounds and supports the birthing apparatus, including actors such as doctors, nurses, midwives, childbearing women, policy makers, as well as feminist theorists. The conversations have resulted in what Kerreen Reiger and Rhea Dempsey describe as the "emerging sense of crisis around childbirth,"[20] mainly from debates on the use of technology in the delivery process—i.e., delivering via natural physiological processes versus intervention with technological aids. While many natural birth activists would push for women to trust in their bodies (who have been taught to trust the medical apparatus instead), opposition not only comes from medical professionals, but also from feminist theorists who are "ambivalent about childbirth developments … seeing natural birth advocates' critiques of technological birthing as essentialist, moralising and patronising towards women's choices."[21] This debate results in a paradox: as women gain more means to help control and take control of their own bodies, they become less psychologically empowered to do so without technological aid. As Reiger and Dempsey describe, "confidence in women's birthing capacity" has declined despite "western women's increased social power and achievement and improved health and living conditions."[22] The point for delivery (in both senses) is not that one side is right over the other, that one should or shouldn't use technology to intervene in the delivery process, but how unsure we have become, individually and collectively, of how to approach the body as it has become separated from our "selves." This may arise because, as Ulmer argues, the "self" as a category for individual identity is shifting to one of "image" as we transition from literate to electrate forms of communication, forms that I will flesh out through the rest of this book. If accurate, such a shift creates other aspects to which an electrate delivery must attend, which will be taken up later.

One aspect to consider, and this especially pertains to rhetorical delivery, is the ability of the body to deliver other kinds of messages beyond those coded in the DNA phenotype of a child. Rhetorical delivery provides a visual track that corresponds to the spoken, and so a body has to produce a particular image, both when static and dynamic, to achieve maximal results. If we take for granted Debord's spectacle, or at least acknowledge a current image-based, celebrity-obsessed culture, then the attention to one's own body (whether in the flesh or a digital, online version), should come as no surprise, especially when thinking about the bodily changes that occur in pregnancy and when delivering a child. "The cultural preoccupation with celebrities, with a tightly controlled, and slender, body image, as well as reliance on technical solutions to bodily difficulties, can all be seen as significant aspects of consumerist society shaping birthing expectations."[23] Here the concerns are not with a delivery that occurs for a special occasion, a special event that is planned such as a public speech, trial, or political campaign, but an everyday delivery in everyday micro rhetorical encounters, ones that may be with oneself as much as with another body. As Susan Bordo argues, a body is a "carrier of culture," whether celebrity or not, and so delivers culture on a daily basis.[24] Or, as Iris Young explores, our experience of our bodies changes in relation to our environment and our specific purposes in those environments and "in light of the projects" one undertakes.[25] Such projects include rhetorical ones, even if the undertaking of argument is unconscious. I address celebrities and the unconscious in greater detail later, but as any acting teacher will likely state, we are all much better actors in "real life" than on a stage, we are all much better deliverers in real life, and so contemporary anxieties and attentions to the body for purposes other than rhetorical delivery may offer insight into how to rethink delivery for electracy (and may very well be rhetorical in their own everyday way).

Perhaps a better term for child delivery—and echoing Brooke on rhetorical delivery—is one of "performing childbirth." Reiger and Dempsey—in trying to stabilize the tension between natural birthing advocates and medical professionals/feminist theoretical camps that place more value in technological intervention—attempt to find a balance in birthing as a performance of the body using Judith Butler's development of gender performance as a relay. A bodily performance helps to provide a more active interpretation of what happens during delivery, as the "philosophical distinction between the inert material body and the lived, experienced body is essential to distinguishing between the processes of being delivered and giving birth."[26] As a counter to the medical regard, the alienation of the body during delivery, a performativity of "being in the body"—one that accentuates "patterns of movement and intentionality"—can shift focus toward considering birthing as an active bodily performance instead of "a passive state of being 'done to' or delivered, though that indeed is often how it is experienced in current medical regimes."[27]

What would "performing childbirth" look like, or how would it look differently than a direct literal interpretation? To develop their term, Reiger and Dempsey turn to artistic and athletic modes of bodily performance. Part of their logic stems from the way that arts and athletics simultaneously intertwine the body with both a physical and cultural performance which, as they argue, also occurs in the process and performance of childbirth. The "lived bodies" of artists and athletes show "the intense effort of undertaking challenging embodied processes and its relevance to birthing," for "conceiving and producing a creative work of theatre, or achieving peak bodily performance in sport, the psychological/physiological processes encountered are highly individual but also involve others."[28] Such a turn is necessary for in delivery the "locus of subjectivity cannot remain in the head, although this is its usual location in western culture" and must be integrated into a mind/body cooperative complex.[29] However, this individual complex must be extended into a larger network (often referred by them as a "holding circle" of support) that creates a larger social assembly working together to "do" delivery. Since, as Reiger and Dempsey argue, the woman's actively taking on the agency and the physical task of birthing is not valued, with supporters or caregivers often reiterating the "cultural message about birth being too difficult to accomplish without medical or pharmacological help," the support of the holding group emotionally holds the fear of the woman during this process, which then "becomes transformed into physiological response."[30] Anyone who has given birth, or been within a "holding circle" of someone giving birth, will probably attest to the importance of having a support network while the mother "does" delivery, support networks that extend well outside of the delivery room proper. However, the limited area of the delivery room provides a space that—while offering a shared location for a support network—quickly marginalizes the network when medical intervention is deemed (often by medical professionals) as the "best" approach to delivering, even if the mother would prefer not to partake (subjectively) in those interventions. The medical regard quickly gazes up and over the one for whom delivery is now being done. While we hardly feel as if the rhetorical deliverer's performance is being "done" for him or her, the network that comes before the act of delivery, the one that forms during, and the one that comes after has as much effect on the performance as the delivery network does for the woman giving birth, offering a variety of feedback loops that not only helps the deliverer adjust her delivery in the moment, but also makes the deliverer herself an audience of the audience's deliverer, making the exact actor in this exchange unclear.

Physiologically, oxytocin plays a major role in delivery, operating in a feedback system based on sensation and pain levels. Clinically speaking, a contraction triggers the release of oxytocin, which decreases the pain and helps trigger another contraction, further triggering a recursive and continual loop. However, oxytocin is released based on external interactions as much as internal processes alone, and thus so is all of delivery, for even bodily reactions that seem autonomous, such as contractions "are directly affected by social interactions."[31] Not only are the physical processes autonomous, but so the emotional responses can happen at an unconscious level, triggering other responses: "These not only enter the body through the senses but also involve unconscious emotional responses."[32] But oxytocin, existing in females and males, plays a much larger day-to-day role, helping to form emotional connections and interactions between people. While a pleasant internal environment during the delivery of a child helps to release oxytocin, the chemical is also released based on the stimuli from external environments, helping humans form feelings and emotions from various interactions so that emotions "are not internal to the individual psyche but flow between people."[33] We can conclude that other forms of interaction among groups of people, such as those that occur in rhetorical delivery, also release or restrict oxytocin and other similar neurophysical chemicals. Thus, delivery delivers oxytocin just as delivery delivers oxytocin (a comparison, not a tautology). One who rhetorically delivers well can produce varying levels of sensation that correspond to the degree that the deliverer triggers in us those relevant pathways. Rhetorical delivery more than resembles the birthing process, but is physiologically tied to the same pathways and is not a simple binary exchange from one to another (or many others), but a constantly negotiated exchange of signals, particularly mood, that results in a larger cybernetic delivery system than has thus far been acknowledged.

Delivering Curve Balls

If Reiger and Dempsey turn to athletic performance to understand the delivery of childbirth, we might also consider how the delivery of various athletic actions, particularly throwing an object such as a ball, can inform rhetorical delivery. A baseball pitcher delivers a fastball, a knuckleball, a slider. A basketball player delivers an alley-oop. A quarterback delivers a pass. Boxers deliver punches.

What are the larger situations in which these deliveries occur? In basketball, a player delivers a pass to another, which if it leads to a basket counts as an assist. The role of the passer here, the deliverer, is one of helping another toward achieving some goal (literally, in this case). In football, the quarterback—when throwing—becomes the intermediary between a center and a receiver. The quarterback doesn't begin with the ball, but moves the ball from a starting point to an ending point and best knows how to read the shifting situation and make decisions about how to best reach a receiver, sometimes sticking with a set plan, and sometimes improvising. All the aspects of delivery that we normally associate with an orator apply here as well, from footwork to vocal volume and enunciation, to the use of eyes, hand gestures, rhythm, dress, and arm movements. Even the celebratory gestures performed by all members of the team create a delivery, but this time in the more rhetorical (as entertainment) sense.[34]

However, in both of these sports, the deliverer can miss his target audience, and the ball can be stolen (basketball) or intercepted (football). Such terms cycle back to how a delivery of electronic messages is often discussed, situations in which email is hacked and information stolen, or a message is intercepted by the "wrong" party. A delivery always has this risk of falling into unintended hands, especially in a rhetorical delivery that is less rule-bound than either of the examples above. The unintendedness of these hands, of course, depends upon point of view. Hamlet most likely felt pretty good after intercepting Claudius's letter to Rosencrantz and Guildenstern, a feeling certainly not shared by the pair who never knew the original, or revised, text of the letter they were to deliver. The issue here has much to do with the delivery reaching an unintended audience and the results that can vary among an inexhaustive degree of possibilities and consequences ranging from an unintended recipient who intentionally tries to intercept the delivery to the unintended recipient who was blind to the entire situation. And, therein, the recipient can be the wrong hands in that there is mal-intent, a resulting delivery ends up used with bad intent, or it may be that the mis-delivery is beneficial, even if not identified as such immediately. Tied to all of these possibilities of delivery is also the failure of delivery to happen at all, the miscarriage of delivery—the delivery that never quite occurs.

As I'll discuss more thoroughly in the postscript, delivery also portends danger for the deliverer, and sometimes, the thing delivered. Not only can a stolen pass or interception reflect negatively on the passer's *ethos qua* passer, but, especially when quarterbacking, the search for a receiver can create a dangerous blind spot that may result in physical harm. This blind spot results from not just the (mis)perception of the quarterback, but the whole network that makes quarterbacking possible, the delivery network of coaching staff, team organization, fellow teammates, equipment engineers, field dimensions, crowd distractions, sideline distractions—a complex ecology of delivery to complete the gesture of a forward pass.

Baseball, however, seems to offer a different curve than either football or basketball. While the pitch needs to reach the catcher, the actual delivery needs to avoid the batter, or at least resist being hit and, unlike other deliveries, not reach home. Within this duel, the pitcher attempts to fool the batter into expecting something other than what he will actually throw, either in the attitude of the ball, or in the location. The goal here is to prevent, as much as possible, the other teammates from doing any work, and in doing so, in striking out batters, solicit the approval of the crowd. In this exchange, we might see the pitcher as not a singular actor, but part of a system with the catcher, a recursive loop, one of collusion and interactivity, inventing together what delivery will work best for a given batter, even if a good delivery is one that misses. But misses what? One should only miss the strike zone if one expects the batter to bite on the delivery. One should only land a pitch within the strike zone if one expects that the batter will miss the delivery. The pitcher, it seems, needs to deliver a ball that either makes the batter overthink, crowding out unconscious instinct, or appeal to unconscious instinct, bypassing critical thought. Either of these deliveries will often be successful and fool the batter into taking an action desired by the deliverer. Through this analogy, we might see that one aspect of rhetorical delivery is about the con, but a con that is usually perpetrated with an accomplice standing behind, or out of view of the audience (in their blind spot). But this partly overlooks the very situation in which the delivery occurs. In this analogy, the pitcher often has an advantageous position; he can surprise the batter, and chances are he will throw more strikes than hits in any given game—the rhetorical power is already on his side, as it were. This aspect should be coupled with other physical and environmental factors—left-handed batters vs. right-handed pitchers, home field advantage, location, weather conditions, pitch count endurance—all material factors that affect the delivery of a ball as they do the ambience of rhetorical delivery.

In such a case, we might ask who is the subject of the at-bat, or if there is a subject? This delivery as "throwing" brings up the question of Heidegger's "thrownness." Delivery in any sense has a relation to *Dasein*, which exists prior to the subject, before the subject and object separate. A being is thrown into a situation, one not of their choosing. This "being-there" opens the site where the subject is open to becoming, an openness-to-being, and has the apparent choice of fallen-ness or being-toward-death. Is this openness not the site of delivery, where an audience opens themselves to becoming based on what transpires at the site? Is this openness not also the open hand of rhetoric, where the deliverer, ideally, *becomes* based on the audience's attitudes and responses? Don't both subjects, like the pitcher and batter (and let's not forget the catcher), become a subjective system where all are thrown under (*subjectum*) the task of understanding (or at least questioning)? Is the act of delivery itself one of revealing the thrownness? As Chung-Hsiung Lai writes,

> One of the major contributions Heidegger makes is his insight of understanding (or questioning) as a primordial mode of human existence.

That is to say, understanding is projective thrownness *(Geworfenheit),* an existential structure of Being. The questioning of Being's meaning as projective thrownness is thus the ongoing experience of Dasein's Being-in-the-world. Thrownness, in view of that, "is meant to suggest the facticity of its being delivered over" (Heidegger 1962, 175). We may therefore assert that the subject is always delivered over as thrownness into the world.[35]

We might combine these terms with another of Heidegger's, *noein,* or apprehending. Any delivery is not just related to thrownness, but also a seizure of understanding, a grasping as one understands how one has been thrown into an inescapable prison and considers the two options that remain. As Heidegger demonstrates in *Introduction to Metaphysics*, language conceals as well as reveals, and so delivery as apprehension provides the deliverance of something else, something that escapes notice, precisely the fact that one has been thrown. One of the criticisms of rhetorical delivery is that it can be manipulative, causing an audience to act in a way it might not if the "tricks" of delivery were not used. Such criticism speaks to the way that the subject of delivery, whatever this may ultimately be within a larger delivery system, is thrown (under), how it comes to apprehend, what it comes to apprehend, and what it fails to apprehend on conscious and unconscious levels. We might conclude then that delivery also throws under the subject, or makes use of subjects that are thrown under, in the sense that delivery often operates on an unconscious level, at a level of emotion that may be felt but not always noticed.

Augmented reality (AR) offers a concept that can help theorize how this unnoticing occurs in digital media, especially media saturated with images. One of the problems in AR is that of registration, matching the virtual with reality so that the two appear as seamless as possible, or at least make the AR asset appear where it's intended to. If a registration error occurs, the user may adapt to it by psychically compensating for the error, making future errors more difficult to notice. Such difficulty primarily arises from "visual capture." As Ronald T. Azuma explains,

> Visual capture is the tendency of the brain to believe what it sees rather than what it feels, hears, etc. That is, visual information tends to override all other senses. When watching a television program, a viewer believes the sounds come from the mouths of the actors on screen, even though they actually come from a speaker in the TV. Ventriloquism works because of visual capture. Similarly, a user might believe that her hand is where the virtual hand is drawn, rather than where her real hand actually is, because of visual capture.[36]

Visual capture suggests that a gestalt occurs among the senses, so that visual stimuli begin to drive what is noticed, how it's noticed, so that we see where sound comes from rather than hear the location. However, rather than just working on how the brain perceives raw data from the environment, we might also attribute visual capture to how this information is eventually processed and incorporated into thought. For instance, we might blame visual capture for the varying perceptions in the famous example of the Kennedy-Nixon televised debate. Those who listened to the debate felt Nixon won, interpreting the audio as McLuhan's hi-definition medium. However, those who watched the debate felt Kennedy did better, perhaps because their listening was overcome by their watching as the image captured their attention. Perhaps this is why the unspoken aspects of delivery can be so powerful, from gestures to facial expressions to gait to clothing— they arrest the audience, they "throw" the audience and make them primarily viewers rather than listeners, when a common sense of all inputs might better serve them.[37]

Returning to sports, we see (literally) this sight dominance take hold in how plays are confirmed through the use of instant replay, replay that relies not on senses of sound, touch, smell, or taste, but on video, the visible, what the officials can see after the play has ended. During the initial viewing the officials have use of their common sense—what all senses combined tell them at once. With rhetorical delivery, these senses further vary in proportion based upon the site and medium used to deliver, but sight has been and remains a dominant aspect of delivery, even though Demosthenes took pains from pebbles to get the sound right. While an electrate delivery, situated within an image-based technology, certainly must continue to attend to the visual, the increased capacity for mixed and multiple modalities requires greater attention to sound, which has unique aesthetic and technical considerations and problems for anyone who wants to write in electrate modes.

Return to Sender

An extended arm; an open palm; gripping a letter between the thumb and fingers: all these articulated movements of limbs and digits signal a gesture of giving up, handing over, delivering a package, a letter, an object, a state of mind. This transitive mode of delivery, of moving objects from one place to another, has become the dominant, most popular use of the term *delivery*. This delivery is also a kind of release, a letting go, and in some ways still a deliverance. Dropping a letter into a delivery box surrenders the letter to an audience, one only intermediary to an intended audience. This transitive act also provides a ritual that frees one of the cyclical burdens that weigh on the psyche, for this delivery enacts a process at the end of which one trusts that the lights will stay on, the door key will still turn, or an application for a better life will be received. This use of delivery is the most prominent as postal services and shipping companies deliver these hopes and fears to our homes and businesses.

This transitive form of delivery provides a concretized relay for rhetorical delivery, and even exhibits some of the same logics of infrastructure that any kind of delivery finds necessary. Like many of the other examples provided so far, this kind of delivery involves a network, a relay of couriers to achieve delivery, paths connecting a series of hubs or nodes. A post office provides a central location for a local area to receive mail, but the effectiveness, the functionality of this office depends upon others in-between it and the origin of the package, since posting requires that there be many posts along the way that can provide shelter, food, and rest for the mailpersons relaying the message from node to node. The term "post" refers not to the thing delivered, but to this network, to the mechanism, originally the series of men on horseback that relays the mail from each to each until it finds its final audience (unless the post should fail), and so the term "post" denotes not that transitive thing, but the transitive process, an act of a hybrid man/animal/machine system and not so simply just a handing over. Or, the post refers to the node in the network that facilitates the intransitive, but is still not the "thing" carried or handed over, such as the literal post, the station, the origin and/or termination of the flow along the postal network. This post is where things begin and end; the post is fixed—hammered, buried, cemented into the ground. Similarly, the term "mail" originally referred not to the individual letters or packages, but the bag in which the letters were stored during transport, a carrier of content whose content was itself a carrier of content. Mail was not the "thing" itself, but temporary memory storage—RAM in the delivery system.

Whereas posts and posting have existed *as* post at least for several millennia (and much earlier in actual practice), the U.S. Postal System began with the second continental congress, with Benjamin Franklin at the helm, becoming the U.S. Post Office Department and eventually the USPS.[38] However, more famous but never formally associated with the USPOD/USPS was the Pony Express. While this iconic delivery system lasted less than two years and was never awarded a government contract to officially deliver mail for the U.S. government, it has helped contribute to the iconicity of delivery in an age of western expansion. The Pony Express, rather than using stagecoaches, relied upon single mounted riders upon single horses, creating a kind of microdelivery. Riders had to weigh less than 125 pounds, and the weight limit on mail was around 20 pounds.[39] However, such a reduction in individual scale could reach great distances quickly, from St. Joseph, MO to Sacramento, CA in ten days. Yet, a diminishment in one size required the increase of another. The 1,900-mile route roughly needed 184 stations, approximately two to twenty-five miles apart, where the rider would stop, exchange horses, and continue on.[40] Although linear and not properly a network, this delivery system comprised a series of nodes that relayed the rider from one post to the next. The success of the delivery—especially within ten days—required that each station attendant be aware of when the rider would arrive so that he or she could prepare the next horse or board the rider in-between divisions. Although separated by great distances, the system needed to have some level of self-awareness.

Perhaps like the lone rhetorical deliverer on stage (or one rhetor in agonistic struggle with another), American mythology has placed the postal delivery man or woman as a model of rugged individualism fighting the elements to guarantee that the mail moves from one state to another. The young, fast rider on the Pony Express came to embody the myth of rugged American individualism often associated with the cowboy and frontier myth, celebrated and romanticized in bygone Pony Express riders (exemplified by William Cody, aka Buffalo Bill). However, this delivery system required an unglamorous network of connections to allow the individual to have any success at handing over the mail to the final recipient. As Lindal Buchanan has shown, rhetorical delivery requires this backstage network of relationships as well, especially for those lacking stature, means, or resources.[41]

This connection to Buffalo Bill should not be overlooked. Cody incorporated the Pony Express into his famous Buffalo Bill's Wild West, circus-like shows that fed the frontier myth and allowed Cody to travel the world, making contacts with popes, kings, and presidents. Cody hired many American Indians for his shows, hoping to offer them better lives, and also hired Sitting Bull to play himself during a reenactment of the Battle of Little Bighorn, with Cody reportedly playing Custer.[42] While Cody delivered through the Pony Express, and delivered American mythology through the ruse of entertainment (which rhetorical delivery has traditionally relied upon), Sitting Bull served as a deliverer in his own community through his role as a shaman, one who can see the invisible problems for a community to help the group solve them (discussed more in chapter 4). Sitting Bull died during a botched attempt by police to deliver him to jail, a decision prompted by the fear that he might join the Ghost Dance movement, which itself aimed to deliver the spirit and human worlds into a reconciliation, creating peace, prosperity, and unity among American Indians, their main problems at the time.

Cody hired Sitting Bull for the *ethos* that Sitting Bull's celebrity and reputation brought to the show—because sending Sitting Bull into the arena delivered a particular message that no other name could. Cody assumed an authentic delivery by having the actual Sitting Bull rather than a simulacra actor portraying Sitting Bull. But even with the actual Sitting Bull, we have to acknowledge that his presence as Sitting Bull relieves Sitting Bull of being Sitting Bull. This is not Sitting Bull; this is still a simulacra of Sitting Bull. Just as—in Don Delillo's *White Noise*—we can no longer see the "most photographed barn in American,"[43] Cody's audience would not see Sitting Bull in this situation because Sitting Bull cannot be authentic here. Like Cody, part of the effectiveness of the postal system relies upon this sending of sender, that the sender is made clear on the envelop and in the contents, so that—if honestly rendered—mail carries more or less importance depending on the author or distributor. This assumption of authenticity is made even if the sender is no longer authentic, for the mail itself relieves the sender from being the sender.

As Derrida has explored with his postal metaphor of writing, the very fact that letters arrive at all only occurs because of the structural possibility that they might not arrive. As Niall Lucy observes, "From this it transpires that every arrival is a special type of non-arrival, such that a letter 'arrives' only by an 'accident' of the post. No letter can be guaranteed a smooth passage from signatory to addressee, and so every arrival is always in some sense accidental."[44] If we extrapolate a postcard to represent any writing that communicates because it can fail to communicate, just as any speech or writing can be misunderstood by the receiver, or intercepted by other audiences (which is another structural possibility of the networked relay system of the postal system), then delivery can only occur given its potential failure to deliver. In addition, since a message's sincerity can be faked to appear genuine, not true but imbued with the appearance of truth, so delivery, as a part of any communicative process, can give way to falsity and lead toward the modern derivative of the Greek term for delivery, *hypokrisis* (i.e., hypocrite). As I'll argue in the next chapter, this misunderstanding of *hypokrisis* provided Aristotle with his chief argument against delivery as a rhetorical canon. However, if the delivery of a postcard, of writing, of speech is accidental to the very structure that makes such actions possible, then the accidental should be accounted for in delivery—not an accounting for that seeks to control and eliminate accidents, but one that encourages accidents toward generative uses. Of course, this very idea is problematic since all delivered writing is necessarily accidental, so it's impossible to make more than what is already delivered. But it is not impossible to recognize delivery without the intentionality and instead as an accident-generative activity, and that all the accidents produced are taken account of in order to mine them for ideas, for collective problem production, recognition, and solution.

Such a distributed practice of delivery is necessary to overcome the abyss of a dead delivery, of a delivery that stops, has stopped, or has never started. As a counter example, mail can be returned if it never reaches its intended audience, making the sender aware of this fact if the letter's destination happens to be to someone to receive it, rather than a dead letter office or unoccupied address. While the post office is present as a post mark and stamp, it becomes an afterthought to the delivery process, invisible in a way that rhetorical delivery is not when performed through an orator or actor. However, does the orator become invisible in other ways? As I will discuss in chapter 2, one could argue that Aristotle would like all aspects of delivery, outside of the presentation of rational argument, to become invisible, to disappear. But delivery has these invisible, subliminal, unconscious elements that feed the audience's desire, that are invisible and unspoken. The orator is invisible even as he or she is seen, as often is the network (the machine of the postal service) that gets the deliverer to the stage in the first place. Delivery is a tension between the seen and unseen, spoken and unspoken, the perceived and unperceived. When this tension reaches a breaking point, the unseen filters into and affects the world of the perceived (although still largely invisible), a condition made manifest in "going postal," when the machine of the delivery service becomes untenable for a particular worker and he or she has a mental breakdown. According to Newman on the television show *Seinfeld*, this happens because the "mail never stops."[45] Or, to quote Mr. Universe from the film *Serenity*, "you can't stop the signal, Mal. Everything goes somewhere, and I go everywhere," a line followed by Mr. Universe finding a subliminal message encoded in an electronic cartoon, a message that previously triggered the telepathic character River to begin killing all those around her.[46] Instrumental logic puts the blame on workplace conditions, and one condition may be this continuity cited by Newman. For Lynn Worsham, "going postal" becomes an uncanny phrase disconnected from its postal origin, a pre-Internet meme, a phrase with circulation transfigured into different contexts with different images of violence. In a networked, information society, in which media is delivered on a nonstop basis, we might wonder what analogous condition to "going postal" is produced within the digital delivery-machine in-between sender and receiver. As I will discuss further in chapter 3, this may be the point at which Deleuze and Guattari's schizoanalysis is needed, for what would Mr. Universe be, what would happen to him, if the signal did stop, and he was then nowhere?

This relationship between sender and receiver suggests, too, that the sender can be considered in another sense. Ulmer notes—through Algirdas Greimas—that traditional narrative elements in a story involve a sender, most often taking the form of the family that instills values into the actant. These values drive much of the character's actions throughout the plot.[47] Before there is a deliverer to send us a message, messages in the form of values are delivered to each of us, determining our behavior and the choices we make. To understand delivery as a rhetorical act (or rhetorical acts in general), attention should be paid to these senders and we should return to them to research how we make collective decisions as a whole, decisions that usually come about after some sender has delivered to a receiver. This afterward of the sender and deliverer's narrative works rhetorically as well. As the Pony Express, long defunct, can no longer generate new parts of its own narrative, it must depend upon the narrative that continues to be told about it by others, and its story continues to be delivered. The most successful deliverers are often those that can tell an entertaining story with which the audience can engage. Moreover, the successful deliverer makes the audience a part of that story so that the narrative continues beyond the performance or transitive hand-off. Delivery is only successful if the audience receives the act and carries it forward. Much of the audience's acceptance of a performance might come from what we consider the more formal rhetorical constructs and arguments of delivery's content, yet much of their inclination to carry on a deliverer's narrative also comes from those unspoken (or unread) elements that make the audience want to act. Delivery is, in some instances, a precursor to exigency, making all receivers into senders, and all senders into receivers.

If we are to place the deliverer in the role of hero/actant in her own narrative, then we might think that what she brings to the audience is the magic elixir in the final scene that will save the community. That is, the deliverer has the answer to the particular problem the community faces, and if the audience drinks the potion that the deliverer has worked so hard to bring them, then all will be restored, exigency nullified. However, because the narrative never really stops, because one delivery only leads to another, then the deliverer's task is not to bring the audience a magic potion, but the more difficult task of convincing the audience to extend this narrative, to keep the sequence of events going. This shifting of delivery as a final act of rhetoric to the middle act then places the deliverer not as Luke Skywalker about to destroy the Death Star, but in Mos Eisley Cantina, trying to convince Han Solo and Chewbacca to take him to Alderaan. His audience becomes the donor of the narrative, a character who can be benevolent, malevolent, or both (Han is a loveable scoundrel). The audience, as donor, tests "the worthiness of the hero to undertake the quest—their desire and their competence."[48] In this capacity, Han tests Luke and Obi-Wan Kenobi: "Well, that's the real trick, isn't it? And it's gonna cost you something extra. Ten thousand, all in advance."[49] If the hero passes the test, as Luke does (through the wisdom of the sage Obi-Wan), the donor provides the magic tool, one that Luke and Obi-Wan were unaware of, given Han's incredulousness that they hadn't heard it: "Fast ship? You've never heard of the Millennium Falcon?" This tool's use "allows the hero to overcome the villain or obstacle causing the conflict and solve the problem motivating the adventure."[50] Despite the tool's intermittent reliability, Han reassures, "I've outrun Imperial starships. Not the local bulk cruisers mind you, I'm talking about the big Corellian ships now."

However, from the point of view of the filmic audience (not Han as Luke's audience), these roles may be reversed. While Luke considered that he was delivering a message (and the droids) to Princess Leia, Han and Chewy were delivering Luke to Alderaan. While Han and Chewy offered transitive delivery to Luke, Obi-Wan, R2-D2, and C-3PO, Luke offered the magic tool of money to Han, his own deliverance: "Those guys must really be desperate. This could really save my neck." As Ulmer writes, whereas one may electrately compose in the "position of the hero, one consults in the position of donor."[51] While the deliverer may see the audience as a donor whose riddle must be solved (through spoken words and the image of the body) and thereby gain acceptance, the audience may see the deliverer in the role of donor, needing their own kind of help, often having to solve the deliverer's riddles to do so, especially when that deliverer is a stand-up comedian.

Stand and Deliver

Perhaps the joke is the closest we have to a modern, aesthetic mode of delivery. As the author Chuck Palahniuk has observed, "I've always thought stand-up comedians were the oral storytellers of our time, because they know rhetoric, they know delivery, they know timing, they know all of these things that you can only learn by telling a story out loud and interacting with an audience."[52] Whereas actors certainly have to deliver lines, and although theaters have more audience engagement than filmic performances, a stand-up comic directly acts with the audience in a way more indicative of a classical delivery that made use of audience interactions. Few of us interrupt and interact with a public speaker at a formal event—a practice often now identified as heckling—but interruptions were common within ancient Greek and Roman orations, particularly those given to a general public; a back-and-forth interplay was part of the delivery process. Such interruptions are also crucial to many non-Western forms of delivery, especially sub-Sahara African traditions of call-and-response, used in religion, government, music, and education as a form of democratic participation. In North America, this practice evolved into modern uses in gospel, blues, R&B, jazz, hip-hop, and other genres. Although the logic of such music is the logic of electrate delivery, I use the comic as a means to illustrate the logic.

While any speaking event can produce laughter, the comic helps his or her delivery by establishing a rapport with the audience, hoping not to be booed off the stage. This relationship is important, but the key to delivering a joke is not the actual punch line (again, referencing the delivery of a blow), but the pause, the beat before the punch line is given. This beat is itself a gap, a space, a silence, an unspeakable moment that allows delivery to occur.[53] This beat is also a rhythm, a kind of dance, and we should note the macaronic pun of pause and *pas*, the French term for "step" particularly relevant in Derrida's discussion of a *pas* (which I'll return to later).

George Carlin perfected the silence of the beat to joke about the unspeakable. In his bit "Seven Words You Can Never Say on Television," Carlin notes and comments upon seven words that the Federal Communications Commission has traditionally censored on broadcast networks.[54] Carlin delivers these words—shit/piss/fuck/cunt/cocksucker/motherfucker/tits—in such rapid-fire, quick succession that it creates a sense of unity not possible with a single utterer and seems like an attempt to sneak the words past the sensors, to fly below their radar. Part of the humor in this routine was the rhythm and tempo in which Carlin delivers the seven words, and although we might say that this delivery erases the gaps between the words, making them almost a singular unit, this kind of delivery also clusters the "heavy" words together, segregating them from the other 399,993 "good" words against which these seven exist in shared isolation.

Carlin's bit is about the bite that these words have, offering that these seven words can deliver at a level of affect beyond the scope of good words: "Those are the heavy seven. Those are the ones that will infect your soul, curve your spine, and keep the country from winning the war."[55] Carlin's joke is very much about delivery, for each of those words is a part of biological delivery systems (either delivery as emission/transmission, missiles, or release): "[fuck] is the beginning of life, and yet it's the word we use to hurt one another." These words are often considered invectives, a term that derives from inveigh and also has a meaning of "carry away." These words deliver, carry away, but also hijack an audience not to a physical place, but a state of mind, one that doesn't soothe, but shocks.

Arthur Koestler has noted—as discussed by Ulmer—that "the best simulation of the experience of original thinking, of having an insight, was getting a joke," and that the timing of a joke, as well as the time required for the audience to get the joke, "simulates the temporality of invention, of grasping the opportunity just when it presents itself."[56] Ulmer goes on to make an important distinction by identifying "the activity in question [getting a joke] not so much as 'creativity' but as 'learning' and 'inventing' (in the rhetorical sense of supplying a reserve with raw materials for composition)."[57] If writing the joke is thought of as a creative activity, I offer that Ulmer's distinction provides an insight into the delivery of the joke and the experience of "invention" that results. Although the audience may not use the raw material from the deliverer to compose, the joke provides material for the reserved audience as they listen, view, and commune with the deliverer, not inventing the joke, but inventing its importance, its effectiveness, and the conclusions that can be derived from the evidence. The proof is not in the logic that ensues from the joke, but in the emotional response that is co-produced with deliverer and audience, so that together the joke becomes co-invented. For the comic and beyond the comic, delivery in general provides the point of group invention, where the deliverer/deliverees work together to produce a reserve of knowledge applicable to not just the individual, but the larger collective. While all forms of delivery have this interaction, an electrate delivery capitalizes on this interaction, hyping the interactivity of a delivery system so that the audience becomes more and more responsible for the deliverable.

The beating the comic gives the audience is meant to stun them, both in the unexpected conclusion that they reach (because they did not think of it themselves) and epiphany of recognition that comes from the punch line. Like dancing, Ulmer uses the logic of the joke as a model for electrate invention, invention that occurs in this epiphany. Because the joke makes use of silence as part of the comic timing, investigating the "mood" that this silence creates proves necessary. Citing Roland Barthes's syntagmatic codes and the moods that André Jolles ascribes to them, Ulmer notes that the mood of "silence" emanates from the riddle in a realist code and the joke in the idealist code. He distinguishes that the riddle contends with what is possible, and thus real, while the joke works without concern for truth, a "what if" that breaks out of reality's constraints. But if the joke is useful for invention, in considering what is and what can be (or cannot be), how does its mood relate?

> What remains unclear in this classification is the precise nature of
> the mood of silence. In the absence of any clue from Jolles, we may

speculate. The mood of a verb "refers to the way writers present their ideas and information," stressing either factuality or counter-factuality, wishes, commands, or questions. But what about the mood of silence? Does it suggest a statement free of the speaker's presence, that is, in which the position of enunciation is left unoccupied? Or, it is not that the enunciation is left unmarked, but that it comes from culture itself, in the cases of the riddle and the joke, from the discourse of the Other (the Symbolic order of the unconscious).[58]

The silence of a joke opens a gap for the audience, to be filled by their common knowledge, and although we might initially think this gap provides the time necessary for the audience to fill in the gap cognitively, it might be more accurate to say that this gap heightens or quickens the affective connection between the audience and the speaker. In terms of rhetorical delivery, this silence provides a sonic gap that allows the audience to concentrate on the orator's physical image, his or her gestures, facial expressions, movements, and all the other visible elements of delivery. The combination of a silence and presence can be used to create an atmosphere through this mood of silence that allows the body to perform other functions not locked into a rhythm of speech. A silence, while it may still have an inaudible rhythm, allows a second rhythm to form with the body. Or, we might also say that this silence is meant to break rhythm, to create a mood in which the audience, no longer grounded in the beat of the deliverer, finds themselves without a drummer, having to fill the gap themselves. The audience becomes temporarily unmoored, disorientated, until the deliverer reels them back like a loosened rope snapped taught.

Ulmer's development of the puncept as an alternative to the concept demonstrates a commitment to the switch logic of the joke. John Allen Paulos explains that "A convenient way to conceive of puns is in terms of the intersection of two sets. A pun is a word or phrase that belongs to two or more distinct universes of discourse and thus brings *both* to mind. The humor, if there is any, results from the inappropriate and incongruous sets of associated ideas jarring each other."[59] Although spoken in one domain of meaning, the logic of the pun (perhaps more than other kinds of jokes) depends on the homonym remaining unspoken for the audience to supply. Or, one meaning is unspoken while the other one explicit. The pun provides a means of reaching down a hand to pull the audience up, a gesture of helping toward education/invention rather than a hand out, or the deliverer installs a switch in the form of a pun that the audience must be able to flip to get the joke. Delivery provides this switch, an up/down interface from above to below, the "de" in delivery and the "*hypo*" in *hypokrisis*. The joke requires this movement from one cognitive domain to another. As Paulos observes:

> To get a joke, one must ascend, so to speak, to the metalevel at which both interpretations, the familiar and the incongruous, can be imagined

and compared … The various interpretations and their incongruity of course depend critically on the context, the prior experience of the person(s) involved, their values, believes, and so on.

The necessity of this psychic stepping back (or up) to the metalevel is probably what is meant when people say that a sense of perspective is needed for an appreciation of humor. It also explains why dogmatists, ideologues, and others with one-track minds are often humorless. People whose lives are dominated by one system or one set of rules are stuck in the object level of their system.[60]

Ulmer surmises that the shape of the joke is the "cusp," the point at which two domains touch and the two levels become communicable with each other. Whereas the deliverer delivers "down" to an audience (not in the sense of condescension), the audience must take a step up, requiring participation from both parties for a delivery exchange to occur.

Ulmer's interest in the joke for developing electracy (making it applicable toward an electrate delivery) is that the joke provides this switch in these cognitive domains for creative thinking within an electrate apparatus in general, and specifically for inventing new forms of rhetoric native to electracy. How might the joke work for delivery? Besides the elements of timing and spoken delivery (which would need a more detailed investigation, moving through each comic's repertoire and delivery, a study made possible because of electronic recording technologies), as well as the important element of silence within that delivery, the joke provides a "cusp" that allows creativity to occur within a group dynamic. If the joke fosters invention precisely because it juxtaposes, touches upon two seemingly disparate domains, then in terms of delivery this is a group invention, happening in a relationship between the deliverer and deliveree(s). If the comic invents the joke, the delivery is itself an inventive process that helps the audience invent the solution on their own—or perhaps more precisely—fosters the conditions (reaching down and helping them up to the metalevel) so they can recognize what was invented. As with enthymatic logic, the more the audience feels that they participate in this exchange, the more likely they are to receive the joke's wisdom.

Because it works in the idealist code, the joke can deliver a kind of non-sense, a "kind of false proof, an abuse of logic."[61] For Ulmer, this application of non-sense provides a key moment for invention in electracy: "Its particular attraction, for a project designed to integrate the cognitive styles of justification and invention, is that wit occurs precisely through the meeting of logical and paleological processes."[62] As Arieti explains:

> In the creation of a joke, the creative process is based on the following: 1) primary-process mechanisms, or cognitive mechanisms that are usually discarded because of their faults, become available to the creative person; 2) out of the primary-process and/or faulty cognitive mechanisms

that have become available, the creative person is able to select those which give the fleeting impression of being valid secondary-process mechanisms. The amused response on the part of the listener occurs when he realizes the invalidity of the thought-process—when he recognizes the logic-paleologic discordance. The creative process of wit consists of putting together the primary- and secondary-process mechanisms and automatically comparing them. The comparison reveals the discordance and provokes laughter.[63]

Implied by Arieti is the audience's role in this creative exchange, so that while the original joke may be invented by the comic, it becomes re-invented, or re-written, when performed before a group. In the delivery of a joke, the process depends no longer on an individual wit, but the wits of the group. While a joke may be in some sense didactic or illuminating, the audience "getting" the joke depends not only on the non-truth value of the joke, its logic (or illogical structure), but on how the comic tells the joke, performing not only the soundtrack of words, but also the image track of his or her entire body. This non-sense is most apparent when comics deliver not through intelligible words—*logos*—but through the unspoken, non-words of non-sense sounds and gibberish (or physical movements), such as Carlin's rapid-fire delivery of the unspeakable seven. As James Sullivan writes about Carlin's seven words routine, "the routine was much more than mere titillation. It was an airtight example of Carlin's belief in the one thing he truly believed in—the power of reason."[64] Perhaps then, the joke was on Carlin, for while his bit provided reasons why these words should not be banned, the ultimate connection, the communication of that reason depended on a comic delivery, delivery that employed the cusp of reason and absurdity of nonsense in terms such as "cheese tits."

The joke provides a deliverance, a freeing of the knots of logic, a magic tool like the sword used by Alexander to cut the Gordian Knot rather than attempt to untie it. Of course, this example demonstrates not that a specific sword is necessary (for instance, an ax should have worked), but a change in gestalt, a new approach. One delivers well when one creates this switch in gestalt, a flip in thinking that allows the audience to see from another perspective. However, the illogic alone doesn't prompt the audience to flip the switch, but the pleasure one often receives when getting the joke, prompting one to attempt to flip in the first place. If there is a mood of silence, then, this mood is one of anticipation for the pay off, one of excitement, a knowledge of a pleasure to come. Beyond nonsense (or through nonsense), the joke provides a *jouissance* to the audience, "what Lacan calls, in a pun, bliss-sense (*jouissance, jouissens*). Bliss-sense names that affective unconscious involved in the logic of identification, transference, and the drives of desire that inform the subject of knowledge, the subject who wants to know,"[65] what an electrate pedagogy "attempts not to strip from learning but to acknowledge and tap for the representation of invention."[66]

As has been noted, but not yet through this term, delivery depends on the bliss-sense, on an unconscious affective register if it's to be effective, which most likely means an integration of the deliverer/deliveree so that a kind of co-delivery occurs. Although Aristotle shunned delivery because of an over-emphasis on emotion, which he felt switched off logic, an electrate delivery would manifest the affective domain toward not (only) the cognitive senses, but emotional senses as well.

Delivery Transmissions

Another way to think about the canon of delivery is through the cannons of delivery. Slings, bows, catapults, firearms, tanks, ships, and airplanes are all missile delivery technologies, extensions of humans that allow them to deliver blows on larger scales, with more accuracy, with more impact, and with faster speeds. The missile provides a mechanism for telepresence, or teleactivity via absence of the sender's proximity. Such advances in delivery have made war both safer and deadlier. This missile allows for the sender to be missed while simultaneously hitting, removing the danger from one side of the exchange but not the other.

Again, this kind of delivery often requires an element of subterfuge, of a delivery that happens "under the radar" through the development of various stealth technologies that make the delivery mechanism invisible from the audience that will eventually receive the message/missile. Stealth fighters and bombers offer examples of an invisible delivery, one meant to be unseen as they deliver their payload. Submarines need not only be invisible, making their particular location unknown to the enemy, but also silent to enemy submarines, invisible to their sonar. Camouflage generally attempts to fulfill this function at the length of light waves visible to the human eye.

Although these delivery technologies need to remain invisible to the instruments that extend our eyes and ears, as well as in-person military engagement, war strategists need the technologies to be visible more generally to the eyes and ears themselves as a way to broadcast their strength and superiority to the enemy and the home front. As Paul Virilio has shown, modern military technology has developed in tandem and in connection with cinema as a way to deliver these images. Warfare, during World War II—as currently—relied on photographic and cinematographic writing practices to gather information, often developing and improving upon these technologies along the way. As Virilio writes, "People used to die for a coat of arms, an image on a pennant or flag; now they died to improve the sharpness of a film. War has finally become the third dimension of cinema."[67] Virilio also notes, citing Sun Tzu, that military force is based on deception, a deception that is itself rhetorical and relies on the delivery of images: "to fell the enemy is not so much to capture as to 'captivate' him, to instill the fear of death before he actually dies."[68] The images of war unleash a "spiritual force" that can work at the level of affect, inside the body rather than upon it. Visual capture, as discussed in connection with augmented reality, dominates sight as a means to dominate the spirit. "Weapons are tools not just of destruction but also of perception—that is to say, stimulants that make themselves felt through chemical, neurological processes in the sense organs and central nervous system, affecting human reactions and even the perceptual identification and differentiation of objects."[69]

The delivery of missiles requires images of the targets of missile delivery, images that are more easily attainable through satellite imagery. But warfare also requires the images of the enemy's delivery systems thereby making delivery itself a target. Area 51 was not a location for extraterrestrial space-craft, but alien aircraft, aircraft that would be strange and invisible to enemy radar. To throw off the Russian spy planes, personnel at Area 51 would place silhouette mock-ups of fake aircraft while the real projects lay under aircraft hangars. Such delivery was truly hypocritical.

The pictures from these spy planes and other image-gathering sources were needed more than ever as successive bombings changed the features of the earth along the warfront, making traditional maps unreliable so that the upturned landscapes "had to be reconstituted with the help of successive frames and shots, in a cinematographic pursuit of reality, the decomposition and recom-position of an uncertain territory in which film replaced military maps."[70] Landscapes were rewritten with the delivery of each ordinance, requiring a redelivery of images to command. The delivery of these images provided a delivery of intelligence, intelligence then used to make practical decisions. The interplay of technology, image, and human systems, all brought together by these various practices of delivery, contributes to a decision-making process that is not unlike that which a rhetorical deliverer facilitates and undergoes, especially among a distributed audience connected by networked systems that may be away from the front lines or the front rows.

If Area 51 was meant to fool the Russians, public displays of military might are meant to bolster support back at home. Especially for an audi-ence overseas, news, stories, and images of the war front become necessary rhetorical tools for keeping a public engaged in their domestic domain of decision-making. Toward this, while the technology of cinematography helps on the battlefield, it also helps to deliver on the home front. As an example of how this delivery occurs, Virilio places notable focus on Fred Astaire, who's "songs and dances … became disguised calls for a new mobilization."[71] In particular, Astaire's movement through dance signals a particular call to war, movement that in Napoleon's words created the very capacity for war:

> Fred Astaire's persistent *charm* doubtless stems from this unsuspected fusion/confusion of 'science' and dance. The thin and glittering hem of his tuxedo, his dancing exhalation of the most everyday steps and body-movements, call to mind that 'hijacking' of the spectator's gaze of which Marey was so fond. When he photographed the movement of white birds or horses, or human subjects with silver strips on their black

clothing, he was making the body disappear into momentary agglom-
eration of sense-data, oscillating between the production of luminous
impressions and that pure fascination which dispels perceptual awareness and induces hypnosis or similar pathological conditions.[72]

This passage needs unpacking, because several terms have ties to other
domains of delivery. For instance, we might understand the colloquial charm
as referring to Astaire's debonair and suave delivery in his romantic come-
dies and musicals, although to charm is to place one under a spell, a kind of
hypnosis, a state beneath consciousness, the place where thrownness occurs.
The original word *charm* meant a chanting or recitation of a magical verse,
or an object that held such powers. While a charm can be an object, subject
to a transitive form of delivery, it's more properly a performance, a delivery
of chanting that results in an enchantment. (The fact that a charm is also an
object is an exception that proves the rule of performance, as the charm-object
is usually a necessary tool to enact the performance of the charm.)

As Virilio describes, Astaire's costume becomes an important part of his
delivery, a key element of his charming performance. But the costume not
only glimmers, it also raps and taps, making the tap shoes a magic tool that
allows Astaire to provide a beat, a rhythm to the image to induce this "pure
fascination." As one follows the tapping beneath the spectacle (literally and
figuratively), syncing with it, the broader "perceptional awareness" dissi-
pates and the audience becomes engaged in the dance with Astaire. Privately,
Astaire preferred to dress in a way that didn't stand out. With his delivery,
his own body became less important than those features of the costume,
causing himself to dissipate with his audience until the performance became
pure motion and fluttering, creating a hypnotic call to war lying underneath
the tap and flash of the dance.

In Virilio's example, this charming dance performs a viewpoint that considers delivery—as Aristotle describes—as a practice of conning. The dance
induces the audience into a state of mind that makes them more perceptive
to a particular message, just as delivery is said to surpass the logical structure of an argument, making bad logic acceptable. In this way we might say
that—using Virilio's term—delivery has the potential to "hijack" not only the
spectator's gaze, but its critical awareness, its "perceptual awareness." How
does this hijacking work with Astaire's dancing? Besides rhythm, Astaire
also relied upon mixing various dance styles, particularly jazz, to keep the
audience "on their toes" about what step would come next in the fluid routine. As Jerome Robbins has stated, "Astaire's dancing looks so simple, so
disarming, so easy, yet the understructure, the way he sets the steps on, over
or against the music, is so surprising and inventive."[73] This last term, inventive, returns us to how dance has traditionally been used when thinking
about writing. Ulmer devotes much attention to dancing in his early work
on electracy (before he coined the term) in *Applied Grammatology*, particularly looking at Derrida's *pas-ne-pas*, the step that is not a step, eventually

moving to Carmen Miranda in *Electronic Monuments*, and offering Elvis's hips in-between the two in *Internet Invention*. However, what is dance's role in delivery? While I discuss dance, Ulmer, and *Applied Grammatology* more in chapter 3, and the importance of rhythm in chapter 4, here I'll simply offer that dance, through its performance before an audience, offers a site of group invention, where the surprises come not for the performer (Astaire painstakingly scripted all his moves and could reproduce every apparent digression with uncanny exactness), but for the audience—as the surprise, a novelty that manifests in their bodies—who may tap along with the dancer or simply feel the moves, especially when the jolt of the unexpected move clashes with their expectation of what should come next.

However, dancing offers a bit more than this. The unexpected movement, pulling the audience in a direction they were not prepared to go, supports Virilio's "hijacking" as way to describe how the audience becomes cognitively lost in its gaze as it becomes pleasantly disorientated. As a biological cell may be "hijacked" by a virus, which then controls the cell and uses it for its own purpose, Astaire—combined with the larger delivery apparatus of suits and sets—attempts to visually capture the viewer and transport them into a different state of mind. "Transport" summons hijack's close association with vehicular delivery, particularly planes. An entire audience can be diverted from their anticipated delivery to an unintended destination. The important functional point of hijacking is that it occurs in transit but with the passenger thinking they are heading for a different destination. A hijacking, from the perspective of the audience, is unforeseen and usually unwanted, and so such hijacking occurs in hypnosis—a hypo-jacking—if to be successful as a delivery strategy, though perhaps an ethically suspect one.

Astaire has often been credited as greatly contributing to how dance appears on film. He was able to develop routines and "gimmicks"—such as dancing on the wall (*Royal Wedding*) or with his shadows (*Swing Time*)— that would only register when viewed through the controlled set construction and postproduction of film. Filmed dance also solves the problem of how a particular dance is interpreted as it can only be seen from the angle of the camera. As Virilio extends, the cinema helps to solve this problem of direct delivery and of the environmental constraints of prior delivery venues. Since no one in a theater sits in the same seat, none experience the same play.

> Cinema solves this problem, however, because what each member of the audience sees from anywhere in the room (or in a country, where there is an audience of millions) is the exact picture taken by the camera ... now there is only one audience which sees and hears exactly as the camera and microphone do.[74]

A mass hijacking also depends on all victims being together and constrained by the same vehicle. As the hijacker, it's much easier to get fifty victims in one bus to do what you want as opposed to fifty victims on fifty different busses. This transition of dance onto film, then, demonstrates the projection of the body as a vehicle for mass hijacking, something not available in previous modes of delivery such as print, and more effective in prior modes of delivering the unspoken characteristics of the body which may be seen, but seen from these individual angles. Although arguments exist that film as an older, non-digital medium is distinct from digital media, we might then turn to Lev Manovich's claim that new media uses the logics and devices of film—thus, the continuation of "dance" into digital media maintains a continuity and provides an important departure point for how to think about dance as a system and mechanism for electrate delivery, not only as a relay of electrate invention.

However—like the relationship between Skywalker and Solo—Astaire was delivered to just as he delivered, and according to Virilio, supported the industrial war machine as an intermediary, translating the desires of the war machine into the desires of the public (as Hearst had done before through images and print). As Virilio writes (referring not to Astaire particularly), because the actor/dancer/singer was simply a part of the delivery-machine, "These film-makers, who seemed to 'hijack' the image as the surrealists hijacked language, were themselves merely being hijacked by war."[75] Ultimately, these various delivery technologies of print and film support other delivery technologies such as the missiles that become guided by the very image technologies that guide the public back home. To talk about these delivery technologies is also to discuss delivery systems—the larger networks that allow for the delivery of a missile to reach its target. We have to remember that the Internet developed from the ARPANET, a network system that was not only designed to keep communications open given a missile strike, but also to allow retaliation by our own missiles, a distributed delivery system that could function even if one part was disrupted. The subsequent creation of the Internet and World Wide Web provides a distributed system of information delivery, missives instead of missiles, but still etymologically and theoretically related. These delivery systems assemble with many other kinds of related technologies, from GPS satellites and GPS guided systems to video games and flight simulators that prepare remote pilots to deliver missile strikes via drones (drones that also carry on the business of capturing images for delivery analysis).

Since "missile" comes from the Latin "mittere"—to send, throw, or cast a weapon—the term missile has a larger sense of throwing, and these missiles are present through our transmissions and eventually, if delivery is successful, a sub-mission of the audience to heed the authority of advice given by the speaker. But the power of transmission (delivery) toward submission is one that is also subliminal, subconscious, so that the audience is not aware that this request of submissiveness (or at least acquiescence) is taking place. Thus, delivery as transmission/submission is often not overt, but covert.

Delivery as transmission requires a new task given the proliferation of ways something can be delivered. As Virilio also explains, once new technologies enabled the military leaders to see and locate the enemy via sonar, radar, and other seeing technologies, the difficult task was no longer trying to guess the unknowable, to but decipher it among all the signals that were newly transmitted:

> visibility and invisibility now began to evolve together, eventually *pro-ducing invisible weapons that make things visible*—radar, sonar, and the high-definition camera of spy satellites … The problem, then, is no longer so much one of masks and screens, of camouflage designed to hinder long-range targeting; rather, it is a problem of ubiquitousness, of handling simultaneous data in a global but unstable environment where the image (photographic or cinematic) is the most concentrated, but also the most stable, form of information.[76]

The delivery-potential of Astaire's dancing comes not in his body's invisibility, for surely one can see it, but how it simultaneously stands out and vanishes among all the other visual elements, all the other "sense-data," the "thin and glittering hem of his tuxedo," the predetermined spontaneity of the tap's rhythm, the musical accompaniment, and all the other visual elements that appear on screen, not to mention the rhythm of the cuts. All these together, like the ubiquitous data of the war image, deliver a mood but make delivery as invention/decision-making difficult because the data can fail to make the mood self-aware to the audience, to produce a self-knowledge that allows one to make a decision in one's best interest, one of the hallmarks of a democratic delivery. The dual technologies of imaging the war and imaging Astaire parallel a similar simultaneity of sense-data that appears in many digital media modes, producing a mood, an emotion, but not always making this conscious to the viewer. While the invisible may become visible, the motivation or workings of triggering this mood may not, producing a kind of delivery that Aristotle rejects. While film and video may visualize the body in a way that print does not afford, that body is still very much invisible like Astaire's, as is the audience's body to themselves when viewing. Delivery, then, has a double-blindness within the larger system that must be addressed to develop any holistic theory on how it might work.

However, a better understanding of what occurs in delivery might not come from the term "hijack," but from abduct. In delivery, an abduction occurs, a leading away, but also a leading under, this subliminal undertaking, a leading of the audience unawares. More broadly, Charles Sanders Peirce has used abduction to identify a "distinctive logical operation," which he describes as "a general prediction without any positive assurance that it will succeed either in the special case or usually, its justification being that it is the only possible hope of regulating our future conduct rationally, and that induction from past experience gives us strong encouragement to hope that it will be successful in the future."[77] Stefan Helmreich, in discussing the complexity of undersea life in his book *Alien Ocean*, uses abduction to denote its centrality to explaining this complexity, and inflects Peirce's definition with the more insidious meaning, "[the] unexpected capture against one's will" by an alien life form.[78] Helmreich uses this combination to theorize the role of microbiologists who research an alien ocean, whereby the scientists often take the role of the extraoceanic alien: "our work might be seen as one style of alien abduction, a venture in which humans, as strangers to the sea, employ a mixture of logic and last-ditch hope to make sense of something unfamiliar."[79] As Sid Dobrin and Kyle Jensen write in their collection *Abducting Writing Studies*:

> In pairing the two definitions together, Helmreich claims that abduction, although pitched toward an uncertain future, dwells in the complexity of the present. This complexity is available only because researchers occupy an intellectual and physical space that estranges the security of their knowledge systems. The hope, of course, is that the experience of estrangement can be understood logically. But Helmreich demonstrates that these alien encounters require unconventional explanations that never fully capture the complexity of the experience.[80]

Delivery often occurs in unknown environments and in unknown moments, moments alienated and alien from what will be, tense moments of unknown abduction to a future time, an unawareness that one has been abducted until after the abduction has occurred. As a logic of the future, abduction provides a useful term through which to think about delivery. If delivery, as I argue, provides a strategy for group invention, abduction provides another term for this strategy, for abduction (usually) requires more than one participant for an abduction to occur. Whenever a group makes a decision, some in the group become abducted. But this decision, because it works toward contingent possibilities, is at best a guess, and as Douglas Walton explains, we abduct whenever we make such an intelligent guess "that is tied to an incomplete body of evidence."[81] Both abduction and delivery are attempts to get hold of unfamiliar, complex, contingent situations where all the facts are unknown and impossible to fully link. Delivery operates amidst this uncertain complexity, and must be reimagined with such complexity in mind.

This chapter has worked through different ways that "delivery" currently circulates, how it comes to represent an action that can be transitive, performative, or both, as Brooke has identified. What these different kinds of delivery tell us is that they often happen collectively, silently, and beneath the level of consciousness, playing on our desires to participate and join in the delivery process. I explore all of these aspects further in the rest of this book. The next chapter, however, will look at other terms that have preceded *delivery* and argue that the original Greek term, *hypokrisis*, best captures what delivery is within our current moment.

Notes

1. Ben McCorkle, *Rhetorical Delivery as Technological Discourse: A Cross-Historical Study* (Carbondale, IL: Southern Illinois University Press, 2012), 2.
2. Collin Gifford Brooke, *Lingua Fracta: Towards a Rhetoric of New Media* (Creskill, NJ: Hampton Press, 2009), 170.
3. Ibid.
4. Alan L. Boegehold, *When a Gesture Was Expected: A Selection of Examples from Archaic and Classical Literature* (Princeton, NJ: Princeton University Press, 1999), 78–79.
5. Alcidamas, *On the Sophists*, trans. LaRue Van Hook, *Peithôs's Web*, accessed July 3, 2015, http://www.classicpersuasion.org/pw/alcidamas/alcsoph1.htm.
6. Boegehold, 80.
7. Raúl Sánchez, *The Function of Theory in Composition Studies* (Albany, NY: State University of New York Press, 2005), 85.
8. Sanchez, 3.
9. *Deliverance*, DVD, directed by John Boorman (1972; Burbank, CA: Warner Home Video, 2007).
10. Eugene M. Longen, "Dickey's 'Deliverance': Sex and the Great Outdoors," *The Southern Literary Journal* 9, no. 2 (1977): 146.
11. Keen Butterworth, "The Savage Mind: James Dickey's 'Deliverance,'" *The Southern Literary Journal* 28, no. 2 (1996): 71.
12. Longen, 146.
13. William Heyen, "A Conversation with James Dickey," *Southern Review*, 9, no. 1 (1973): 154–155.
14. R. Barton Palmer, "Narration, Text, Intertext: The Two Versions of Deliverance," *Struggling for Wings: The Art of James Dickey*, ed. Robert Kirschten (Columbia, SC: University of South Carolina Press, 1997), 202–203.
15. Ibid., 203.
16. Lynn Clark Callister, "Cultural influences on pain perceptions and behaviors," *Home Health Care Management & Practice* 15, no. 3 (2003): 207.
17. Margaret Mead, *Male and Female* (New York: Perennial, 2001), 57.
18. Judith Walzer Leavitt, "How Did Men End Up in the Delivery Room?," *History News Network*, September 6, 2009, http://historynewsnetwork.org/article/116291.
19. Iris Marion Young, *On Female Body Experience: "Throwing Like a Girl" and Other Essays* (Oxford, UK: Oxford University Press, 2005), 55.
20. Kerreen Reiger and Rhea Dempsey, "Performing Birth in a Culture of Fear: An Embodied Crisis of Late Modernity," *Health Sociology Review* 15, no. 4 (2006): 364.
21. Reiger and Dempsey, 364.
22. Reiger and Dempsey, 365.
23. Reiger and Dempsey, 366.
24. Susan Bordo, *Unbearable Weight: Feminism, Western Culture, and the Body* (Berkeley, CA: University of California Press, 1993), 287.
25. Iris Marion Young, "Lived Body vs Gender: Reflections on Social Structure and Subjectivity," *Ratio* 15, no. 4 (2002): 415.
26. Reiger and Dempsey, 368.
27. Ibid.
28. Ibid., 369.
29. Ibid., 368.

30. Ibid., 370.
31. Ibid., 368.
32. Ibid.
33. Ibid., 367.
34. In professional road cycling, the winner of the race will often make a gesture that resembles the one used in American football for "touchdown": in cycling, this gesture is called "posting."
35. Chung-Hsiung Lai, "Re-writing the Subject: The Thrownness of Being in the Multicultural Condition," *Canadian Review of Comparative Literature/Revue Canadienne de Littérature Comparée* 30, no. 3–4 (2003): 496.
36. Ronald T. Azuma, "A Survey of Augmented Reality," *Presence* 6, no. 4 (1997): 367.
37. As an experiment to see and experience the effects of this kind of visual capture, try the following: sit on the floor with your back against a wall or something firm. Extend your legs out in front of you, feet together. Then take your cell phone, turn on the camera and point it at your legs. Pull the camera back close enough to your face so that you can see the image of your feet on the screen, but if you twist your ankles outward so your feet point out, you can't see them beyond the phone. Then slowly rock your feet out and in, from feet parallel pointing up to feet pointing in opposite directions away from each other. Keep the motion going watching only on the screen. Soon the experience between what you feel your feet doing and what you see your feet doing will begin to switch and disconnect.
38. The first logo for the USPOD (1782), appropriately enough, used the image of Mercury, the messenger of the Greco-Roman gods. In 1837, the USPOD changed the logo to an image of a rider on horseback similar to that created and used by the short-lived Pony Express. Rather than a stagecoach, railcar, or steamboat, the U.S. Post Office Department tapped into the American mythology that would eventually take hold after the Pony Express. Current logos for the USPS (used beginning in 1970), however, have incorporated the bald eagle, solidifying its association with the U.S. government, but also the swiftness of the eagle's flight, pushing the dromosphere of delivery ever faster. However, we must also remember that a return to the eagle is also a return to classical mythology, as the eagle is the bird of Zeus, who can also deliver through electricity (the need for the Pony Express was made obsolete by the telegraph), and uses his eagle to deliver punishment of Prometheus. We must remember this because—as will be discussed in the postscript—delivery, like deliverance, has risks and a duplicity that must be considered before put into practice, even rhetorical delivery.
39. Glenn Danford Bradley, *The Story of the Pony Express* (Chicago, IL: A.C. McClurg, 1913), 55.
40. See Raymond W. Settle and Mary Lund Settle, *Saddles and Spurs: The Pony Express Saga* (Lincoln, NE: Bison Books, 1972), 113–143.
41. See Lindal Buchanan, *Regendering Delivery: The Fifth Canon and Antebullum Women Rhetors* (Carbondale, IL: Southern Illinois University Press, 2005).
42. See Louis S. Warren, "Cody's Last Stand: Masculine Anxiety, the Custer Myth, and the Frontier of Domesticity in Buffalo Bill's Wild West," *Western Historical Quarterly* 34, no. 1 (Spring 2003): 49–69.
43. Don Delillo, *White Noise* (New York: Penguin, 2009), 12.
44. Niall Lucy, *A Derrida Dictionary* (Oxford, UK: Blackwell, 2004), 96.
45. *Seinfeld*, episode no. 57, first broadcast February 18, 1993 by NBC, directed by Tom Cherones and written by Larry David, Jerry Seinfeld, Larry Charles, Bruce Kirschbaum, and Peter Mehlman.

46. *Serenity*, DVD, directed by Nicholas Meyer (2005; Hollywood, CA: Universal Studios, 2008).
47. See Gregory L. Ulmer, *Internet Invention: From Literacy to Electracy* (New York: Longman, 2002), 186.
48. Ibid., 180.
49. *Star Wars, Episode IV: A New Hope*, DVD, directed by George Lucas (1977; Los Angeles, CA: Twentieth Century Fox, 2004).
50. Ulmer, *Internet Invention*, 180.
51. Ibid.
52. Quoted in William Leith, "A Writer's Life: Chuck Palahniuk," *The Telegraph*, October 21, 2003, accessed July 23, 2015, http://www.telegraph.co.uk/culture/books/3604888/A-writers-life-Chuck-Palahniuk.html.
53. The fact that "outer space" itself is silent helps deliver an intrigue about an environment that negates spoken language, a quality we often equate to humanness.
54. George Carlin, "Seven Words You Can Never Say on Television," *Class Clown*, © 2000, 1972 by Eardrum Records, 92923–2, compact disc.
55. Carlin.
56. Gregory L. Ulmer, *Teletheory* (New York: Atropos, 2004), 77.
57. Ibid.
58. Ibid., 72.
59. John Allen Paulos, *Mathematics and Humor* (Chicago, IL: University of Chicago Press, 1980), 61.
60. Ibid., 27.
61. Ulmer, *Teletheory*, 76.
62. Ibid.
63. Silvano Arieti, *Creativity: The Magic Synthesis* (New York: Basic Books, 1976), 112.
64. James Sullivan, *7 Dirty Words: The Life and Crimes of George Carlin* (Cambridge, MA: Da Capo Press, 2010), 4.
65. Ulmer, *Teletheory*, 79.
66. Ibid.
67. Paul Virilio, *War and Cinema: The Logistics of Perception* (London: Verso, 1989), 106.
68. Ibid., 8.
69. Ibid.; Such "targeting" of a fear of death also uses sound. In the film *Top Gun*, the character Cougar, a U.S. Naval Aviator, becomes panicked once he hears the tone of the enemy's missile lock on his fighter jet, made all the more terrifying since he cannot maneuver to see the enemy jet behind him. The lingering fear drives him to resign his post.
70. Ibid., 99.
71. Ibid., 13.
72. Ibid., 13–14.
73. Quoted in John Mueller, *Astaire Dancing: The Musical Films* (London: Hamish Hamilton, 1986), 18.
74. Virilio, 50.
75. Ibid., 26.
76. Ibid., 89.
77. Charles S. Peirce, *The Essential Peirce: Selected Philosophical Writings, vol. 2*, ed. Peirce Edition Project (Bloomington, IN: University of Indiana Press, 1998), 299.
78. Stefan Helmreich, *Alien Ocean: Anthropological Voyages in Microbial Seas* (Berkeley, CA: University of California Press, 2009), 173.

79. Ibid., 194.
80. Sidney I. Dobrin and Kyle Jensen, *Abducting Writing Studies* (Carbondale, IL: Southern Illinois University Press, forthcoming).
81. Douglas Walton, *Abductive Reasoning* (Tuscaloosa, AL: University of Alabama Press, 2005), 3.

Bibliography

Alcidamas. *On the Sophists.* Translated by LaRue Van Hook. *Peithôs's Web.* Accessed July 3, 2015, http://www.classicpersuasion.org/pw/alcidamas/alcsoph1.htm.

Arieti, Silvano. *Creativity: The Magic Synthesis.* New York: Basic Books, 1976.

Azuma, Ronald T. "A Survey of Augmented Reality." *Presence* 6, no. 4 (1997): 355–385.

Boegehold, Alan L. *When a Gesture Was Expected: A Selection of Examples from Archaic and Classical Literature.* Princeton, NJ: Princeton University Press, 1999.

Bordo, Susan. *Unbearable Weight: Feminism, Western Culture, and the Body.* Berkeley, CA: University of California Press, 1993.

Bradley, Glenn Danford. *The Story of the Pony Express.* Chicago, IL: A.C. McClurg, 1913.

Brooke, Collin Gifford. *Lingua Fracta: Towards a Rhetoric of New Media.* Creskill, NJ: Hampton Press, 2009.

Butterworth, Keen. "The Savage Mind: James Dickey's 'Deliverance.'" *The Southern Literary Journal* 28, no. 2 (1996): 69–78.

Callister, Lynn Clark. "Cultural influences on pain perceptions and behaviors." *Home Health Care Management & Practice* 15, no. 3 (2003): 207–211.

Carlin, George. "Seven Words You Can Never Say on Television." *Class Clown.* © 2000, 1972 by Eardrum Records. 92923–2. Compact disc.

Delillo, Don. *White Noise.* New York: Penguin, 2009.

Deliverance. DVD. Directed by John Boorman. 1972; Burbank, CA: Warner Home Video, 2007.

Dobrin, Sidney I. and Kyle Jensen. *Abducting Writing Studies.* Carbondale, IL: Southern Illinois University Press, forthcoming.

Heidegger, Martin. *Introduction to Metaphysics.* Translated by Gregory Fried and Richard Polt. New Haven, CT: Yale University Press, 2000.

Helmreich, Stefan. *Alien Ocean: Anthropological Voyages in Microbial Seas.* Berkeley, CA: University of California Press, 2009.

Heyen, William. "A Conversation with James Dickey." *Southern Review,* 9, no. 1 (1973): 135–156.

Lai, Chung-Hsiung. "Re-writing the Subject: The Thrownness of Being in the Multicultural Condition." *Canadian Review of Comparative Literature/Revue Canadienne de Littérature Comparée* 30, no. 3–4 (2003): 495–503.

Leavitt, Judith Walzer. "How Did Men End Up in the Delivery Room?" *History News Network.* September 6, 2009. http://historynewsnetwork.org/article/116291.

Leith, William. "A Writer's Life: Chuck Palahniuk." *The Telegraph.* October 21, 2003. Accessed July 23, 2015. http://www.telegraph.co.uk/culture/books/3604888/A-writers-life-Chuck-Palahniuk.html.

Longen, Eugene M. "Dickey's 'Deliverance': Sex and the Great Outdoors." *The Southern Literary Journal* 9, no. 2 (1977): 137–149.

Lucy, Niall. *A Derrida Dictionary.* Oxford, UK: Blackwell, 2004.

McCorkle, Ben. *Rhetorical Delivery as Technological Discourse: A Cross-Historical Study*. Carbondale, IL: Southern Illinois University Press, 2012.

Mead, Margaret. *Male and Female*. New York: Perennial, 2001.

Mueller, John. *Astaire Dancing: The Musical Films*. London: Hamish Hamilton, 1986.

Palmer, R. Barton. "Narration, Text, Intertext: The Two Versions of Deliverance." In *Struggling for Wings: The Art of James Dickey*, edited by Robert Kirschten, 194–203. Columbia, SC: University of South Carolina Press, 1997.

Paulos, John Allen. *Mathematics and Humor*. Chicago, IL: University of Chicago Press, 1980.

Peirce, Charles S. *The Essential Peirce: Selected Philosophical Writings*. Vol. 2. Edited by Peirce Edition Project. Bloomington, IN: University of Indiana Press, 1998.

"Postal Insignia." *United States Postal Service*. 2015. https://about.usps.com/publications/pub100/pub100_082.htm.

Reiger, Kerreen and Rhea Dempsey. "Performing Birth in a Culture of Fear: An Embodied Crisis of Late Modernity." *Health Sociology Review* 15, no. 4 (2006): 364–373.

Sánchez, Raúl. *The Function of Theory in Composition Studies*. Albany, NY: State University of New York Press, 2005.

Seinfeld. Episode no. 57, first broadcast February 18, 1993 by NBC. Directed by Tom Cherones and written by Larry David, Jerry Seinfeld, Larry Charles, Bruce Kirschbaum, and Peter Mehlman.

Serenity. DVD. Directed by Nicholas Meyer. 2005; Hollywood, CA: Universal Studios, 2008.

Settle, Raymond W. and Mary Lund Settle. *Saddles and Spurs: The Pony Express Saga*. Lincoln, NE: Bison Books, 1972.

Star Wars, Episode IV: A New Hope. DVD. Directed by George Lucas. 1977; Los Angeles, CA: Twentieth Century Fox, 2004.

Sullivan, James. *7 Dirty Words: The Life and Crimes of George Carlin*. Cambridge, MA: Da Capo Press, 2010.

Ulmer, Gregory L. *Applied Grammatology: Post(e)-Pedagogy from Jacques Derrida to Joseph Beuys*. Baltimore, MD: The Johns Hopkins University Press, 1984.

———. *Internet Invention: From Literacy to Electracy*. New York: Longman, 2002.

———. *Teletheory*. New York: Atropos, 2004.

Virilio, Paul. *War and Cinema: The Logistics of Perception*. London: Verso, 1989.

Walton, Douglas. *Abductive Reasoning*. Tuscaloosa, AL: University of Alabama Press, 2005.

Warren, Louis S. "Cody's Last Stand: Masculine Anxiety, the Custer Myth, and the Frontier of Domesticity in Buffalo Bill's Wild West." *Western Historical Quarterly* 34, no. 1 (Spring 2003): 49–69.

Yancey, Kathleen Blake. *Delivering College Composition: The Fifth Canon*. Portsmouth, NH: Boynton/Cook, 2006.

Young, Iris Marion. "Lived Body vs Gender: Reflections on Social Structure and Subjectivity." *Ratio* 15, no. 4 (2002): 410–428.

———. *On Female Body Experience: "Throwing Like a Girl" and Other Essays*. Oxford, UK: Oxford University Press, 2005.

2   Reclassifying Delivery

> For Theophrastos, mastery of *hypokrisis* involved harmonizing the movement of the body with the 'tone' of the *psychê* ... Theophrastos accepted what Aristotle could not accept, namely the importance of the visual, physical elements in performance.
>
> —David Wiles, *The Masks of Menander*[1]

> *Hypokrisis, Hypokrisis, Hypokrisis.*
>
> —Demosthenes

If chapter 1 sought to stir and remix delivery, to declassify and interrogate the term, and determine what it can tell about the current state of delivery, this chapter turns to classical terms for delivery—such as *hypokrisis*, *actio*, and *pronuntiatio*—to investigate their original use as rhetorical techniques. However, rather than a simple rehashing and summary, my goal is to problematize the way the field usually understands this rhetorical tradition—to re-classify the classical—and to suggest that older ways of thinking about delivery have much to offer an electrate delivery. Any chorographic study of delivery requires we think about the whole of delivery, and so this chapter adds to that conversation begun in chapter 1.

In a larger context, the theorists of delivery discussed below—especially classical theorists of delivery such as Aristotle, Cicero, and Quintilian—provide the contrast against which an electrate delivery might be developed. That is, if—as Ben McCorkle argues—the adoption of new writing technologies becomes primed by delivery, changing the practices and function of delivery in this process, then the adoption of alphabetic writing by the Greeks (and the later development of print) changes communication of information from one kind of body (human) to another (non-human media). Delivery methods developed for alphabetic writing technologies no longer favor the body, a medium reintroduced by visual media. However, the contrast that classical scholars provide contains elements of delivery that have been abandoned or neglected and which might be useful for a digital delivery, gaps that might be remixed to provide the invention of a delivery suited for electracy. When considered amongst the contrasts of oral, literate, and electrate language apparatuses, Aristotle's theories of delivery leave clues for how a delivery might work when contextualized within a digital media environment.[2]

Aristotle, Cicero, and Quintilian offer possibilities in their prescriptions. Aristotle, trying to exclude the accident from rhetoric, acknowledges the role of delivery only with great hesitation. Cicero notes its importance and goes further by extending categories of delivery practices glossed over by Aristotle. Quintilian provides even more guidance, offering pedagogical practices and head-to-toe instructions for how to deliver well. However, they all provide a kind of delivery that suits either an oral context, or an oral-literate, almost pre-electrate hybrid. That is, Aristotle acknowledges delivery only so that he may advise against its use (ideologically speaking, but not practically), while Cicero and Quintilian make use of the voice and image of the speaker (the poetic aspects) when delivering rhetoric. In the gaps between their techniques, or in asking the question—"what is that for us?"—we can find practices in this classical contrast that might be useful toward a delivery that uses not only the literate technology of the book, but one that uses image technologies combined with the digital Internet in addition to the identity and institutional formations that coevolve with language technology.

These three classical thinkers, then, provide a distinction for what a delivery-for-us does not want to do while at the same time, through a grammatological reading, perform exactly those aspects which can be adapted for an electrate language apparatus. In one sense, Aristotle, Cicero, and Quintilian have delivery all wrong at the same time that they (collectively) have it all right. They all point out that delivery is the most important aspect of rhetoric, but they all examine different aspects of delivery that were most appropriate for their situations. The program for an electrate delivery circulates among all of these theorists, but is suppressed by the need to use it according to either an oral scenario or for the written word, where Aristotle tried to incorporate it but failed. However, Aristotle's student, Theophrastos, is said to have developed a more comprehensive theory of delivery than his teacher.[3] But just as the voice disappears on the air, so has Theophrastos's works about delivery, and all we know of them comes from classical references to his supposed treatise. Here, then, I will not attempt to recreate Theophrastos's work, but to extrapolate what delivery might be for electracy: to do for electracy what Theophrastos tried to do for an emerging literacy. In other words, my point in teasing out some of the following classical elements of delivery is not to take them literally (that is exactly the opposite of what I want to do), but to look at how they might provide an analogy or relay for practices that an electrate delivery should assimilate.

My methodology does not consist of an archival categorization of the different practices of delivery taught or recommended by these classical teachers and orators, although I do provide a somewhat detailed examination of their advice. Rather, as I explain in the introduction, my method is grammatological, letting the metaphors and terminology do the work for me. This methodology in looking for these gaps comes from Ulmer's work in *Applied Grammatology*. Ulmer advocates that one needs to examine "every manner of inscription, circulating in the universe of discourse as an interruption, a disturbance that excites (incites, not insights), generating 'information.'"[4] Toward this, Ulmer argues that we should explore the metaphors of different domains and discourses "in order to decompose or unfold and redirect the possibilities of meaning inherent in the material."[5] Although we have no actual classical bodies to study (only texts that tell us how such bodies should speak, gesture, move, dress, etc.), the descriptions can still provide information, and we can bootstrap the literate archive to find out what it knows. I begin this chapter by looking at the metaphors within classical conceptions of delivery and ask where those metaphors lead for a system of delivery more useful for a rhetorician that requires not only her own body for delivering, but the prosthesis of digital technologies, a cyborg body that functions differently from the classical orator. Because Aristotle provides the chief icon (along with Socrates and Plato) of literacy—or if you will, literacy's celebrity—I begin with him in order to establish the contrast against which an electrate delivery might be constructed.

Aristotle and *Hypokrisis* (Getting Under His Skin)

"It is interesting that Aristotle, who rarely holds back from being the first to investigate a subject or to formulate the art of practice, dismisses this one as too vulgar to be worthy of his attention."[6] According to Don Bialostosky, *hypokrisis* posed a difficult problem for Aristotle, who never quite developed its theory as he did the other rhetorical parts: "It is rare to see him take as many conflicting turns of evaluation as he does in the brief section in which he takes up the topic."[7] In the *Poetics*, Aristotle writes a more straightforward account of *hypokrisis*, where "his deprecation of its importance for poetics is accomplished in a dismissive rhetorical question, while his referral of the topic elsewhere is relatively neutral."[8] In chapter 19 of the *Poetics*, Aristotle dismisses delivery as rhetorical by classifying its elements, such as diction, and "Modes of Utterance," under a separate poetic delivery category: "But this province of knowledge belongs to the art of Delivery and to the masters of that science."[9] The poet who writes the lines must not be responsible for whether a poetic line is a "command, a prayer, a statement, a threat, a question, an answer, and so forth. To know or not to know these things involves no serious censure upon the poet's art."[10] The actors of such poems must know how to deliver the lines, not the poet, and, Aristotle argues, "we may, therefore, pass this over as an inquiry that belongs to another art, not to poetry."[11] As Bialostosky points out, Aristotle refers this mode of speaking "to an 'art of Delivery' that belongs in neither poetics nor rhetoric."[12] *Hypokrisis* belongs to the actors, not to the poets: let them deal with it. For Aristotle, delivery becomes a domain of rhetoric that should remain unspeakable.

Aristotle cannot decide whether to classify delivery as an art or a science, and this indecision reveals his crisis with *hypokrisis*. This terminological chaos might simply be due to carelessness by Aristotle, or such categorical confusion might be a slip that shows his uncertainty and difficulty in developing a theory and practice for *hypokrisis*. George Kennedy, in his translation of *On Rhetoric*, notes that Aristotle's "negative attitude toward delivery probably also derives from Plato," specifically, Plato's view that "political oratory under democracy had become a form of flattery and that it offered entertainment to the mob" rather than a reasoned debate based in *logos*.[13] Aristotle contends with *hypokrisis* in more detail in *On Rhetoric* than in the *Poetics*, but, as Bialostosky describes, "his tone vacillates"[14] as Aristotle acknowledges *hypokrisis*'s role in rhetoric, but simultaneously laments its necessity. *Hypokrisis* "has the greatest force" but its effectiveness in oration is due to "the sad state of governments."[15] However, while *hypokrisis* "seems a vulgar matter when rightly understood ... one should pay attention to delivery, not because it is right but because it is necessary, since true justice seeks nothing more in a speech than neither to offend nor to entertain."[16] Aristotle would prefer a rhetoric that could rely upon *logos* alone ("for to contend by means of facts themselves is just"[17]), since the rest of rhetoric is merely ornament, extraneous to the pure argument ("everything except demonstration is incidental"[18]). Yet, "because of the corruption of the audience," *hypokrisis* "has great power."[19]

Aristotle perceives *hypokrisis* with a hue of deceit (one that stays with us in the word's English derivative "hypocrite"), and his analysis of *hypokrisis* supports this: "Even in regard to tragedy and rhapsody, delivery was late in coming to be considered; for originally the poets themselves acted their tragedies. Clearly there is something like this in rhetoric, as in poetics."[20] When performed by the author of a play, *hypokrisis* seems more authentic, and does not require a developed skill set. However, this division of labor between the poet (mind) and actor (body) establishes a schism in the development of a literate delivery that Plato laments in the *Phaedrus* when a man's speech becomes divorced from his person via alphabetic writing. Aristotle considered that an author speaking one's own texts was not much different than just merely speaking, and as Kennedy notes, "Thus there was no need to consider the oral interpretation of a play separately from the presentation of it by the author. With occasional exceptions, plays were only performed once, but written copies were available to the reading public."[21] Kennedy also confirms that "the prevailing meaning of *hypokrisis* in Greek is 'acting' and the regular word for an actor is *hypokrites*."[22] According to this vernacular meaning, then, the delivery of a speech becomes complicit with delivering lines in theatre, and thus the rhetorical canon of delivery (as we understand this canon within the context of modern rhetorical studies) becomes synonymous with acting, which would not necessarily be "deceitful" except that during his time logographers wrote speeches for others who would then have to "act" those speeches, and some orators took acting lessons from both tragedians and comedians, thus concealing their "true" essence. *Hypokrisis* becomes an acting of the *logos*, a performance of the word, words that are not one's own, sometimes using a "body" that is not one's own. Such "deceit" itself is not necessarily negative or positive, but rather a form of othering as a rhetorical strategy distinguished as negative or positive through context and use. That is, one becomes something other than an "authentic" self to foster *hypokrisis*, and so we should read "deceit" as the rhetorical attempt to create this alterity rather than assume that it must carry negative baggage.

But Aristotle does view *hypokrisis* with a negative understanding of deceit, and Kennedy further illustrates Aristotle's disposition toward *hypokrisis*, which shifts from an "authentic" acting to a deceitful kind: "Aristotle has remarked in 2.8.14–15 on gestures used by people in affliction, which were probably sometimes acted in court."[23] Aristotle notices a schism between truth and appearance when such speakers distort their *ethos* in order to win sympathy (which resembles techniques that Aristotle advocates in Book 2 of *On Rhetoric*, techniques that explain how to affect the emotions of the audience). In Book 3, as it pertains to *hypokrisis*, Aristotle provides only a brief summary of the techniques involved in acting:

> It is a matter of how the voice should be used in expressing each emotion, sometimes loud and sometimes soft or intermediate, and how the pitch accents [*tonoi*] should be entoned, whether as acute, grave, or circumflex, and what rhythms should be expressed in each case; for [those who study delivery] consider three things, and these are volume, change of pitch [*harmonia*], and rhythm.[24]

Aristotle mentions here only the auditory aspects of delivery, those concerned with how a speaker orally performs the speech and sounds to an audience. However, he neglects to mention anything about the gestures used to act out a speech. Boegehold points out that in large spaces, the audience probably could not readily see such delivery aspects such as facial features: "The shadows and nuances of facial expression, effective as they are in close quarters, are lost when much of the audience sits too far away to see the expression on the orator's face."[25] Large spaces—such as those where the *ekklesia* would meet—would require that other visual performances of the body, such as gesture, become more important in such venues: "Speakers accordingly had to move their heads and hands and bodies to be fully effective."[26] Through his attention to speech, neglecting the other aspects of the visible body to the audience, Aristotle reveals his bias for the word, and his own anxiety for what he feels are extrinsic properties not proper to rhetoric. His omission of gestures forces us to consider the absence of the visible, which requires attention in a shift from book to screen culture.[27]

Aristotle would prefer only to consider the logical essence of an argument. However, the accidental traits of rhetoric haunt him. When in the form of writing alone, speeches can appeal more to reason. But when orally recited, "written speeches have greater effect through expression than through thought."[28] His unease with *hypokrisis* appears again when he considers pedagogy: "The subject of lexis, however, has some small necessary place in all teaching; for to speak in one way rather than another does make some difference in regard to clarity, though not a great difference; but all these things are forms of outward show and intended to affect the audience. As a result, nobody teaches geometry this way."[29] Geometry, a logical construct, does not require pedagogical ornament in the classroom. However, by arguing in the section on *hypokrisis* that "outward show" and "affect" are undesirable, Aristotle undercuts his own argument on rhetoric that he develops earlier in his text. Again, as Bialostosky writes:

> these gestures would retract not just attention to delivery but to every-thing beyond arguments from logos in the *Rhetoric*; indeed, the turn to geometry would retract all the probabilistic arguments that Aristotle has carefully developed for the kinds of questions rhetoric ordinarily addresses. He seems to be struggling here to name a rational discourse of sufficient power and purity to dismiss definitively the inescapable but apparently scandalous irrational force of delivery, which seems even more troubling in the province of rhetoric than in that of poetics.[30]

Aristotle, based on Bialostosky's reading, wants to exclude the accidental traits of rhetoric to arrive at a purer, more "literate" form of rhetoric, a rhetoric of pure reason that involves just "the facts themselves" and can "dismiss" the irrationality of the affective elements delivery can afford. This irrational force of delivery threatens this pure reason, but if he excludes it in total he dismantles much of his argument that other rhetorical aspects, predominantly those that affect an audience's emotions, should be available to the speaker.

These emotional appeals primarily appear in Book 2 of *On Rhetoric*. Aristotle's stance toward *hypokrisis*, then, as it pertains to emotions, seems antithetical to this earlier argument where he lists propositions for the definition and causes of various emotions and how to address them in rhetoric.

> The emotions [*pathe*] are those things through which, by undergoing change, people come to differ in their judgments and which are accompanied by pain and pleasure, for example, anger, pity, fear, and other such things and their opposites. There is need to divide the discussion of each into three headings. I mean, for example, in speaking of anger, what is their state of mind when people are angry and against whom are they usually angry and for what sort of reasons; for if we understood one or two of these but not all, it would be impossible to create anger. And similarly, in speaking on the subjects discussed in other emotions.[31]

Whereas Aristotle disapproves of delivery as *hypokrisis*, that is, as an acting equivalent to defrauding, he sees the value of understanding emotion to the extent that a rhetor may either elicit or at least take account of mood ("state of mind") when inventing a speech. However, the way that Aristotle accounts for emotions with *heuresis* is quite different from how he approaches them in *hypokrisis*. It seems that as long as the argument is constrained to the writing, the words of the speech, then emotions are necessary, or at least acceptable. Yet, when other factors such as pitch, rhythm, or tone are introduced, these non-graphic elements have too much power over *logos* in persuading an audience.[32] This emotional element (*pathos*) of rhetoric, especially as it manifests through the image of the body, provides an abandoned thread that can benefit electrate delivery.

Aristotle's anxiety coincides with an originary moment for literacy, most notably analyzed by Martin Heidegger. In *Introduction to Metaphysics*, Heidegger offers that the feature of literacy that the Greeks used to confront the natural world (*phusis*) was *logos*, which becomes reduced to "word" or "language." However, Heidegger tells us that *logos* originally meant "gathering." That is, the Greeks gathered things that they saw and put them into relationships with each other based upon categories. Category systems, however, can differ. Once the Greeks had the recording device of alphabetic writing, they began to gather according to words and essences, and categories became literate. At this point, *logos*-as-gathering and *logos*-as-word collapsed into a single meaning, the latter eclipsing the former:

> *Logos*, in the sense of saying and asserting, now becomes the domain and place where decisions are made about truth—that is, originally, about the unconcealment of beings and thus about the Being of beings. In the inception, *logos* as gathering *is* the happening of unconcealment; *logos* is grounded in unconcealment and is in service to it. But now, *logos* as assertion becomes the locus of truth in the sense of correctness.[33]

The literate way to connect things in the world (and thus gather them) was through the copula, which Heidegger identifies as the verb "is," and which creates essences through this linking. The "is" places things into categories, into fixed states of being. This linking excludes the accident as an important element of being, one that Heidegger tells us to rescue. One of the most important features of the poetic is *doxa*, for this is what the poet works with, what we notice, the already known. The *doxa* gathers accidents and is an accident itself. If Heidegger is not after literate essence, then one must look for the accidental, the opinion, the view of something other than the necessary—the *hypokritical*. Like *logos*, *hypokrisis* the term collapses into the essence of "acting," cutting off other ways of being that *hypokrisis* reveals.

Aristotle's dilemma, his tracing and erasure of *hypokrisis* (rooted in this new metaphysics of essences), mimics a dance, or more accurately, a two-step. In *Applied Grammatology*, Ulmer makes a creative case for the way that Derrida often evokes dance metaphors to create a dancing effect in his texts, especially when Derrida analyzes other texts such as those of Mallarme, and this "reversal of the analogy between syntax and dancing helps to decipher what is taking place."[34] In looking at Derrida's "Pas," a step that is not a step, Ulmer notices how Derrida structures his syntax to create a shuttling effect (which he identifies earlier as a pattern important to Derrida).

> A phrase like "*pas d'au-dela*" (undecidable between a "step beyond" and "no beyond") perfectly states the simulacrum of movement in the space of writing (the taking place of the place itself, which goes nowhere). The "step" that does not walk, in the syntax explored in "Pas," ... suggests that what is involved here might be easier to dance than to explain or describe.[35]

Aristotle also creates a shuttling effect, dancing around *hypokrisis* (which is itself, in its bodily aspect, concerned with movement as well), weaving back and forth, toward and away from it, flirting with it at times but ultimately rejecting it as an undesirable component of rhetoric—yet accepting it as necessary, given the "sad state of governments." Thus, *hypokrisis* is an accidently necessary dance partner, or perhaps a necessary accident, but one that Aristotle would rather pass off and forget altogether. Because of this, *hypokrisis*, even though in the international language of theory, does require a Rosetta stone, or at least an application of grammatology.

If Aristotle dances around *hypokrisis*, snubbing it, what can the jilted term itself tell us that he will not? If we return to this transformational moment for *hypokrisis*, what paths might it take other than "acting"? Starting etymologically, the prefix, *hypo-* translates from Greek into several meanings: under, beneath, down, from below; underhand, secretly; in a subordinate degree, slightly. "*Krisis*" derives from the verb *krinein*: to decide, determine, judge. The sense in which the term comes to mean "acting," then, would seem to be something like "to undercut one's judgment," in that acting has the ability to fool, to represent as truth what is false, to swindle. The English derivative "hypocrisis" has this meaning—dissembling: "To alter or disguise the semblance of (one's character, a feeling, design, or action) so as to conceal, or deceive as to, its real nature; to give a false or feigned semblance to; to cloak or disguise by a feigned appearance."[36] *Hypokrisis* makes what seems seem something else. It operates below *doxa*, or transforms what would seem into another seeming. *Hypokrisis* adds accidents to accidents, which may be why Aristotle found it so troubling.

Turning to the English derivative, *hypokrisis* (as hypocrisy) denotes this dissembling. Where does dissembling lead? At first, it suggests the kind of hypocrisy common in the current vernacular: one who says one thing but does another. In this way, one disguises one's true nature. One "acts" a way different from her/his essence: they are uncanny, out of their being.

But one can also merely "appear" different, which becomes an act of representation, of resemblance. But when one "sembles" (the obsolete root of dissemble), one already appears: "To be like, resemble; to seem, appear."[37] Why, then, does *hypokrisis* dissemble? Why the "dis"? Dissemble suggests a double appearance, or an undoing of appearance, a return from appearance. However, this is not a turn to the "truth," but rather a means of a non-representational writing; *hypokrisis* is a writing without a clear inscription, a clear trace, for the trace disappears on the air even as it becomes affect. *Hypokrisis*, as it dissembles, disses the appearance that passes for truth. It is to resemble not.[38] But if *hypokrisis* is a writing of disappearances, can we make it appear and turn it into a writing practice?

"Semble" also means "to bring together."[39] A dissembling disperses what has been gathered. Within the rhetorical canons, *hypokrisis*, literally, delivers what was invented, arranged, styled, and memorized. It circulates this work of the author/speaker to an audience. This, it seems, is at the heart of *hypokrisis* as delivery. Of course, writing alone becomes its own deliverer. A shopping list can deliver; the author and the audience, in this case, is the same. So why *hypokrisis* at all? Aristotle seems to be correct in wanting to dismiss it from rhetoric, especially as it pertains to literacy. However, although literacy does not support *hypokrisis*, *hypokrisis* supports affect, and thus still finds a place within the oral applications of literacy. But "dis" does not just convey an undoing, but also a "twiceness." That is, *hypokrisis* disseminates, it disperses what was gathered, but it also gathers again. An orator gathers his audience as it hangs on his words. He tries to gather their opinions into his own. He tries to disseminate his own feelings while collecting theirs, a process that flows back and forth as an audience affects the speaker and the speaker affects them in turn.

But back to *hypokrisis*. Because *krisis* derives from *krinein* (to decide, determine, judge), *hypokrisis* not only operates on the surface, on the seems (seams) of the speaker's voice and image, but also below, or under, judgment. Moreover, the form of *krinein* within *hypokrisis* is that of the middle voice, and connotes "crisis." That is, *hypokrisis* names the level at which it works—it operates on the level of the unconscious, underneath those faculties that we use to judge, determine, and decide. *Hypokrisis* does not deal with *logos* because it operates at the level of *hypologos*, beneath the "truth" at the same time it operates at the surface of the truth. *Hypokrisis* is an unspeakable form of delivery because it works beneath the word. Thus, there is no getting under what seems in order to get to the bottom of things, for under the bottom is the unconscious. Going back to dis-sembling, the judgment of *hypokrisis* comes from *Dis*, the realm of the underworld, and becomes exploited in the commercialization of unconscious desires through the fantasy worlds of entertainment institutions.[40] *Hypokrisis* is a judgment that operates "from below." Instead of the head, *hypokrisis* operates on the visceral, the lower, abject faculties of reason. Moreover, *hypokrisis* through "dissemble" also represses this unconscious: "To pretend not to see or notice; to pass over, neglect, ignore; To shut one's eyes to the fact." *Hypo-krisis* deals with blindness (*ATH*), with the dumbness of the unconscious that we know is there, but that we pretend does not exist: delivery denied.

How does one deliver from below? An electrate delivery should not per-petuate such blindness, but deliver these "semblances" and make them vis-ible to the audience. An electrate deliverer does not just gesture in the air within *hypokrisis*, but writes with the gesture—she uses the tools of digital technologies to write the unconscious and make the invisible appear. An electrate delivery provides another *hypokrisis* that would allow a delivery of desire, to de-suppress the faculties of thinking that literacy does not support. Toward this decomposition of *hypokrisis*, what would a *hypo-hypokrisis* tell us? That is, what is the unconscious of the word that can point toward forming a new *hypokrisis*? For starters, Ionic meanings of *hypokrisis* don't immediately include "acting" as such: "In Ionic ... the word and its cor-relative verb *hypokrinomai* have the dialogically central sense of 'reply' or 'answer,'" and the root *krisis* "carries the rhetorically central senses of choice, decision, judgment, and the related senses of trial or dispute and the issue of trials and disputes."[41] *Hypokrisis* provides the interface for a communal practical reason where the process of delivery is intended to lead toward group problem solving. "The verb *krino* can mean 'to question,' as *hypokrinomai* can mean 'to answer,' making such paradigmatic dialogic interchange available along with the paradigmatic situation of rhetorical debate and decision in the same word history."[42] *Hypokrisis* answers the call of the unconscious, and tries to question and answer the various desires at play when confronting a situation; it interrogates mood. But this inter-rogation is not categorical—it does not attempt to eliminate "irrelevant" moods. Thus, distinguishing or separating (*krino*) in this case relates to the space of *chora* rather than the place of *topos*. *Hypokrisis* does not suggest the analytical separation available through literacy, but a decision based upon the gathering of *pathos* in addition to *logos*, a gathering where all moods contribute to a decision, fostering group decision-making at the level of affect.

Even more telling, modern-day uses of *hypo* provide clues to the spirit of an electrate *hypokrisis*. I mention them now to circulate their uses in this context, but will return to them later. An obsolete example of hypo appears as a synonym for melancholy: "Morbid depression of spirits."[43] This term sometimes relates to the idea of "hypochondria," but suggests a psycho-logical depressive state more akin to our current notion of depression (the gloomy underworld of Hades). While perhaps less severe than depression, Ulmer notes a similar condition that appears as the dominant mood of Japan in the term wabi-sabi: "Wabi-sabi is the cultural mood of Japan, its default aesthetic, developed over centuries, being to that civilization what the Classi-cal Greek principles of harmony, proportion, and the like are to the West."[44] In recent American culture, Ulmer identifies a similar aesthetic emerging as "the blues" which comes from jazz: the experience of feeling happy to feel sad. We also see here, in this originary moment for a Western rhetoric, how Aristotle sought to suppress the emotional aspects of rhetoric, or at least those most unlikely to be controlled by *logos* (such as style), in favor of another aesthetic. However, these latent forms of hypo still exist, or emerged in later formations. Thus, hypo in this sense connects the term back to emotion, the primary faculty upon which Aristotle believes delivery works.

Hypo also plays an important role in the development (and delivery) of images in film and photography. "Hypo" is a slang term for sodium hyposulfite, a photographic fixer used to develop photographs, which was invented by John Herschel, also the inventor of the term "photography" (as well as "negative" and "positive" as they relate to photographic film).[45] The fixing process, which Herschel helped to improve, is used in all common modes of photography that use film, and is used as the final step of developing a photograph, the same terminal step that most have viewed delivery as holding in a rhetorical development. Without "hypo" or *hypokrisis*, neither image nor speech would come to presence. Hypo also shows how the objective senses, in this case sight, are dependent upon the chemical, or at least, in this instance, a chemical process that is required to bring an image into being, or in other terms, transform a latent image into a visible image, in essence, delivering the visible aspect.

A third meaning of hypo is its slang use as a hypodermic needle, which is a delivery method for medication or other substances into the body (under the skin).[46] *Hypokrisis*, in theory, delivers "information" rather than substances, be it the message composed by the other rhetorical canons, or more unpalatable to Aristotle, the accidental traits of a message. Or rather, it uses accidental traits to deliver the essential. *Hypokrisis* uses emotion as its point (Barthes's *punctum*), its needle, to deliver emotion, to "get under one's skin," and cause an emotional disturbance and release the chemicals in the body that influence emotion. As mentioned in the previous chapter, oxytocin is usually released by chemical and psychological delivery systems between bodies and not from medical technologies.[47]

However, the hypodermic needle is not simply used to deliver a drug, but for the "rapid delivery of a drug," and ties into one necessary aspect of an electrate delivery. If one needs to reason at the speed of light, Ulmer's *reasoneon*, or flash reason,[48] then delivery must also work at a comparable speed, and needs a rapid delivery system in order to help groups collectively reason at such velocities. The hypodermic needle as metaphor, within the auspices of new media, was also conceptualized in the 1940s and 1950s as a strategy for delivering information. Known as the "Hypodermic needle model,"[49] the strategy held that the intended message sent out by mass media is directly received and wholly accepted by the viewer. This theory became debunked as research determined that mass media is more selective on individuals, and that a predetermined response cannot be produced.[50] But, isn't this the same for pharmaceuticals injected into the body as well? Drugs sometimes have selective effects on patients, and one drug does not work for all. But the mediascape delivers information ubiquitously, and creates a virtual panacea to immunity by saturating the infosphere with many kinds of "drugs." As an antidote, electracy might develop its own practice of delivery that would be as effective at detoxifying the collective body. An electrate delivery needs to be as much anti-delivery as pro-delivery; or, delivery must be self-injected by the specific audience.

Hypokrisis puts judgment under the skin, just not the kind of judgment that Aristotle had in mind. But the needle can also extract. It can take fluids from the body, and use them elsewhere. Can *hypokrisis* extract, and if so, what? Does a speaker not extract sighs, cheers, laughter, boos, and gasps from an audience, and then adjust the delivery accordingly? A new *hypokrisis* should extract affect and show it before the viewer, entering them in a feedback delivery loop. Again, delivery should get under the skin and discover/reveal what was (placed) there originally. Ulmer has created a method of invention (e.g., the mystory) that allows for an individual to do just this. The epiphany, the ah-ha!, or even the "huh?" is the created and creative response from such an extraction.[51] How, then, does an individual do this for a larger audience within a rhetorical exchange? Or, does the group do this for itself with the "deliverer" in a much different role than traditionally understood? How does an individual extract and recognize group desire, a collective unconscious that is currently dumb (at the affective level), and dissemble the semblance? At stake here, as well, is a kind of metaphysics for the unconscious, a delivering of what is unspeakable in itself. If Ulmer shows how we can invent from the unconscious, how can we deliver from it? How can we deliver to it, at least in a way that doesn't collapse delivery with the pejorative sense of rhetoric as manipulation? Delivery occurs at the level of desire, and the rhetor must deliver desire, but a productive desire invested in the needs and wants of the audience. This delivery does not persuade one to adopt a course of action, but co-invents in the group's self-interest.

The *Rhetorica ad Herennium* and Cicero's Flute

Another detailed account of *hypokrisis* (now through the terms *actio* and *pronuntiatio*) appears in the Latin text *Rhetorica ad Herennium* (*RaH*),[52] which defines delivery as "the graceful regulation of voice, countenance, and gesture,"[53] and breaks these elements further into the aspects of "Voice Quality and Physical Movement."[54] Voice Quality has three aspects, "volume, stability, and flexibility";[55] the first comes primarily from "nature" alone, but the other two may be developed by declamatory exercises, or by hiring "those skilled in this art." Vocal flexibility is perhaps the most malleable, and the one that *RaH* devotes the most attention to, breaking it into eight subparts: the dignified conversational tone, explicative conversational tone, narrative conversational tone, facetious conversational tone, sustained tone of debate, broken tone of debate, hortatory tone of amplification, and the pathetic tone of amplification.

In addition to voice, the *RaH* provides more detail on the physical aspects of delivery than does Aristotle, and states that physical movement "consists in a certain control of gesture and mien which renders what is delivered more plausible."[56] The physical aspects of delivery, then, should provide the words with credibility, perhaps imparting *ethos* to the speaker. The speaker must act the part that s/he plays, becoming believable when speaking, making the audience believe that the speaker believes what s/he says. *RaH*'s prescription on this kind of physicality, this kind of "acting," is more nuanced than Aristotle's, who saw the necessity in developing delivery, but found it rather distasteful. *RaH*, on the other hand, fully prescribes techniques for delivery, but notes that one must disguise them when performing, so not to look like one is performing: "the gestures should not be conspicuous for either elegance or grossness, lest we give the impression that we are either actors or day labourers."[57] Here, the concern lies less with a falsity of the argument, a distortion of the truth, than with being seen as a lower class of citizen. In ancient Rome, actors were an abject class, among the ranks of prostitutes, so that *hypokrisis* here is not just a swindling or dissembling of the audience, but a kind of decision-making that happens from the abject class, from the bottom up rather than the top down.

RaH posits that delivery is more complicated than "acting," or at least describes this complexity in more sophisticated ways than Aristotle was able to, breaking down various techniques of voice and movement and then synthesizing them. For example, *RaH* gives this advice on how to combine voice with gesture for one of the voice tones:

> It seems, then, that the rules regulating bodily movement ought to correspond to the several divisions of tone comprising voice. To illustrate: (1) For the Dignified Conversational Tone, the speaker must stay in position when he speaks, lightly moving his right hand, his countenance expressing an emotion corresponding to the sentiments of the subject—gaiety or sadness or an emotion intermediate.[58]

Delivery, in this case the combination of sound and movement, becomes a kind of song and dance, one that, like Astaire's, attunes the speaker's body and voice with the audience's expected unexpectedness. The symbol for delivery should not be any particular extension of the body, such as a megaphone, but a tuning fork. For while Aristotle has his own hesitations at theorizing *hypokrisis*, *RaH* also finds difficulty in trying to tune a theory of delivery and describe proper delivery techniques through words: "I am not unaware how great a task I have undertaken in trying to express physical movements in words and portray vocal intonations in writing. True, I was not confident that it was possible to treat these matters adequately in writing."[59] However, whereas delivery is nearly as unwritable for *RaH* as it is for Aristotle, though for different reasons, *RaH* can point the way toward methods or practices that will help develop an electrate delivery: "Yet neither did I suppose that, if such a treatment were impossible, it would follow that what I have done here would be useless, for it has been my purpose to suggest what ought to be done. The rest I shall leave to practice."[60] Studying doesn't improve delivery, but active practice does. To learn *actio*, one must be active. The constant performance of performance makes one a better orator, in both voice and movement. The pedagogy that *RaH* prescribes cannot use writing or speaking alone: *actio* must be acted, must be shown.

After this advice, *RaH* proclaims one important maxim for those who wish to achieve effective delivery: "This, nevertheless, one must remember: good delivery ensures that what the orator is saying seems to come from his heart."[61] Ultimately, again, delivery comes down to acting, and not just "half-hearted" acting, but fully committed, "good" acting. Unlike Aristotle, who dislikes the accident of delivery but views it as a temporary necessity as long as men are corrupt, *RaH* makes the claim that delivery only needs the appearance of essence, it only needs to "seem" as if the orator speaks from the "heart."[62] Effective delivery, then, depends upon a seam that seems, and this seeming depends upon the *doxa*, opinion—what constitutes believability to the audience. What seems to seem, then, is not the authenticity of character or an argument, but the authenticity of emotion, what is felt.

Augmenting the advice given in the *RaH*, Cicero provides his most detailed account of delivery in *De Oratore*. Cicero makes very clear in the section he devotes to delivery (as well as throughout the work) of his thoughts about this part of rhetoric: "Without it, even the best orator cannot be of any account at all, while an average speaker equipped with this skill can often outdo the best orators."[63] While invention, as a canon, gathers materials into topics, themselves categories, on which an orator should speak, delivery is a canon of gathering people. That is, delivery's purpose is to collect the listeners, not only to listen, but to agree.[64] But the way that delivery gathers is not through *logos*, but through *pathos*, emotion. In Cicero's time, delivery was still required because of, as Aristotle complained of his own time, "the sad state of governments and people." Not all citizens may be as intelligent as Cicero, but delivery works not on the head, but the soul, which "affects everyone, because everyone's soul is stirred by the same feelings."[65] *Pathos*, via delivery, provides the unconcealment of the poetic in Heidegger's emerging-abiding sway; *pathos* uncovers what *logos* conceals. This is not to say that *logos* is lost or irrelevant or unnecessary, but that it is not suited for gathering "souls" the way that it gathers other kinds of information. Rather than gathering "nature," delivery requires a trip to the domain of the underworld (the unconscious) to gather the "human nature" of souls. As these "souls" shift online, everting from the body into other networks, new methods of soul-gathering become necessary for delivery to occur.

In Book 3 of *De Oratore*, Antonius, countering Crassus, argues about the merit of knowing civil law, and whether it behooves the orator to memorize this topic before going into court. Although he feels every orator should know as much as he can,[66] Antonius notes that the orator already has so many aspects of his craft to consider, that he must be judicious in how he allocates his time among all of these subjects.[67] Rather than knowledge of particular kinds of law, Antonius would have the orator study voice and gesture, even to the detriment of the knowledge of civil law. Among these, Antonius vacillates on which should be studied more, gesture or voice. One needs "graceful gestures," though to study as an actor would be overkill.[68] He goes on to point out the importance of voice as well,[69] but recommends that an orator not become a "slave" to vocal training, like Greek tragic actors, who practice every day for several years, and before performances practice voice exercises.[70] Voice and gesture require so much time for training that civil law has no time left. But unlike voice and gesture, knowledge of law "can be acquired in broad outline without instruction."[71] And unlike civil or other kinds of law, which can be learned as needed from books or experts for a particular case, voice and gesture cannot be learned this way, they cannot "be picked up all at once or drawn from somewhere else."[72] Delivery, then, becomes a technique, a skill set, a kind of knowledge that an orator must practice to gain proficiency, a technique that cannot be simply spoken as knowledge, but one that must be embodied over time.

Antonius elevates the importance of delivery because legal books can do the other kind of thinking for the orator, or, in other words, the prosthesis of literacy can do the legal thinking, and so mastering this kind of knowledge is not as important for the orator as the physical aspects of "being" that he extends in the court room. In addition to excellent delivery, he needs only an excellent ability to navigate the database which, although slower than contemporary searching, can be perused "instantly if you like."[73] Moreover, the database of civil law need not be done by the orator, but can be done by legal aids, "assistants who are experts in the law."[74] Antonius shows us that literate knowledge itself is not as necessary for argument as delivery is, for the orator need not even have her/his own best argument (this is not new to legal cases, of course, for logographers in ancient Greece often wrote speeches for clients). But delivery in this case is not one based in a pure orality, but one more fully supplemented by the prosthesis of literacy. For a new practice of electrate delivery to emerge, one that (literally) *incorporates* the body again through digital technologies, delivery needs its own electrate prosthesis.

This dialogue between Antonius and Crassus also stresses an aspect of general writing relevant to digital media. In *Applied Grammatology*, Ulmer describes Derrida's attempt to write—within the technology of the book (*Glas*)—multiple tracks that play simultaneously. He discusses the implications that such writing has for digital media forms of writing, especially the dual writing of audio-visual mediums where one writes a verbal and visual track side-by-side, a structure "simulated by *Glas*," but "In book form, the two tracks of *Glas* are spatially distributed, allowing only analytic access to the two scenes,"[75] unlike audio-visual media, where the verbal and visual track play at the same time. Delivery, which is explained by its dual terms in Latin (*pronuntiatio* and *actio*), is performed in two (or more) tracks: the verbal and the visual. If the script provides multiple tracks and directions for a film's production, then delivery performs those multiple tracks within an aural/visual context. Cicero explains that neither voice, gesture, nor expert knowledge is enough to persuade an audience, but that all must "play" at the same time for delivery to be successful. Thus, delivery requires a narrative track (expert knowledge), a sound track (voice/tone), and a visual track (gesture) in order to achieve maximum effectiveness. An electrate delivery through digital media cannot simply be spoken, but must be shown and felt in a way not optimized by print forms of delivery.

The *RaH* describes these different tracks and how to combine them. The one "track" that Cicero adds is that of the face. If delivery operates not on intellect, but the soul, then the "face is an image of the soul, while the eyes reflect it."[76] This idea that the eyes project an image of an inner soul was not new, but Cicero's explication on how to use this "image" is more detailed than any other account, for no other part of the body "can produce as many varying signs as there are feelings in the soul."[77] The eyes become the signature, a sign with a floating signified, which can be used repeatedly to deliver different affects, to create a mood or tone without the use of voice.

> nature has actually given us eyes, as it has given the horse and the lion their manes, tails, and ears for indicating our feelings. So the most effective element in our delivery, next to the voice, is the expression on our face; and this is controlled by our eyes.[78]

Although voice produces the soundtrack, the face, directed by the signifying eyes, becomes the image track. The face projects the unconscious, what lies beneath (the soul). Malcolm Gladwell, in *Blink*, uses Paul Ekman's work on facial expressions and emotion to explain that the face tells the truth when we consciously lie, and that only the best actors can control these involuntary (unconscious) motor reflexes.[79] Acting, *hypokrisis*, tries not only to reveal the unconscious, but sometimes cover it up.

Cicero's analysis of the voice track breaks down the different kinds of sounds into discreet categories that might be combined depending on the desired emotion. Each emotion depends on the right composition of sound effects. Anger requires "high and sharp, excited, breaking off repeatedly," while "lamentation and grief require another kind of voice, wavering in pitch, sonorous, halting, and tearful."[80] Fear uses a voice "subdued, hesitating, and downcast," while happiness is a tone that is "unrestrained and tender, cheerful and relaxed."[81] He goes on to list the tonal requirements for energy, distress, and others in addition to these. Again, looking at the voice as one part of a multi-track delivery system, the voice provides information based on affect, not unlike how a film can use a single image but conjure up different emotions depending on the background music. What Cicero describes, then, is a category system for mood based upon sounds, which he likens to music: "The entire body of the human being, all facial expressions and all the utterances of the voice, like the strings on a lyre, 'sound' exactly in the way they are struck by each emotion."[82] Delivery is not spoken, but sung. However, despite the use of instruments to discuss delivery, Cicero's chief metaphor in developing each category is not music, but painting, as each gesture and sound "are at our disposal to be varied at will in delivery, just as colors are in painting."[83] The musical qualities of voice require a layering effect, just as paints on a canvas; so does all the elements of delivery in general. Delivery requires a layering of different verbal and visual elements that literacy has difficulty (even in *Glas*) reproducing.

Cicero leaves the section on delivery with an interesting anecdote. Crassus speaks on the proper use of voice, how to use it in a manner that preserves and cares for it. During this discussion, he tells the story of Gaius Gracchus and his use of a flute to aid him in delivery:

> When he was addressing a public meeting, he always had someone standing inconspicuously behind him with a little ivory flute, a skillful man who would sound a quick note that would either rouse him when his voice had dropped, or call him back when he was speaking in a strained voice."[84]

The man with flute becomes an integral part of the performance as a delivery aid, a prosthetic that provides a bio-cybernetic feedback loop to help Gracchus regulate his delivery. Of course, the flute alone isn't the whole of the feedback system, but also the "skillful" someone who operates the flute, and who gauges if and when Gracchus strays in voice. And all three—Gracchus, the flute, and the flute player—operate according to an established network with certain parameters and behavioral codes. Delivery, therefore, is not just communal in the sense of a gathering around an orator, but that gathering—illustrated by this example of the flute player—provides feedback to the orator who delivers according to a specifically designed system, where delivery is also delivered to the orator. An electrate delivery would not just make the "subject" responsible for delivery, but crowdsource to make the audience responsible as well. That is, the audience should all be flute players.

Delivery depends on an attunement with the audience, but this audience must be skillful and knowledgeable about their shared, participatory role in the delivery. The story of the flute seemed important enough to Cicero that he not only explains its use, but calls attention to it through Caesar's pleading for him to discuss it further.[85] Crassus explains that each voice has a middle range, and the flute is designed to maintain this moderation:

> there is a certain limit to raising the voice ... Beyond this the flute will not allow you to go, while it will also call you back when you

are actually reaching this limit. Likewise, at the other end of the scale, when you are dropping your voice there is also a lowest sound, and this you reach step by step, descending from pitch to pitch. By this variation, and by thus running through all the pitches, the voice will both preserve itself and make the delivering pleasing. And while you will leave the man with his flute at home, you will bring with you to the forum a feeling for these things, derived from practice.[86]

In *Applied Grammatology*, Ulmer points out that electracy (though he introduces the term in later writings) writes in the middle voice. That is, it is an auto-communication (an action done to oneself), a writing of oneself and one's particular situation. The flute is a prosthetic device for finding the middle voice (in this case, literally), and provides practical reason for the best delivery decisions. An electrate delivery, as well, would be a delivery in the "middle," whether that middle voice occurs on the individual or collective level. It is conceivable, then, that delivery can occur between one's selves. But besides just being in the middle voice, it is clear that delivery has to do with taste, with aesthetics, what is "pleasing." And whereas Cicero advises one not to bring the flute player along, and instead "leave the man with his flute at home" after an orator has sufficiently mastered the practice, an electrate delivery—one that requires a network to support digital technologies—would do the opposite: don't leave the prosthesis at home, but let the prosthesis leave home without you.

Quintilian's Body Language

If Cicero's contribution to gesture is to focus on the face, then Quintilian extends this theory by analyzing gesture according to a whole body, moving from the head down to the feet. Starting at the head, which "occupies the chief place in Delivery,"[87] Quintilian describes that it should be used to mark time with a gesture and as a gesture,[88] but that the head cannot be used as the sole means of gesturing.[89] Furthermore, if the head is chief, then the "face is sovereign" for it captures the audience's attention "before we start to speak" and "often replaces words altogether."[90] Cicero writes much already about the face, but Quintilian adds that the eyelids, cheeks, and eyebrows add service to the face because they "shape the eyes and command the forehead."[91] Quintilian then moves on to a brief discussion of the blood, which controls the forehead when it blushes from shame or "disappears altogether in an icy pallor when fear puts it to flight."[92] The face, to the extent that it can change color via blood, provides the interface between inside/ outside, or between the *hypo* and *hyper*, as what's underneath comes to the surface but never wholly appears—it is only indexed by the color change. Sometimes this subcutaneous aspect is difficult for the deliverer to contain, so to control the image produced by such facial elements, one aspect of theatre that Quintilian mentions in this section is the mask. Whereas others who write about delivery disparage the use of the mask by actors, Quintilian notes how it may be used, like Gracchus's flute, as an aid for delivery, and in this case, emotion, as theatrical actors "borrow extra emotion from masks."[93] The mask provides a prosthesis for emotion—it does the work of delivering emotion for the actor so that he may focus on other aspects of performance, just as the flute aids the orator in controlling his voice.

Quintilian moves from the head/face complex into the neck, shoulders, and arms (where he mostly describes posture and exercises to keep good posture), into the hands which possess infinite movements, and rather than simply match the words spoken by the deliverer, "speak for themselves."[94] Whereas languages differ among peoples of different nations, he writes that the hands seem to provide a universal language across different cultures.[95] Of course, hand gestures are not the same across different cultures, but the important point here is that Quintilian sees a nonverbal system of communication operating within delivery, not just as a supporting track, but one that can be understood by itself, unspoken, without the accompaniment of a soundtrack. Turning again to the question of prosthetics, how can digital technologies augment the hand so that such delivery can be extended through delivery-networks? A simple answer seems to be the computer mouse and the pointer/hand it controls, but we might also ask how can the hand (literally, the digits) be amputated and sent off along with the flute to deliver without the speaker?[96]

Two smaller contributions that Quintilian makes, without really making much contribution at all (at least it seems), are in his analysis of the nose and the lips. His remarks demonstrate more how not to use them in order to avoid a negative effect rather than for any positive gain as they usually signify "derision, contempt, and disgust."[97] One should not "wrinkle the nostrils" nor wipe one's nose. Regarding lips, they should mostly go unnoticed and do not help the speaker, even when speaking.[98] However, the nose and the lips provide yet another departure toward an electrate delivery, one that would attempt to make use of the chemical senses that Ulmer finds Derrida wanting: "Derrida's project to displace the dialectic includes an attempt to isolate the specific features of those senses that have not been conceptualized—taste in particular, and smell—and to pose them as an alternative, as models of thinking and writing, to the distancing, idealizing notions based on sight and hearing."[99] Quintilian (as does Cicero) judges delivery by taste: a good voice is often described as "sweet," and unlike acting, oratory has a "different flavour: it does not wish to be highly spiced."[100] The nose and the lips, then, become the organs by which to judge a good delivery, and if a deliverer is not to make use of these when performing, how will he know whether he "stinks" or not? An electrate delivery needs to make use of the chemical senses, whether those chemicals are registered by the nose and mouth, or just the ones that we register with emotion (e.g., serotonin, dopamine, endorphins). The tendency to describe delivery in terms of taste, yet deny those organs needed to judge it (including

Quintilian's exclusion of eating and drinking itself during delivery), again shows the tension begun with Aristotle in trying to account for delivery within literacy, or at least an oral performance based out of literate logic.

Quintilian often analogizes delivery to music and musical instruments in particular: "The voice is indeed like the strings of an instrument."[101] Just as music moves emotions according to tempo, delivery uses tempo differently depending on the context and content. A quick delivery is used "to pass rapidly over things, to pile up details, and to hurry on," while a slower delivery is used "to insist, to emphasize, and to drive points home."[102] But if the voice is an instrument, it needs a player to pluck at its strings or play its keys. Or, it needs a conductor (in the sense of an orchestra conductor, but also one who inferences via conduction). The movement of the hands represents a conduction of the musical track of the orator's voice. The conductor may conduct with the hand using the baton, making use of the other hand only in an ancillary way; such is the case with delivery: "The left hand never rightly makes a Gesture on its own, but it often lends support to the right."[103] The musical terms used for the purpose of conduction (beat and tempo, dynamics, articulations) correspond to those aspects that an orator should have in making sure his speech is well articulated, that his voice raises or lowers for the correct occasion, or that he stresses the correct words for emphasis. Quintilian finds that using gestures to help "conduct" oneself is an error for delivery, as poor orators visibly mark the stresses of their speeches with gestures, subordinating gestures to the rhythm of the speech.[104] And prior to giving the speech, when the speech is being written, Quintilian finds it a fault when students develop their sentences while rehearsing gestures in order to make the sentences "fit the way in which the hand is to fall."[105] So unlike a conductor that directs an orchestra or a choir, the orator conducts himself, both in the composing of a speech and its delivery. Whereas the gestures might be visible to the audience, and might elicit that which is inexpressible through language, the orator also directs his performance, even if he means for his gestures to follow his words. Thus, feedback occurs between speech and gesture, both influencing each other, making it difficult to tell which is really controlling the other. However, the outcome, the signal that indicates the system is working correctly, is not a result of "understanding," but an infusion of pleasure. Within this system the orator must maintain a middleness (Cicero's flute): "The first rule of correct Delivery is evenness. Speech must not be jerky."[106] At the same time, "The second requirement is variety."[107] The key to delivery, then, is a proper aesthetics that is balanced, sung-in-the-middle range. Through these aesthetics, the output of the system does not just provide pleasure to the audience, but also to the speaker, and "revives" him by "giving him a change of work."[108] The speaker's outputs become his inputs.

However, although an orator's rhythm and sweet voice may sound like music, Quintilian advises against actually speaking in song.[109] His aversion toward this style of delivery stems from Aristotle's fear—*hypokrisis*'s roots in acting. "What is less becoming of an orator than a theatrical recitation which sometimes sounds like the excesses of a drunken orgy or a riotous party?"[110] Or, perhaps what is worse, musical theatre, as an orator makes a shambles of emotional delivery and "destroys the very dignity of the court by a sort of naughty song and dance act."[111] From the head to the feet, song possesses the ability to transform the speaker from a controlled orator to one controlled by the rhythm and tune, overcome by the feedback loop that sends him into a frenzied, unbecoming state.

Quintilian advocates a balanced oratory that is musical, but without singing. But in fact, some singing often occurs in delivery. Orators do this because the feedback they receive from such practice is pleasurable: "no one dislikes the sound of his own singing."[112] If one sings too much, one becomes addicted "to the pleasure of listening to sounds that soothe their ears wherever they are."[113] Whereas not the same biological process, infant delivery and the delivery of song both connect to the body's oxytocin production system. The study of music and the body has shown a deep connection between the production of oxytocin with singing or playing an instrument. Empirical studies by Christina Grape *et al.* have shown that among both amateur and professional singers, "Oxytocin concentration levels increased significantly in both groups after a singing lesson."[114] Delivery delivers pleasure, even if that music is the blues (a mood of music often described as happiness at feeling sad).

Quintilian dislikes marking time (rhythm) with the body, as did Cicero: "No twiddling of the fingers, no marking the rhythm with the finger joint."[115] Deliverers should maintain a pose and a use static flexing, appearing more like a statue. However, as already seen, when the music starts, dancing soon follows for bypassing the oxytocin circuit is difficult. Thus, we arrive at the bottom of the orator, his feet, which control stance and gait.[116] At first, Quintilian wants to separate oratory from the theatre, and so footwork appropriate to the stage would not be appropriate in court. However, as he goes on, it is clear that besides merely providing instructions on how not to step, delivery has its own moves:

> when you put your weight on the left foot, it is bad to raise the right, or keep it poised on tiptoe. Holding the feet too far apart is unsightly if you are standing still, and almost indecent if combined with movement. A step forward is quite in order, so long as it is opportune, short, and well controlled.[117]

Quintilian emphasizes control of movement as becoming of an orator, and proper etiquette, such as not turning one's back to the judges, moving at an angle, and maintaining proper eye level.[118] Thus, specific moves become necessary to maneuver throughout the court, particularly slow, gradual, and controlled movements.[119] Yet, "Some people jump back: this is simply ridiculous."[120] Moderation in movement is the advice that Quintilian provides to keep the orator from looking "ridiculous." A slow, methodical movement by the feet prevents one from stamping the foot too much, or marking time through too much rhythmic movement and delivering oneself into song and dance.

If Quintilian's discussion of the hands seems to resemble a kind of conducting, his detailed suggestions on an orator's footwork seem like choreography, or an anti/counter-choreography. What Quintilian really derides, and again, what Aristotle wanted to eliminate from delivery, is any aspect of noise in rhetoric. Whereas Aristotle saw acting and emotion as an uncontrolled element of rhetoric, and hence a noise, Cicero and Quintilian seem to think that they can control such noise and turn it into music, music that is not noise. Quintilian dislikes the sing-song style of delivery because it can devolve into this kind of noise, where the orator no longer controls the delivery, but the delivery controls the orator. As Jeffrey Henderson notes, it is unimportant if the locations where he finds such singing and dancing "is a gambling house or a place where long-skirted dancers perform, it is evidently a noisy place, and that is Quintilian's point."[121] When singing and dancing take place, the spectacle becomes unbecoming, more of a Bacchic performance, and the delivery becomes noisy (and probably messy). The orator may feel the rhythm and understand the unspeakable, but the danger is not that the audience will not understand, but that they will: "castanets and cymbals were a public nuisance: a censor closes the places down, because he cannot help dancing to the beat himself as he passes by."[122] In advocating a sweet voice and fluent gestures, then, Quintilian (and to some extent Cicero) flirts with moving from literacy into something else entirely: the pure aesthetic. This, as it pertains to rhetoric, was Aristotle's ultimate anxiety.

Finally, in addition to song and dance, Quintilian gives advice on the performance element that is especially relevant to an electrate delivery: the look. Ulmer theorizes that "the look" is the category of individual identity formation that occurs in electracy, just as the spirit was to orality and the self to literacy. Quintilian often teaches against appearing "unsightly" (*deforme*) to others, and goes on to provide specific advice about several aspects of an orator's "look" beyond voice and gesture. "As for dress ... it should be distinguished and masculine."[123] Dress need not be special, but particular styles can improve the orator's effectiveness: "Toga, shoes, and hair invite criticism both for too much care and for not enough."[124] Like all aspects of rhetoric, the orator must adapt dress to the rhetorical situation: "There are some features of dress which have themselves changed somewhat with the changing times."[125] Quintilian's look has to do with fashion, and not just fashion for fashion's sake, but how it will improve or detract from oratory. The speaker must find, just like his tone and movement, a middle-look that appears fashionable but not "over-made" (it "must be neither too tight nor too loose"), or else the audience will attend too much to gossip about "what he is wearing" rather than the substantive quality of his speech. The speaker should also not wear too much jewelry,[126] and some garments must be avoided altogether: "The short cloak, like leg-bandages, scarves, and ear-protectors, is only excusable by illness."[127] The orator must properly hide the body beneath the toga. However, once the initial "look" is given, the orator can disrobe during the actual delivery (first impressions really are the most important), for "almost by the beginning of the Narrative, it is quite proper for the fold to slip, apparently accidentally, off the shoulder."[128] As the speech continues into the Arguments and Commonplaces, "You can pull the toga away from the throat and the upper chest with the left hand, for everything is now hotting up."[129] The initial dress advice Quintilian gives makes the orator look more like a celebrity on the red carpet, complete with advice on hair, jewelry, dress, and intentional wardrobe malfunctions than a rhetorician. "And when the great part of the speech is over ... almost anything goes—sweat, fatigue, disordered clothing, toga loose and falling off all round."[130] No wonder Demosthenes practiced declaiming while running; as Quintilian describes it, oratory is an athletic endeavor. Although Quintilian denounces the orator whose movements devolve into dancing, he finds no problem in moving toward nudity in the court. This is an exaggeration of course, but like Aristotle, again, Quintilian finds himself in his own crisis when trying to account for what elements of the body should be used in delivery. And again, these accidents are all necessary because of the affect they deliver. Unlike Pliny, who advises not to "disturb the hair" when wiping sweat with a towel, Quintilian thinks that "disheveled hair has some emotional impact, and wins approval just because trouble seems to have been forgotten."[131] Quintilian does not provide the essentials of delivery, but the accidental traits, and more specifically, his own aesthetics for what makes a good deliverer. For us, his orator equates to our celebrity, from A list to D. The question for an electrate delivery, then, is how do we each bring out our own "celebrity" in order to better deliver through digital technologies?

Delivery, ultimately, is this incarnation—not necessarily into celebrity—but the incarnation of *being* into a body, and then out of a body. Aristotle wanted the logic of literacy, what he saw as pure being, an essence of an argument, to incarnate into a body and come forth from an orator (one colored by *ethos*), just as a logical argument can be read from a book. However, the human body is full of accidents: it never exists only as Plato's "featherless biped" (debunked by Diogenes). Even the current scientific essence of a body, DNA, is full of necessary accidents in order for being to strive within the body (Heidegger's *Dasein* or Spinoza's *conatus*). This very striving occurs when an orator tries to deliver a speech; it is never just an act, but a struggle, an attempt to incarnate a "soul" into being, a soul that incarnates the speaker, which the speaker tries to disseminate and incarnate into the audience. The orator is trying to deliver, to birth, a new being, and it is impossible for delivery to be without accidents as long as a human being delivers it. Delivery needs these accidents, for it interfaces with other humans, who are designed to respond to such accidents. This delivery depends not just on the speaker, but the audience as well, so that delivery needs multiple bodies in order for this incarnation to occur. Delivery's Necessary Accidents (another kind of DNA) are essential in rhetoric too for these accidental births to occur. Within digital media and technologies, the image and the participation of the audience disrupts the essence of literate logic in print so that a "logical" delivery-machine like the book cannot deliver accident-free. We need to look at the site of the body and what it can tell us about how the accidents of an electrate apparatus can be used to deliver being. However, this being-becoming-body is not the incarnation into a human body of an oral delivery, but a posthuman body of a digital delivery-machine, a cybernetic body connected in multiple ways to the Internet. Bodies such as these become integrated into desiring-machines and require a new logic for their operation. By turning to Gilles Deleuze and Félix Guattari and their theories of desiring-machines and schizoanalysis, the next chapter offers an example of such a logic for a digital delivery-machine.

Notes

1. David Wiles, *The Masks of Menander: Sign and Meaning in Greek and Roman Performance* (Cambridge, UK: Cambridge University Press, 1991), 21.
2. I use the concept of language apparatus as derived from media studies. In this context, a language technology functions within a social machine that includes a matrix of technology, institutions that develop and determine practices for that technology, and the individual and collective identities that evolve and develop within their interaction.
3. Given that Theophrastos's name translates into something like "sweet voiced," his attraction to delivery should not be surprising if considered in a mystorical context.
4. Gregory L. Ulmer, *Applied Grammatology: Post(e)-Pedagogy from Jacques Derrida to. Joseph Beuys* (Baltimore, MD: The Johns Hopkins University Press, 1984), 314.
5. Ibid.
6. Don Bialostosky, "Aristotle's *Rhetoric* and Bakhtin's Discourse Theory," in *A Companion to Rhetoric and Rhetorical Criticism*, ed. Walter Jost and Wendy Olmsted (Oxford, UK: Blackwell, 2004), 397.
7. Bialostosky, 396.
8. Bialostosky, 396–397.
9. Aristotle, *Poetics*, trans. S. H. Butcher (Mineola, NY: Dover, 1951), 1956b.
10. Ibid.
11. Ibid.
12. Bialostosky, 396.
13. Aristotle, *On Rhetoric: A Theory of Civic Discourse*, trans. George Kennedy (New York: Oxford University Press, 1991), 195 n.7.
14. Bialostosky, 397.
15. Aristotle, *Rhet.*, 1403b.
16. Ibid., 1404a.
17. Ibid.
18. Ibid.
19. Ibid.

20. Ibid.
21. Ibid., 195 n.4.
22. Ibid., 195 n.2.
23. Ibid.
24. Ibid., 1403b.
25. Alan L. Boegehold, *When a Gesture Was Expected: A Selection of Examples from Archaic and Classical Literature* (Princeton, NJ: Princeton University Press, 1999), 6.
26. Ibid.; Boegehold also points to Aeschines 1.25, who "implies that orators addressing the assembly should keep their hands to themselves." To illustrate his point, Aeschines references "a statue of Solon standing in the Agora on Salamis as having been fashioned after the living Solon. This misstep opens him up to ridicule from Demosthenes in due course…and a lessons to be drawn from the exchange is that by the fourth century, orators were not constrained to keep their right hand under their cloak" (Boegehold, 6 n.3).
27. If the gesture must be used in larger spaces, how much must the body move in infinite spaces, such as those online?
28. Aristotle, *Rhet.*, 1404a.
29. Aristotle, *Rhet.*, 1404a.
30. Bialostosky, 397.
31. Aristotle, *Rhet.*, 1378a.
32. These elements are non-graphical through the writing technology of the alphabet, but visible through other writing modes.
33. Martin Heidegger, *Introduction to Metaphysics*, trans. Gregory Fried and Richard. Polt. (New Haven, CT: Yale University Press, 2000), 198–199; emphasis in original.
34. Gregory L. Ulmer, *Applied Grammatology: Post(e)-Pedagogy from Jacques Derrida to. Joseph Beuys* (Baltimore, MD: The Johns Hopkins University Press, 1984), 182.
35. Ibid.
36. *Oxford English Dictionary*, 2nd ed., s.v. "Dissemble."
37. *Oxford English Dictionary*, 2nd ed., s.v. "Semble."
38. *Oxford English Dictionary*, 2nd ed., s.v. "Dissemble."
39. *Oxford English Dictionary*, 2nd ed., s.v. "Semble."
40. The Walt Disney Company's New York Stock Exchange symbol is DIS.
41. Bialostosky, 394–395.
42. Ibid.
43. *Oxford English Dictionary*, 2nd ed., s.v. "Hypo."
44. Gregory L. Ulmer, *Internet Invention: From Literacy to Electracy* (New York: Longman, 2002), 52.
45. *Oxford English Dictionary*, 2nd ed., s.v. "Hypo."
46. Ibid.
47. Of course, medical interventions can deliver oxytocin and related chemicals artificially.
48. See Gregory L. Ulmer, *Electronic Monuments* (Minneapolis, MN: University of Minnesota Press, 2005).
49. This model is also known as the hypodermic-syringe model, transmission-belt model, or magic bullet theory.
50. See Paul Felix Lazarsfeld, Bernard Berelson, and Hazel Gaudet, *The People's Choice: How the Voter Makes Up His Mind in a Presidential Campaign* (New York: Columbia University Press, 1944), 151.

51. Ulmer, *Internet Invention*, 61–64.
52. Although the *Rhetorica ad Herennium* was originally thought to be written by Cicero, many classicists now believe that another author wrote it. Rather than an author's name, then, I will refer to the text itself to identify the author of its citations, and abbreviate the title to *RaH* through the rest of this chapter.
53. *Rhetorica ad Herennium*, I.1.10.
54. Ibid., III.11.19.
55. Ibid., III.11.20.
56. Ibid., III.15.26.
57. Ibid., III.15.27.
58. Ibid., III.15.26.
59. Ibid., III.15.27.
60. Ibid.
61. Ibid.
62. Ibid.
63. Cicero, *On the Ideal Orator (De Oratore)*, trans. James M. May and Jakob Wisse (New York: Oxford University Press, 2001), III.213.
64. Or, delivery may also foster disagreements and contrasts, generating new perspectives.
65. Cicero, *De Oratore*, III.223.
66. Ibid., I.250.
67. Ibid., I.250.
68. Ibid., I. 251.
69. Ibid.
70. Ibid.
71. Ibid., I. 252.
72. Ibid.
73. Ibid.
74. Ibid.
75. Ulmer, *Applied Grammatology*, 147–148.
76. Cicero, *De Oratore*, III.221.
77. Ibid.
78. Ibid., III.221–223.
79. See Malcolm Gladwell, *Blink: The Power of Thinking Without Thinking* (New York: Little, Brown and Company, 2005), 197–214.
80. Cicero, *De Oratore*, III.217.
81. Ibid., III.219.
82. Ibid., III.216.
83. Ibid., III.217.
84. Ibid., III.225.
85. Ibid., III.226.
86. Ibid., III.227.
87. Quintilian, *The Orator's Education*, Vol. 5, ed. and trans. Donald A. Russell (Cambridge, MA: Harvard University Press, 2001), XI.3.68.
88. Ibid., XI.3.69–70.
89. Ibid., XI.3.71.
90. Ibid., XI.3.72.
91. Ibid., XI.3.77–78.
92. Ibid.
93. Ibid., XI.3.73–74.

94. Ibid., XI.3.85–87.
95. Ibid.
96. This question will be discussed more in chapters 5 and 6.
97. Ibid., XI.3.80–81).
98. Ibid.
99. Ulmer, *Applied Grammatology*, 34.
100. Quintilian, *The Orator's Education*, XI.3.182.
101. Ibid., XI.3.40.
102. Ibid., XI.3.111.
103. Ibid., XI.3.114.
104. Ibid., XI.3.108.
105. Ibid., XI.3.109.
106. Ibid., XI.3.43.
107. Ibid.
108. Ibid., XI.3.44.
109. Ibid., XI.3.57.
110. Ibid., XI.3.57.
111. Ibid., XI.3.58.
112. Ibid., XI.3.58–60.
113. Ibid.
114. Christina Grape, Maria Sandgren, Lars-Olaf Hansson, Mats Ericson, and Töres Theorell, "Does Singing Promote Well-Being?: An Empirical Study of Professional and Amateur Singers During a Singing Lesson," *Integrative Physiological & Behavioral Science* 38, no. 1 (2002): 65.
115. Quintilian, *The Orator's Education*, XI.3.122.
116. Ibid., XI.3.124–125.
117. Ibid., XI.3.125.
118. Ibid., XI.3.112–113.
119. Ibid., XI.3.127–128.
120. Ibid.
121. Ibid., 114 n.39.
122. Ibid.
123. Ibid., XI.3.137.
124. Ibid.
125. Ibid.
126. Ibid., XI.3.142.
127. Ibid., XI.3.144.
128. Ibid., XI.3.144–145.
129. Ibid.
130. Ibid., XI.3.147–148.
131. Ibid., XI.3.148–149.

Bibliography

Aristotle. *On Rhetoric: A Theory of Civic Discourse*. Translated by George A. Kennedy. New York: Oxford University Press, 1991.
———. *Poetics*. Translated by S. H. Butcher. Mineola, NY: Dover, 1951.
Bialostosky, Don. "Aristotle's *Rhetoric* and Bakhtin's Discourse Theory." In *A Companion to Rhetoric and Rhetorical Criticism*, edited by Walter Jost and Wendy Olmsted, 393–408. Oxford, UK: Blackwell, 2004.

Boegehold, Alan L. *When a Gesture Was Expected: A Selection of Examples from Archaic and Classical Literature*. Princeton, NJ: Princeton University Press, 1999.

Cicero. *On the Ideal Orator (De Oratore)*. Translated by James M. May and Jakob Wisse. New York: Oxford University Press, 2001.

Gladwell, Malcolm. *Blink: The Power of Thinking Without Thinking*. New York: Little, Brown and Company, 2005.

Grape, Christina, Maria Sandgren, Lars-Olaf Hansson, Mats Ericson, and Töres Theorell. "Does Singing Promote Well-Being?: An Empirical Study of Professional and Amateur Singers During a Singing Lesson." *Integrative Physiological & Behavioral Science* 38, no. 1 (2002): 65–74.

Heidegger, Martin. *Introduction to Metaphysics*. Translated by Gregory Fried and Richard Polt. New Haven, CT: Yale University Press, 2000.

Lazarsfeld, Paul Felix, Bernard Berelson, and Hazel Gaudet. *The People's Choice: How the Voter Makes Up His Mind in a Presidential Campaign*. New York: Columbia University Press, 1944.

Quintilian. *The Orator's Education*. Vol. 5. Edited and Translated by Donald A. Russell. Cambridge, MA: Harvard University Press, 2001.

Rhetorica ad Herennium. Translated by Harry Caplan. Cambridge, MA: Harvard University Press, 1954.

Ulmer, Gregory L. *Applied Grammatology: Post(e)-Pedagogy from Jacques Derrida to Joseph Beuys*. Baltimore, MD: The Johns Hopkins University Press, 1984.

———. *Internet Invention: From Literacy to Electracy*. New York: Longman, 2002.

Wiles, David. *The Masks of Menander: Sign and Meaning in Greek and Roman Performance*. Cambridge, UK: Cambridge University Press, 1991.

Part II

Who Delivers?

In the biopic, Demosthenes has just won the court case against his uncles and the story now shifts to Act II. He begins his career as a logographer and advocate, mostly working on private suits. However, he becomes more and more interested in public affairs and gives his first political speech, *On the Navy*, which will launch him into the political arena. As Phillip Harding explains, "Demosthenes was in many ways the very model of modern democratic politicians"[1] and needed both an issue and an image. Later, his issue would become the threat of Macedonia. His image was that of integrity (he did not accept bribes) and of the wise sage: "he chose to project himself as the people's counsellor (*symboulos*), whose main qualities were wisdom; that is, he saw what others did not see."[2] Although his speeches are unsuccessful, we see his character develop and he eventually challenges Eubulus, the most powerful statesman of the period. During this act, Demosthenes notes that Philip of Macedonia is preparing to build an empire and begins to warn Athens of the invasion to come.

We also see the thrill that both the audience and Demosthenes get from a well-delivered oration (and the displeasure of poor ones), even if these speeches don't always succeed in terms of policy or votes. Delivery is about producing an emotion, but also feeling and affect, terms that are often taken synonymously but can have particular meanings in certain contexts. Within a context of delivery, it's important to unpack and develop these terms to have a more sophisticated understanding of what happens when a speaker delivers words and images from a body. The character of Demosthenes embodies a desire of delivery as much as a delivery of desire. To support such a reading, many historical anecdotes abound about his devotion and dedication to overcoming his natural impairments that would make him an otherwise poor speaker. Cicero advised his student orators to "press forward night and day" in their vocation as did the famous Athenian Demosthenes, who "surmounted natural drawbacks by diligent perseverance ... at first stuttering so badly as to be unable to pronounce the initial R. of the name of the art of his devotion."[3]

In addition to the public performances shown in Act II, Demosthenes also works behind the scenes. To create the conditions for delivery, we see Demosthenes tinkering with various contraptions in order to build machines for delivery. Another historical anecdote from Cicero reveals that Demosthenes would put pebbles in his mouth, and in a single breath, practice delivery, sometimes while walking uphill.[4] These pebbles become a kind of machine, like the "stone-sucking machine" that Deleuze and Guattari write of the stones of Beckett's *Malloy*.[5] Demosthenes sucks his stones, not for the pleasure of sucking on stones, but for the pleasure of the process, the process of becoming his desire, which for him, is becoming orator.

But this simple machine is but one of a montage of machines. For practicing his gestures, to be "seemly," Quintilian tells us that Demosthenes made use of a mirror in order to view his delivery and plan his movements.[6] Also, because it was unseemly to shift one's shoulders during delivery, Demosthenes suspended a spear above a small platform and practiced delivery, feeling the spear's point if he shifted his shoulders too much.[7] And in order to study, to break off from the world, Demosthenes made use of a primitive sense-deprivation chamber where he could hear no external sounds, nor see any extraneous surroundings.[8] Alternatively, Demosthenes also overloaded his senses, in perhaps one of the best known scenes of his training, an inspirational shot for the film. Although a "great lover of seclusion," he would deliver down at the beach "against the crash of the waves, to accustom himself not to be frightened by the roar of the assembly."[9]

This biopic, of course, would hopefully help us ask questions about the historical trajectory of delivery into its current state. The next two chapters address three questions about a delivery of digital technologies: 1) who or what kind of person delivers; 2) exactly what do they deliver; and 3) how do they manufacturer this delivery? To begin answering these questions, chapter 3 offers that the deliverer doesn't deliver any particular informational content, but a nexus of emotion, feeling, and affect, doing so through a logic of Deleuze and Guattari's theories of desiring-machines (assemblages) to create a delivery-machine complex. As a model for the kind of actor a digital deliverer might emulate, chapter 4 shows how the figure of the shaman provides an analogy for how a deliverer serves as a medium, connecting the audience to an invisible world of consequential affective states toward solving issues important to local communities.

Notes

1. Phillip Harding, "Demosthenes in the Underworld: A Chapter in the *Nachleben* of a *Rhētōr*," in *Demosthenes: Statesman and Orator*, ed. Ian Worthington (New York: Routledge, 2000), 247.
2. Ibid.
3. Cicero, *De Oratore*, trans. E. W. Sutton and H. Rackham (Cambridge, MA: Harvard University Press, 1942), 1.61.260–261.
4. Ibid., 1.61.261.
5. Gilles Deleuze and Félix Guattari, *Anti-Oedipus: Capitalism and Schizophrenia*, trans. Robert Hurley, Mark Seem, and Helen R. Lane (Minneapolis, MN: University of Minnesota Press, 1983), 3.

6. Quintilian, *The Orator's Education*, Vol. 5, ed. and trans. Donald A. Russell (Cambridge, MA: Harvard University Press, 2001), XI.2.67.68.
7. Ibid., XI.3.130–131.
8. Ibid., X.3.25.
9. Ibid., X.3.30.

Bibliography

Cicero. *De Oratore*. Translated by E. W. Sutton and H. Rackham. Cambridge, MA: Harvard University Press, 1942.

Deleuze, Gilles and Félix Guattari. *Anti-Oedipus: Capitalism and Schizophrenia*. Translated by Robert Hurley, Mark Seem, and Helen R. Lane. Minneapolis, MN: University of Minnesota Press, 1983.

Harding, Phillip. "Demosthenes in the Underworld: A Chapter in the *Nachleben* of a *Rhētōr*." In *Demosthenes: Statesman and Orator*, edited by Ian Worthington, 246–271. New York: Routledge, 2000.

Quintilian. *The Orator's Education*. Vol. 5. Edited and Translated by Donald A. Russell. Cambridge, MA: Harvard University Press, 2001.

3   Becoming Delivery-Machine—
Emotion, Feeling, Affect

The Internet provides a delivery system for pathological states of mind.
—Phillip Adams

To face the assembly, Demosthenes relied upon machinic assemblages of different kinds, and although not schizophrenic in a clinical sense, practiced a kind of schizophrenic production. Demosthenes needed to couple with the various machines he either found or devised in order to enact a process that eventually produces another process. To be sure, the natural elements that Demosthenes used constitute as much of a machine as a flute or a computer, but how he assembled these machines, and how he incorporated them into his body, is more important than what they were made of. That is, how he tapped into the underlying codes for using the machines, as well as the affective flows produced from coupling with these machines, are the salient factors for how delivery might make use of the machines of digital technologies toward electrate forms of delivery.

The goal of delivery and of the schizophrenic are the same: they both seek to produce desire. The orator in classical Athens sought to persuade an audience based upon the speaker's desire, and to do this, the desire must be extended to this audience. The very desire to speak was also indicated and questioned by the presiding officer of the ancient Greek assembly, who asks "Τίς ἀγορεύειν βούλεται;" ("Who wishes to speak?").[1] When delivering, Quintilian says that the orator must make himself believe in what he says in order to convince his audience that they should feel it, too. Such feigned desire is nonetheless still desire, and at this level it matters not if what one "says" is different than how one "acts" as long as one "feels." This orator, desiring an outcome, seeks to persuade the listeners to share in this outcome, to also desire it, thus, the output of desire becomes an input, and the process perpetuates. This is no less true for any of the three species of rhetoric. A deliberative speech shares the same desire for a particular solution to a problem. Socrates is negatively influencing our youth. What should be done about it? One speaks, "I desire him to be put to death." For epideictic rhetoric, one desires to praise Pericles for feats in battle: an agreement over such feats must begin and end with the desire to also praise him. Forensic discussions deal with the desire to find the truth about past events. The orator must convince the audience that finding the truth is important, that it is desirable, before anyone would agree to look for it. Logical arguments have little effect at this level of discourse. Simply informing an audience of the facts, even if credible, is not enough. They must be made to believe—they must desire such knowledge, and so such desire much be delivered, in one way or another.

When Ulmer looks at the modern disaster in *Electronic Monuments*, he observes that with the news of a disaster, the media fail to deliver desire and creates its own kind of schizophrenic with the split coming between knowledge and belief, primarily because the information overload provided by media coverage becomes "unreceivable at the level of belief ... Such is the scission of our time—the disjunct between knowledge and experience, between collective history and individual existence."[2] The media creates what Ulmer refers to as compassion fatigue. Knowledge persists about a whole host of problems, but few have the desire to do anything about the problems. If rhetoric exists at all as a tool for democratic institutions, to find solutions to collective problem solving that are in the best interests of the people, then rhetoric must attend to belief, and the beliefs that we hold are often tied directly to our individual desires. The trick, rhetorically, is to tie the other problems of the world with the beliefs people have, or, to their desires that influence what they believe. But such beliefs and desires do not always appear at a conscious level of debate. Thus, rhetoric needs to attend to the unconscious.

This is what delivery has always done. And as delivery has delivered the unconscious, it has always been performed not in terms of a whole body, but as an assemblage of body parts—as a delivery-machine. This break-up may be from the whole of rhetoric itself, which is used precisely to break wholes of language/argument into parts for criticism and pedagogy. The five canons of rhetoric are an exemplar of rhetoric's aims. Thus, Cicero and Quintilian's pedagogical breakdown of how the body should deliver never rests upon an organic whole, but proceeds through the different sub-machines and how each of them functions. The voice, the head, the face, the arms, the hands, the eyebrows, the eyes, the feet—and then the nonhuman prostheses such as clothing and flutes. The deliverer draws upon whichever machine is necessary to enact the feeling desired in his audience. Aristotle's body without organs writhes because it wants to be organless, but rhetoric has sensations and requires that organs develop. The Latin usage of *actio* to describe the action of delivery informs thinking about delivery as primarily a process, a production made by such machines.

To be sure, delivery-machines have the ability to augment the physical capabilities of the body. The microphone, the Internet, the webcam: all of these help the speaker connect with the perceptive hardware of a desired and desiring listener. They amplify sound, zoom the image, or teleport presence. However, what is the wetware that determines how these machines become connected? If delivery operates at the level of the unconscious, what is the unconscious logic that might guide how delivery-machines become joined? If delivery delivers desire, the unconscious, both uncovering what lies beneath as well as injecting it and placing it there, then any logic at which these machines work must deal with the unconscious. Deleuze and Guattari, specifically in their work *Anti-Oedipus*, provide a theory of desire and machinic assemblage that can complement the work with unconscious writing practices and psychoanalysis already done by Ulmer with what they call schizoanalysis. If invention operates at the individual level, and psycho-analysis can inform the invention process for the individual, allowing them to write the unconscious, the linking of multiple individuals into groups— the effect of delivery—requires an addition to psychoanalysis so that the group subject might write the larger group unconscious. Such writing cer-tainly requires the techniques put forth by Ulmer for invention, but delivery also requires a new logic aimed at the machines used to make such con-nections. Deleuze and Guattari's theories of how desiring-machines operate become an important relay for the logic of delivery-machines.

Emotion, Feeling, Affect

As discussed in chapter 2, delivery is deeply implicated with emotion. The premise of Aristotle's complaint with *hypokrisis* is that it appeals to the wrong kind of emotion—base emotion that overpowers reason. This distinc-tion between different kinds of emotion begs further questioning of emotion, particularly how different forms of emotion influence delivery, nuances and distinctions which have not yet been addressed by other theories of delivery. It would be incorrect, of course, to say that rhetoric doesn't contend with and appropriate emotion in more general ways. From its roots in ancient Greece, at least, rhetoric has attended to the emotional quotient of the audi-ence. Likewise, rhetoricians and theorists have composed volumes on the effect of the emotions on rhetoric and rhetoric on emotions.

For this project, I'm more interested in the interrelationship between emotion and the delivery process of rhetoric, for although a rhetorical pro-cess must develop and invent the best emotions for a situation, delivery must actually make those emotions manifest in the audience, and emotions are often talked about in such "summoning" terms. For instance, George Kennedy defines *pathos* as the "emotion that the speaker can awaken in the audience."[3] As I'll explore later, this emotion is already present, latent, subliminal, and unspoken in the audience, something for *hypokrisis* to dig out and make present, make appear; however, this awakening itself can also be done subconsciously.

Much of Book 2 of Aristotle's *On Rhetoric* describes the ways that a rhetor might employ emotion to persuade his audience. Such emotional appeals, as discussed in chapter 2, seem a bit disingenuous when decrying the use of emotion to win over an audience, at least when such emotion supplants the reasoned, best argument. As Gisela Striker points out, while

Aristotle describes different types of emotion (anger, for instance), he doesn't provide a general definition of what he means when he writes "*pathe*":

> Aristotle usually begins each chapter with a definition and then tries to derive from it the answers to the questions "from what," "regarding whom," and "in what kind of state of mind" an emotion will arise. He offers no general definition of what a *pathos* is, and he usually does not try to argue for the correctness of his definitions.[4]

At this point, however, it's important to consider that Aristotle might actually be discussing emotion that is different in kind rather than degree, and this difference in kind, I argue, is one of the chief characteristics of delivery. That is, while the spoken aspects of a rhetorical exchange focus on one kind of emotional current, the aspects of delivery work upon another. Although invention might develop emotional appeals, only delivery can employ other kinds of psychic and bodily sensations: feeling and affect. It thus becomes important to tease out the differences identified among emotion, feeling, and affect and to understand the role that each might play for delivery.

Emotion and Feeling

First, let's consider the differences between emotion and feeling. Emotion, as Kenneth Burke has discussed, is primary. Emotion becomes the raw material that helps develop feelings. As John Voris describes it, "Emotions serve as a sort of, 'Feelings Factory.'"[5] Emotions help humans react to immediate conditions on the ground, to make instantaneous decisions of fight or flight. Emotions recognize the materiality of the world and help to establish an attitude toward that material reality.

If emotion is primary, feeling is secondary, it is learned. Feeling bridges a primary emotion with a cognizant recognition of context. Feeling can change based on situation and environment. Whereas the image of a shark may produce the emotion of fear, the feeling of panic will only be felt when one sees the shark with him or her in the water, and not on television or hanging dead from a marina scale. Or, an ichthyologist working in the water with the shark might experience this fear, but may not worry about being attacked because of experience or deeper understanding of the fish. The emotional response is channeled into feeling based on prior experience and knowledge. Feeling becomes triangulated with prior theory.

In *On Rhetoric*, the term Aristotle most uses for emotions is *pathos*, a Greek word well known to rhetoricians and one that can be translated as emotion, feeling, passion, and suffering. Unlike *hypokrisis*, which developed the meaning of "acting"—even though its roots suggest a more sophisticated definition—*pathos* has developed multiple meanings, collapsing different kinds of "feeling" into a single term. This may be one reason why theories of delivery have failed to provide a more detailed treatment of how it impacts the audience and what exactly the deliverer does with emotion.

In the case of delivery, the speaker should attempt to provide a connection between the emotion of the audience and the feeling that should be felt, or that the speaker would like the audience to feel. The deliverer, then, summons an emotion and delivers the feeling. That is, the rhetorician makes a conscious attempt to generate an emotion and link that emotion to a particular feeling, a feeling that would then be directed toward a particular action that the speaker wants the audience to undertake. Thus, while Aristotle thought emotion was important in the inventional stage of rhetoric, it's also important within the group context as delivery provides the transition from an individual invention to a group invention.

It is important to note, then, that we can think of delivery as non-instrumental. Delivery seeks not to deliver a speech or information as such, but to guide the audience toward this process of invention. In other words, delivery is not delivered for its own sake, or for the sake of the speech, or for the sake of the audience hearing the speech, or even for the sake of the audience to make an immediate decision, although that is sometimes what audiences do. Emotion is primary to delivery, then, because it is also non-instrumental—it functions despite not often serving the goal it enacts. As Nico Henri Fridja describes of the misdirection of emotion:

> At some moments when observing behaviour, that behaviour seems to come to a stop. Effective interaction with the environment halts and is replaced by a behavior that is centered, as it were, around the person himself, as in a fit of weeping or laughter, anger or fear. Or interaction with the environment may go on but seems particularly ineffective. When someone smashes the dinner plates, the broken plates would hardly seem to be the end result the person had in mind. Other behaviour that invites emotion words seems to contain a surplus that is not needed for the end result: superfluous emphasis in speed and scope of movement, or hesitation and undue toning down, or a smile that, in someone who is stroking a child, does not add to the tenderness of the touch.[6]

Perhaps this is one of the problems Aristotle has with delivery—its superfluousness. Delivery contains an excess that is not needed when simply persuading someone of some information, of some argument. Of course, speed, slowness, destruction, and a smile do add to their respective situations because humans truck in emotions. But from a Vulcan point of view, such behavior seems illogical. However, as Patrik N. Juslin and John A. Sloboda write, "There is some consensus that the primary function of emotions is to guide behaviour; emotions evolved because they enabled successful interaction with the environment."[7] What does rhetoric, and especially delivery, do other than to guide behavior based on changing environmental conditions?

She who taps into the emotions of the audience best persuades them of a successful path through the environmental problem and thus shapes their behavior.

But just as emotion can be used to gain goodwill and help execute delivery, injecting the wrong dose, the wrong concoction, can cause the audience to turn against the deliverer (how many of us are unhappy when a delivery service brings us the wrong package, or no package at all?). As Longinus warns us:

> Playing tricks by means of figures is a peculiarly suspect procedure. It raises the suspicion of a trap, a deep design, a fallacy. It is to be avoided in addressing a judge who has power to decide, and especially in addressing tyrants, kings, governors, or anybody in a high place. Such a person immediately becomes angry if he is led astray like a foolish child by some skillful orator's figures. He takes the fallacy as indicating contempt for himself. He becomes like a wild animal. Even if he controls his temper, he is now completely conditioned against being convinced by what is said. A figure is therefore generally thought to be best when the fact that it is a figure is concealed.[8]

Was Aristotle once duped by an orator, leading to his reaction to a delivery that appeals to non-instrumental emotions rather than those that have logical bearing on the situation? Based on his comments in Book 3, he would seem to agree with Longinus's admonishment of those who would lay emotional traps for an audience, pitfalls that hold back the logical working through of an argument so that an emotional swelling moves the audience. However, again, are we talking about different kinds of psychic sensations, lumping them all together under *pathos*? Because feeling, which comes forth from emotion, requires a logical connection with prior theories, it is not at all the same degree of unconscious emotion that a more primary mode of emotion might produce. Following Longinus's train of reason, the figure that "tricks" has to do so through *hypokrisis*, so that the audience is unaware of the judgment he or she is making about the figure.

What I have been describing as "group invention" might also be called practical wisdom (*phroenesis*) because, in most cases of delivery (especially deliberative rhetoric, but also in forensic and epideictic), some decisions must be made about what course of action to take. Invention may either be rhetorical, developing ideas that respond to the deliverer (even if not articulated), or the invention of the course of action. It is at this point in the delivery exchange that the emotions come to bear on the action and not simply in the transference from one body to another. Striker reminds us that Aristotle argues "The person of practical wisdom ... must start reasoning from the premise that such-and-such, whatever it may be, is 'the end and best.'"[9] However, a person who is not "morally" good will not act in the best way for two possible reasons. A bad person will not recognize a situation that needs intervention and fail to act, or a bad person, when told the best course of action to take, will not recognize this action as the best. As Striker contends, "The first interpretation brings out the cognitive element; the second, the motivational role of emotional dispositions for moral character."[10] She further elaborates:

> It is the right kind of emotional disposition that enables the morally virtuous person to see or recognize what is best in any situation. A bad person, by contrast, might be described as morally blind: not only will she fail to notice the relevant aspects of a situation but even if someone told her "what is best," she might fail to recognize it as the best.[11]

Of course, we may debate about what makes a good or bad person, and the criteria for each term may be completely flipped if not nuanced out of effective use. In either case, the role of the deliverer is to deliver the appropriate emotion for the situation, either by reasoning one toward another emotion (as Aristotle states, emotions can be persuaded by reason although not being reason-based), or by abducting or hijacking and replacing one emotional state for another. The deliverer must be able to see what the audience cannot see, to feel what they cannot feel. This feeling can be feigned, as emotion and feeling need not be authentic. However, if a bodily sensation such as affect is pre-conscious, is there a way where "good" can come from focusing on an affective mode of delivery, whatever "good" may mean?

Affect

This third kind of emotion, then, is affect. What role does affect play, and how does it differ from emotions and feelings? Keith Oatley and Jennifer M. Jenkins identify affect as a more general term than emotion.[12] As Juslin and Sloboda write, affect "refers to the positive or negative valence of the emotional experience. Many researchers consider affective valence as the most basic feature of emotional life, and believe that affect is phylogenetically and ontogenetically more primitive than emotion."[13] So if emotions are a feeling factory, affect provides the substrate, the general condition that makes emotion possible. Affect is not an emotion factory per se, but affect provides the current that allows emotions to exist. Affective flows can become emotional, which then can manifest into feelings, but neither are necessary outcomes of such affective flows. This is an important difference between emotion/feelings and affect. Eric Shouse identifies this difference as one of consciousness:

> An affect is a non-conscious experience of intensity; it is a moment of unformed and unstructured potential. Of the three central terms ... feeling, emotion, and affect—affect is the most abstract because affect cannot be fully realised in language, and because affect is always prior to and/or outside of consciousness ... Affect is the body's way of preparing itself for action in a given circumstance by adding a quantitative

dimension of intensity to the quality of an experience. The body has a grammar of its own that cannot be fully captured in language because it "doesn't just absorb pulses or discrete stimulations; it infolds contexts ..."[14]

To illustrate the differences between the three, Shouse relies upon the case of an infant, which he explains does not yet have language or biography, so even though parents describe their newborns as having feelings, they are really displaying affect. To express feelings, one must be able to check the emotional sensation against prior knowledge and give it a label—in other words, one must be able to speak this kind of emotion.

Shouse also offers a different way to tease out emotion and feeling, circling back to affect. Although Voris notes that emotions are a feeling factory, Shouse suggests that emotions provide external displays of feeling. That is, facial features, gestures, and other body language provide an index of feeling, an index he labels emotion. An infant, because of this lack of biography of language, has only body language (and unspoken cries or utterances). Thus, the "emotions of the infant are direct expressions of affect."[15] These "direct expressions" provide the space in which delivery (*hypokrisis*) works as it attempts to produce a visual track that bypasses the construction of feelings through verbal (or written) discourse. This difference between the affect→emotion complex and the emotion→feeling complex corresponds, again, to Aristotle's unclarified distinction between the structured, argumentative appeals to language-constructed feelings and the unfiltered emotional displays of unspeakable affect.

The infant, freshly delivered, teaches us about delivery. Their emotions (indexes of affect) are not meant for themselves, but for the parents. Studies by Paul Ekman and others have shown that when we express emotion in public, we often do so for the sake of those around us rather than indicating genuine feelings. We express different emotions in private than we might when around others. If witnessing a harrowing accident while in a group, we feign despair or disgust even if we really feel a sense of schadenfreude. The affect-facial circuit can bypass feeling altogether if for the sake of an external audience (or one's own superego). One may feel one way, but show a different emotion. This is what *hypokrisis* has eventually come to mean through its Anglicized form hypocrite. Yet feeling, which is speakable, operates on a different level than an emotionally expressed affect. If so, then one who acts differently than one says may be a hypocrite, but what if she simply expresses only one track while keeping the speakable feeling silent? This may be hypocritical in the pejorative sense, rhetorical in a positive sense, or simply a communicative impasse where what one would say regarding one's feelings, if present, have nothing to do with the emotional act displayed on her face.

This visual display of affect, if not primarily meant for she who expresses it, is mainly intended for others. To reiterate Shouse, even though an infant has no feelings, "almost every parent will state unequivocally that their child has feelings and expresses them regularly."[16] A deliverer, then, uses affect, displayed through non-verbal cues, to prepare the audience for the content, which is no longer the most important part of delivery. Whereas content itself can prepare the audience for more content (as when an introduction hints at bad or good news to come, priming emotion and steering it toward a desired feeling and course of action), affect is best gained through the unspoken language of the body. Such delivery may occur through speech, but it is the unspoken elements of speech that are most important. Delivery, generally, is in every way a language of the body, even when that body becomes technologized through ink and paper or electricity and silicon.

More importantly than emotion or feeling, what delivery delivers is an affective experience, something that cannot be well codified in language (if at all). When an infant makes an emotional indication of affect, the audience may make his or her own face as well, a face that reports the affective response that has been triggered. If the audience has a biography and language, such affect may then develop into an emotion-based feeling factory, for the audience may recall their own experience with such affective states, or what they interpret those states to have been. But this circuit happens prior to the language of speech, a circuit that delivery tries to tap prior to the delivery of language.

To be sure, feeling, emotion, and affect are always intertwined within a nexus in delivery, but delivery, especially delivery as *hypokrisis*, capitalizes on affect as a way to conduct affect below the threshold of judgment. To understand how this nexus interacts within the body of the deliverer, we can examine contemporary theories of affect and how such affect is produced. Toward the end of this chapter, I will turn to Deleuze and Guattari's theories of affect, especially when filtered through the condition of schizophrenia, as well as Ulmer's conception of affect as mood. But first, I need to tease out two more kinds of sensation related to affect: mood and the sublime.

Mood

There is another related term also influenced by delivery: mood. Ekman and Davidson argue that mood differs from emotion in three primary ways. First, moods last much longer than emotions. A mood may linger for hours, weeks, or months while emotions are fleeting by comparison, more tied to short-term situations. Second, researchers of emotion often find that emotions have some sort of trigger event, some clear stimulus, while moods often do not have a clear reason for their manifestation. Third, such researchers also have found that emotions "are accompanied by distinctive facial expressions while moods are not."[17]

These are just a few characteristics, but ones that might be interesting to think of in terms of delivery. Most acts of delivery are themselves short, probably no longer than an hour or two, but possibly as quick as the download rate of the audience. For any of these situations, though, delivery works in the moment on emotions. The word, intonation, gesture, or expression are all meant as stimulants to drive affect toward becoming particular emotions, eventually manifesting into individualized feelings. However, mood is more related to the initial affective current that underflows throughout the delivery process and performance. Although the duration of delivery includes micro-deliveries that act on particular emotions, the total flow is one of affect directed into a mood, a mood that sustains the viewer throughout the smaller undulations of emotions. If the emotions are the melody of the song, then the mood provides the beat that anchors the song as a whole.

Perhaps more interesting for delivery, then, is how mood and emotion differ in their function. Davidson contends that "emotions bias action, while moods bias cognition."[18] Delivery attempts to fulfill two functions. One is to get the audience to act in some way. Of the emotional appeals made by the deliverer, those that work on emotion (as opposed to affect or mood) would seem best suited to rile the crowd into action. Or, as Sloboda and Juslin explain, "Emotions arise most often when adaptive action is needed."[19] However, delivery also aims to foster group invention, using the conduct of the deliverer (for the deliverer conducts the audience with emotion as well as words) as the material to act collectively, action that must first be considered—not just logically, but also affectively. The deliverer establishes a mood that helps to foster the conditions for this cognition, a cognition of the body as well as the mind. Or, we should tweak Davidson's diction toward a word that includes a mode of thinking that occurs with the body as a whole. In any case, as Davidson offers, mood "serves as a primary mechanism for altering information-processing priorities ... Mood will accentuate the accessibility of some and attenuate the accessibility of other cognitive contents and semantic networks."[20] And, as Davidson also states, moods can increase the likelihood that one emotion will be triggered over another:

> Moods provide the affective background, the emotional color, to all that we do. Emotions can be viewed as phasic perturbations that are superimposed on this background activity. To the extent that moods are continually present, it can also be said that our cognitive processes are always biased or modulated.[21]

If emotions are feeling factories, then affect might be considered a mood factory, although affect can be turned toward emotions/feelings as well. Or, if emotions arise before feelings—which can be uttered since they require language and history—mood perhaps is the most speakable form of affect. I will turn more to mood later, but this initial description should be considered when the term appears in the rest of the text.

Sublime

Somewhere in this matrix of emotion, feeling, affect, and mood emerges another term that has rhetorical history: the sublime. Older rhetorical theories about the sublime as a means of moving an audience have similarities to the conceptions of affect and mood discussed above. Such theories also have implications for media beyond the body. For instance, Longinus compares the delivery tactics of Demosthenes to those of light and painting. When painting figures, Longinus notes, "one can wrap that figure in a grandeur of sublimity and emotion, so that these latter aspects dominate the reception of the figure itself." Moreover, the emotional reaction conceals its own cause:

> The artifice of the trick is lost to sight in the surrounding brilliance of beauty and grandeur, and it escapes all suspicion. 'By the men of Marathon ...' is proof enough. For how did Demosthenes conceal the figure in that passage? By sheer brilliance, of course. As fainter lights disappear when the sunshine surrounds them, so the sophisms of rhetoric are dimmed when they are enveloped in encircling grandeur. Something like this happens in painting: when light and shadow are juxtaposed in colours on the same plane, the light seems more prominent to the eye, and both stands out and actually appears much nearer. Similarly, in literature, emotional and sublime features seam closer to the mind's eye, both because of a certain natural kinship and because of their brilliance. Consequently, they always show up above the figures, and overshadow and eclipse their artifice.[22]

Longinus's analogy to painting is telling for a digital sublimity and delivery, for he simultaneously provides rationale and logistics for how speaking the sublime is like showing the sublime, which can then circle back to electrate concerns with the image and how delivery was and has become unspeakable. Or, delivery in this case might also be unshowable. The actual artifice of delivery disappears and the audience becomes unconscious of this process, when done well at least. Most importantly, however, is the emotional state of the audience, who is left feeling good, even if the content itself is rather dim.

Longinus also makes some interesting comparisons between Demosthenes and Cicero that inform the different ways that emotion can be delivered. In discussing the role of the sublime in oratory, Longinus notes that:

> Demosthenes has an abrupt sublimity; Cicero spreads himself. Demosthenes burns and ravages; he has violence, rapidity, strength, and force, and shows them in everything; he can be compared to a thunderbolt or a flash of lightening. Cicero, on the other hand, is like a spreading conflagration. He ranges everywhere and rolls majestically on. His huge fires endure; they are renewed in various forms from time to time and repeatedly fed with fresh fuel.[23]

One point we can derive from Longinus is that both examples provide valid logics of delivery, as both speakers were highly effective in their eras.

Demosthenes provides a flash of sensation, whereas Cicero delivers a steady source of heat, one that will last. Although delivery is analogized to natural forces, Longinus also describes the sublime as a force of nature (a comparison made by many authors writing about the sublime). This force of nature, whether a fire, a deep ocean, a hurricane, or some other natural aspect that delivers the sublime, is usually never a discrete part of nature, but rather a larger system composed of many parts taken in as a whole. This is why, rhetorically, the sublime chiefly manifests at the point of delivery. Unlike the other parts of rhetoric, such as invention and arrangement, which Longinus tells us are only noticeable when viewing the speech in its entirety—so that one can see how all the parts go together—"Sublimity ... produced at the right moment, tears everything up like a whirlwind, and exhibits the orator's whole power at a single blow."[24]

Given the description above, it might be easy to say that the sublime can be an effect of an emotional appeal or of a mood, given that the abruptness of Demosthenes's delivery seems more like the quick strike of emotion rather than the sustained duration of mood. First, the quick strike of Demosthenes's delivery might seem like the quick appeal to emotion with an identifiable stimulus. However, the quick strike of lightening, or the whirlwind of a tornado, represents not quickness itself but the power of transformation. We can think of Dorothy being delivered to Oz as a metaphor for how delivery uses the sublime to transport an audience. Second, as Longinus sees it—even if a specific feature can be pointed to—the sublime has no specific requirements to make it felt, as Patricia Bizzell and Bruce Herzberg note: "this impact cannot be directly tied to any stylistic features."[25] If delivery starts in the undercurrents of consciousness via *hypokrisis*, it hopes to achieve, but probably rarely does, a *hyperkrisis* in the sublime.[26] Although "subliminal," *hypokrisis* via the sublime contains within itself the hyper and suggests a transcendence. As such, Longinus found the sublime superior to mere persuasion:

> For the effect of genius is not to persuade the audience but rather to transport them out of themselves. Invariably what inspires wonder casts a spell upon us and is always superior to what is merely convincing and pleasing ... [The sublime exercises] an irresistible power of mastery and [gets] the upper hand with every member of the audience.[27]

Although Longinus mainly writes about a literary-based rhetoric, we can imagine this audience as the audience Aristotle considered when chastising delivery as "acting"—especially as Longinus goes on to state that, as Pernot puts it, the "sublime cannot be bothered with exactitude and correctness."[28]

Renato Barilli, working through Longinus, helps to illustrate how comfortable Longinus is with rearranging rhetorical principles and grammatical practices of his time to forge his own bolts of sublimity. As might be expected to develop sublimity, Longinus focuses on *pathos*, but not one that is initially aimed at the audience—rather, an appeal to *pathos* within oneself as deliverer. The orator "must manifest his own pathos, in order to convey it to the audience … To show that one is inspired by strong passions is itself a persuasive argument."[29] Such autopoietic *pathos* moves beyond hypocrisy, as the deliverer must first genuinely feel that which he intendeds to invest within his audience; the manifestation of the affective current must originate from the deliverer. For the current to flow, it must originate somewhere. Even if the deliverer is a capacitor and not a battery, he provides a relay switch to direct the current. *Logos*, the word, takes a back seat to *pathos*, for the most important rule is to be concise and direct so the speaker does "not hinder the flow of emotional intensity."[30] Such concision erases words not in favor of logical clarity, but affective efficiency.

Like affect and mood, sublimity is an unspeakable kind of emotion, and Barilli shows how rhetorical delivery through *hypokritical* sublimity is literally unspeakable when done well, praising Longinus for writing a work that "marks the victory of silence, the absence of words as a tool of persuasion."[31] As Blaise Pascal has offered, "La vraie eloquence se moque de l'eloquence" ("True eloquence scoffs at eloquence").[32] This aphorism becomes even more visible, and more inaudible, when we remember that much of delivery was (and is) visual in nature. If Aristotle based rhetoric on what rhetoric studies identifies as the rhetorical triangle of *logos*, *ethos*, and *pathos*, "we may say that in this case everything is centered on pathos."[33] To take effect then, the silence that manifests the sublime needs "as guarantee a filling of strong feelings … In this way, in line with Pascal's statement, even the absence of *logos* can sometimes be a tool of persuasion."[34] And this bare idea must be unspoken, or spoken as little as possible, for sublimity to take effect. "Better a style that sometimes is not impeccable but that can rise to the heights of pathos than a style displaying a smooth technical mastery but offering only an elegant and cold homogeneity with no soul."[35]

Although Longinus is not referring to delivery specifically, the kind of composition he proposes—its invention and lack of style—are all tied to the end act of delivery, how these words will be delivered to an audience and thus move them toward sublimity. It's no surprise, then, that he turns to the figure of the runner, a performative deliverer, in order to make his point: "just as you deprive runners of their speed if you tie them together, emotion equally resents being hampered by connecting particles and other such append-ages."[36] Here, Longinus is referring to his dislike of connecting participles and conjunctions "on which the Attic school relied for the construction of discourses with symmetry, shrewdness, clearness, and agility."[37] Language can get in the way of emotion, or perhaps a certain kind of language that is built upon literate construction before being delivered orally. Perhaps what Longinus is really getting at is trying to style a speech that still relies upon the human body for delivery rather than a printed, paper-based body, one that has no other way to deliver than through alphabetic transcription. And whereas Longinus is against appendages, I would argue that such appendages pertain only to the cluttering of language rather than the appendages necessary for the body to deliver.

Instead of these connecting bits of language, Longinus "prefers solutions that are technically simpler but also more solemn,"[38] establishing a mood rather than a thought. As Barelli tells us, Longinus prefers techniques such as hyperbaton, or the Yoda approach: "Ready are you? What know you of ready?" This term literally translates to a step (*bainein*) over or above (*hyper*). The words take a step, a step that is important to the dance of delivery already discussed in Astaire and which I'll return to later. As "above," the technique provides a step up toward the sublime of elevation. Longinus also tended to substitute plurals in place of singular words and other infringements of language. "These are little infractions that recall the ones on which Freud's psychoanalysis or Spitzer's stylistic analysis will concentrate to find the symptoms of the unconscious (which is a good contemporary heir to the pathos preached by the author of the Sublime)."[39] These little infractions also recall the ones Ulmer uses, building on psychoanalysis toward developing an electrate mode of invention. In fact, Longinus's overall goal seems to be similar to Ulmer's wish to break the compassion fatigue that prevents intervention and participation in solving individual and communal problems. In his own situation, Longinus is trying to counter an audience's "boredom," trying to "overcome this plight by teasing and by pleasing the audience's curiosity through an immoderate search for the new."[40] Like Ulmer, Longinus seeks to create epiphanies, eureka moments, and such "immoderate" techniques are similar to the wordplay of a pun or a joke (Ulmer's puncept). And although these techniques are useful to invention, they also (although, perhaps, only through invention) contribute toward developing an electrate delivery, especially if what is delivered is not "words" per se but, more importantly, affect, mood, or sublimity, modes of sensation that can only exist once the flow of emotions is transferred between bodies, even if that transference is between the bodies of I to I. For, as described above, the deliverer doesn't (only) deliver to the audience, but helps deliver from within himself and to himself. In this way, the deliverer becomes a medium rather than a transitive partner, an idea tangentially discussed by Aristotle:

> Aristotle highlighted this fundamental idea: persuasion requires exploiting the forces already present in the listener. The good orator knows the cognitive competencies and pertinent mental associations of those listening to him. He builds on preexisting ideas and recognized values, and in this way he can effect the mystery of persuasion: to induce someone to think something he was not thinking before.[41]

Whereas any rhetorical act can be said to induce such an effect, and although the process of invention might be the initial step in which these competencies and associations are thought through, it's only in the delivery that the induction occurs, an induction that is really a hypoduction leading to *hypokrisis*. For if the deliverer is meant to conjure up what is already in the listener, the emotions that the deliverer expresses in face or gesture are those that the audience would expect, tied to the emotion that they would expect, or that they would not expect, yet an expected unexpecting, as one listens to a joke in order to not expect the punchline and thus receive pleasure. The deliverer expresses his own inner emotions to express the audience's. The deliverer induces the audience to feel something they were not feeling before.

All in all, however, we need to question what a contemporary emotional or affective state might mean compared to what Greeks or Romans might have meant. This isn't to say that one emotional state is highly different from another, but that some differences might ensue, especially if we consider a repression and resurrection of emotion from print to electronic media.

> The prerogatives of the emotions, imagination, and affectations do not filter through the mesh of the typographic cage: they are left out and excluded, whereas in a world where orality was the norm there were not separate channels for *docere* and *movere*: both were spontaneously mixed, to the point that the attempt to distinguish between them would have been considered an abstract and derivative undertaking. McLuhan goes so far as to say that through these processes of fragmentation "modern" civilization has created the unconscious; that is, it has legitimized the repression of an entire instinctual area, which is contrasted with the geometrical and rational spaces expressed through the Gutenberg technology.[42]

Perhaps we do not need to question emotions themselves but how we learn to think with emotions, and how we can and should communicate with them. The move to print stripped the body from delivery, or stripped delivery from the body, and with it the kind of affective current that the body can deliver. Certainly print can evoke emotions, feeling, and mood, but not in the same way as visual or tactile forms of delivery. While a term like "digital literacy" seems oxymoronic, a term like "emotional literacy" seems even more so. But whatever this "emotional literacy" is, it could be argued (as I will below) that print has developed an emotional dumbness that very much resembles many of the symptoms of certain kinds of schizophrenia. Thus, Barilli's turn to McLuhan makes good sense, for a numbing does occur for delivery when print attempts this kind of emotional work (or removes the need for such work), a numbing upon the body and upon the ability to receive affective states. Digital technologies, which create new possibilities for bodies, require their own means of reception.

To investigate an electrate delivery is to help fulfill the promise that Barilli sees for digital media technologies, as he expresses their importance for delivery through the term *actio* and performance, which would be taken up later by Brooke. Since "A certain technological order, print, has caused this disease,"[43] it is up to rhetoricians of digital technologies to develop a logic to rebalance the body, although this balance won't be the same as pre-print.

> What reemerges is the possibility of a way of speaking that includes all of its aspects, speaking in the fullest sense of the word: the speaker may be entirely present in body and soul, intellect and senses ... Now rhetoric returns also as action, as a mode of delivering words, or managing and acting. It is a performance, an action that has a not insignificant degree of well worked out artistry. It is the reemergence of sounds, and not only of sight, that in fact had accompanied the strong development of rhetoric throughout antiquity. This return is also an attempt on the part of our civilization to undertake a sort of psychoanalysis of itself in order to recover the sensory dimension, the libidinal erotic pleasure of the word—its "presence," to borrow a term from a scholar close to McLuhan: Walter Ong.[44]

Rightly so, Barilli is starting to make the distinction between a pre-print, print, and post-print rhetoric in which the spoken body disappears into the page and then reemerges through audio-visual and electronic technologies. However, Barilli's work was published in 1989 and just preceded the explosion of digital and networked technologies that would become the digital Internet and World Wide Web. The possibilities that Barilli forecasts are still present, but his analysis needs tweaking. If delivery in print was truly "unspoken," one can see a move back toward the spoken as the voice reunites with the body through audio-visual communication. However, "words" are not all that become spoken. In fact, they may be more unspoken than ever as the focus turns toward the dynamic body that is also made present as image, particularly video, as well as non-bodies designed through animation or other aesthetic production methods. Or, it is not the spoken word, but the elements that accompany the word, such as pitch, tone, rhythm, or volume. So while Barilli is uniquely insightful in offering how a technologizing of words beyond the technologies of print may help to "recover the sensory dimension," the presence of the body reemerges in more complex ways that allow for a variety of senses and kinds of sensations to manifest.

Schizophrenia

Schizophrenia can be one of those touchy subjects that is hard to discuss in the abstract—i.e., not related to any particular clinical case—especially when trying to use theoretically the condition and the symptoms of the medical disorder. Certainly, many people are afflicted with schizophrenia, or have loved ones who suffer from its effects. The disease can thus become hard to use when suggesting that it serve as a model to study something else, such as understanding the human relation to capitalism or when trying to craft a logic of digital media. However, at the risk of being insensitive, I offer that there are some sound neurophysiological reasons why attributes of schizophrenia might prove desirable as a relay for understanding an electrate delivery, despite the legitimate cautions against doing so.

New research into schizophrenia suggests that the condition results from something that goes wrong only because it goes so right (in other words, too much of a good thing). Whereas the barriers of "language" that had traditionally set *Homo sapiens* apart from other species have been challenged and partially perforated, "creativity" is touted as another specifically human trait that makes the species unique. Humans create, invent, and manipulate, allowing them to alter and change their environment as far as such creativity will go. Thus, this trait has been environmentally selected for throughout human evolution. Schizophrenia, it would initially seem, is a condition that would hurt chances of survival, but it can actually be described as creativity run amok and has historically appeared and been revered by many cultures, often showing up in the figures of shamans, healers, and medicine men. Such figures were thought to have special powers and abilities of communicating with the spirit world. The figure of the psychologically tortured artist comes out of this tradition as well, and thus a myth developed that associated mental disease, particularly bipolar disorder and schizophrenia, with creative genius. While scientists have set out to debunk some of these myths—for certainly most creative people do not have such psychological disorders— neuroscientist Rex Jung and his colleagues have found that a correlative connection does seem to exist between schizophrenia and creativity.

> We set out to disprove some of the myths that we thought existed, but, again, something surprising happened and we needed to follow the data. We found something surprising, that the region in which our subjects had lower fidelity, if you will, of white matter was precisely the same region that subjects, patients with bipolar disorder and schizophrenia had lower white matter fidelity. And these were subjects that performed high on our creativity measures, so there might be a continuum of creativity and psychopathology. What others have hypothesized of psychosis might be an overshoot of something that is evolutionarily useful, like creativity. Why does psychosis and psychopathology persist in the gene pool when it's such a devastating disorder socially, and interpersonally, and occupationally? It may be because creativity is so highly valued evolutionarily that there's occasionally overshoots into psychosis.[45]

Schizophrenia sticks around because its condition, although debilitating in other ways and in this extreme form, provides unrestrained creativity. The reverence of figures such as artists and shamans makes sense as a visible valuation of this trait. And while such creativity might be good for inventing individually, the role of these figures is to make this creativity useful for the group and put it into the practice of delivery. Based on Jung's comments, this isn't to say that schizophrenia is particularly desirable to have as an individual, but that those more positive characteristics are useful to study, and in this context, specifically useful to study in order to arrive at a more general theory of delivery. What is there about schizophrenic logic and behavior that can teach us about what it means to think and communicate at a level of creative affect beyond what is thought to be normal? There's something partially beneficial within schizophrenia even if it's harmful as a whole.

Central to Deleuze and Guattari's conception of schizophrenia, especially as an alternative to thinking about psychoanalysis, is language. For Freud, schizophrenic language exhibits a disorder of affect and desire. It is precisely this categorization that Deleuze and Guattari work against. As Rosi Braidotti explains, the important aspect of Deleuze and Guattari's critique of psychoanalysis is turning a negative understanding of schizophrenic language into positive use: "Refusing to interpret desire as symptomatic of 'lack' or to use a linguistic paradigm that interprets desire through the system of metaphor and metonymy, they insist we understand desire in terms of affectivity, as a rhizomic mode of interconnection."[46] For Deleuze and Guattari, schizoid language is not a disorder, but an order, or perhaps better put, a logic of sensation and desire. A schizoid language provides the key for creating affective connections, for making affect visible, or speaking the unspeakable. Affect and desire are not suppressed, but created. And although Deleuze and Guattari refer to the spoken language so attended to by psychoanalysis, a language of digital technologies can take this term more broadly to include a language of the networked body, for the way that the schizophrenic operates is not only through language, but through building machines.

Whereas psychoanalysis usually casts the abnormality of mental disorders as itself normative, so that the normal is never the pathological, Deleuze and Guattari show the complicity of the state and the medical regard with such separation and repression: the schizophrenic does not attempt to repress his body, but has that body repressed in turn.

> The double burden that comes from medicalising emotions and affects, in conjunction with reducing sexual expression to genitalia, leaves bodily affects and intensities in an impoverished state. Their theory of the Body without Organs (BwO) not only critiques psychoanalysis' complicity in repression but the functionalist approach to human affectivity as well.[47]

Turning toward writing studies and working through Frederic Jameson's similar understanding of schizophrenia, Jeff Rice explains that "schizophrenic writing is not in need of 'therapy' or of a cure; it is not indicative of 'morbid content' but rather makes 'available more joyous intensities' that displace 'older affects of alienation and anxiety.'"[48] We can see this organization of desire also as a manifestation of delivery via print. With written speech, delivery becomes relegated to a reduced eye-ear circuit: the subject reads and "hears" within the brain what the eye sees. The mouth is disconnected from this delivery, especially after Augustine makes the move to read silently, further interiorizing and insulating delivery to the individual. Delivery via print, in an almost literal sense, truly becomes unspeakable. In terms of expressing desire through the body, this lack of speech now creates a triple burden, for to speak at all through a schizophrenic logic disrupts delivery within the psychoanalytic system. As an alternative, Deleuze and Guattari recast "unruly desire in terms of schizoid flows."[49] For delivery, the interconnection through flows is the key. The expression of the affective circuit strives not toward invention (although one can certainly invent in such a way, and that is, after all, what delivery does), but toward sharing this expression through the circuits created within the desiring-machine, a process that I will pick up again toward the end of the chapter. For now, I ask the question: Is delivery about the not normal? The unexpected? The WOW! If invention for Ulmer is about the eureka! and the Huh?!, is delivery about the WTF! or "look at this!"? If so, then we must look at the non-normal traits as defined by the medical establishment and determine how they might fit into a general theory of delivery.

The schizophrenic and schizophrenia are not necessarily the same. The former defines the creator of flows of desire, while the latter defines a clinical condition of the person who is stopped from her desiring production. It is this latter definition that often conditions the way we understand the schizophrenic. And although Deleuze and Guattari's understanding of schizophrenia's causes provides this initial relay into understanding what the schizophrenic can teach us about delivery, the clinical understanding of the schizophrenic's "symptoms" also provides a way to understand how clinical schizophrenia informs classical theories of delivery, and why they have become more or less useless for the body attempting to deliver within a digital environment.

Traditional characteristics of schizophrenics reveal several aspects of a differently abled individual who would not be able to deliver very well, at least according to Cicero and Quintilian's methods. Schizophrenics have no voice. They cannot pronounce that which they think, because what they think is inaccessible to their body, and their body is inaccessible to what they think. They cannot think through feeling. If they try to declaim their words, it is possible that "word salad" comes forth (Freud might say word diarrhea) rather than the musical intonations of a classically trained orator. The schizo has not the smooth starts and stops, the carefully raised and lowered tones of a well-trained mouth/ear complex, but the fits and starts, breaks and flows of one who cannot enunciate the desired words. What follows is a breakdown of the schizo's breakdowns, and how they might be indicative of, or relayed toward, an electrate delivery.

Positive Symptoms

Delusions: "fixed beliefs that are not amenable to change in light of conflicting evidence."[50]

- *Persecutory delusions*: "(i.e., belief that one is going to be harmed, harassed, and so forth by an individual, organization, or group)."[51] Living now not only in a society of the spectacle, but also the society of surveillance and of big data, such belief is not necessarily false, generally speaking. However, the condition of a general paranoia does not preclude some from still seeing such a condition as a positive symptom of schizophrenia in others. A collective paranoia might include those engaged in classic conspiracy theories (JFK assassination, UFOs, 9/11), but also the celebrity's condition of constant gossip about themselves. Celebrity gossip creates the appearance that "people are doing things" even if there is no evidence. For better or worse, this appearance, and the corresponding belief in it (rightly or wrongly), should be accounted for in a logic of electrate delivery.
- *Referential delusions*: "(i.e., belief that certain gestures, comments, environmental cues, and so forth are directed at oneself)."[52] It should come as no surprise that one would believe this in a digital media environment. Messages everywhere constantly gesture and clamor, not for the attention of the person next to me, but for MY attention. The schizo might be more aware of this than most, but this is no reason for institutionalization. Good delivery of such messages should target "me." But besides an understated enthymatic attempt to influence one's desire to buy in the advertisement, journalism often directly asks viewers to respond to prompts, send in citizen videos of both news and opinions, and to blog or tweet their thoughts. The media, while trying to be both immediate and effaced, collapses that space by direct appeal to the viewer, not just as consumer, but as producer (or perhaps the term "prosumer"). Such use of digital technologies taps into the schizophrenic's need to create desiring-machines, and territorializes the flows by seeming to deterritorialize them at the same time.
- *Somatic delusions*: "focus on preoccupations regarding health and organ function."[53] Somatic delusions do not just happen to the individual body, but also the socius, the collective body. Not only does media shift back and forth on whether the latest drug or diet are good or bad for the individual, but also about what is good for the socius. However, the beliefs are false only in that their frame of reference, how they ask the question, creates a serious blind spot, a spot that Ulmer details extensively in *Electronic Monuments*, which I'll return to in the postscript.
- *Grandiose delusions*: "i.e., when an individual believes that he or she has exceptional abilities, wealth, or fame)."[54] The culture of celebrity, of not just the idea that everyone has fifteen minutes of fame, but that such fame can become extended through digital technologies, relies on

the idea that anyone can become an instant celebrity in a moment. In fact, the celebrity (as Ulmer notes), the look, is one of the chief identity formations within electracy. One of the most reliable ways to generate celebrity, for both the already-celebrity as well as the wannabe, involves the hoax or the gag. YouTube, Facebook, Twitter, and other social media platforms, through a viral method that mimics Jim Ridolfo and Dànielle Nicole DeVoss's concept of rhetorical velocity, provide vehicles for this gag to deliver and promote such delusions.

Hallucinations: "perception-like experiences that occur without an external stimulus ... They may occur in any sensory modality." It would make sense that the schizophrenic would be able to sense things beyond what other people cannot. Not only does the schizophrenic have the advantage of being able to connect to her/his desiring-machines, creating other experiences unavailable to those whom the socius territorialize, but they also have a metaphysics based less on literate logic and more on that of the poetic (how else could they create their machinic assemblages?). As Rice notes, the "schizophrenic marks a cultural condition that affects a variety of practices where referentiality is questioned."[55] The schizophrenic is not hermeneutic, but heuretic, constantly making things, things other people might not be able to see, hear, touch, smell, or taste. The task would be to take such practices and to make these "hallucinations" appear for the group, using them to create a practice for delivery that would generate mass hallucinations, not for control, but to investigate the idea of collective/cultural hallucination and lead toward group invention.

Disorganized Thinking (Speech): "typically inferred from the individual's speech. The individual may switch from one topic to another (*derailment* or *loose associations*). Rarely, speech may be so severely disorganized that it is nearly incomprehensible and resembles receptive aphasia in its linguistic disorganization (*incoherence* or 'word salad')."[56] Again, the apparent disorganization results not from the point of view of the schizophrenic, who requires multiple lines of flight to make machinic assemblages, but from the blind spot of the observer, from this description, the clinician, whose bias toward a literate understanding of the behavior produces the appearance of disorganization. And it is not that such behavior is not disorganized, for it most certainly is in the sense that the schizophrenic must disorganize the body without organs, the organization of organs without becoming an organism. Thus, when undergoing treatment by an analyst, as Deleuze and Guattari explain in *Anti-Oedipus*, what seems like disorganized word salad cannot be used in the psychoanalytic formula of daddy-mommy-me (although this perhaps still has merit because we believe that it does), and the analyst cannot look for Freudian slips. The schizo does not have Freudian slips; he or she cannot engage in wordplay. Instead, speech itself is nothing but wordplay, all slippage, all flows, and so the play aspect disappears and turns into serious business, a business of desire—she puts play to work. For the clinician evaluating the schizo, the logic of the pun inherent to the schizophrenic voice becomes unnoticeable and suppressed. Contrasted with "word salad" is cognitive slippage, "where categories and lists become overly broad as concepts unrelated at first glance become related through tangential connections":

> "List some types of cars."
> "Let's see, there's Ford, Chevrolet, Toyota, Japan, Rising Sun, Hiroshima, Atomic Bomb, Enola Gay, oh and Miata."[57]

The problem is not the slippage, for a logic indeed operates within cognition that produces this speech. Rather, the problem is the blind spot produced by the logic of category systems: literacy. Science, one of the byproducts of literacy, is too invested in the logic to see that the response to "List some type of cars" is not categorical but poetic (categorical still, but of a different kind). It is nothing more sophisticated than a stream of consciousness, or perhaps, stream of unconsciousness. It is this unconsciousness that delivery must deliver, and the apparent disorganization used by the schizo can become a strength of delivery rather than a weakness.

Grossly Disorganized or Abnormal Motor Behavior (Including Catatonia): "*Catatonic behavior* is a marked decrease in reactivity to the environment. This ranges from resistance to instructions (negativism); to maintaining a rigid, inappropriate or bizarre posture; to a complete lack of verbal and motor responses (mutism and stupor)."[58] A seemingly paradoxical symptom of schizophrenia, where the behaviors appear more to fall in line with bipolar disorders. However, such behavior can be thought of in two ways. The first has to do with the general dumbness of society (or for McLuhan, numbness), what Ulmer identifies as *ATH*, the condition of a blindness showcased in Greek tragedy.[59] Our current societal *ATH* manifests because we are unaware of how our actions mismatch our supposed values, or the fact that we overlook abject values and fail to recognize our behaviors that, in a disorganized way, contradict those values. An example Ulmer gives is traffic accidents, which he says should be memorialized to officially commemorate those who've sacrificed their lives so that we may drive as freely as we do. The catatonia symptom appears in the "compassion fatigue" that sets in due to the presence of an information overload and twenty-four-hour news cycle that wears out any motivation to act. We are presented with so many disasters and problems that must be dealt with that it stifles any call to action—where to start?—thus effectively putting society into a stupor.

Negative Symptoms

Alogia: "manifested by diminished speech output."[60] Literally, without speech, how is the schizo to speak before the assembly? Aren't there many ways to speak? It is assumed that one without speech, without *logos*, is also one without logic, without content, without anything to say. However, nothing could be further from the truth. Alogia is not alogical, but for the schizophrenic operates under its own logic. The flows of words dry up, but the flows appear elsewhere in unspoken ways of acting. While oral speech may decrease, productivity as a whole does not, unless, of course, the desiring-production of the schizo is blocked and she is reduced to an "autistic rag."[61] Although this may seem antithetical to the concept of delivery, it is not necessarily up to the deliverer to make the message appear to the audience, but make the audience responsible for the delivery as well. The whole system of deliverer-audience needs a shared metaphysics. This metaphysics would not be alogical, but a logic apart from *logos*. For, if the schizo seeks to deliver desire, as delivery itself has always strived for, then the literate content contained in words is only secondary to the machinic function it serves, and words, if thought of as containers or vehicles, might not be the best way to deliver such "information."

Diminished emotional expression: "includes reductions in the expression of emotions in the face, eye contact, intonation of speech (prosody), and movements of the hand, head, and face that normally give an emotional emphasis to speech."[62] Here we have all the classical components of delivery, but affectively flattened. The question, again, is how does a schizophrenic, given her/his dearth of ability to deliver like a Demosthenes because of the failure of the face, voice, eyes, and other bodily movements, provide us with a model for how to deliver? If a schizophrenic is bodily dumb and affectively dumb (a redundancy), then why study one for digital forms of delivery? As Deleuze and Guattari show us, machines are meant to wear out, but it is the breaking of desiring-machines that serves as the key for creating flows of desire. The schizo, methodically, knows how to break the flows, breaking the machinic assemblages in favor of others. Because the schizo's bodies is, for lack of a better term, broken, he is familiar with how to break, and also because of his brokenness, finds it necessary to create desiring-machines to augment his body and create conditions for affect to occur. This is necessary for society as a whole given its general condition of schizophrenia, and the affect flattening that appears most notably in the condition of compassion fatigue.

Avolition: "a decrease in motivated self-initiated purposeful activities."[63]Relatedly, Ulmer provides the following characteristic of compassion fatigue: "We know more about worldwide catastrophes than ever before, and care less. Or rather, we are unable to conjoin our intellectual understanding and our emotions, and this disjunction of discursive and pathic knowledge is systematic, structural, and seemingly irreducible."[64] What Ulmer describes here is analogous to the reduction of affect in the schizophrenic, the lack of will to do anything, even if the knowledge about what and how is present. This problem at large plagues social activists about a host of issues. One can "know" that the phenomenon is occurring, but be too emotionally dumb to do anything about the problem (emotional dumbness = avolition). What avolition is for the individual, compassion fatigue is for the collective, but with the individual still important and a key for such delivery of affect. What delivery must do (which ties into the larger invention of electracy as a whole) is to deliver that affect to both the individual and the collective, or make them interested enough (Longinus's problem with boredom) to deliver for themselves. As Ulmer notes, part of the issue is the emotional reduction that takes place within literacy, the "very pathetic sentimental emotional 'fallacies' of propaganda against which critical reason constructed an entire logical defense."[65] In electracy, these fallacies become a "needed point of departure for a new mode of reason."[66] Delivery's function becomes delivering the desire back into such debates, so that the clinical condition of avolition, which occurs not as symptom of schizophrenia per se, but due to the schizophrenic's blockage from her desiring-machines, may be overcome.

Cognitive Symptoms

Cognitive symptoms traditionally associated with schizophrenia include disorganized thinking, slow thinking, difficulty understanding, poor concentration, poor memory, difficulty expressing thoughts, and difficulty integrating thoughts, feelings, and behavior.[67] Besides the symptoms associated with the body, we often associate schizophrenia with the cognitive symptoms that the schizo possesses or lacks. Again, such cognitive problems are only symptoms if we identify them from the perspectives of literacy or orality. Thinking that appears to be disorganized under a literate apparatus has its own organization under an apparatus of electracy. Poor memory has been associated with literacy going back to Plato. However, perhaps the last item (difficulty integrating thoughts, feelings, and behavior) is where the true schism occurs from the standpoint of trying to solve problems of public policy, and the place of delivery. As Ulmer writes, collectively we have difficulty when attempting to "conjoin our intellectual understanding and our emotions,"[68] thus revealing our collective schizophrenia. We cannot systematically connect information with emotion, integrating what we know with what we feel, and then create new behaviors based on this integration (the delivery of invention). While literate rhetoric has, for the most part, jettisoned delivery via the body in favor of delivery via the book, affect has mostly been jettisoned along the way because the book was never an adequate substitute for the body. However, digital technologies afford the opportunity not to replace the body, but to offer new kinds of bodies via machines through which the schizo may attach and reinvent the methods of delivery while still striving toward this same goal of a mind/body/machine integration.

Schizophasia, as one of the symptoms of formal thought disorder within the schizophrenic, is understood as a disorder when language is taken for its representational mode. A famous question is posed to schizophrenics: "Why do people believe in God?" Some replies include:

- "Because He makes a twirl in life, my box is broken help me blue elephant. Isn't lettuce brave? I like electrons, hello."
- "Tissues without a triangular head lice be it with controller is the noodle man of ice pops and radio yes thanks."
- "So even with I but he river flow amber rod with it."
- "You know bear mama said just keep boxing bitches."
- "Where is narwhal pretty rhombus with monocle kitty."
- "Has anyone really been far even as decided to use even go want to do look more like?"[69]

What does the voice of schizophrenics deliver at the same time it fails to deliver? If the voice of a schizo fails to deliver, it is only that it fails to deliver a literate logic. This is not to say it does not fail to deliver other kinds of logics as well. Again, the point is not to become schizophrenic in a pathological way, but to invent with their logics how delivery might occur in digital environments and with digital technologies that require hacking, code switching, and the reorganization of flows. However, would we recognize such logics, probably more poetic logics, if we heard them? If not, how can we design delivery-machines that can aid both the audience and the speaker so that what is noticeable (the breakdown of literate logic) becomes hidden so that the unspoken and unnoticeable (a nonliterate logic) might emerge? In other words, how can we create a prosthesis that puts such statements in an other-context so that the "meaning" that one derives from them is the intended state of mind, or mood—the unspoken quotient that delivery offers? Such unspoken delivery seeks not to "tell" the audience something, but to quicken the creative flow of collective invention and problem solving.

Delivery-Machines

Given these symptoms, it would seem that the schizophrenic is the least capable to deliver according to the classical pedagogy outlined by Cicero and Quintilian. The physical limitations alone would prohibit her from developing a strong voice, clear pronunciation, timely gestures, and other elements of bodily delivery. However, the point is not to take the schizophrenic's condition literally, but to learn how she compensates through her processes, and more than compensate, develops a different logic. The point Deleuze and Guattari make throughout *Anti-Oedipus*, and in other writings, is that the body for all of society is dumb: we don't have a general logic of affect. While the logic of literacy has hypertrophied the left brain, the right brain has withered. The schizophrenic, according to Deleuze and Guattari, has a logic to find (produce) desire, to deliver it to herself, and to put it into action through her desiring-machines (also, assemblages). As Christian Hubert explains, rather than identify desire "with lack, with the law, or with the signifier" as psychoanalysis does, Deleuze and Guattari link desire with production, specifically the production of desire through the productive unconscious.[70] "Desiring machines are the site of that production," and all machines are connected with each other, creating a network of machines, with each machine as a node that breaks the flows from one machine to the next, while itself producing flow.[71] Collectively, then, desiring-machines can be put to the service of building delivery-machines not only individually, but also collectively as a network of delivery, the vector that delivery has traditionally taken.

Although some of the clinical symptoms of schizophrenia above appear as one way to consider this "disorder," Brian Massumi surmises that for Deleuze and Guattari, echoing Braidotti, schizophrenia is not a pathological disorder. Neither should my use of schizophrenia be construed as pathological in nature; instead, the schizophrenic can teach us about delivery, how she is able to connect with the outside world despite the apparent inability to enact the necessary bodily processes as understood within a literate selfhood: "For [Deleuze and Guattari], the clinical schizophrenic's debilitating detachment from the world is a quelled attempt to engage it in unimagined ways. Schizophrenia as a positive is inventive connection, expansion rather than withdrawal."[72] In the schizophrenic's attempt to expand, to connect, we can find instructions for how to deliver in a digital environment where identity and thinking is as much within cyberspace as it is outside of and beyond the body (and, as I'll discuss in chapter five, outside cyberspace again). The schizophrenic, through desiring-machines, provides a relay for how a body connected to multiple prostheses might create multiple vectors of delivery.

Moreover, the kind of schizophrenia discussed by Deleuze and Guattari is simultaneously an invention and a delivery, and both canons occur at once. However, delivery pushes invention to the final step, just as the schizophrenic process does with the idea. For the experimental nature of the schizophrenic "is only effectively expansive if at every step it is also a relay away from ideas into action."[73] The schizophrenic process is pragmatic. This, in many ways, is also true of delivery, or at least the desired outcome of delivery, which is rhetorical at the level of affect. Layered onto *logos*, delivery attempts the pragmatics of a logic of sensation, to help (or manipulate) an audience to feel a particular sensation about the question of debate, directing them toward one or another contingent outcome. Delivery, like the schizophrenic, relies upon a process that must be enacted—thus, not just *hypokrisis*, but also *pronuntiatio* and *actio*, which is why, perhaps, delivery has taken so many different terms throughout its history, and why McCorkle describes such history as schizophrenic.[74]

While Deleuze and Guattari approach schizophrenia non-pathologically, they approach the machine non-metaphorically. They are very clear to explain that desiring-machines are, in fact, real machines, which they define as a "system of interruptions or breaks" that respond to environments and material circumstances.[75] The machines we are considering here are those that may be used to deliver, but it is complicated, if not impossible, to extract these kinds of machines from any other kind of machine, for they are really one in the same. That is, desiring-machines are always delivering-machines. The question becomes, how can these machines be put to use so that, in conjunction with the literate forms of persuasion already available to us, we can use them within a new domain of electrate delivery?

Assembling the Code

Deleuze and Guattari explain that every machine already has codes built into it, including codes recorded into the body.[76] Such machines don't merely stand as signs, but as relationships, and relationships denote not a thing, but a process. The intricate connections between an organ and a body, or other organs, allow it to tap into many flows, and may "waver" between functions it already has, or take on new ones. For delivery, any organ's use is only limited by the imagination of the deliverer. One can use a gesture just as well as the voice, the hand, or the mouth, speak with one's hands or gesture with one's mouth, to deliver a message—*actio* can be performed in many ways. The pedagogical question becomes the functional question: "What flow to break? Where to interrupt it? How and by what means?"[77] An electrate delivery becomes less how to move one's body than how to make one's body flow among many machines.

Perhaps one of the most important characteristics of desiring-machines is that they work not according to a stringent code, a program that controls their operation, but that their processes and functions require a larger network that takes advantage of chance (the accident, the contingent). One of the advantages of DNA is that it is 75 percent redundant, which allows for it to have a glut of information that is not responsible for any process at a particular time. This "surplus value" allows its "microscopic cybernetics" to be ready and available for environmental conditions should they arise.[78] If an organism (in this case) had only the single code available, it could not be as selective, and might be selected against. Deleuze and Guattari make this point by looking at allosteric protein. The function of its interactions, because it has no chemical commitments in the body, allow it to be more adaptive to the environment should conditions change, and if the changes it makes to adapt are advantageous, selected for genetically.[79] Thus, the glut of DNA in DNA allows for unlimited ability to form and test new cellular networks and "elaborate the huge network of cybernetic inter-connections."[80] This dynamic and variable collection of possible connections is characteristic of all the stages from molecular to molar, and appears in all machines. The codes in these machines, rather than signifying some operation, are really "nonsignifying elements" that only create meaning on larger scales in the aggregate.[81] The signification of these codes can only occur when coupled and interlinked with the rest of the system. DNA requires this redundancy in order to function.

The important feature of such code is not its "information" purpose, but its functional purpose, specifically the "extra features" it might enact based on its available redundancy. Deleuze and Guattari describe code's surplus value as a different kind of surplus value beyond its use in Marxist economics. Rhetorically, the surplus value is what delivery adds, specifically to uncover the surplus in each of us. This is what is left over when *logos* is exhausted. While the sur- signifies super-, it really denotes sub-, the values hidden at the unconscious level, which a schizophrenic logic can reveal as a *hypokritical* logic, as chains of code may appear as "characters from different alphabets in which an ideogram, a pictogram, a tiny image of an elephant passing by, or a rising sun."[82] Within these chains, codes mix together as letters, syllables, details from family members, accidental traits from childhood, all blending and "extracting" a surplus value from each other, "just as the orchid code 'attracts' the figure of a wasp: both phenomena demonstrate the tracks, and of selections by lot, that bring about partially dependent, aleatory phenomena bearing a close resemblance to a Markov chain."[83] While Deleuze and Guattari offer a series of signifiers via alphabetic text to represent this chain, we can represent such a chain just as easily through the metaphysics of science via a DNA sequence or a string of binary code. The latter becomes the digital code through which a new kind of delivery occurs. Moreover, the rhizome between the orchid and the wasp may be analogized between the deliverer and the deliveree, requiring the former to develop the proper desiring-machine for delivery to occur.[84]

These chains rely on gaps, the schizzes that form, schizzes that are the "locus of continual detachments" that "must not be filled in" but kept open for the rearrangement of codes.[85] The schizzo as engineer does not place machinic blocks where she desires them, but must launch them, throwing different blocks together over distances.[86] The blocks are not so much placed as delivered, for delivery inheres in this distance, this schiz that must be crossed but not filled. And as Deleuze and Guattari note, each brick is not homogeneous, but inscribed with a multitude of alphabetic symbols and "various figures, plus one or several straws, and perhaps a corpse."[87] Each brick contains a heterogeneous mixture not unlike the mixture of elements found in digital media, which contains a multitudinous array of material.

Moreover, the bricks and their assemblage also resemble digital technologies rather than analog structures: "This is the second characteristic of the machine: breaks that are a detachment, which must not be confused with breaks that are a slicing off."[88] Machines are made of digital pieces, digital chains that can be combined and recombined, detached and reattached, not amputated and left to rot. Even when analogical in appearance, the analog part functions as a digital component.

Thus, if this schizo is an engineer, she is a digital engineer, a d-engineer (one that de-engineers the digital), and a d-engineer of codes. How does the schizo go about this de/re/coding? The schizo's strategy is to break apart the codes at hand, often unified codes previously assembled by those in power, taking these codes "off in every direction in order to create a new polyvocity that is the code of desire."[89] The schizo, as a coder, is a writer, a rewriter, and she rewrites using the method of cut-and-paste, taking parts of would-be analog productions and creating a digital collage. The schizo uses machines to write with, to decode and recode, to inscribe, delivering them to new locations. "Every composition, and also every decomposition, uses mobile bricks as the basic unit."[90] In terms of digital technologies, the brick is the byte, and as Ulmer might see it though Derrida: "The first step of decomposition is the bite."[91] This is the first step of the schizo in her recording process, and also, as Ulmer explains, one of the salient features of Derrida's writing and his theory of iterability, particularly a "biterability" of the bite: "Derrida says one must realize that 'the object of the present work, its style too, is the 'morceau' [bit, piece, morsel, fragment; musical composition; snack, mouthful]. Which is always detached, as its name indicates and so you do not forget it, with the teeth.'"[92] The mechanisms for those working in alphabetic text, the "teeth" for writers like Derrida, "refer to quotation marks, brackets, parentheses" that hold and separate language.[93] These bites are Deleuze and Guattari's bricks, which the schizo takes apart at the edges, and perhaps center, of the social codes. The schizo is a citing-machine (and thus a biting-machine), and takes those pieces away to make other kinds of machines. And lest we forget that what Derrida describes is a kind of machine, we should remember his vision in *Glas*:

> I see rather … a kind of dredging machine. From the hidden, small, enclosed cabin of a crane I manipulate levers from afar … I plunge a steel mouth into the water. And I rake the bottom, and pick up rocks and seaweed which I carry back to dump on the land while the water rapidly falls back out of the mouth.[94]

Derrida and his machine integrate some of the same elements as Demosthenes: rocks in the mouth and parts from the sea. These machines don't merely deliver, they *hypokricize*.

While Cicero's mouth declaims and enunciates, one of the important features for delivering desire to the schizo is this bite, a kind of lip maneuver of which Quintilian would never have approved. The schizo bites the bricks, or bytes, in order to decompose and then recompose her machine, all the time using other machines to do the biting. And to be sure, this effect concerns not just the schizo in her local element, but has a delivery effect over distance. Citing Constantin von Monakow's term *diaschisis* ("shocked throughout") to describe how an injury in part of the brain can affect the whole or a distant part, Deleuze and Guattari explain that this injury can travel through other kinds of networks as well and "thus gives rise at a distance to phenomena that are incomprehensible from a purely mechanistic (but not a machinic) point of view."[95] Given our present metaphysics of network, this can easily be read as how the digital schizo creates machines that deliver in a digital environment. Although the machines seem to only have immediate connections to other machines, the spans of these connections actually have global potential. However, beyond both digital networks and the metaphor of network, a more appropriate metaphor might be felt, a smooth but heterogeneous and non-identical material that resembles an "anti-fabric" that "implies no separation of threads, no intertwining, only an entanglement of fibers obtained by fulling."[96] The materials of felt are not woven, but natural or artificial fibers pressed together under heat and moisture so that the fibers (often wool or acrylic) hook together and tangle like Velcro. When conjoined, the material of felt can then be formed into shapes. This concept is developed by Ulmer, as he provides a way to construct cognitive, networked "felts" and put them to use toward an image logic, adopting this term since it "carries the overtones of emotions, of feeling (I felt the punctum)."[97] Ulmer, in his initial use of felts, relies on them for purposes of invention, for fulling out the biographical/historical constellation of one's mystory to reveal what the unconscious has otherwise hidden. The "hook and eye" of the fibers provide the place where the machines may connect, and these interstices need not be physical in the sense of Velcro, but graphic traces that hook the eye. In this way, machines tap into the codes of other machines (i.e., the posthuman machine) and break and create flows. Just as the individual can construct a felt that fulls the unconscious layers onto other graphic traces, the group can create felts filled out with a group unconscious. Writing felts, then, is a process of delivery when it occurs at the group level.

The bite is not always, if ever, swallowed—it is always vomited and reused toward the schizo's purpose. The brick/bite/byte, because of its (b)iterability once detached, "may also continue to function in the absence of its context."[98] This bite that occurs in the decomposition of the social code has everything to do with the decomposition that Ulmer finds in Derrida. In addition, as it is technically regurgitated once bitten, the morsel becomes vomit. As Ulmer explains, reading Kant,

> The split between all opposed values passes through the mouth, whether sensible or ideal, judging the good and the bad ... Against Kant's 'exemplorality' (exemplary orality) concerning taste in the ideal

sense, having to do with singing and hearing, without consumption, Derrida raises the question of 'distaste,' or rather, disgust (degout).[99]

As we know, the mouth is one of the main conduits of the oral deliverer (although not necessarily the most important), not just because the content that comes out, but the articulation of that content (how as opposed to what). For Ulmer, the question of the mouth's content, the question of taste, "has to do with the relation of Kant's 'exemplorality' to the structure of the *gustus*—the relations among the palate, lips, tongue, teeth, throat—in short, the *articulators*,"[100] the very structure that an orator like Demosthenes depended upon. But there is an excess with the mouth, for not all can be swallowed. "'And what of this excess with regard to what is called the mouth?' Derrida's response is an inverted duplication of the question. If taste orders a system of pleasure of assimilation, the excluded will be that which cannot be digested, represented, spoken. What cannot be swallowed is what 'makes one vomit.'"[101]

Does the deliverer vomit? Can the articulators do nothing more than to provide an excess that is nothing more than the vomi? For Aristotle, the answer to this question might be yes, it's all excess. Other than thought alone, which would be preferred, all else is but extraneous material best vomited and never assimilated, just as if the nutritious parts of food might be assimilated into the body and all of the nonessential chemicals could be regurgitated and left out. But how would any of that taste? "The vomi explicitly engages not the 'objective' senses of hearing and sight, not even touch, which Kant describes as 'mechanical,' all three of which involve perception of or at surfaces, but the 'subjective' or 'chemical' senses of taste and smell."[102] Ulmer shows how Derrida offers the chemical senses as a way to breakdown the object within a new philosopheme of decomposition. "The organ of this new philosopheme is the mouth, the mouth that bites, chews, tastes: the organs of speech in the mouth and the throat are examined now for their metaphoric potential in terms of their other function—not to exclude speaking in the way that the orthodox philospheme of the voice-ear circuit excludes eating, but to 'think' their 'surplus.'"[103] The vomi provides that surplus, the surplus that leaves a sweet or bitter taste in the mouths of the audience that determine whether or not they "like" what they see and hear (what they feel). Demosthenes could sugarcoat and help the medicine go down and, according to Longinus, make the audience unaware that there was any sugar added. However, although the words may go down the ear pathway of the circuit, if done well, the unconscious—the vomi—is what comes up. When Deleuze and Guattari ask—"Should one, or should one not, suffocate from what one eats, swallow air, shit with one's mouth?"[104]— the answer might be yes, we should deliver the shit, the vomi, all of what's underneath, and add this to the track of "clean" literate logic.

This vomiting occurs at both ends of the sender-receiver circuit, as the vomi and shit flow from each. But in terms of the schizo as deliverer, to ask that she bite is to ask too much. Instead of the bite, the schizo prefers to nibble, only sampling what is available. From these nibbles, these tastings, the schizo can construct larger bites, but such is not necessary. Operating within the digital, the schizo works with the bit, the 1 or the 0, not the full byte, the full string of numbers within a code. Instead, the schizo strings together her own series of bits making her own bytes. And just as the schizo-deliverer nibbles when inventing, so too does she vomit just a nibble. It is not that this is all she is capable of, for she could expel the full assortment of nibbles, and does in a very scattered way. However, to be effective, any one particular line of flight is best delivered via the nibble. It is not in the schizo's interest to deliver a full speech, the way that Demosthenes might have done. It is not even in the schizo's interest to deliver the out-of-context sound bite, which on its own seems small enough to work at a molecular level. No—the schizo delivers at the micromolecular level, a level so small that it goes straight to the unconscious, straight to the viscera, bypassing the audience's ears and mouth altogether: a mouth-stomach machine. Via Barthes, we would identify this as a stinging detail. Instead of the sound bite, the schizo delivers the sound bit, picking up on a single word, a single tag, tearing it off and riffing it into a new design, delivering the one-word micromolecule directly to the gut. The trick for digital delivery is not delivering a speech at a time, but a single word or hashtag.

Machining the Unconscious

Deleuze and Guattari make it clear that their use of physics is not just a metaphor to describe the unconscious, but that the unconscious and intensities that affect it are "matter itself."[105] Thus, when they describe the machines that affect the unconscious, the machines themselves are more than metaphysical. They explain how such machines can be physical and affect desire, and how they might function to do so: "A machine works according to the previous intercommunications of its structure and the positioning of its parts."[106] However, a machine, as part of its reproduction, requires someone to build and operate it, or at least provide the programming that allows it to auto-function. Then how could a machine produce desire? Through an interplay of human vitalism and machinic mechanism, between a vital unity and structural unity, machines gain life from the living.[107] Machines use humans as a prosthetic to gain their own vitality. But desire is always external to the machine, as the machine either helps to effect desire through its processes, or because the machine is only built as a means to an end, so that any "link between the two remains secondary and indirect, both in the new means appropriated by desire and in the derived desires produced by the machines."[108] Desire can deliver machines, and machines can deliver desires, but never in a primary relationship. They depend upon a third intermediary. Or, rather, desire always exists; machines just let us notice it. They help, literally, to deliver the unconscious.

At least, so it would seem. As an example, Deleuze and Guattari point toward Samuel Butler's text "The Book of Machines." Butler's argument appears to contrast the machinic and vitalist arguments, but eventually pushes them to a point of "dispersion." For Deleuze and Guattari, Butler provides a way of thinking about machines that extends their argument of desiring-machines, for he doesn't view machines as simply extensions of man, but "really limbs and organs lying on the body without organs of society" that are available to those who have the power and means to acquire and attach to their own bodies.[109] We can see the ethics of desiring-machines taking shape. Likewise for organisms, Butler can't see them as simply machines because a typical body has so many different kinds of parts (parts for moving, for chewing, for holding, for digesting, for seeing, for talking, etc.) that they "must be compared to very different parts of distinct machines, each relating to the others, engineered in combination with the others."[110] Butler's double movement eventually pushes Deleuze and Guattari's main point about machines, that to say that they can only reproduce through the "intermediary of man" misses the point that reproduction requires an entire network, for the machine and the man as well as the bee and the clover.[111] Each are part of the reproductive system of the other, and as I discuss in chapter one, machines are certainly part of modern human reproduction and delivery. Thus, humans are part of a machine's reproductive system. This line of thought also informs the rhizome which Deleuze and Guattari will develop, especially the image of the wasp and the orchid, where a surplus value of code is captured by one machine into itself.[112] The point for delivery has to do with the machines it uses: Gracchus's flute is a simple machine that depends on humans for reproduction, but together entwined produce something that is external to both: sound. The sound, the tone, depends upon the breath that goes forth, and the pleasantness of that sound is dependent upon the human playing it. However, within the flute's physical properties—which determine a range for its limit and use—is also the knowledge of scale and pitch, which is not immediate to the deliverer looking for the right range, and so has a built in aesthetic constraint of desire, passing on that same scale of desire to the deliverer, creating the expectation of a certain kind of deliverable. These physical properties themselves are also affected by context, such as altitude, pressure, temperature, or humidity, and something else is delivered if the instrument goes out of tune.

Michael Pollan makes a similar argument in his book *Botany of Desire* where he explores the co-evolutionary relationship of humans and four plants: apples, tulips, marijuana, and potatoes, which he links to four basic desires of humans: sweetness, beauty, intoxication, and control. Humans manipulate these species to best deliver these desires, constructing an interlinked organism like Butler describes. In fact, Pollan refers to man as a "human bumblebee," using the example of Johnny Appleseed who spreads the seeds of apple trees about the countryside, so that these trees in turn provide the fruits of his desire. Besides merely disseminating these species, man also manipulates them at the genetic level, at the level of coding, so that the desire that each plant represents is fully manifest. It is not just a baseline level of sweetness, beauty, intoxication, or control that Johnny is after—he is striving for the plant to embody such feelings to the essence of each. Such an exchange is not one-sided, for the plants also benefit from this exchange and use humans as much as humans use plants. From the apple's perspective, although its fruit is harvested, it was able to reproduce in places that it wouldn't have otherwise had access to without the help of Johnny, thereby adding to its reproductive success and constructing a reproductive rhizome in the mold of Butler's bee/clover analogy, or Deleuze and Guattari's orchid/wasp. Through this relationship, which is worked out at both the molar and molecular (and micromolecular) levels, the desire of both organisms is attained (at least, to a certain degree), and delivery flows two-ways. Butler's passage is most important for what it "blossoms into," which is showing the true relationship between desire and machines. As Deleuze and Guattari explain, after the unity of the machine and unity of the living human have been dispatched, then the connection between the machine and desire becomes clear, for "the machine is desiring and desire, machined. Desire is not in the subject, but the machine in desire."[113] Desire calls forth its own machine to be built; it must deliver its own machine, a machine that in turn will help deliver it. The deliverer becomes the intermediary ("off to the side") that helps the process along.

Desiring-machines are molecular, opposed to the molar machines (social, technical, organic). However, molar machines reterritorialize the flows of desiring-machines into their own, creating unity among machines, but a unity that is forced, a desire no longer of the schizo but of the capitalistic urge to merge and assemble, to gather other machines, created by others, into one's own. The problem occurs when these machines enter molar scales and determinant conditions, static organizations where breaks can no longer occur. When machines aggregate into these larger molar scales, something becomes lost, because these machines cease to function as desiring-machines: "It is only at the submicroscopic level of desiring-machines that there exists a functionalism."[114]

The molar aggregates, like the molars in the mouth, are incapable of taking bites, making selections to taste, working at this submicroscopic scale. Whereas molars may make bites more digestible, and whereas they may release taste by crushing a food's casing or increasing its surface area (turning a bit into a morsel), they are not as precise as the incisors, mix tastes together, and grind and homogenize the food before sending it to the gut. At this point in the gastro-intestinal track, the sampling is over, for the journey across the tongue has ended. There is nothing left to do but to swallow. This molar mashing, this unifying, is abhorrent to the schizo, who delights in the tasting of many things. If she were to become full, then the desire to taste would end. The schizo must stay hungry, continue to nibble and nibble, bite after bite. Moreover, the deliverer must keep the audience hungry. These bites, these nibbles, are a salient feature of a digital delivery. For delivery-machines deliver not by molar aggregates of gigabytes, and not even by the individual lines of bytes, but by the bit that the mouth nibbles away. A 0 here, a 1 there. The schizo-as-deliverer does not want to organize the crowds the way that the fascist would, but summon smaller groups, according to whatever rhizomatic complex that emerges, according to what delivery-machines are desired.

Delivery Without Organs

To bite in the first place, to nibble and taste, the schizo needs a body to which the teeth attach, a mouth of some sort which contains the tongue. This "body" is not that of an organism but a body without organs (BwO). "What exactly is a 'BwO?'" Brian Massumi writes that a "body" is an "endless weaving together of singular states, each of which is an integration of one or more impulses."[115] For example, different stimuli create different vibratory regions which pick up these stimulating vibrations, creating different "zones of intensities." Then, "Look at the zone of intensity from the point of view of the actions it produces": this viewpoint gives us an "organ."[116] Next, find the viewpoint of "the organ's favorite action, and call it an 'erogenous zone.'"[117] If the body is still, suspended, taking no action, then "intensity = 0" and you have a BwO, a body that ceases to maintain any essential functions or identity, one instead that is "outside any determinate state, poised for any action in its repertory; this is the body from the point of view of its potential, or virtuality."[118] To deliver, the deliverer maintains a BwO that is adaptive, able to create any organ when necessary, to feel what is necessary, as if performing a gesture. This condition is one reason why delivery-machines are needed.

However, we can also consider the audience as the BwO that the deliverer must address and develop ways, as delivery-machines, to make desire and affect flow. Thus, it may not be clear which, at any point, offers the BwO to be assembled with machines, and the two may alternate depending on the encounter. The problem, however, is that the BwO does not want an assembly with desiring-machines. "Every coupling of machines ... becomes unbearable to the body without organs."[119] The BwO would rather remain at intensity = 0 than become organized. To resist connections and differentiated flows, it offers a substance difficult for making attachments, one that is "smooth, slippery, opaque, taut" and presents "a counterflow of amorphous, undifferentiated fluid."[120] Deleuze and Guattari see "primary repression" as this initial attempt of the BwO to resist organization, to resist assembling with desiring-machines.[121] This is the audience who does not answer the door for the deliveryman, afraid of what he brings, or the monarch who kills the messenger with bad news, attempting to kill the news as well. The BwO wishes to stay at intensity = 0 while the desiring-machine wants to add its bit of desire +1 to form a new code.

To bypass this apparent conflict, the BwO appropriates the production of the desiring-machine toward its own use, which is to remain unaffected.[122] If desiring-machines continue to constantly disturb the BwO, it will make the best of it, so that the "organ-machines now cling to the body without organs as though it were a fencer's padded jacket."[123] While the BwO began by being repulsed by the desiring-machines, a strange attraction now takes place so that the net effect of this interaction is that the BwO "serves as a surface for the recording of the entire process of production of desire" making it seem that the BwO produces desiring-machines from its undifferentiated surface.[124] As desiring-machines couple themselves to the BwO, they do so as "so many points of disjunction, between which an entire network of new syntheses is now woven, marking the surface off into co-ordinates, like a grid."[125] The grid creates a layout not of the linear "and then," but allows for the schizophrenic "either ... or ... or." Such a recording process allows for decision-making to be slippery, like the surface of the BwO, for although "the 'either/or' claims to mark decisive choices between immutable terms ... the schizophrenic 'either ... or ... or' refers to the system of possible permutations between differences that always amount to the same as they shift and slide about."[126]

The 'either ... or ... or' system resembles a digital code, and it is important for the schizophrenic, and thereby the deliverer, to be able to operate at this level. Because not only must the schizo be able to recognize the existing social codes, but also develop his own. The first part of the schizo's strategy is to be able to play the same games as the psychoanalyst, but introducing "a few tricks of his own."[127] Ultimately, though, such is merely play, for the schizo "has his own system of co-ordinates for situating himself at his disposal" as he forms and attaches codes in a much different way, toward different goals.[128] The schizo takes the ready-made codes available and transforms them into his own, again, taking a bit here and a bit there, scrambling codes, shifting between codes, and making a new code.[129] Although the coding method of the schizo might seem counterintuitive for a deliverer, constantly switching back and forth, this variation is actually beneficial (Quintilian tells us that variety is the "second requirement" of delivery), not only in a digital environment that constantly changes, but to reach diverse audiences that might otherwise be unreachable. An electrate deliverer would need to have a variety of codes available, be able to make use of them all at once, constantly creating new microstrands of codes for diverse groups— not just humans and posthumans, but nonhumans as well.

Because the act of production is simultaneously a recording process, the inside becomes the outside, and is folded back onto the body of the schizo so that the output also becomes an input, and delivery is always a self-delivery. In order for this to occur, a deliverer needs to be a BwO, but at the same time make use of desiring-machines so that this production/recording process occurs in such a way that creates the very possibility for the slipperiness and fluidity of the coding process, which gives the schizo-deliverer such flexibility. "Although the organ-machines attach themselves to the body without organs, the latter continues nonetheless to be without organs and does not become an organism in the ordinary sense of the word. It remains fluid and slippery."[130] While the deliverer's body is always connected to machines, it is always also detaching from machines, and maintains a BwO that can adapt. As the audience is also a BwO, new machines can (and must) be constantly built and developed in order to create the appropriate organ needed to feel, to sense whatever affect must be delivered.

Cicero and Quintilian suggest that a speaker's own emotions are secondary to the emotions required by the situation. The deliverer must make themselves feel the same emotion they want the audience to feel, whether or not they do so intrinsically. Cicero argues that an audience cannot feel the emotion of a speech unless these same emotions are "imprinted and branded onto the orator himself."[131] These emotions, again, exist at two levels—a coded level of the unconscious (the imprint), and an external image of the emotion (the brand). If these emotions do not exist for the orator, he must arouse them in himself just as much as in the audience, for Cicero found that faking emotion never seemed to work, for every time he aroused emotion in an audience, he discovered that he had become "thoroughly stirred ... by the same feelings to which I was trying to lead them."[132] Not only must the deliverer make the audience develop the necessary organs needed to feel, but she must develop them as well. And although the techniques by which the orator comes to feel these emotions may seem artful and "artificial," the actual intensities themselves are not, for they are sensations that are as real as any other, pre-conscious affects rather than learned feelings. The orator's body, then, must be a BwO through which she can be artful, and arouse the emotion not just extrinsically, but intrinsically as well. Such practice is incumbent upon an electrate delivery, which must be able to switch between internal codes and external surfaces, or external codes and internal surfaces, which are really the same for the BwO.

In his translation notes of *A Thousand Plateaus*, Massumi provides a working definition of affect/affection as it relates to Deleuze and Guattari's treatment of the concept:

> Neither word denotes a personal feeling (*sentiment* in Deleuze and Guattari). *L'affect* (Spinoza's *affectus*) is an ability to affect and be affected. It is a prepersonal intensity corresponding to the passage from one experiential state of the body to another and implying an augmentation or diminution in that body's capacity to act. *L'affection* (Spinoza's *affectio*) is each such state considered as an encounter between the affected body and a second, affecting, body (with body taken in its broadest possible sense to include "mental" or ideal bodies).[133]

Here, affect dissociates from both emotion and feeling, similar to the move made by Shouse. As Massumi identifies, and as in delivery, affect relates not simply to a thing, but an action, a process. Through this definition, it's easy to connect the general flow of affect between bodies to a directed flow of affect through the process of delivery. As a form of group invention, delivery seeks to produce the epiphanic moment, an A-Ha! when the solution is realized based on the inputs from the speaker, but in a lightning strike of the sublime. The deliverer delivers an intensity from his body to those in the audience (or from an audience's body to themselves), moving them from one experiential state to another, providing this augmentation (and sometimes diminution) in the audience's ability to act once the delivery has ended. This delivery doesn't end, but continues to transfer from body to body, trickling, dripping, vomited, flowing from one to another. The means and pace of this affective transfer changes with digital technologies, but the basic premise is the same: delivery is affect, and affect is delivery.

Finally, the key to selecting and producing these emotions lies in philosophy, specifically the philosophy that lies around the human heart and mind: psychology. Cicero, throughout *De Oratore*, stresses how important it is for the orator to study philosophy and understand the role emotions play in driving people to act, and these emotions will only be generated if the orator understands the full gamut of human behavior and the "causes by which feelings are stirred or calmed."[134] The orator must understand not only the conscious workings of the mind, but the unconscious as well, and how an orator's body can untap, dredge up, and stir the unconscious sensations lurking below. Feelings and emotions, yes, but also affect. Delivery contends not only with the surface of the soul, the "logical" arguments that he must make, but requires the deliverer to dig deep. And why stir? Why arouse? Because the root of those feelings that often lie at the bottom, in the unconscious, are those reached by *hypokrisis*. However, whereas Cicero's orator must be well versed in philosophy, if not a philosopher as well, a deliverer working with a BwO must also be an engineer, and know how the assemblage of various parts will stir emotions and make them appear so that desire can flow. An electrate delivery adds Deleuze and Guattari's schizoanalysis as a necessary field about which the rhetor should attend. However, this rhetor, this deliverer, is a complicated entity, and exists in at least as many parts as there are members of her audience. The deliverer is herself distributed, and may not be—effectively—a single person at all. Delivery requires the assembly of a particular kind of "subject" that does the delivering, which I take up in the next chapter.

Notes

1. Aeschines, *The Speeches of Aeschines*, trans. Charles Darwin Adams (Cambridge, MA: Harvard University Press, 1919), 1.27.
2. Gregory L. Ulmer, *Electronic Monuments* (Minneapolis, MN: University of Minnesota Press, 2005), xxx.
3. George A. Kennedy, *A New History of Classical Rhetoric* (Princeton, NJ: Princeton University Press, 1994), 5.

4. Gisela Striker, "Emotions in Context: Aristotle's Treatment of the Passions in the *Rhetoric* and History Moral Psychology" in *Essays on Aristotle's* Rhetoric, ed. Amélie Oksenberg Rorty (Berkeley, CA: University of California Press, 1996), 287.

5. John Voris, "Difference Between Emotions and Feelings," *Authentic Systems*, July 3 2009, accessed June 12, 2013, https://www.authentic-systems.com/featured-articles/difference-between-emotions-and-feelings/.

6. Nico Henri Fridja, *The Emotions* (New York: Cambridge University Press, 1986), 2.

7. John A. Sloboda and Patrik N. Juslin, "Psychological Perspectives on Music and Emotion." *Music and Emotion: Theory and Research*, ed. Patrik N. Juslin and John A. Sloboda (Oxford, UK: Oxford University Press, 2001), 83.

8. Longinus, "On the Sublime," in *The Rhetorical Tradition*, ed. Patricia Bizzell and Bruce Herzberg (New York: Bedford/St. Martin's, 2001), 17.1.

9. Striker, 298.

10. Ibid.

11. Ibid.

12. Keith Oatley and Jennifer M. Jenkins, *Understanding Emotions* (Oxford, UK: Blackwell, 1996), 29–30.

13. Sloboda and Juslin, 75.

14. Eric Shouse, "Feeling, Emotion, Affect," *M/C Journal* 8, no. 6 (Dec. 2005), accessed July 9, 2014, http://journal.media-culture.org.au/0512/03-shouse.php.

15. Ibid.

16. Ibid.

17. Richard J. Davidson, "On Emotion, Mood, and Related Affective Constructs," *The Nature of Emotion: Fundamental Questions*, ed. Paul Ekman and Richard J. Davidson (New York: Oxford University Press, 1994), 51.

18. Ibid., 54.

19. Sloboda and Juslin, 75.

20. Davidson, 52.

21. Ibid.

22. Longinus, 17.1.

23. Ibid., 11.4–5.

24. Ibid., 1.4.

25. Patricia Bizzell and Bruce Herzberg, ed., *The Rhetorical Tradition* (New York: Bedford/St. Martin's, 2001), 345.

26. *Hypsos* is translated here as "height" or "elevation."

27. Laurent Pernot, *Rhetoric in Antiquity*, trans. W. E. Higgins (Washington, DC: The Catholic University of America Press, 2005), 139.

28. Ibid., 140.

29. Renato Barilli, *Rhetoric*, trans. Giuliana Menozzi (Minneapolis, MN: University of Minnesota Press, 1989), 21.

30. Ibid., 22.

31. Ibid., 21.

32. Blaise Pascal, *Pensées*, Vol. 1 (Oxford, UK: Oxford University Press, 1812), xxxiv.

33. Barilli, 21.

34. Ibid.

35. Ibid., 22.

36. Ibid.

37. Ibid.
38. Ibid.
39. Ibid.
40. Ibid.
41. Pernot, 43.
42. Barilli, 124.
43. Barilli, 125.
44. Ibid.
45. "Rex Jung on Neuroscience of Creativity," by Jim Fleming, *To the Best of Our Knowledge*, National Public Radio, November 25, 2012, http://www.ttbook.org/book/rex-jung-neuroscience-creativity.
46. Rosi Braidotti, "Schizophrenia," in *The Deleuze Dictionary*, ed. Adrian Parr (Edinburgh, UK: Edinburgh University Press, 2005), 240.
47. Ibid., 241.
48. Jeff Rice, *Digital Detroit: Rhetoric and Space in the Age of the Network* (Carbondale, IL: Southern Illinois University Press, 2014), 174.
49. Braidotti, 240.
50. American Psychiatric Association, *Diagnostic and Statistical Manual of Mental Disorders: DSM-V* (Washington, DC: American Psychiatric Association, 2013), 87.
51. Ibid.
52. Ibid.
53. Ibid.
54. Ibid.
55. Rice, 174.
56. *DSM-V*, 88.
57. "Cognitive Slippage," Project Gutenberg Self-Publishing Press, accessed July 20, 2015, http://self.gutenberg.org/articles/cognitive_slippage.
58. *DSM-V*, 88.
59. Ulmer, *Electronic Monuments*, xxv.
60. *DSM-V*, 88.
61. Gilles Deleuze and Félix Guattari, *Anti-Oedipus: Capitalism and Schizophrenia*, trans. Robert Hurley, Mark Seem, and Helen R. Lane (Minneapolis, MN: University of Minnesota Press, 1983), 19–20.
62. *DSM-V*, 88.
63. Ibid.
64. Ulmer, *Electronic Monuments*, 61.
65. Ibid., 62.
66. Ibid.
67. *DSM-V*, 88.
68. Ulmer, *Electronic Monuments*, 61.
69. Nancy C. Andreason, "Thought, Language, and Communication Disorders. I. Clinical Assessment, Definition of Terms, and Evaluation of their Reliability," *Archives of General Psychiatry* 36, no. 12 (Nov. 1979): 1315.
70. Christian Hubert, "Desiring Machines," Christian Hubert Studio, accessed June 20, 2015, http://christianhubert.com/writings/desiring_machines.html.
71. Ibid.
72. Brian Massumi, *A User's Guide to Capitalism and Schizophrenia: Deviations from Deleuze and Guattari* (Cambridge, MA: MIT Press, 1992), 1.
73. Ibid., 1.

74. Ben McCorkle, *Rhetorical Delivery as Technological Discourse: A Cross-Historical Study* (Carbondale, IL: Southern Illinois University Press, 2012), 2.

75. Deleuze and Guattari, *Anti-Oedipus*, 36.

76. Ibid., 38.

77. Ibid.

78. Ibid., 298.

79. Ibid., 288.

80. Ibid., 288–289.

81. Ibid., 290.

82. Ibid., 39.

83. Ibid.

84. The example of a Markov chain is also telling because a Markov chain must be "memoryless" as the selection process can only be determined by whatever state exists at the present time; there is no code from the past, although such code can lead one back into the past. Google's algorithm for PageRank is a Markov chain, attending to the present moment of page relationships. Google's Sergey Brin and Larry Page have stated "PageRank can be thought of as a model of user behavior. We assume there is a 'random surfer' who is given a web page at random and keeps clicking on links, never hitting 'back' but eventually gets bored and starts on another random page."; Sergey Brin and Lawrence Page, "The Anatomy of a Large-Scale Hypertextual Web Search Engine," Stanford University Infolab, accessed August, 28, 2015, http://infolab.stanford.edu/~backrub/google.html.

85. Deleuze and Guattari, *Anti-Oedipus*, 39.

86. Ibid., 39–40.

87. Ibid., 40.

88. Ibid., 39.

89. Ibid., 40.

90. Ibid.

91. Gregory L. Ulmer, *Applied Grammatology: Post(e)-Pedagogy from Jacques Derrida to Joseph Beuys* (Baltimore, MD: The Johns Hopkins University Press, 1984), 57.

92. Ibid., 57–58.

93. Ibid., 58.

94. Jacques Derrida, *Glas* (Paris: Galilée, 1974), 229.

95. Deleuze and Guattari, *Anti-Oedipus*, 40.

96. Gilles Deleuze and Félix Guattari, *A Thousand Plateaus: Capitalism and Schizophrenia*, trans. Brian Massumi (Minneapolis, MN: University of Minnesota Press, 1987), 475.

97. Ulmer, *Electronic Monuments*, 166–167.

98. Ulmer, *Applied Grammatology*, 58.

99. Ibid., 56.

100. Ibid.; emphasis in original.

101. Ulmer, *Applied Grammatology*, 56.

102. Ibid., 57.

103. Ibid.

104. Deleuze and Guattari, *Anti-Oedipus*, 38.

105. Ibid., 283.

106. Ibid.

107. Ibid., 284.

108. Ibid.

109. Ibid.
110. Ibid.
111. Ibid., 285.
112. Ibid.
113. Ibid., 285–286.
114. Ibid., 288.
115. Massumi, *A User's Guide to Capitalism and Schizophrenia*, 70.
116. Ibid.
117. Ibid.
118. Ibid.
119. Deleuze and Guattari, *Anti-Oedipus*, 9.
120. Ibid.
121. Ibid.
122. Ibid., 11.
123. Ibid.
124. Ibid.
125. Ibid., 12.
126. Ibid.
127. Ibid., 14.
128. Ibid., 15.
129. Ibid.
130. Ibid.
131. Cicero, *On the Ideal Orator (De Oratore)*, trans. James M. May and Jakob Wisse (New York: Oxford University Press, 2001), II.189.
132. Ibid.
133. Deleuze and Guattari, *A Thousand Plateaus*, xvi.
134. Cicero, *De Oratore*, I.53–54.

Bibliography

Aeschines. *The Speeches of Aeschines*. Translated by Charles Darwin Adams. Cambridge, MA: Harvard University Press, 1919.

American Psychiatric Association, *Diagnostic and Statistical Manual of Mental Disorders: DSM-V*. Washington, DC: American Psychiatric Association, 2013.

Andreason, Nancy C. "Thought, Language, and Communication Disorders. I. Clinical Assessment, Definition of Terms, and Evaluation of their Reliability." *Archives of General Psychiatry* 36, no. 12 (Nov. 1979): 1315–1321.

Barilli, Renato. *Rhetoric*. Translated by Giuliana Menozzi. Minneapolis, MN: University of Minnesota Press, 1989.

Bizzell, Patricia and Bruce Herzberg, ed. *The Rhetorical Tradition*. New York: Bedford/St. Martin's, 2001.

Braidotti, Rosi. "Schizophrenia." In *The Deleuze Dictionary*, edited by Adrian Parr, 240–243. Edinburgh, UK: Edinburgh University Press, 2005.

Brin, Sergey and Lawrence Page. "The Anatomy of a Large-Scale Hypertextual Web Search Engine." Stanford University Infolab. Accessed August, 28, 2015. http://infolab.stanford.edu/~backrub/google.html.

Cicero. *On the Ideal Orator (De Oratore)*. Translated by James M. May and Jakob Wisse. New York: Oxford University Press, 2001.

"Cognitive Slippage." Project Gutenberg Self-Publishing Press. Accessed July 20, 2015. http://self.gutenberg.org/articles/cognitive_slippage.

Davidson, Richard J. "On Emotion, Mood, and Related Affective Constructs." *The Nature of Emotion: Fundamental Questions*, edited by Paul Ekman and Richard J. Davidson, 51–55. New York: Oxford University Press, 1994.

Deleuze, Gilles and Félix Guattari. *Anti-Oedipus: Capitalism and Schizophrenia*. Translated by Robert Hurley, Mark Seem, and Helen R. Lane. Minneapolis, MN: University of Minnesota Press, 1983.

———. *A Thousand Plateaus: Capitalism and Schizophrenia*. Translated by Brian Massumi. Minneapolis, MN: University of Minnesota Press, 1987.

Derrida, Jacques. *Glas*. Paris: Galilée, 1974.

Ekman, Paul and Richard J. Davidson, ed. *The Nature of Emotion: Fundamental Questions*. New York: Oxford University Press, 1994.

Fridja, Nico Henri. *The Emotions*. New York: Cambridge University Press, 1986.

Hubert, Christian. "Desiring Machines." Christian Hubert Studio. Accessed June 20, 2015. http://christianhubert.com/writings/desiring_machines.html.

Kennedy, George A. *A New History of Classical Rhetoric*. Princeton, NJ: Princeton University Press, 1994.

Longinus. "On the Sublime." In *The Rhetorical Tradition*, edited by Patricia Bizzell and Bruce Herzberg, 346–358. New York: Bedford/St. Martin's, 2001.

Massumi, Brian. *A User's Guide to Capitalism and Schizophrenia: Deviations from Deleuze and Guattari*. Cambridge, MA: MIT Press, 1992.

McCorkle, Ben. *Rhetorical Delivery as Technological Discourse: A Cross-Historical Study*. Carbondale, IL: Southern Illinois University Press, 2012.

Oatley, Keith and Jennifer M. Jenkins. *Understanding Emotions*. Oxford, UK: Blackwell, 1996.

Pascal, Blaise. *Pensées*. Vol. 1. Oxford, UK: Oxford University Press, 1812.

Pernot, Laurent. *Rhetoric in Antiquity*. Translated by W. E. Higgins. Washington, DC: The Catholic University of America Press, 2005.

Quintilian. *The Orator's Education*. Vol. 5. Edited and Translated by Donald A. Russell. Cambridge, MA: Harvard University Press, 2001.

"Rex Jung on Neuroscience of Creativity." By Jim Fleming. *To the Best of Our Knowledge*. National Public Radio. November, 25. 2012. http://www.ttbook.org/book/rex-jung-neuroscience-creativity.

Rice, Jeff. *Digital Detroit: Rhetoric and Space in the Age of the Network*. Carbondale, IL: Southern Illinois University Press, 2014.

Shouse, Eric. "Feeling, Emotion, Affect." *M/C Journal* 8, no. 6 (2005). Accessed July 9, 2014. http://journal.media-culture.org.au/0512/03-shouse.php.

Sloboda, John A. and Patrik N. Juslin. "Psychological Perspectives on Music and Emotion." In *Music and Emotion: Theory and Research*, edited by Patrik N. Juslin and John A. Sloboda, 71–104. New York: Oxford University Press, 2001.

Striker, Gisela. "Emotions in Context: Aristotle's Treatment of the Passions in the *Rhetoric* and History Moral Psychology." In *Essays on Aristotle's Rhetoric*, edited by Amélie Oksenberg Rorty, 286–302. Berkeley, CA: University of California Press, 1996.

Ulmer, Gregory L. *Applied Grammatology: Post(e)-Pedagogy from Jacques Derrida to Joseph Beuys*. Baltimore, MD: The Johns Hopkins University Press, 1984.

———. *Electronic Monuments*. Minneapolis, MN: University of Minnesota Press, 2005.

Voris, John. "Difference Between Emotions and Feelings." *Authentic Systems*. July 3, 2009. Accessed July 24, 2014. https://www.authentic-systems.com/featured-articles/difference-between-emotions-and-feelings/.

4   Becoming Shaman—Delivering the Invisible

There's an old romantic idea in German, *das Volk dichtet*, which says that the ideas and poetry of the traditional cultures come out of the folk. They do not. They come out of an elite experience, the experience of people particularly gifted, whose ears are open to the song of the universe. These people speak to the folk, and there is an answer from the folk, which is then received as an interaction.

—Joseph Campbell, *The Power of Myth*[1]

Demosthenes's success as a deliverer depended upon his ability to tap into the emotions of his audience, to understand the pathic potential in a given rhetorical situation—to be empathic, sympathetic, pathetic. For his situation, delivering before a present and collected audience, Demosthenes's body was enough to fill the space with his presence.[2] However, the body requires new machinic-assemblages to become present again over the vast distances across which it must now deliver. What the body did for orality, and what the technology of alphabetic print did for literacy (the page, of course, arranged as a "body"), we must now do for electracy. Moreover, because of the distance across which we must now deliver, the body has become apathetic. Affect is still present, but in a diminished state, for the machines we build numb those parts that feel, or overload the affective circuits. Thus, this distance does not just include physical space, but the psychic spaces that exist within these physical spaces. While Barilli was hopeful that electronic technologies would help restore the psychic aspects of delivery (and rhetoric), it has not yet done so. In addition, since the space across which delivery must work exists with time, we not only need the ability to flash forward—to allow for a deliberative rhetoric—but also the ability to join different states of psychic time (memory) and apply them within an instant (Ulmer's flash reason). Thus, in addition to the other pathic attributes, what we now need is to be telepathic—we need to deliver affect across space(s).

Demosthenes often stands as the deliverer-par-excellence, if not for actual, acclaimed ability at oration then at least for the celebrity status that such acclaim has endowed him with. Yet, Demosthenes—and the whole Western tradition of delivery coming from Demosthenes, Cicero, Quintilian, and others—does not serve as the best model to deliver telepathos within a digital, networked society. While their oral traditions certainly made use of visual elements, a better model for an electrate-deliverer appears in the figure of the shaman, a deliverer that provides a relay for how to straddle both the oral and literate apparatus and move forward into an electrate logic.

As a relay, shamanism makes sense since ghosts and spirits are real, or, at least, have real effects. The image of Alexander Gardner certainly haunted Barthes even though he had died years before Barthes had ever known of him. Ghosts of actors long dead appear to us through old (and sometimes new) films. For the WWII war room, Virilio explains that the airwaves and heads of pilots became filled with the voices of chattering commanders and colleagues, "ceaselessly followed by these off-stage voices," to the point that they could "visualize the audience in the operations room" where "female assistants contributed to ... the derealization of a battle in which ghosts played an ever greater roll ... and ghostly radar images, voices and echoes came through on the screens, radios and sonars. The projection of light and waves had replaced the old projection of arrows and javelins."[3] The continued visualization (and now auralization) of the war required a new logic of seeing what could not be directly seen.

Delivery has always involved these kinds of weapons, as discussed in the first chapter. These spears, daggers, or arrows that shamans had to help navigate were weapons that threatened individuals and whole communities. It should come as little surprise then that these military weapons, and their effects, produce some of the same kinds of effects among communities and within individuals, such as in conditions we now recognize as Post Traumatic Stress Disorder. Shell shock, hallucinations, emotional numbness—a new affect impresses a soldier's soul that makes it difficult to understand and thus communicate, to deliver. And Virilio finds it "curious" that new weapons of war, both projectile ordinance and telecommunication networks, were "being produced by the Hughes Aircraft Company, whose celebrated founder, Howard Hughes, had directed a film in 1930 about a First World War bomber crew (*Hell's Angels*). This schizophrenic magnate ... built an industrial empire by associating ... by associating cinema and aviation."[4] These delivery machines, as Virilio shows, are all implicated with the same kind of logic that digital technologies use in order to deliver, and perhaps his curious fact is not so curious, only illuminating. It takes the schizophrenic's logic to divert the flows of entertainment into war and back again, summoning one into the service of another.

Thus, the shaman provides an apt analogy for this project because of his association (accurately or inaccurately) with several aspects of our own situation. First, shamans provide a service to their community, much like the rhetorical deliverer, that allows the community to solve problems collectively. Shamans also, by serving as an intermediary between physical and psychic worlds, explore the unconscious states of both individuals and communities (which, in effect and affect, are often the same). But in this capacity as intermediary, shamans perhaps provide their most important function as a relay by showing how to enter into and navigate alternate, often invisible worlds that affect the common physical world that we normally experience: they have telepathic powers. This spirit world that the shaman must navigate is analogous to our image-saturated networked society, what some might term the society of the spectacle, and the shaman's logic can offer us instructions helpful to delivering with digital technologies in, through, across, around, and underneath digital environments.

The Shamanic Artist

Often overlooked among many of his other prognostications and sound bite theories was McLuhan's focus upon the artist as the herald for what electronic technologies might mean for those who adopt them: "in the electric age ... the artist is indispensable in the shaping and analysis and understanding of the life of forms, and structures created by electric technology."[5] The artist shows us what cannot be readily seen, both as a warning of what might come, but also by inventing new ways to use these technologies:

> It is the artist's job to try to dislocate older media into postures that permit attention to the new. To this end, the artist must ever play and experiment with new means of arranging experience, even though the majority of his audience may prefer to remain fixed in their old perceptual attitudes.[6]

As such, the artist's job is to tinker and enter into new assemblages with media (in this case, electronic media) to deliver what others cannot see or yet understand. In this role, the artist provides an intermediary position not unlike the role of the deliverer. In fact, she is a deliverer, not of the transitive type (although this too), but toward fostering invention among a collective, of developing a course of action, of suggesting what may lie ahead.

As Gordon Teskey has shown, this more formal role of the artist as intermediator begins with Milton who "represents a watershed in the seventeenth century, and, therefore, in the history of art in the West, in which the artist begins to play a new and unfamiliar role, as one who mediates spiritual power."[7] How does the artist mediate this power? "Like a shaman."[8] Teskey makes this leap from Milton to shaman through another shaman/artist, Joseph Beuys, who was himself saved by and trained as a shaman before going to art school. One of Beuys's best known edicts—"jeder Mensch ist ein Künstler"—or "every person is an artist," suggests that everyone has the potential to become an artist and serve as a shaman to his or her community. "For every person, aided by magical substances deployed in the spiritual practice of art, may become a means of communicating cosmic energy,"[9] and the more artists the better, contends Teskey, for "the better it will be for the planet."[10] Beuys's statement could be also be restated as "every person is a deliverer," especially through this understanding of a deliverer as shaman, for the three terms are nearly interchangeable.

Rather than make large pieces of art for museums and small distributions, Beuys's logic was one of the schizo, to bite off smaller morsels and spread them widely. He "moved to small works—multiples—to obtain the widest possible dissemination of cosmic warmth and so remain, as he put it, in touch with people."[11] Unlike artists previous to Milton, who created art without undergoing the experience that was intended for the audience, today's artist, stemming from Milton and working through Beuys, "undergoes an experience on our behalf and does not so much represent as mediate that experience to us, so that we seem to participate in it."[12] This experience is of the deliverer who must make himself feel the sensations and intensities he wishes his audience to feel, for the two must experience them together, the audience participating in the performance. Affect transferred through delivery cannot be represented, only communicated. "What is communicated is, in the first instance, simply the excitement of creating,"[13] the same excitement that the schizo-deliverer experiences through the process of delivery.

If Teskey noticed the role that Milton and subsequent artists play as modern-age shamans, then McLuhan notices the same role for artists within an electronic age. We can deduce that the unseen spirit world that a shaman navigated has parallels to the electronic media that so worried McLuhan. Like the shamanic spirit world, an ability to see, think, and feel in multiple senses allows one to communicate with this parallel dimension.

> The effects of technology do not occur at the level of opinions or concepts, but alter sense ratios or patterns of perception steadily and without any resistance. The serious artist is the only person able to encounter technology with impunity, just because he is an expert aware of the changes in sense perception.[14]

Echoing Teskey, the artist is able to tap into those elements of experience that are typically unseen, sense what is nonsense, and make that experience sensible to a larger audience. This isn't to say that the artist has the final say on what to make of that experience, only that he begins the delivery process, one that continues once the audience takes it up. In this role, the artist-shaman provides an important figure for electrate delivery, as a model for an electrate deliverer, for the electrate artist-shaman employs the logic of schizo necessary to mix the full array of media and networks to divert their flows according to the desired affective situation. "In our age artists are able to mix their media diet as easily as their book diet."[15]

But in addition to navigating an invisible space, the shamanic artist can also navigate across time, a Janus-like figure who can look behind and ahead at what may come, transforming this vision into something that the audience can see and hear. "Artists in various fields are always the first to discover how to enable one medium to use or to release the power of another."[16] Whereas delivery had undergone a bodiless transition and was produced through the words of print, which "encouraged artists to reduce all forms of expression as much as possible to the single descriptive and narrative plane of the printed word,"[17] the range of electronic communications technologies has opened new possibilities, first taken up by artists: "The advent of electric media released art from this straitjacket at once, creating the world of Paul Klee, Picasso, Braque, Eisenstein, the Marx Brothers, and James Joyce."[18] It matters not whether these artists actually worked within electronic media—being prescient and aware of the emerging logics of electronic media was enough to influence their work and make them sense new possibilities. "The artist picks up the message of cultural and technological challenge decades before its transforming impact occurs. He, then, builds models or Noah's arks for facing the change that is at hand."[19]

Shamanic Properties

Shamanism has parallels in many cultures, even those without strong evidence of shamanistic origins. For the ancient Greeks, the closest analogous figure would seem to be the oracles. Many similarities existed in the oracle of Delphi and what we know about shamanism: the trance-like state that the priest or priestess underwent, the sometimes use of hallucinogenic agents to create such a state, and the use of divination and shamanism toward practical reason. However, another parallel is that of the deliverer, with Piers Vitebsky's discussion of a shaman's performance sounding very much like Cicero on delivery: "The shaman's activities depend closely on the ability to sweep the audience along with the power of his or her performance, which must have its effect both on the audience and on the shaman."[20] While shamanism is a broad (perhaps too broad) concept that incorporates many cultures and most continents, my borrowing of the practice(s), like Teskey's, is more comprehensive than specific, and while I provide some specific examples from specific cultures, these examples aren't meant to be representative of every mode of shamanism. Rather, they represent those practices that can help us develop an electrate delivery system.

In general, for shamanistic cultures, the universe is not just composed of the physical world, but of a cosmos composed of many layers of worlds, or layers of reality. The shaman is a figure that can travel to and from these other layers through a variety of techniques, and thus serve as an intermediary between his or her community in the immediate, lived, physical world, and these other "spirit" worlds. "Shamanic logic starts from the idea that the soul can leave the body."[21] Although death eventually greets everyone, "the experience of dreaming is taken to show that the soul can also wander independently and return without causing death."[22] Although the term "shaman" is often used synonymously with medicine-men, magicians, witch doctors, and other such figures who often operate outside established spiritual institutions, the shaman performs his or her specific function unlike many of these other cultural figures. As Mihály Hoppál explains, the shaman's role is to understand and preserve the complex codes of his or her community, and to help the community navigate those codes depending upon a given situation.[23] Thus, in one of its contested translations, "shaman" means "one who knows,"[24] for the shaman knows better than anyone else (for this is his or her profession) how to master these codes. As a profession and practice, shamanism is always practical, attempting to solve problems by manipulating the various codes.

The shaman doesn't choose his or her profession; it chooses him. Shamanism is a calling, often resisted by the one called into service. This resistance often causes the would-be-shaman significant distress, both mentally and bodily, until he finally accepts the role. One reason for this resistance is the dangerous initiation that the shaman must undertake to become shaman, which is a rather gruesome affair. The Siberian shaman Dyukhade, with a stoat and mouse as a guide, traveled to the underworld to contend with his illness (the calling to be a shaman). After entering different tents of madness, learning about different diseases, instructed by cliffs how to use the earth, Dyukhade was

> dismembered by an otherworldly blacksmith, who seized him with tongs the size of a tent, cut off his head, sliced his body into pieces, and boiled the whole lot for three years. Then he put the head on his anvil and hammered it, dipping it in cold water to temper it. He separated the muscles from the bones, and then put them together again. He covered the skull with flesh and rejoined it to the torso. He pulled out the eyes and replaced them with new ones. Lastly, he pierced Dyukhade's ears with his iron finger and said that, now, he would be able to hear the "speech of plants." After this, Dyukhade found himself on a mountain. Soon after, he woke in his own tent.[25]

The shaman becomes nothing but a skeleton, completely devoid of a body, until the spirits teach him his craft and rebuild his body into one that can mediate between worlds. The shaman's story is one of ultimate body modification. In the process of becoming a shaman, a deliverer for his people, the shaman undergoes a deliverance from the body, and in the end is re-delivered in the delivery metaphor of rebirth. Here, the skeleton becomes code-like, giving form to the context; indeed, in adults, blood cells are produced within the bone marrow and serve as the paradigmatic source of DNA (though any cell contains DNA). Maureen B. Roberts places the shaman's initiation and his/her wounding within a larger mythic context, noting other figures that have undergone similar trauma, such as Osiris and Dionysus's dismemberments, Psyche's journey to the underworld, or Prometheus's daily suffering from the beak of Zeus's eagle—the Titan who delivered fire (knowledge) to humans. The body is continually stripped down in the process of the "psyche's ultimate goal of attaining wholeness, centredness [sic] and integration," for "fragmentation is a blow to the hubris of the stable ego, which must relinquish its sense of a fixed identity and must eventually step aside in order to allow the paradoxical Self to displace it as the centre of consciousness."[26]

In order to become whole, the body must undergo trauma, for in this wounding the body learns how to join with its machines to find true deliverance. This trauma allows the shaman to have his power through a new "mental strength" via this "mental disturbance" and "controlled disintegration which is always followed by a reintegration into someone more powerful and more whole."[27] This wholeness, however, is not assembled for the sake of physical integrity, but toward flow so that the entire body becomes a mechanism through which the flow may go.

This kind of shamanic initiation, this becoming shaman, presents an important parallel between the shaman and Deleuze and Guattari's Body without Organs. Furthermore, the stripping away of organs, making it necessary to learn to attach new ones, provides the shaman with a form of schizophrenic logic, knowing when/how to attach machines to the body and create new organs for specific situations. Because of their experience of a Body without Organs, the shaman shows us a praxis of schizophrenia, especially mirroring the schizo-logic espoused by Deleuze and Guattari as discussed in the previous chapter. While Deleuze and Guattari observe the advantages of schizophrenic logic for a capitalistic society and theorize a method in schizoanalysis by which such a logic might be developed, the shaman as schizo exhibits a schizo-logic for his own environment. Although our own situation is one of late capitalism linked with digital networks and images, shamanism can offer a mode of schizoanalysis prior to literacy, a method of attaching machines and creating assemblages from oral traditions that provides a point of departure for digital machines that often allow us to enter into different places of existence.

The schizophrenic nature of the shaman's performances and way of interacting with the world has historically linked the celebrity of shamanism with schizophrenia and mental disorder, so it should come as no surprise that the shaman can offer us something toward a schizo-logic, the logic that Deleuze and Guattari notice in our modern, clinically diagnosed schizophrenics. As Vitebsky argues, symptoms of clinical schizophrenia closely parallel bouts of shamanic "madness," especially terrible hallucinations and the disintegration of personality. However, unlike the idea of the schizophrenic that Deleuze and Guattari argue against (even if indirectly), i.e., the schizo that is diseased and without a logic, the shaman has a very specific method for inducing and controlling her schizophrenic states. Unlike the untrained schizophrenic, whose attention becomes scattered, the shaman can control his or her concentration, and even enhance it toward a particular purpose. The shaman is in control of delivery, using a schizo logic for the benefit of the community rather than the schizophrenic who is "trapped inside a private experience, almost to the point of autism."[28]

The shaman, unlike the general schizophrenic, is honored rather than ostracized because of her ability to enter into a schizo state on demand. Socially, the shaman and the schizophrenic occupy much different positions: "The shamanic personality is moulded by the culture, and shamans are 'mad' courtesy of the culture and on the terms of that culture."[29] Two societies treat each differently depending on their values, and "One becomes a hero, the other a hospital patient."[30] Unlike the general schizophrenic, "The shaman lives on the brink of the abyss but has the means to avoid falling in."[31] This position of hero, the shaman becoming local celebrity, puts her in another position that allows her to become the chief deliverer of knowledge for her community. And this is not just any knowledge, but practical reason, what an individual or the whole community should do given a particular situation. The shaman is not only one who knows, but one who knows what to do, and in turn gets others to heed her advice. The shaman delivers *actio* and the desire to act.

Thus, the shaman represents the schizophrenic that is not feared or clinically treated, but revered, even though the shaman also lives a very normal life, often only becoming shaman when a problem arises and the community needs help. The community then turns to their schizophrenic, who in his shamanistic role delves completely into his inward self, to find the problem's desire within the unconscious. Joseph Campbell describes this role of the schizo: "The shaman is the person, male or female, who … has an overwhelming psychological experience that turns him totally inward. It's a kind of schizophrenic crack-up. The whole unconscious opens up, and the shaman falls into it."[32] How that psychological experience happens can differ from culture to culture. The point for delivering desire is that we turn it into a method for rhetoric, to use such practices for communal problem solving. One of these practices includes approaching a problem from the unconscious as well as conscious aspects of thinking, providing a point of view not just from the physical world, but the metaphysical world.

The shaman, then, possesses these unique powers which makes her useful to study toward an electrate delivery within a digital culture, one that through digital technologies of linking, visualization, mobile networks, and other methods of creating virtual worlds, requires delivery in multiple realities. What follows is a more in-depth analysis of where the shaman delivers (his spirit world which is analogous to our digital infosphere) as well as how the shaman delivers (using a logic that is analogous to Deleuze and Guattari's schizoanalysis, a combination of the Body without Organs with desiring-machines to form assemblages, which is how one may deliver with/in digital environments). In this analogy, of course, I'm not attempting to celebrate or romanticize either schizophrenia or shamanism (of which there are many kinds/degrees of both), but to learn from their logics toward a new mode of delivering with digital technologies and in digital environments. It is unimportant if shamans were truly schizophrenic: what matters is the logic they provide under analogous conditions.

The Spirit World

The shaman does not operate in the physical world alone, but also in other "spirit" worlds. These worlds act upon each other in daily existence, and shamanic cultures needed to invent a way to coexist with these other worlds and the spirits that reside in them. For shamanic cultures, spirit becomes a being's *Being*, as well as a kind of consciousness, and living things and objects in the physical world each have their own consciousness. With this consciousness, spirits can act upon humans and spur events in shared, everyday existence. Spirits have human emotion and emotions toward humans, including love and compassion, but also "hunger, jealousy and pride, and so can attack us and eat us or drive us mad."[33] Although such a metaphysics might seem too vitalistic for contemporary purposes, it provided the shaman with a way to act upon a larger world, or multiple worlds, that often acted upon his human society. Although seemingly mystical at times, shamanism is always practical.

The quality of a creature or object's spirit depends upon this practicality. A large animal spirit, such as a bear, can be used for aggressive attacks, whereas a small animal spirit, such as a mouse, can be used to access small spaces. The spirits of objects are likewise practical according to purpose. Although useful at times, however, the properties of these spirits still "may overwhelm us." Shamanic metaphysics becomes a category system for contending with the overwhelming forces of nature, a way to understand and cope with this power, similar to the mythologies of other cultures, such as the Greeks. And just as the Olympian deities had emotions that stirred the seas, lands, and skies, so forces that affect shamanic cultures have similar environmental properties that can either destroy or support life according to the temperamental mood of such forces. These worlds, thus, interact and often join, for an individual "consciousness of spirits can merge into human consciousness."[34] What the shaman provides, then, is a human figure that can become an intermediary between the human and spirit worlds.

The spirit world is not static. Shamans adapt their practices to changing environments over time or place (one only has to research the many kinds of shamanistic practices that have developed over the world), for with changes in the physical world come changes in the spirit worlds. This is true of a digital, networked society as well, in which the spirit world has reopened through the eversion of the Internet, the Internet of Things, and what David Rose refers to as "enchanted objects,"[35] requiring us to contend with spirits once again. The spirit world for the shaman, this other world to which the shaman journeys, is analogous to the digital image environment in which we find ourselves, but also the codes that undergird the digital network. Whereas the images themselves may be apparent to us, the actual affect they produce remains within the invisible (or unconscious) world. It makes no difference if spirits are "real" or not—it only matters that spirits are real for the shamanistic cultures that believe in them and who then have to find practical solutions for dealing with them. Thus, it makes no difference if images are "spirits" or not: what matters is that they have effects/affects that are analogous to spirits in shamanic cultures.

Toward this analogy, the spaces in which both spirits/images live mimic each other. Although the shaman may be capable of accessing other worlds, this often occurs within a parallel, geographic space, planes of existence overlaid upon each other. The shamanic cosmos is built in layers, with one on top of the next; this universe is flat rather than geographically removed, occupying the same space. The shaman has specific practices that allow him to make this invisible world visible, to merge different layers of reality just as his own body was split and put back together again. Such spaces can be thought of as our current concepts of the conscious and unconscious, two ways of being in the world that exist in one physical location (the brain/body). If delivery, in a transitive context, consists of moving objects from one place to another, then the shaman transports from one space to another. However, the shaman also delivers in the same sense that classical delivery does: he delivers from the unconscious world to the conscious; he performs *hypokrisis*. Shamanic thinking holds that the spirit dimension is always in co-existence with everyday reality (it is, thus, part of everyday reality), but it is "largely hidden ... because it expresses not the surface appearance of things but their inner nature. Thus to a shamanic culture there is more to reality, especially to its conscious aspect, than that which meets the eye and the other ordinary senses."[36] At its best, delivery reconciles the conscious and unconscious, making the invisible visible, and allowing another mode of decision making to exist alongside pure, literate reason (i.e., the best logical argument). However, at its worst, delivery unleashes spirits from the unconscious that we cannot see nor do anything about, causing us to act against our own best interests. These were the spirits that Aristotle warned against, but Nietzsche for: "Be careful in casting out your devil 'lest you cast out the best thing about you."

Attitudes toward images often mirror reactions to the idea of spiritual phenomenon. Shamanic cultures treat spirits as having very real and physical relationships with the immediate visible world in which those cultures find themselves, even if most of the people can't see the spirits. A culture of the digital image is a bit opposite, but still analogous. We see and are affected by images everywhere, but we are blind (*ATH*) in the sense that we don't know what to do about them. In other words, we still need a mediator to discern what these image/spirits want. W. J. T. Mitchell, in his book *What Do Pictures Want?*, addresses this question from the viewpoint that images have both lives and desires, and examines the "varieties of animation or vitality that are attributed to images, the agency, motivation, autonomy, aura, fecundity, or other symptoms that make pictures into 'vital signs,'"[37] by which he means that pictures are not just representations of living things, but are representations that are living as well: "If the question, what do pictures want? makes any sense at all, it must be because we assume that pictures are something like life-forms, driven by desires and appetites."[38]

Mitchell notices and questions the power images still have over people, how we sometimes act as if pictures were living, as if they have their own desires, demands, arguments, and power over our actions. As such, images have all the capabilities and agency within a digital image environment as do the spirits for shamanic cultures. However, while those seeking the shaman do so because they believe in the powers of spirits, those perceiving images today do so in a manner akin to how they perceive spirits, which is by often rejecting the role spirits play in shamanic cultures as relevant to their own; in other words, while shamanic cultures acknowledge the existence of spirits and behave toward them congruently with such beliefs, we typically refute that images have the power that they do, noting that inanimate objects have no real power other than what we consciously or unconsciously give them. For the most part, we might replace "pictures" with "spirits" and reflect the same modern attitude about the latter. The final question Mitchell poses is how to hold a "double consciousness" toward images and other visual representations and media "vacillating between magical beliefs and skeptical doubts, naïve animism and hardheaded materialism, mystical and critical attitudes."[39] What we have lost is the ability to recognize that it doesn't matter if images/pictures/spirits are alive in the biological sense, but that they still affect us and require not simply a logical dismissal, but a way to accept them and deal with them at the affectual level on which they operate.

The answer that Mitchell gives further justifies my use of shamanism as an analogy toward a logic of digital delivery. "The usual way of sorting out this kind of double consciousness is to attribute one side of it (generally the naïve, magical, superstitious side) to someone else, and to claim the hardheaded, critical, and skeptical position as one's own."[40] We see this behavior happen often, as when some strange phenomenon, such as alien sightings, happens to someone with no belief in the phenomenon only to see the non-believer become a convert, if not totally obsessed by the experience. The spirits have possessed them. This person then becomes an easy target for another skeptic. But there are "many candidates for the 'someone else' who believes that images are alive and want things: primitives, children, the masses, the illiterate, the uncritical, the illogical, the 'Other.'"[41] Expert opinions have developed a number of ways to associate different groups of people with such magical beliefs, such as the anthropologists aligning such beliefs with the "'savage mind,' art historians to the non-Western or premodern mind, psychologists to the neurotic or infantile mind, sociologists to the popular mind."[42] However, as Claude Levi-Strauss and others have argued, the "savage mind" has much to teach us about our own minds, and what our own minds might become (or how we should attempt to make them). Many regard shamanistic cultures (and the schizophrenic) as falling within the category of those with "savage minds," but their situation with spirits teaches how we might adapt our thinking about modern spirit-images, for as Mitchell surmises, this double consciousness is a "deep and abiding feature of human responses to representation. It is not something we 'get over' when we grow up, become modern, or acquire critical consciousness."[43]

It is not that Mitchell literally believes that images want things, but he argues that "we cannot ignore that human beings (including myself) insist on talking and behaving as if they *did* believe it."[44] The same situation manifests in shamanic cultures: it doesn't matter whether or not any particular member of the shamanic community actually believes in spirits, in the spirit world(s), or not. The important features of such communities are that they *behave* as if the spirits really do exist, and their survival as a culture depends upon this behavior. Do people in shamanic cultures really suffer because malicious spirits hurl poisonous darts at them? No. Or Maybe? However, the shaman is still able to provide relief to the suffering patient. Even if we don't believe that images actually want anything from us, or that they lack means to do us harm, they still affect us, and we need a practice to deal with them in the practical way that the shaman does. If we replace the spirit with the image, shamanic practices offer a relay for how to contend with images. Images have the ability to deliver, just as spirits do; the trick, like the shaman's tricks, is to figure out how to make the images work for us, to become image helpers, rather than benign but useless, or worse, malicious images that, as Mitchell argues, want something from us.[45]

Rather than destroy images, though, as the shaman might attempt to destroy either rival spirits or shamans—stripping them down to their own bones so they can no longer reconstruct themselves and thus stealing the soul away from their body—we must use images and digital technologies as if they were our own spirit helpers. As Deleuze and Guattari instruct, if we want to deliver the unconscious then we must build desiring-machines to produce delivery-machines. McLuhan also notes the machinic interaction with media: "by continuously embracing technologies, we relate ourselves to them as servomechanisms. That is why we must, to use them at all, serve these objects, these extensions of ourselves, as gods or minor religions."[46] Humans become the servo-mechanisms of their technologies, as the "Indian is the servo-mechanism of his canoe, as the cowboy of his horse, or the executive of his clock,"[47] or of the shaman and his spirits. To deliver the unconscious, the desire of an individual or group, we must also understand the desires of those machines to which we attach. Shamans understand this when negotiating with their spirits. Mitchell suggests that rather than destroy images we should attune to them, to "play upon them as if they were musical instruments."[48] We must, just as Cicero and Quintilian recommend, learn to produce a sweet sound.

Mitchell notes Aristotle's recognition of the poetic nature of the image, which are "themselves products of poetry, and a poetics of pictures addresses itself to them ... as if they were living beings, a second nature that human beings have created around themselves."[49] Whether images are actually "living" or not doesn't matter, because they still have what Mitchell calls "lives." The question we need to ask about such images is not the rhetorical or hermeneutic, not how they work or what they mean, but what do they want, what do they ask of us, and how do we answer. Part of my question here asks how they work (or how we can work with them), yet this question in turn depends on the poetic question, because an image's desire influences the situation and helps determine the rhetorical response.

But pictures, like people, don't always know what they want, and have trouble expressing it when they do, for the message they express is not necessarily what they desire from us or the desire they create in us, "it's not even the same as what they say they want."[50] Just like people, "they have to be helped to recollect it through a dialogue with others."[51] Not only just like people, but along with people. Images and people form assemblages that can deliver not only the unconscious for the viewer, but for the image as well—for the image has its own unconscious as does the viewer in the spirit world. The desiring-machine complex that the two form helps to deliver (or at this point, perhaps, invent, produce) what each desires. The picture's want is the insertion point for the desiring-machine to connect. The image does not always sting us (although this is another point of conduction); sometimes the image beckons us as though pulling us with a thread. Here the question is not one of representation, the image is not a carrier of some literate kind of information, but a spirit that desires, that wants. Mitchell offers a different approach to image investigation, one not focused on representational qualities, but one where we should "question pictures about their desires instead of looking at them as vehicles of meaning or instruments of power."[52]

To play Mitchell's game, "What do pictures want?," is to engage in a game of practical reason—attempting to solve a problem toward some potentially beneficial outcome. This game is one of the shaman, and the motivation behind the game is the shaman's motivation as well, which is to make the invisible visible, or sensible in some way. For Mitchell, images have become invisible due to their very ubiquity, rendering them effectively transparent. Or, even though we see them, they are in some sense taken for granted. Asking this question of images is an attempt to make their presence and effects opaque and also to "turn analysis of pictures toward questions of process, affect, and to put in question the spectator position: what does the picture want from me or from 'us' or from 'them' or from whomever?"[53] We can easily substitute the keywords in this sentence and complete the analogy: Both attempt to make the invisible visible through either a game of inquiry or a shamanistic practice. Of course, Mitchell is only one of the more recent image theorists to suggest the effect an image-saturated society has for us. No doubt that we can find many parallels between a shamanic worldview and the descriptions of our current image society. For example, according to Barthes, we sense the affect of images as a sting, a *punctum*.[54] Shamans often have to contend with stings, fighting off evil spirits who sling arrows or barbs. Shamans, however, are able to use their own arrows to fight back against these spirits. We need our own means of arming ourselves, which is to say, to provide practical solutions to think with/against images, but more specifically, the infinitely delivered and alterable digital image. Borrowing from advertising speak, Mitchell notes that images "have legs": "that is, they seem to have a surprising capacity to generate new directions and surprising twists ... as if they had an intelligence and purposiveness of their own."[55] Images don't just have legs, but wings, beaks, claws, tails, and teeth. Becoming a shaman, we must use them to become our own wings and claws, and when necessary (using the logic of the schizo), bite them back.

The Shaman's Machines

We have already looked at the various machines that Demosthenes used to deliver. His machines, although not always present at the scene of his speech's delivery, are present at his own delivery, his own deliverance. Contrasted to Deleuze's loss of speech later in life, Demosthenes reportedly had an absence of clear voice early in life, as Plutarch reports his habit of stuttering.[56] To free him from his own body's affliction, he devised to use the earth, from surf to stones, as machines that would deliver desire to him should he practice with them enough. But such desire is not inherent in the machines themselves; rather, it becomes a byproduct of an interaction. Demosthenes did not desire the stones, but the process that would become of them, the becoming-orator that they offered. Such a relationship is not one (only) of fetish, the desire for the object, but the interaction-into-being that such a relationship promises—the relationship itself.

Demosthenes's relationship with his tools (we might call them training aids, although they are much more) extends beyond his own body once he steps before the assembly and begins to speak. At such a point, his being becomes integrated with the audience into a true assemblage, for all the traces of his desiring-machines are with him and become true delivering-machines. Through his machines, he has attuned himself with his body so that the sound he produces has the highest potential of resonating with the audience, to teleport his intensities from his own body into others through the sound of his voice and the sight of his gestures. He becomes machine, and his machine is a descending-machine that retrieves *hypokrisis* in others. When successful, the group no longer acts as individuals, but makes a collective decision. As Aristotle laments, this is not always based on literate reason, but often on affective sensations: Demosthenes attempts to become desiring-machine so that he can create desire in others, create the desire for others to join Demosthenes-as-desiring-machine into a larger assembly (assemblage) with a shared desire, even if—as so many desires are—that desire is conflicted with itself. Demosthenes then succeeds at becoming a delivery-machine.

The shaman uses his or her machines in much the same way. The shaman seeks to reach the unconscious spirits within herself so that she can interact with invisible spirits in present and alternate realities or worlds. This variety of present worlds mirrors the future contingent worlds that an orator wishes to paint for the audience. A shaman also deals with future, contingent worlds, but interacts with present alternate realities to help create practical reason regarding those contingencies. Of course, whether or not shamans "actually" accomplish this linking with alternate dimensions/universes depends on one's metaphysics. Even if we take physicist Hugh Everett's theory of many worlds seriously, what he calls his "relative state" formulation,[57] a literate metaphysics would view the shaman's experience of relative states with skepticism, judging any possible correspondences between her visions and future events as mere coincidence—a lucky prediction—or an accidental alignment. But still, the shaman becomes spirit, becomes something more when she couples with her many tools to become, like Demosthenes, a desiring-machine that seeks to deliver a message from an invisible world. And these tools and machines are crucial for enacting delivery, for "Without the necessary accessories the shaman could not enter the underworld."[58]

Drum

One of the chief musical tools of many shamanic cultures is the drum. This instrument helps create a connection between the shaman and the spirit world and also establishes a connection between himself and his audience. The drum does this by providing a rhythmic device which helps the shaman enter a state of trance. More than any other instrument, and in nearly every shamanic culture, "the drum is the shamanic instrument par excellence."[59] Roger Finch asks if a shaman can enter his necessary trance-like state without the aid of this machine: "Instances reviewed where genuine trance was attested all involved music: drumming, drumming and singing or, in the absence of a drum, at least rhythmic choral singing."[60] The shaman's drum is not just a musical instrument, but also a portal or gateway to the spirit world: "the most important object is the drum which symbolizes the universe as well as countless other things."[61] Of instrument classification, the drum is a membranophone, and produces its sound through a skin that vibrates when struck. This membrane separates an inner world from an outer one, and through proper rhythm, allows the shaman to transport his spirit from this world to another.

The material of the drum's membrane is specific to the shaman. Most drums are made by stretching the hide of an animal over a shell or structure, and most shamans can narrate how their drum came into being. An Altaic shaman can give "the details of the animal's birth ... its parents and its life until it was hunted down, so both the shell and the skin of the drum contain magico-religious elements which enable the visionary to undertake his ecstatic journey."[62] The historiography inscribed in the drum provides a knowledge necessary for the shaman, and the drum animal becomes the shaman's primary spirit-helper in the spirit world.

A drum must be made from an animal, for the ability to drum is an animalistic ability that humans have either lost or never developed, so that they must recreate this ability with a musical prosthesis. Certain fish, such as red and black drum, are able to produce a drumming sound, and some primates have special organs used to achieve this effect. For instance, the howling monkey has a hollow hyoid bone that it uses to produce a bass-like sound. It can drum from its interior to exterior, the opposite direction in which a shaman works. The monkey, as we shall see later, has many built-in tools and appendages which the human must adopt.

The shaman who drums experiences enhanced perception, and is trained to look for the minute details with this power, helping everyone else follow along. Most people's sense of tempo has a variance of about 4 percent, meaning they can sing a song within 4 percent of its tempo, but also cannot very well distinguish the difference between 96 and 100 beats per second; however, most professional or trained drummers would be able to make this distinction, as "their job requires that they be more sensitive to tempo than other musicians, because they are responsible for maintaining tempo when there is no conductor."[63] The shaman uses this sense of rhythm to help lead himself and his audience toward a solution to a problem. To do so, he must synchronize himself and the audience with the spirit world. And it is the drum beat, rhythm, that most strongly links the shaman with his audience, creating a group organism that begins to function as one.

> We all know the contagious effect strong musical rhythm has, at least on susceptible individuals who find it difficult not to move their heads or their legs in unison with the rhythm ... Recent evidence suggests that such coupling of internal rhythms to external drivers ... might be present at a very early age ... If there is, indeed, a fundamental tendency for synchronization of internal biophysiological oscillators to external auditory rhythms, such coupling may provide a promising explanatory venue for the emotion-inducing effects of music.[64]

Such synchronization is important for thinking through the rhythms of an electrate delivery, where time seems to be compressed to nanoseconds, yet regular daily rhythms occur, not only natural rhythms that persist, but digital rhythms of posts, updates, crawling robots, and other synchronizations with which an electrate delivery must attend. Of course *kairos* is important, but also a digital *kairos*, one that contends with code as well as humans.

While drumming, the shaman engages in a finely tuned performance, a term that links the shaman's activity with delivery. Rather than a set piece of music, the performance is variable, adaptable, and unique. Rather than a recording, the performance is live, and, therefore, can be better described in terms of jazz or groove. "Groove has to do with a particular performer or particular performance, not with what is written on paper."[65] To work well, such music must be unexpected, like the punchline of a joke, as already discussed. Although a shaman becomes the servomechanism that drives his drum, creating a rhythm-machine, "groove works best when it is not strictly metronomic—that is, when it is not perfectly machinelike."[66] Such changes in groove are primarily made by the drummer "who changes the tempo slightly according to the aesthetic and emotional nuances of the music; we say then that the rhythm track, that the drums, 'breathe.'"[67] When the drums have breath, then they can begin to work on the affective connections with the audience: "Music communicates to us emotionally through systematic violations of expectations ... Music is organized sound, but the organization has to involve some element of the unexpected or it is emotionally flat and robotic."[68] This unexpectedness found in groove is unspoken, unconscious, and so works at an affective level:

> Effective music—groove—involves subtle violations of timing. Just as the rat has an emotional response to a violation of the rhythm of the branch hitting his house, we have an emotional response to the violation of timing in music that is groove. The rat, with no context for the timing violation, experiences it as fear. We know through culture and experience that music is not threatening, and our cognitive system interprets these violations as a source of pleasure and amusement. This emotional response to groove occurs via the ear-cerebellum-nucleus accumbens-limbic circuit rather than via the ear-auditory cortex circuit. Our response to groove is largely pre- or unconscious because it goes through the cerebellum rather than the frontal lobes.[69]

These transformational effects help foster a kind of affective invention, but unlike a singular invention often ascribed to the solitary writer, rhythm also serves delivery in another way: it groups. First music groups cognitively, allowing the listener to remember much more than if the ungrouped items were heard distinctly. The rhapsode, perhaps a descendent of the shaman, is able to remember the long verses of the epic poem thanks to this feature, because the words are arranged according to a rhythm that makes units of words more memorable. As a principle of delivery, we might extrapolate this technique to examine how grouping of all sorts of elements allows the audience to remember and connect to a deliverer's performance or communication.

Within his own delivery, the shaman uses the drum to help tell a narrative. The shaman-drum machine creates a rhythm "as an aid in developing the state of mind necessary for the trance on the part of the shaman or for hypnotic influence on the patient."[70] The drum affects both the shaman and his audience. "The rhythm of the drum excites the shaman, as well as controlling the psychic state of the audience."[71] As a visual track, the drum itself may also tell a story. The drum is often embellished with artistic representations, like Achilles's shield, which both plays a part as immediate protection on the battle field, but also contains wisdom in its telling of histories. Drums are decorated with symbols and adorned with other objects that the shaman suspends from its body. These embellishments are not just aesthetic but important in the shaman's delivery system, for the visual texts that accompany the drum's sound provides a metaphysical context for the shaman's work. In Siberia, for instance, the drum's decoration depicts a scene of the cosmos, representing the "sky, earth, and underworld,"[72] and helps to show what cannot be spoken over the rhythmic drumming. By itself, the drum provides a multimedia text; but when coupled with the shaman as a prosthetic machine, it becomes a more complex delivery-machine used to reach the spirit world.

The drum's waves do not affect the ear alone, but transport the whole body. As Carl Seashore explains, rhythm "finds resonance in the whole organism,"[73] and is what motivates the delivery-machine to form, to act, and to produce a rhythm that will make others act.

> It is not a matter of the ear or the finger only: it is a matter of the two fundamental powers of life, namely knowing and acting. And, therefore, indirectly it affects circulation, respiration, and all the secretions of the body in such a way as to arouse agreeable feeling. Herein we find the groundwork of emotion; for rhythm, whether in perception or in action, is emotional when highly developed, and results in response of the whole organism to its pulsations. Such organic pulsations and secretions are the physical counterpart of emotion. Thus, when we listen to the dashing billows or the trickling raindrops ... we feel ourselves into them, and there is rhythm everywhere, not only in every plastic part of our body, but in the world as we know it at that moment.[74]

The human-drum-machine produces a delivery mechanism that transports one to another world. This is one reason why many shamans correlate drums with the transportation features associated with their materials or shape. For instance, a drum made from the skin of a wild reindeer may be used by a shaman to "ride" to other worlds. If not a wild animal, the drum may represent a domesticated, or saddled, animal. The drum provides a tele-machine that, like our current electronic tele-machines, performs dual functions in how it reduces space and transports across worlds; the drum both allows the user to travel to new places and bring beings from other places: it both travels and hosts.

It is music itself, however, that opens up the space between the physical and the spiritual, what a Western metaphysics might call life and death. Music provides the vibrations needed to trigger the death themes necessary for the shaman to enter the other worlds. Music offers a kind of becoming, a becoming-music that Deleuze and Guattari find facilitates a line-of-flight because it offers a something-else beyond simply sound-expression: "a child dies, a child plays, a woman is born, a woman dies, a bird arrives, a bird flies off. We wish to say that these are not accidental themes in music ... they are something essential."[75] For the shaman, these are often the problems they must deal with: the death of a child; the mourning mother; the assemblage with a spirit-animal, such as a bird, to fly off, become the child, and communicate as the child with the mother. But in these themes, delivered by their musical expression, is a "'danger' inherent in any line that escapes, in any line of flight or creative deterritorialization,"[76] and this is why the shaman faces danger whenever she or he attempts to visit the spirit world on behalf of her community, "the danger of veering toward destruction, toward abolition."[77] The shaman's use of music "gives us the taste for death; not so much happiness as dying happily, being extinguished,"[78] which is one of the shaman's functions as psychopomp, making sure that the spirits are now content, and that the living are content with their loved one's transition.

The drum works by creating an altered state of consciousness for the shaman, an event somewhat scientifically supported by psychological experiments that demonstrate "drumming harmonizes neural activity in the brain with the vibrational frequency of the sound."[79] The shaman often uses a rhythm of 3–4.5 beats per second to enter into an altered state of consciousness and visit "other realms and realities, thereby interacting with the spirit world for the benefit of their community."[80] And although neurophysiologists might contend that the drumming produced by the shamanic-drum machine produces an altered state of consciousness by which the shaman slips into a trance, we might also say that the drum allows the BwO to develop a deterritorialized organ that allows an escape from the body. The power of the drum can have fascist effects, to be sure, which "draws people and armies into a race that can go all the way to the abyss."[81] However, music can be used to free one's own soul from the body itself and "dispatches molecular flows."[82] Rather than rely on the body's own drum, the heart, which might produce a rhythm up to 200 beats per minute (bpm) given strenuous exercise, the shaman relies on the prosthetic machine of the drum in order to achieve a greater, superhuman rhythm of up to 270 bpm. The shaman, using the drum, can produce another organ that allows her to transcend the limits of her own body and temporarily (though sometimes accidently permanently) escape it. The drum aids in deterritorializing (hacking) the body's own biological codes.

The shaman does not join with the animal-via-drum in order to imitate it—nor is the drum, covered in the animal's skin, meant to imitate or represent the animal—but this imitation factors into becoming "like a finishing touch, a wing, a signature."[83] Deleuze and Guattari offer the example of Alexis the Trotter, who imitated a horse by running like a horse, and also "whinnied, reared, kicked, knelt, lay down on the ground" like a horse.[84] However, "he had a deeper zone of proximation or indiscernability"[85] than what these external imitative indexes might suggest, and was at his most horseful when he played the harmonica "because he no longer needed a regulating or secondary imitation … and played the instrument twice as fast as anyone else, doubled the beat, imposed a nonhuman tempo."[86] Instead of moving like a horse, music provides the human-horse-attunement necessary to sync the spirits of the human-harmonica-horse-machine that allowed Alexis to become-animal, and which allowed him to take on the human activity of playing a harmonica at a nonhuman, or superhuman, rhythm. "Alexis became all the more horse when the horse's bit became a harmonica, and the horse's trot went into double time."[87]

In this altered state of coding, a rearranging of DNA, an altered state of consciousness develops. And what the shaman becomes through music more than the child, more than the woman, is his animal, and more specifically, his helper-animal. "Music takes as its content a becoming-animal ... takes as its expression soft kettledrum beats ... and the birds find expression in *gruppeti*, appoggiaturas, staccato notes that transform them into so many souls,"[88] which is how the shaman is able to gather other souls around his spirit-helper. But the shaman must be cautious as the music changes him, or else he risks leaving his body forever. During this exchange, the helper-animal also becomes shaman, and the drum, the permeable membrane of the animal skin on which the shaman beats, provides the linkage. However, this linkage occurs only when activated by the vibrations it puts forth, and the shaman is "deterritorialized in the bird, but it is a bird that is itself deterritorialized, 'transfigured,' a celestial bird that has just as much of a becoming as that which becomes with it."[89] The musician does not "imitate the animal," she becomes-animal at the same time that the animal becomes since becoming is "always double."[90] The spirit-helper faces a much greater danger than the shaman: it risks becoming reterritorialized back into a body and losing the freedom it had died to achieve.

The drum itself is digital, and not just because it is made of the bite, the skin torn from an animal. The drum, when combined with its operating system (or servomechanism) of the player, sends out digital signals. Whereas the individual vibrations produced by a drum may technically be considered as continuous and thus analogue, the drum only fulfills its function as a rhythm-machine by producing many discontinuous beats to create the rhythm; the experience that these beats are so close together as to seem continuous does not make them less digital, for it is, of course, the gaps, the silence between the beats that permits rhythm in the first place. These beats become the bits through which the drum reaches its audience, the silent gaps the schizzes, and although a single beat/bit might permeate the air, rhythm is not produced until another beat/bit is transmitted, and then another, and another. The drum makes use of discrete beats, sounds that are not sustained by the player, as might be found in a woodwind instrument. When stricken, the beat lasts only as long as the skin continues to vibrate, and then must be struck again, another bite by the player's digits to produce another beat (bit). Continuously pressing on the drum's skin will not sustain the vibration—the skin must be torn into again. Rather than operating by the modern convention of one's and zero's, the drum operates according to beats per second.[91] The shaman's drumming code is roughly 3–4.5 bps.

And it is no wonder that we need these kinds of musical augmentations, for music saturates the universe, which is "made of refrains" and has a "power of deterritorialization permeating nature, animals, the elements, and deserts as much as human beings."[92] Humans may be able to codify music, develop category systems for it, but this does not make us innately musical, it leads to "overcoding" which is "even the opposite of having an advantage," trending toward a music of "factories and bombers."[93] While the shaman uses her drum to harmonize with the environment, Deleuze and Guattari's humans have mechanized music in order to destroy and exploit it. They require the poetic in order to deliver alternatives, to view, invent, and then communicate unseen possibilities. To do so, the technology of non-music must be coupled with music's sound logic in order to capacitate humans with the ability to deterritorialize their own flows and attune with an affective cosmos, one that cannot be spoken as such, but felt through rhythm, noting that the rhythm may be seen and not heard.

Finally, the drum is both a writing instrument and substrate. The word membrane derives from the Greek word *membranos*, which translates to parchment. The drum's membrane does not only produce sound, but provides a surface on which to produce marks. Such marks include the picto- and ideographic mythologies written on its outer surface, but also bear the trauma performed on the originary animal, and the reverberating, disappearing marks of vibration that reappear elsewhere within the body of the shaman and/or audience as psychic marks, the marks necessary to provide a code that transports the shaman elsewhere and allows him or her to interact with otherworldly spirits. As much as the shamanic experience is a performative one, it is very much a recorded, written one, and the drum provides one of the many surfaces which become this delivery-machine's textual substrate; these texts on the shaman's drum do more than add ornamentation but are each a quality that "functions only as a line of deterritorialization of an assemblage, or in going from one assemblage to another."[94] The drum, through both its visual and acoustic effects, provides points-of-attachment that further provide points-of-departure. These marks provide memories, which are not for remembering per se but for creating openings to the spirit world, openings that appear because of the larger delivery-machine made possible by the attachment points that the marks provide: "a quality never functions for itself or as a memory, but rather rectifies an assemblage in which it is deterritorialized, and, conversely, for which it provides a line of deterritorialization."[95] For the shaman, a key to performing delivery— to delivering oneself to the spirit world, and thus ultimately delivering a solution to the community—is memory.

Costume

For Quintilian, the dress of the orator provided important clues to the speaker's *ethos*, and one had to take care in one's appearance.[96] The habit of delivery may offer credibility, yet it may also provide a glimpse through to an interiority that may be a speaker's undoing. Like the drum, the clothing—or costume—that a speaker chooses to wear becomes a permeable membrane through which the spirit may pass. However, Quintilian's actual advice on what to wear is rather brief but specific, as we've already seen, and consists of general rules for toga etiquette, jewelry wear, and hair grooming.[97]

But Quintilian's conservative approach to dress is a bit misleading, for its decorative use only pertains to the early parts of the orator's performance; as a speech proceeds it's normal to undress.[98] The orator works himself into such a frenzy at times that the garment necessarily falls away as the orator heats up and begins to sweat from the exertion of delivery.[99] Such a description sounds more like the shaman in his or her frenzied chant than the controlled orator, master of delivery. Instead, the toga appears to aid in heating the orator, in raising the temperature of the body so that the body itself can warm up and better deliver, much like an athlete warming up prior to an event. The toga becomes an aid to body temperature regulation, itself a second skin that may be removed (to a point) when necessary.

For the Roman and Greek orator, the body is inescapable, and the classical garments worn highlight this fact. While the toga, in Quintilian's case, does offer some short-term benefit to the orator, as described above, it eventually becomes a hindrance and burdens the body as the orator finds it a nuisance and struggles with it while maintaining control of the rest of his delivery. This is not to say that the goal of delivery should be a transcendence of the body, but instead the use of the body to deliver the unconscious rather than exhibiting the conscious attention to contend with it.

In contrast, the shaman never fights with her own costume, but becomes with it a delivery-machine. In fact, the costume becomes a sacred space for the shaman's work, so that while Demosthenes might enter the assembly space, the shaman becomes the assembly space by donning her elaborate costume. The costume itself might be made up of few or many materials. To be sure, some shamans don so little paraphernalia that a simple piece of headwear such as a scarf can hardly be said to constitute a costume. However, for many shamanic traditions, the costume encompasses the whole world. Most Siberian shamans perform in "some ritual costume or equipment which distinguished them from other people on sight,"[100] visually marking their profession. Toward this, S. M. Shirokogoroff writes that "there is no shamanism without paraphernalia,"[101] and Hoppál comments that "symbols make a shaman."[102] Such garb might include "a gown or kaftan … ornamented with embroidery, tassels or metal pendants, and a headpiece decorated with hangings, ironworks, feathers or fur."[103]

Such costumes could be heavy—up to forty kilograms when including the headpiece, amulets, metal ornaments, and other objects—but the clothing, for the purposes of delivery, weighs less to the shaman than does the comparatively lightweight toga for the Roman. Much of this weight hangs in the form of metal: "A good shaman's garment is decorated with forty to forty-five pounds of iron; these metallic ornaments are said to resist rust and each possesses a soul."[104] Many of the metallic elements consist of metal disk "mirrors" that, depending on the shaman, serve a variety of purposes.

These mirrors may be used to "see wandering spirits and to hold helpful spirits ... drive off evil spirits who fear their own reflection, or are used like armor to protect the navel or heart from attack by hostile spirits."[105] For our own spirit world, the most immediate analogy that presents itself is that of virus protection against computer malware. However, such defenses only project one part of the human-computer interface. The images themselves, to the extent that they become a kind of spirit that wants something from us, still have the opportunity to affect us. Delivery has always been dangerous, and what new defenses must we develop to protect an electrate deliverer from new risks they might face in digital environments?

The costume differs from shaman to shaman, as they all have unique needs to fulfill their function in the community. Each shaman has a costume that is attuned to this community, to the known collective universe, and those universes known to the shaman through his travels. The costume provides a "sitemap" of sorts that details the metaphysics of the community. At the same time, the costume is independent, possessing its own power from its own in-dwelling spirits. When the shaman dons her costume, she literally invests herself with spirits. "By means of the costume the shaman is transformed into a superhuman being before the assembled people; thus the shaman becomes that which one displays."[106] The shaman becomes a focal point, an image or icon for the community. She becomes celebrity.

As Caroline Humphrey describes, the objects that make up the costume have a specific "construction which was a conscious appropriation of powers. It had its own space (the back-pad), time (the twelve-year straps, the days of the year, shells), roads (the cart-track straps and the rainbow streamers), and vehicle (the drum)."[107] The costume itself becomes a world for not only the shaman to inhabit, but also for the audience to view and help share in the experience. The costume provides the background narrative by incorporating "the idea of the renewal (the antlers ...) and mysterious metamorphosis-birth (the cuckoo-chick which emerged in the nest of a different species),"[108] as well establishing the shaman as a location in space-time or "as a socio-political arena, the armed citadel ... the shaman's plaques, arrowhead, etc. were a comment on time, since the ancient objects were fixed to a gown representing years and months."[109] If the shaman is actually going into another world, then he and his costume become a sort of monitor for viewing from the outside.

Nganasan shamans have reported using the disks to "break the ice" when going to the "Lower World of the dead,"[110] but they also say that the disks are there for artistic reasons. So in addition to its functional purpose, the costume does have an aesthetic dimension. Tara Maginnis likens the shaman's costume to that of the actor's, extending the performative action of the shaman's delivery, not unlike the mask used by the actors of ancient Greece. The costume is powerful in its own right, "capable of assisting the shaman to complete a total internal and external transformation," and its function most closely resembles the use of costumes by actors through which the performer "assumes another personality or acquires other personal attributes by the process of donning the costume and expressing the character of the being the costume represents."[111] Aristotle should not have pushed delivery away from acting, but toward it, using the methods of acting, including costume, in order to achieve a greater performative effect (and affect). *Hypokrisis*, as identified with acting, is indeed an apt name after all for delivery. To what extent, then, can this analogy be played out with the actor/celebrity of today, where donning the identity of actors themselves rather than becoming-actor for oneself is the proper mode of transformation? In other words, is it enough to mirror oneself on those who are actors already, or must one become an actor oneself rather than let others act for us?

As mentioned earlier, the shaman, during his or her initiation, becomes nothing but a skeleton. While this de-organing removes his or her own organs, it provides a blank slate for attaching other organs, many of which his original body was already without (Dyukhade notes that he was given extra bones and muscles) and so the de-organing caused no ill-effects. With this stripping away of the flesh, the shaman becomes an empty canvas on which to arrange the parts of the costume. More specifically, the shaman's costume becomes a choral space, a cut-and-paste text, and resembles many pieces by avant-garde collagists of the twentieth century. Joseph Cornell, especially, was able to make desiring-machines that functioned in the way of the shaman's costume. Like the shaman and his tools, and in the shamanic role of Teskey's Milton, Cornell used his collage boxes to search, both for "what the world looks like, how far man can see … man's attempt to understand and then represent the universe"[112] as well as the invisible, "to what cannot be seen, to what lies beneath the surface."[113] Just as the shaman's costume provides a metaphysical map of the outer and inner worlds, Cornell's Soap Bubble Sets were "concerned with the heavens, seas and earth—the 'created Universe'"[114] and his own relationship to it. Cornell created these sets as cognitive maps (many of which contained pieces of actual maps) by combining different created and found objects such as "wine-glasses … sea-shells, cork balls or stoppers, glass marbles, natural sea-sponge, driftwood and wooden cylinders," with pipes "flanking either side of a central map."[115] Shamans also made use of found materials, and attached these objects to their costumes as well as those specifically developed for particular purposes. Such objects include "old horse brasses,"[116] an "old brass Soviet army button, added to the mix of metal amulets,"[117] and "small copper wheels taken from watches."[118] These found objects, although perhaps not having the same meaning for a shaman's culture as the culture from which they came, provide a variety of associations and open up possibilities for lines of flight. Cornell chose not to disguise what many of his objects were for this reason: "A map drawn by a cartographer is precise in its rendering, it has been used by travelers or explorers through time and it displays a known and specific way of depicting the world."[119] However, "An object like a cotton reel or a piece of driftwood allow, by being more everyday, the possibility of a different range of associations entering into the assemblage."[120] Although the shaman needs to know how to navigate the spirit world, she also needs to be able to explore new visions and to provide the audience with new opportunities through which to share those visions.

Like Cornell's boxes, no two costumes of the Siberian shaman's are exactly alike, or even closely alike, for each are constructed specifically by each shaman according to his or her history and experiences with various spirits. When Johann-Gottlieb Georgi tried to sketch the dress of Russian inhabitants in 1776, "he had to illustrate eight completely different styles of shaman's costumes to show what he had seen in just a few regions."[121] Likewise, Shirokogoroff writes of southern Evenks that "there are no two absolutely similar cases of paraphernalia observed in the individual cases of shamans, even within the same ethnical unit."[122] Thus, while some symbols and objects appear across many shamanic cultures and costumes, the meaning may change across locations, and between individual shamans. As Cornell constantly reworked many of his boxes, often asking to have boxes back once given away so that he might append them, the shaman often makes and remakes his costume throughout his life. Indeed, Cornell's boxes, like the shaman's costume, "are clearly part of a process; they exude stillness, timelessness, yet are manifestly stages in a voyage."[123] The costume becomes revisable and becomes more powerful as the shaman gains increased experience. Although shamans initially learn how to begin their costume from traditional knowledge, they learn "from the spirits who help them, and many costume features are intended to physically represent attributes of animals that the shaman has been allowed by his animal spirits to acquire for use in the other words."[124] The shaman and his costume mimic the narrative of the hero and her journey, who acquires more power as she defeats adversaries, and gains important items such as "magic tools." And to illustrate how important the costume is as a prosthetic machine, the shaman may also lose powers without the costume: "There is a recorded incident in the eighteenth century of a Tungus shaman who lost all his powers after a group of professors from the West stole his costume."[125] Thus, "A shaman's equipment is an extension not only of the shaman's person but in particular of his or her capacity to act. The carved, weasel-like Alaskan *kikituk* ... summarizes the certain powers in its owner's mind and communicates these to the audience."[126] The costume, like the drum, provides a prosthesis to the shaman that allows him or her to have nonhuman powers, powers that he delivers on behalf of the audience.

What is most important for us about the shaman's costume, however, is not only the assemblage-makings that it can teach us, but this use of assemblages to "go before" the shaman, allowing the assemblages to perform actions on the user's behalf, doing things and going places the shaman cannot. Rocks, crystals, plants, and animals are all important because, similar to helper spirits, they "endow the shaman with something of their own properties, and may perform actions on the shaman's behalf."[127] Secondly, the costume provides not only a cosmology for the audience, but also a map for the shaman's own use so that he can navigate the other worlds. The costume becomes a map, but one enriched with myth and narrative, as well as the shaman's own history and relationship to the cosmos. Thus, in some ways the costume-as-map is mystorical, documenting the shaman's relationship to his oral language apparatus and using it as a compass to make decisions to help his community. We each need to map our own cosmos, our own pathways through a society of digital networks and images and create a costume that can help us leave the body and deliver in other worlds, or have parts of the costume deliver for us.

Fringe

Besides the larger pieces such as the drum and headgear, an element of fringe—such as the iron disks—makes up much of the rest of the shaman's costume. As already demonstrated with the metal disks, this fringe provides the organs that attach to the shaman's BwO, necessary because the shaman's own body had been reduced to a skeleton. Complementing the audio track of the drum, the fringe provides visual points of assembly, the linking nodes, for the shaman-machine to connect with the different worlds and spirits to make up a larger, networked delivery-machine.

This fringe manifests in many kinds of materials, such as "fur, leather, fabric, or even beads ... individually sewn on strings, tassels, or bundles of strings."[128] This fringe appears across the costume, including the headgear, where the fringe hides the shaman's face from evil spirits when he travels to the world of the dead. The shaman's headgear is one of the more important elements of shaman's costume as it holds much of his power. Many shamanic cultures believe the chakra located near or above the head provides a connection to the center of the universe, and thus a gateway for the soul to leave the body. Thus, the headgear "closes up the hole at the top of the head through which the soul may escape."[129] Soul loss is particularly dangerous for the shaman, whose spirit might be captured by hostile spirits while on a spirit journey. Thus, it is important to make sure the head/face area is protected. This particular feature is interesting when relayed to our current situation, where the seeming anonymity of cyberspace—where the face and identity can remain hidden— provides different subjectivities for behavior. As with the shaman, different identity signatures appear, such as the avatar, and become a new face for inhabiting electronic environments.[130]

Fringe is abundant on the body garment and provides the lines of flight for the shaman's travels, allowing great opportunity to journey to different realms. The mode of travel depends on the spirit animal—if a bird, then the garment will be heavily adorned with feathers, all of which may be needed to create sufficient psychological lift. The shaman's fringe helps him connect with his animal spirit to produce this mobility so that "the fringes on the arms of the garment allow the wearer to fly to the other world with the aid of the animal spirit."[131] Many other animals may be attached as well, for a variety of purposes. When displayed properly, the costume signals to the spirit helper that the shaman is friendly, and the spirit offers assistance.

Perhaps the most iconic fringe, though—that is, the one that seems most representational within a single object—is the amulet. These amulets, made of many kinds of materials, "may be in abstract shapes or stylized forms representing boats, faces, fish, animals, snakes, breasts, six-fingered hands, or humans."[132] As the shaman's costume grows throughout his career, the shaman may also add or remove these amulets depending on the particular function that he needs to carry out. For instance, a shaman among the Alaskan Eskimo may make use of a carved wooden or ivory effigy of a weasel, kept on his person, that could then be used as needed to "heal patients by using it to bite the spirits attacking them" or delivered to kill an enemy "by burrowing into his body to the heart."[133] These amulets, like all elements of the shaman's costume, have a very practical use as they help direct or enhance natural forces toward processes they already support, such as rain for farming or fertility for child bearing. Amulets may also be used for protection against evil spirits, and are still used in modern societies with shamanic traditions. Anthropologist Susan Rasmussen observed—during the Taureg uprisings of the 1990s—that "A small child, whose father had been shot by soldiers, wore a bullet as an amulet to protect himself against the same fate."[134]

From the Latin *amulētum*, it would seem that an amulet can be "any object—a stone, a plant, an artificial production, or a piece of writing—which was suspended from the neck, or tied to any part of the body" for "counteracting poison, curing or preventing disease, warding off the evil eye, aiding women in childbirth, or obviating calamities and securing advantages of any kind."[135] A possible Arabic cognate, "hamalet," defines objects such as "that which is suspended" and generally means any kind of object which is "a carrier, bearer."[136] The amulet, like all objects used by the shaman, provides an external organ through which he can function in a way unavailable to him without its aid. The amulets literally suspend from the body, not unlike Deleuze and Guattari's description of a stone-machine, or the "organ-machines" attached to the fencer's jacket or "pinned onto the jersey of a wrestler who makes them jingle as he starts toward his opponent."[137] Amulets provide nodes through which to network with other parts of the environment that remain hidden without their use. Like a metaphor, they carry the shaman across to an affective state she or he could not otherwise arrive at.

It is this function, more so than its use as an apotropaic device, that informs the amulet's potential as a totemic augmentation. Totemic objects are primarily used by individuals and small groups within tribal settings for identification purposes. The totem may help define the individual or tribe and give them a proper name, which may also be a group name, as when we say some individual is a Democrat or Republican. The totem as emblem often appears in amulet form on the shaman's costume, not necessarily to provide himself with a proper name, but to give a proper name to his spirit-helpers and help to bring those spirits into the larger community as kin. Whereas the amulet wards off evil, it also attracts friendly spirits as well as cultural knowledge to the group who witnesses the shaman's performance. As Mitchell describes, totems are inferior compared to other beings, usually "animal, vegetable, or mineral, rarely human, they are things which are adopted as counterparts to people, a kind of society of things we can use to think through what a human society is."[138] As Mitchell explains, a totem usually derives from found items taken from the natural environment, usually of common experience. These found objects provide identify formation when they become totems. Mitchell further identifies friendship (within which he includes kinship) with totemism, which he also defines as "the image practice that signifies the clan, tribe, or family … the word means, literally, 'he is a relative of mine.'"[139] The amulet hails, and like the corporate brand or logo, provides a recognizable icon for gathering. The amulet, as a totemic carrier, collects friends.

The amulet-totem provides an image-artifact for creating complex group desiring-machines because it avoids the Oedipal tangle often found with the fetish object. An image is fetishistic "when it is the object of fixation, compulsive repetition, the gap between articulated demand and brute need, forever teasing with its *fort-da* of lack and plenitude."[140] In contrast, the totem is not longed-for by the individual, or even the "national individual" that creates national fetishism, but a different kind of group desire. As Andrew McLennan notes, "fetishism is totemism minus exogamy and matrilineal descent."[141] While the fetish object, the partial body part or detached thing, may seem more applicable to the construction of the desiring-machine, it is only so to the extent that the fetish helps to understand (invent) which parts might go together; the fetish does not provide a means for linking those objects. Totemism, more than fetishism, relates to the situation of the schizo and the shaman, both of whom use these objects not because they long for the object, but because they provide points of transition from one desire to the next. This is not to say that fetishism and traditional psychoanalytic techniques do not offer means of invention, for Derrida and Ulmer have certainly shown that they do, especially toward electracy. However, for terms of delivery, the totem offers more potential than the fetish, precisely because it offers a way to reconnect the individual to the group so that a collective decision might be made.

Whereas the totem offers a shared object for the community to form around, the shaman's amulets and overall costume also serve as a totem for the spirits. The shaman uses his amulets to tell the spirits that he is a friend of theirs, and asks for their assistance. His totems provide an interface through which to connect with the invisible, and he uses totems as prostheses that go before him into the spirit world, for their powers "take flight" before he is able to alter his consciousness and enter into a trance. For although the shaman makes a totem, or finds one and adds it to his family of totems, "they take on an independent life. They seem to create themselves, and to create the social formations that they signify."[142] This feature of the totem, its ability to deliver before the deliverer, is a salient feature needed for an electrate delivery. The Israelites fashioned the golden calf to "'go before them' as leader, predecessor, and ancestor that has begotten them as a people."[143] As I offered when discussing Gracchus's flute, the deliverer needs to make use of tools that can deliver without him. The literate form of this is the letter, even when in electronic form. However, a letter does not address the contemporary, spirit world of networked digital images and other digital agents, some of which may be used to deliver for the deliverer, and some which may actually stand in the way of delivery.

How to find or create totems in electracy? For the most part, Ulmer's mystory and electronic monument (MEmorial) provide inventional methods for seeking the totems used to create collaged emblems made of found "objects." Such inventional methods correspond with those of the shaman with his deliberate attempt to make the invisible visible, or to deliver the unspeakable. As Teskey points out, and as seen in Cornell, artists prime themselves to find the accidental, the "'happy accident' ... that artists have always prepared themselves to recognize."[144] When we find the totem, though, the next task is not only to compose with it, but then to deliver such compositions back to the community so that collective decision making can occur. The closest deliberate practice toward accomplishing this is Ulmer's electronic monument (MEmorial), but other practices must be developed as well. The main point of this book is to identify what an electrate delivery might look like, and offer some theoretical underpinnings of its functioning. However, more specific practices must be invented in order to craft a rhetorical delivery with digital technologies.

Becoming Shaman

In the previous chapter, I discussed the role of the vomi; for the shaman, the stomach and the vomi it contains serve an important role in his or her delivery. As Vitebsky writes of the cultures in the Peruvian upper Amazon, one of the powers that a shaman keeps is "a thick white phlegm in the upper part of his stomach, which is the most vital part of the body."[145] This phlegm "contains spirit helpers, which the shaman calls upon for healing, as well as magical darts which he fires into victims to harm them."[146] Although a white phlegm is sometimes associated as sperm, coming from organs often prominent in Freudian psychoanalysis, for this particular shaman the important organ is the gut and the juices it contains. Other organs, especially the heart and brain, are given prominence in the knowledge they impart to the person; however, for the shaman it is this gut, intuition, a kind of knowledge passed off as less important within a literate metaphysics. For the shaman, the gut holds a phlegm called *yackay*, etymologically traced to the verb for "to know." The phlegm, the *yackay*, is yucky, not only in its physical form, but also in the kind of knowledge it contains, a deeper knowledge of the unconscious. As such, the *yackay* "represents power as knowledge. The magical substance, the helping spirits and the darts are just three aspects of the same shamanic power, which in turn consists of knowing how the world really is and how to manipulate its processes."[147] The shaman relies on helpers to deliver his knowledge, prostheses that do some of the work for him, all in order to manifest the power he is able to summon. And this *yackay* is not just practical for the shaman operating on a communal problem, but is also pedagogical as the shaman—like a bird to its chicks—regurgitates some of the phlegm for his student to drink, passing on knowledge and power in doing so. The phlegm, like many of the tools of the shaman, can either help or hurt, depending on how it is used.

We often make such claims of modern deliverers. These vehicles for information, whether it is a politician or a media outlet, can either harm or help their audiences, depending on the level and aims of the propaganda they use to persuade. Again, this returns us to Aristotle's main complaint about delivery: orators didn't rely on their arguments alone, but used the body (in multiple ways) to add value to their content, to tap into the unconscious of the audience and persuade them toward a course of action that might not be in their best interest. Delivery, then, is about regulating behavior, which is often examined and adjusted at the individual level through psychotherapy (toward the literate self) in one-on-one sessions, or mass produced and delivered to us like a pizza, as though we were individuals first and foremost. But unlike psychotherapy, which is chiefly concerned with healing the psyche (cold soul) of the individual, the work of the shaman functions within a group context and the soul of the collective. As Vitebsky explains, the tools and techniques of the shaman are amoral, but when put into communal practice "much shamanic activity is concerned with morality, and many areas of social behaviour may be regulated and arbitrated through the shaman. In this respect the shaman is not so much a psychotherapist as a sociotherapist."[148] The shaman attends to the values of the society, and delivers/reifies those values through his prescriptions: "When the *vegetalista's* patient was wrenched from his mermaid lover, restored to his family and forbidden ever to go fishing again, the diagnosis and treatment were a reminder of a man's duty to stay with his family."[149] Like orators deliberating over a proper course of action, the shaman must deliver the proper course of human behavior in order to keep balance in the society, and attending to one member attends to the whole as a single sick person indicates not just an individual problem, but a cosmic, universal one: the micro and macro healed together. Such sicknesses and acts toward healing affect not just this reality, but all realities, for "a wrong action in one realm may have a bad consequence in another."[150]

The shaman's tools provide not only a means of attachment, but also a means of attunement, of tuning the resonance of the unconscious to that of the drum, so that the healer becomes the feeler. Through Heidegger, Ulmer has written extensively on the need for attunement within an image society, for, as he argues, one of electracy's chief logics is attuning one's state of mind to an emerging digital environment. As Rodolphe Gasche writes of attunement (*Stimmung*),

> The three essential determinations of *Stimmung*—Dasein's thrownness or facticity, the disclosure of its being-in-the-world as a whole, and the fact that something can "matter" to it—constitute existentially Dasein's openness to the world. In *Stimmung*, in the attunement of a state-of-mind, Dasein, which experiences *itself* always already factically (knowingly or not), is shown to be capable of being "affected" by the world and of directing itself toward things in a world that in every case has already been disclosed to it. Dasein's being-attuned in a state-of-mind is the existential a priori of all possible linkage, connecting, or relationship.[151]

Ulmer might say that the shaman becomes a bachelor machine, "possessed by and articulating the collective multiplicities passing through 'me.'"[152] Or as Deleuze and Guattari write, "When a statement is produced by a bachelor or an artistic singularity it occurs necessarily as a function of national, political, and social community, even if the objective conditions of this community are not yet given to the moment except in literary enunciation."[153] To create this attunement, one must calibrate the vibrations of one's machines so that they resonate the "sweet sound" of delivery. Of course, sweetness is a matter of taste, opinion, in both quality and quantity. Moreover, this vibration is not just a singular vibration but also a rhythm of vibrations. The point is to create a vibration in "me" that also affects others, attuning one's own mood to the audience, and vice versa. The deliverer as shaman is not as concerned with the individual as with the whole, noting that the two are networked and never really separate.

The total ensemble of the shaman and his delivery-machines exists not as some sort of organic whole; it does not exist as an organism, but of a collection of molecules that make a machinic hole through which the shaman may enter the spirit world. So while the bird is an important animal for the shaman, representing the flight from the body, Deleuze and Guattari suggest that another animal might better represent our situation:

> the reign of birds seems to have been replaced by the age of insects, with its much more molecular vibrations, chirring, rustling, buzzing, clicking, scratching, and scraping. Birds are vocal, but insects are instrumental: drums and violins, guitars and cymbals.[154]

A shaman uses many instruments to become-animal with her spirit-helper, and creates an orchestra. If our spirit-animal is the insect, how do we summon it? What is our drum that links us with it? Such a union is necessary, for the insect helps us to bear witness, to deliver the invisible, providing a perspective we cannot see without its compound eyes or the algorithms of search engine spiders that help us draw from Web portals our online que-ries. Insects, those that bite us and those that bite the bits in our computers, become, if only in metaphor, the new spirit-animals, particularly Web spi-ders and other unseen algorithmic spirits that help us deliver through digital technologies.

Or, is this a deterministic reading and the bird is still available to us? Is the phrase "ants marching" a true description of unthinking, unfeeling humans progressing through the "rat race"? Or, correspondingly, does the "hive mind" of other insect colonies adequately describe the current situation? Do we collectively follow orders or follow the crowd of public opinion, thoughts which may not be in our best interests, both collectively and individually? Does the "web" provide a trap where we are caught to be consumed by other insects, if we are not ourselves the spider? The point for digital technologies and environments is that these worlds are filled with spirits (and apparently, insect-spirits), no less real (in fact, more so) nor less dangerous than those spirits that the shaman encounters when he or she enters a trance and leaves the body. For shamanistic cultures, all beings have a soul that gives them Being, just as all objects have a literate essence within literacy. Even Web robots have Being, and we have to attune with these spirits and try to make them friend rather than foe, a topic I will visit in the next chapter.

To be sure, shamanism has not entirely left us, and the practical reason that it provided is still needed. But shamanism—as we find it in hunting and oral societies—is also outdated and nonfunctional; for the language appa-ratus we find ourselves in, literacy transitioning to electracy, has a different set of problems and thus requires different kinds of solutions. However, sha-manism has also functioned under many political and social systems, not just hunting societies. Because of its adaptability to a diverse range of cultures and climates, shamanism still persists. And as Teskey has pointed out, we still have our shamans in the form of artists, and we still have anxieties about the world, which have shifted from "hunting to floods and crop failure, pass-ports and permits, and passing exams or finding a job."[155] What I suggest is not that we bring back shamanism as a religion, not the shaman of preliterate cultures, but the logic that Deleuze and Guattari notice in the schizophrenic, which shamanism has turned into a fully developed system of delivering that which is invisible. The next section of the book, chapters 5 and 6, begin to examine, in direct and indirect ways, contemporary spirit worlds, shamans, and their spirit helpers, how they make digital tools and costumes, and how these figures perform their shamanistic functions and facilitate new modes of delivery. Yet, even as the modes and tools change, the goals remain the same.

Notes

1. Joseph Campbell, *The Power of Myth* (New York: Anchor Books, 1991), 107.
2. Of course, Demosthenes made use of machines prior to his performance, and also during his performance through the space of the assembly, which becomes

enmeshed into the larger machine by which he delivers and thus becomes a machine, a prosthesis, itself.

3. Paul Virilio, *War and Cinema: The Logistics of Perception* (London: Verso, 1989), 95.
4. Ibid., 106–107.
5. Marshall McLuhan, *Understanding Media: The Extensions of Man* (Cambridge, MA: MIT Press, 1994), 65.
6. Ibid., 254.
7. Gordon Teskey, *Delirious Milton: The Fate of the Poet in Modernity* (Cambridge, MA: Harvard University Press, 2006), 2.
8. Ibid.
9. Ibid., 2–3.
10. Ibid., 3.
11. Ibid.
12. Ibid.
13. Ibid.
14. McLuhan, 18.
15. Ibid., 53.
16. Ibid., 54.
17. Ibid.
18. Ibid.
19. Ibid., 65.
20. Piers Vitebsky, *Shamanism* (Norman, OK: University of Oklahoma Press, 2001), 52.
21. Vitebsky, 14.
22. Ibid.
23. Mihály Hoppál, *Sámánok Eurázsiában* (Budapest: Akadémiai Kiadó, 2005), 15.
24. Ibid., 14.
25. Patrick Harpur, *The Secret Tradition of the Soul* (Berkeley, CA: Evolver, 2011), 169–170.
26. Maureen B. Roberts, "Embracing the Fragmented Self: Shamanic Explorations of the Sacred in Schizophrenia & Soul Loss," *Jung Circle*, August 22, 1998, accessed March 5, 2010, http://www.jungcircle.com/embrace.html.
27. Vitebsky, 139.
28. Ibid., 138.
29. Ibid., 139.
30. Ibid.
31. Ibid.
32. Campbell, 107.
33. Vitebsky, 12.
34. Ibid., 13.
35. See David Rose, *Enchanted Objects: Design, Human Desire, and the Internet of Things* (New York: Scribner, 2014).
36. Vitebsky, 18.
37. W. J. T. Mitchell, *What Do Pictures Want?: The Lives and Loves of Images* (Chicago, IL: University of Chicago Press, 2004), 6.
38. Ibid., 6.
39. Ibid., 7.
40. Ibid.

41. Ibid., 8.
42. Ibid.
43. Ibid.
44. Ibid., 11.
45. Although I have used the term *image* here, digital technologies present the opportunity for all sorts of spirits.
46. McLuhan, 46.
47. Ibid.
48. Mitchell, 26.
49. Ibid., xv.
50. Ibid., 46.
51. Ibid.
52. Ibid., 36.
53. Ibid., 49.
54. See Roland Barthes, *Camera Lucida: Reflections on Photography*, trans. Richard Howard (New York: Hill and Wang, 1982), 43–59.
55. Mitchell, 31.
56. Plutarch, *Lives*, Vol. VII, trans. Bernadotte Perrin (Cambridge, MA: Harvard University Press, 1919), *Life of Demosthenes* 6.4.
57. See Hugh Everett, "'Relative State' Formulation of Quantum Mechanics," *Reviews of Modern Physics* 29 (1957b): 454–462.
58. Margaret Stutley, *Shamanism: An Introduction* (New York: Routledge, 2003), 39.
59. Vitebsky, 78–79.
60. Roger Finch, "Drumming in Shamanistic Rituals," in *Shamanism: An Encyclopedia of World Beliefs, Practices, and Culture*, Vol. 1, edited by Mariko Namba and Eva Jane Neumann (Santa Barbara, CA: ABC-CLIO, 2004), 100.
61. Stutley, 39.
62. Ibid., 40.
63. Daniel J. Levitin, *This is Your Brain on Music: The Science of a Human Obsession* (New York: Penguin, 2006), 59.
64. Klaus R. Scherer and Marcel R. Zentner, "Emotional Effects of Music: Production Rules," in *Music and Emotion: Theory and Research*, ed. Patrik N. Juslin and John A. Sloboda (New York: Oxford University Press, 2001), 371–372.
65. Levitin, 166.
66. Ibid., 167.
67. Ibid., 168.
68. Ibid., 168–169.
69. Ibid., 188.
70. Spencer L. Rogers, *The Shaman, His Symbols and His Healing Power* (Springfield, IL: Charles C. Thomas, 1982), 36.
71. Stutley, 39.
72. Rogers, 36.
73. Carl E. Seashore, *Psychology of Music* (New York: Dover, 1967), 143.
74. Ibid., 143–144.
75. Gilles Deleuze and Félix Guattari, *A Thousand Plateaus: Capitalism and Schizophrenia*, trans. Brian Massumi (Minneapolis, MN: University of Minnesota Press, 1987), 299.
76. Ibid.

77. Ibid.
78. Ibid.
79. Vitebsky, 81.
80. Melinda Maxfield, "The Journey of the Drum," *ReVision* 16, no. 4 (1994): 157.
81. Deleuze and Guattari, *A Thousand Plateaus*, 302.
82. Ibid., 309.
83. Ibid., 305.
84. Ibid.
85. Ibid.
86. Ibid.
87. Ibid.
88. Ibid., 304.
89. Ibid.
90. Ibid., 305.
91. Literally—*cor*—with the heart and mind.
92. Deleuze and Guattari, *A Thousand Plateaus*, 309.
93. Ibid., 309.
94. Ibid., 306.
95. Ibid., 309.
96. Quintilian, *The Orator's Education*, Vol. 5, ed. and trans. Donald A. Russell (Cambridge, MA: Harvard University Press, 2001), VIII *prooem.* 20.
97. Ibid., XI.3.138.
98. Ibid., XI.3.144.
99. Ibid., XI.3.147–148.
100. Ronald Hutton, *Shamans: Siberian Spirituality and the Western Imagination* (London: Hambledon and London, 2001), 78.
101. Sergei Mikhailovich Shirokogoroff, "Preliminary Remark 102. To Chapter XXIV," *Pscyhomental Complex of the Tungus*, Vol. 3, Shirokogorov.ru, 2015, accessed July 20, 2015, http://www.shirokogorov.ru/s-m-shirokogorov/publications/psychomental-complex-tungus-03/102.
102. Mihály Hoppál, "Shamanism: Universal Structures and Regional Symbols," in *Shamans and Cultures*, ed. Mihály Hoppál and Keith Howard (Budapest: Akadémiai Kiadó, 1993), 191.
103. Hutton, 79.
104. Stutley, 76.
105. Tara Maginnis, "Costume, Shaman," in *Shamanism: An Encyclopedia of World Beliefs, Practices, and Culture*, Volume 1, edited by Mariko Namba and Eva Jane Neumann (Santa Barbara, CA: ABC-CLIO, 2004), 59.
106. Stutley, 71.
107. Carolina Humphrey and Urgunge Onon, *Shamans and Elders: Experience, Knowledge, and Power Among the Daur Mongols* (Oxford, UK: Clarendon Press, 1996), 208.
108. Stutley, 71.
109. Ibid.
110. Maginnis, 59.
111. Ibid., 57.
112. Lindsay Blair, *Joseph Cornell's Vision of Spiritual Order* (London: Reaktion Books, 1999), 189.

113. Ibid., 189.
114. Ibid., 191.
115. Ibid., 192.
116. Maginnis, 59.
117. Ibid.
118. Stutley, 79.
119. Blair, 202.
120. Ibid.
121. Maginnis, 58.
122. Shirokogoroff.
123. Blair, 204.
124. Maginnis, 59.
125. Ibid.
126. Vitebsky, 82.
127. Ibid.
128. Maginnis, 59.
129. Stutley, 60.
130. Of course, many other data traces appear (or remain hidden) and are recorded with every action online, the sub (*hypo*) workings of the computer and network.
131. Maginnis, 60.
132. Ibid., 59.
133. Vitebsky, 83.
134. Susan Rasmussen, *Healing in the Community: Medicine, Contested Terrains, and Cultural Encounters among the Taureg* (Westport, CT: Bergin and Garvey, 2001), 184.
135. James Yates, "Amuletum," in *A Dictionary of Greek and Roman Antiquities*, ed. William Smith (London: C. C. Little and J. Brown, 1853), 91.
136. *Oxford English Dictionary*, 2nd ed., s.v. "amulet."
137. Gilles Deleuze and Félix Guattari, *Anti-Oedipus: Capitalism and Schizophrenia*, trans. Robert Hurley, Mark Seem, and Helen R. Lane (Minneapolis, MN: University of Minnesota Press, 1983), 11.
138. Mitchell, 122.
139. Ibid., 75.
140. Ibid.
141. Andrew McLennan, quoted in Claude Lévi-Strauss, *Totemism*, trans. Rodney Needham (Boston, MA: Beacon Press, 1963), 13.
142. Mitchell, 105.
143. Ibid.
144. Ibid., 124.
145. Vitebsky, 24.
146. Ibid.
147. Ibid.
148. Ibid., 112.
149. Ibid.
150. Ibid., 114.
151. Rodolphe Gasche, *Of Minimal Things: Studies on the Notion of Relation* (Stanford, CA: Stanford University Press, 1999), 116; emphasis in original.
152. Gregory L. Ulmer, *Electronic Monuments* (Minneapolis, MN: University of Minnesota Press, 2005), 154.

153. Gilles Deleuze and Félix Guattari, *Kafka: Toward a Minor Literature*, trans. Dana Polan (Minneapolis, MN: University of Minnesota Press, 1986), 83–84.
154. Deleuze and Guattari, *A Thousand Plateaus*, 308.
155. Vitebsky, 33.

Bibliography

Blair, Lindsay. *Joseph Cornell's Vision of Spiritual Order*. London: Reaktion Books, 1999.

Campbell, Joseph. *The Power of Myth*. New York: Anchor Books, 1991.

Deleuze, Gilles and Félix Guattari. *Anti-Oedipus: Capitalism and Schizophrenia*. Translated by Robert Hurley, Mark Seem, and Helen R. Lane. Minneapolis, MN: University of Minnesota Press, 1983.

———. *Kafka: Toward a Minor Literature*. Translated by Dana Polan. Minneapolis, MN: University of Minnesota Press, 1986.

———. *A Thousand Plateaus: Capitalism and Schizophrenia*. Translated by Brian Massumi. Minneapolis, MN: University of Minnesota Press, 1987.

Finch, Roger. "Drumming in Shamanistic Rituals." In *Shamanism: An Encyclopedia of World Beliefs, Practices, and Culture*. Vol. 1, edited by Mariko Namba and Eva Jane Neumann, 95–100. Santa Barbara, CA: ABC-CLIO, 2004.

Gasche, Rodolphe. *Of Minimal Things: Studies on the Notion of Relation*. Stanford, CA: Stanford University Press, 1999.

Harpur, Patrick. *The Secret Tradition of the Soul*. Berkeley, CA: Evolver, 2011.

Hoppál, Mihály. *Sámánok Eurázsiában*. Budapest: Akadémiai Kiadó, 2005.

———. "Shamanism: Universal Structures and Regional Symbols." In *Shamans and Cultures*, edited by Mihály Hoppál and Keith Howard, 181–192. Budapest: Akadémiai Kiadó, 1993.

Humphrey, Carolina and Urgunge Onon. *Shamans and Elders: Experience, Knowledge, and Power Among the Daur Mongols*. Oxford, UK: Clarendon Press, 1996.

Hutton, Ronald. *Shamans: Siberian Spirituality and the Western Imagination*. London: Hambledon and London, 2001.

Lévi-Strauss, Claude. *Totemism*. Translated by Rodney Needham. Boston, MA: Beacon Press, 1963.

Levitin, Daniel J. *This is Your Brain on Music: The Science of a Human Obsession*. New York: Penguin, 2006.

Maginnis, Tara. "Costume, Shaman." In *Shamanism: An Encyclopedia of World Beliefs, Practices, and Culture*. Vol. 1, edited by Mariko Namba and Eva Jane Neumann Fridman, 57–60. Santa Barbara, CA: ABC-CLIO, 2004.

Maxfield, Melinda. "The Journey of the Drum." *ReVision* 16.4 (1994): 157–163.

McLuhan, Marshall. *Understanding Media: The Extensions of Man*. Cambridge, MA: MIT Press, 1994.

Mitchell, W. J. T. *What Do Pictures Want?: The Lives and Loves of Images*. Chicago, IL: University of Chicago Press, 2004.

Plutarch. *Lives*. Vol. VII. Translated by Bernadotte Perrin. Cambridge, MA: Harvard University Press, 1919.

Quintilian. *The Orator's Education*. Vol. 5. Edited and Translated by Donald A. Russell. Cambridge, MA: Harvard University Press, 2001.

Rasmussen, Susan. *Healing in the Community: Medicine, Contested Terrains, and Cultural Encounters among the Taureg*. Westport, CT: Bergin and Garvey, 2001.

Roberts, Maureen B. "Embracing the Fragmented Self: Shamanic Explorations of the Sacred in Schizophrenia and Soul Loss." *Jung Circle*. August 22, 1998. Accessed March 5, 2010. http://www.jungcircle.com/embrace.html.

Rogers, Spencer L. *The Shaman, His Symbols and His Healing Power*. Springfield, IL: Charles C. Thomas, 1982.

Scherer, Klaus R. and Marcel R. Zentner. "Emotional Effects of Music: Production Rules." In *Music and Emotion: Theory and Research*, edited by Patrik N. Juslin and John A. Sloboda, 361–392. New York: Oxford University Press, 2001.

Seashore, Carl E. *Psychology of Music*. New York: Dover, 1967.

Shirokogoroff, Sergei Mikhailovich. "Preliminary Remark 102. To Chapter XXIV." *Pscyhomental Complex of the Tungus*. Vol. 3. Shirokogorov.ru. 2015. Accessed July 20, 2015. http://www.shirokogorov.ru/s-m-shirokogorov/publications/psychomental-complex-tungus-03/102.

Stutley, Margaret. *Shamanism: An Introduction*. New York: Routledge, 2003.

Teskey, Gordon. *Delirious Milton: The Fate of the Poet in Modernity*. Cambridge, MA: Harvard University Press, 2006.

Ulmer, Gregory L. *Electronic Monuments*. Minneapolis, MN: University of Minnesota Press, 2005.

Virilio, Paul. *War and Cinema: The Logistics of Perception*. London: Verso, 1989.

Vitebsky, Piers. *Shamanism*. Norman, OK: University of Oklahoma Press, 2001.

Yates, James. "Amuletum." In *A Dictionary of Greek and Roman Antiquities*, edited by William Smith, 91. London: C. C. Little and J. Brown, 1853.

Part III

How to Deliver?

In the transition between the second and third acts of the biopic, Demosthenes's audience listens to him deliver his *First Philippic* and ignores his warnings. As a consequence, Athens is late in preparing for Philip, and the two sides broker an uneasy treaty. In his position of shaman, Demosthenes "saw what others did not see,"[1] he was able to see the invisible forces and desires brewing to the north, but he failed to make this visible to his fellow citizens. Demosthenes realizes that if he is to survive, and Athenian democracy as well, he must change his rhetorical tactics and be less polemical, more subtle, and adjust his delivery accordingly. As Edmund M. Burke writes, Demosthenes had "to adjust his voice, to become less partisan in tone."[2] So Demosthenes waits and saves his most effective speech, the *Third Philippic*, for the right time, the *kairotic* moment for its delivery. After this speech, Demosthenes becomes the dominant force in Athenian politics and turns the narrative against the pro-Macedonian faction of Aeschines.

Act III presents this victory as a false resolution, and those in the theater—if they didn't know already of Demosthenes's life—might expect the ending to be near, the triumph of Greek democracy. However, this victory is short lived, and the falling action depicts the unraveling of Demosthenes's own desires and eventually his life. But this act also shows Demosthenes in the frantic act of assembling alliances, creating networks to turn against Philip, to keep the Macedonians at bay. He works to help Athens form alliances with Euboea, Megara, Achaea, Corinth, Acarnania, and Thebes. Delivery shifts away from the immediate concerns of the *ekklesia*, of a macro-delivery that addresses large crowds, to micro-deliveries, with Demosthenes attempting to persuade smaller groups or individuals to make choices and then in turn become deliverers themselves, establishing a viral message. Demosthenes builds networks. Even if scale and technology differ, the logic is similar.

Part III, then, looks at two ways to consider the future of delivery, how digital technologies rely upon a logic that is both new and classical. New, in that delivery technologies such as digital networks, algorithms, and communication platforms help change the way delivery occurs, and classical in that a logic of networks, of backstage relationships, of having others help in the delivery process, still pertains. Digital technologies allow delivery to be literally unspoken and also for a spoken word to continue in echo, without being spoken again. Chapter 5 first looks at these networks and backstage relationships, pointing to a concept of network developed by Jeff Rice in *Digital Detroit*, Lindal Buchanan's insights into how women orators relied upon such assemblages to deliver in the nineteenth century, and how modern networks are everting, creating delivery-networks through digital technologies into everyday space, in a way similar to how the shaman's spirits can exist in multiple worlds at once. Chapter 6 then turns to the posthuman and how machinic assemblages with digital technologies fundamentally change how we might think of the deliverer, particularly through the work of Eduardo Kac, with an eye to how this lineage is the natural outcome of the practices Demosthenes started in his own time.

Notes

1. Phillip Harding, "Demosthenes in the Underworld: A Chapter in the *Nachleben* of a *Rhētōr*," in *Demosthenes: Statesman and Orator*, ed. Ian Worthington (New York: Routledge, 2000), 247.
2. Edmund M. Burke, "The Early Political Speeches of Demosthenes: Elite Bias in the Response to Economic Crisis," *Classical Antiquity* 21, no. 2 (2002), 188–189.

Bibliography

Burke, Edmund M. "The Early Political Speeches of Demosthenes: Elite Bias in the Response to Economic Crisis." *Classical Antiquity* 21, no. 2 (2002): 165–193.

Harding, Phillip. "Demosthenes in the Underworld: A Chapter in the *Nachleben* of a *Rhētōr*." In *Demosthenes: Statesman and Orator*, edited by Ian Worthington, 246–271. New York: Routledge, 2000.

5 Delivery-Networks

Engaging with spaces means being more than a spectator.

—Jeff Rice, *Digital Detroit*[1]

One of the roles of the new digital humanities in our present moment might be to help us all learn new ways to see some of these hitherto unseen (but always-present) dimensions of mixed-reality existence, the people, places, and things opened up by the conjunctions of the digital and the physical.

—Steven E. Jones, *The Emergence of the Digital Humanities*[2]

A speaker can no more be eloquent without a large audience than a flute player can perform without a flute.

—Cicero[3]

To talk about delivery is to talk about networks, but to talk about networks is also to talk about environment, as well as to understand that delivery happens within broader spaces, places, and nonplaces, even if those spaces are locations that humans can't "step" into, such as Internet packets, routers, servers, cables, wireless systems, and the like. A digital deliverer couples with these objects to become a delivery-machine; or, perhaps, a more accurate description of the kind of machine they produce is a delivery-network. But whereas digital networks certainly function as a technology of contemporary delivery, this delivery relies not just on technological networks, but other kinds of networks, so that a broader network epistemology becomes inherent and necessary when understanding the functions of delivery no matter the technology. In a larger sense, then, not only have machines often played an important role in performing the rhetorical act of delivery, but the most basic technology of delivery has historically been networks, which—although existing in different technological form from contemporary computer-based networks—were even required of ancient Greeks to successfully enact delivery, and as Lindal Buchanan has shown, required of nineteenth century women orators to reach the podium at all. By examining various forms of networks that have historically aided delivery—from classical Athens to present day—this chapter argues that such comparisons can teach us how contemporary networks allow delivery to occur in ways that extend beyond the invisible (and even visible) theories of "network" that commonly circulate in contemporary rhetorical theory, to expand the very idea of network into something more dynamic and more complex than we have previously assigned to the metaphor.

"Network" can be a slippery term, and, as I attempt with delivery in the first chapter, I hope multiple theories of network will ultimately prove useful for thinking about logics of delivery-networks. For the most part, the immediate theory of network that I use in this chapter centers on the kind of network explored by Jeff Rice in his book *Digital Detroit*. A network is not a specific technology, or to borrow from systems theory, the structure of a network can be composed of numerous substances. A network can be electronic, as in digital computing, but also biological, as in a brain's network of neurons. Networks, of course, can be made up of many brains, and these two structures can (and do) overlap to form more complex networks. But all networks, to be networks, have the same function, and if both this structure and function have a foundation, then Rice contends that the "very many is the basis of network rhetoric," and he sees this very many playing an important role in "spatial storytelling and construction."[4]

In *Digital Detroit*, Rice applies the metaphor of the network to how he sees Detroit, producing "a mapping of Detroit as a network."[5] Rather than a fixed place with fixed boundaries and identities, Rice shows the fluidness of relationships and meanings as they filter through his own personal experience of Detroit. Each dweller of Detroit imagines and invents Detroit, and it becomes an interactive network as individuals access differently its database of icons, images, history, infrastructure, and narratives. Space and place are not fixed, but fluid, and they can be manipulated depending on how one selects the inputs of the city as database.

But to say that a network is "fluid" might seem at first to be a contradiction. The database operates as more of a fluid that individualized networks pass through to select items from the database than a network in itself. Networks are usually structured tools that are applied to a fluid. A database only becomes a network once these items are placed in a relationship, in Rice's case, by an individual moving through space. Although networks can be reconfigured, they are initially established with a particular structure to serve a particular purpose. Nets themselves work to deliver a variety of materials, mostly animals, and are so constructed to target particular species, particular audiences. The configuration of the net itself determines the target of species to be delivered into the net, as nets are made of different materials with different size meshes to include certain species, but also exclude them. A net with large mesh might be good for catching cod, but not minnows. Some nets include other components such as Turtle Excluder Devices which specifically remove such animals (for good reasons) from the network. But such exclusion might be developed for unethical purposes, and so any metaphor of networks, including delivery-networks, needs to consider how networks formed intentionally or unintentionally include or exclude based on how they are constructed. That is, to create a delivery-network, one also needs to attend to the empty spaces between the parts of a network that allow unwanted audiences to pass through, and consider the implications for such gaps. If the schizzes between bits of code and the silent gaps between drum beats provide locations for attachment, what do the spaces in-between networks provide?

So if we are to juxtapose terms such as "fluid" and "network" together, then it must be in the sense that a multitude of networks exist along the same plane of immanence, much like the multiple, overlapping spirit worlds of the shaman, which might be fluidly navigated, one network to the next. Given Rice's description of the network, this is a given, as each individual is herself an affective net that catches items from the surrounding database. Each individual builds his or her own network, but can also move among, or coexist in, other networks. These networks attach, overlap, forming a network of networks. Each network might require its own logic of delivery, while internetwork delivery might require a delivery of meta-networks. The "how" of this action is a central question for a digital delivery.

Although grounded in Detroit, Rice produces a generalizable theory of networks that can be applied to other networks. But what he also shows is that although we have now come to nearly synonymize network with digital technology, the network can also exist without such particular technologies, even though digital technologies exponentially increase the amount and kinds of networking that can now occur. Such non-digital networks also affect non-digital performances of delivery, and can inform how digital networks could or should be used for digital delivery. In other words, a continuity exists with network and delivery, that networks were always in some sense at play when delivery was required. I bring this up not only to point out such historical roots in the network, but to better understand how digital networks might or might not be used in a contemporary moment.

In addition to the "very many," Rice also defines the network in terms of motion which "operates by movement, not fixity,"[6] and applies to our movements "within information and spaces simultaneously."[7] Motion and movement, too, are key features of delivery, moving breath to deliver words, moving one's body to move the audience, or moving letters from one location to another in a postal network. It's fitting, after all, that acting and delivery had become conflated for Aristotle and the Greeks in the term *hypokrisis*, and that Bruno Latour refers to agents as actors within a network: "As soon as actors are treated not as intermediaries but as mediators ... they render the movement of the social visible to the reader."[8] This making-visible is the process of delivery as I have defined it, making the *hypo hyper*. Moreover, Latour acknowledges the linage of acting with theatre, attending to the unconscious element at play in discerning the source of the actor's motivations: "To use the word 'actor' means that it's never clear who and what is acting when we act since an actor on stage is never alone in acting."[9] Likewise, to use the world "delivery" means that it's never clear who and what is delivering when we deliver because a deliverer is never alone, but always part of a delivery-network.

What Rice, Latour, and others demonstrate is that, even in the situation of the shaman, the whole network of things and associations delivers together as a "very many" in motion, and that these vary many must stay in relation to each other or delivery is lost. As Latour describes, discussing the technology of plug-ins, this interconnectedness is needed to make a decision—for delivery to transpire: "The crucial point is that you are sustaining this mental and cognitive competence as long as you subscribe to this equipment."[10] Delivery requires the apparatus, the machine, the network. The deliverer must plug-in to the delivery-networks that are necessary to reach an audience, but the audience too must plug-in to some part of this network. As the network requires very many plug-ins, each affecting the delivery process, delivery is not simply a single or closely coordinated set of actions, but "a string of actions where each participant is treated as a full blown mediator."[11] Every piece is a deliverer, especially within a networked environment where every mediator has, or has the potential to have, actionable options to participate in the delivery process. The shaman mediates between some entities and others, and is aware that those entities can themselves be mediators, thus the reliance upon helpful spirits and the avoidance of harmful ones.

Actors operate within environments, but they also construct environments, and such environments should be considered as one of these actors (or a macro-actor made up of micro-actors). Various environments have historically factored into delivery, from the environments that Demosthenes used pre-delivery, to Greek spaces and amphitheaters, law courts, the Roman Forum, as well as media-based environments such as sets and sound stages. With current digital technologies embedded in mobile computing devices and, increasingly, everyday objects, contemporary networks make all networked spaces into delivery environments, and all are increasingly more active, more in motion. For Rice, such an active environment constitutes a whole city, Detroit, which becomes "an actor mediating a variety of meanings and interactions," and not an immobile location driven by a "grand narrative. Instead, it is an account, albeit a complex one, that embodies the rhetorical characteristics of 'the very many.'"[12] Before returning to Rice and networks composed of digital technologies—particularly mobile computing, ubiquitous computing, and networks everting into an Internet of Things—I first want to consider historical environments and how they have aided the delivery process.

Delivery Environments

Several examples, from classical Athens to present day, demonstrate the extent to which environments have been altered and manipulated to increase the effectiveness of delivery. The Pnyx—a small hill southwest of the Acropolis that became the official spot where the Greek *Ekklesia* convened and most of the major political contests took place, including those of Demosthenes's—was significantly altered at least three different times.

Literally meaning "tightly packed together,"[13] the size of the Pnyx varied at different points in its constructions, but roughly held 6,000 audience members, the number needed for a quorum when making a voting decision. Located near the Agora, the original Pnyx made use of the natural landscape of sloping rock, probably lightly altered to remove some high and low spots. It included a low retaining wall to help support an earth terrace and included a level area for the speaker.[14] However, around 400 BCE the Pnyx was substantially changed.

> The auditorium of Pnyx II was very different. The natural slope of the hillside was reversed by heaping up a mass of earth filling. This huge earthen embankment was supported by a semicircular retaining wall. Access to the auditorium was provided by two stairways along the retaining wall to the north east and north west. The new auditorium sloped from north east to south west. Now those attending had their backs turned to the Agora and were sheltered against the north wind, but they faced the sun. The platform was moved to the center of the semicircle. The high semicircular retaining wall closed the auditorium to the west, north, and east.[15]

The main differences between the Pnyx I and II, then, were that the Greeks turned an open space (that could be expanded) into a closed one, limiting the space's capacity and separating those inside from non-participants that simply gathered to listen and observe. Part of the reason for closing off all sides of the Pnyx II, argues Mogens Herman Hansen, was to limit entry and ensure the distribution of assembly pay.[16] Generally, eligible citizens were required to attend if they were one of the 6,000 marked or given a *symbola* (a small token handed out to the *ekklesiastai*) and were paid for their attendance. Around the time of the renovations between Pnyx I and Pnyx II, this payment was raised from one to three obols. Hansen argues that this increase in pay coincided with the renovation of the Pnyx in order to limit the number of citizens entering the space, making sure that only the required quorum of 6,000 received payment for participation, reducing excess attendees that might eat into the public coffers. It paid to be an audience member, but the economics thereby limited who could legitimately participate, and the different networks of politics, citizenship, finance, and oratory converged in the design of this delivery environment.

While the Greeks attempted to separate the inside from the outside of the Pnyx when it came to people, they failed when it came to sound. Classical Greek spaces, such as the Pnyx, were large, open, and susceptible to weather. As Gregory Aldrete explains, classical orators, both Greek and Roman, might have adopted the United States Postal Service (USPS) motto: weather was no excuse, and an orator might have to deliver in any conditions.[17] Such circumstances make Demosthenes's training seem even more practical, and as Quintilian advises, bad weather does not mean that an advocate can abandon their client; one must be prepared for bad weather, whether in a glaring "sun, or on a windy, a wet, or a sweltering day."[18] Such weather, especially wind, produces sound that drowns out the orator's voice. Christopher Johnstone writes that the Pnyx, during the early fifth century at least, "may have been acoustically defective and therefore problematic as an auditorium for deliberative oratory."[19] The seating size of the first two Pnyx constructions was over 30 meters from the speaker's platform to the back of the structure. Although the Pnyx, after its first major renovation, was renovated to account for "at least one principal source of difficulty—the wind,"[20] with the prevailing direction in Athens now and then being from the northeast, it still "presented a considerable challenge to the speaker."[21] Recalling an anecdote with students, in which he delivered part of Demosthenes's "First Philippic" to a group of twenty-three students who positioned themselves along the back of the amphitheater, Johnstone notes that volume was the most important training an orator could have to deliver in such a space:

> I had to maintain a level of volume that amounted almost to shouting in order to be heard even by auditors who were only three-quarters of the distance to the perimeter of the *cavea*. To have sustained the required level of vocal output for an extended period—even for fifteen or twenty minutes—would have been very challenging physically ... The physical demands—on the vocal cords, on the diaphragm—are daunting. Clearly, if an aspiring 5th-century orator was to be trained to perform adequately in such a setting as the Pnyx, he must have been encouraged to consider (and to practice) vocal volume.[22]

In addition, volume must also be combined with proper pitch. A voice with a pitch too low would not reach the edge of the space, or become unintelligible during its travel, compared with a voice in the middle range (~150 Hertz). An orator delivering in the Pnyx (and similar spaces) had to train his voice to stay within this range, and at loud volumes: "the aspiring Athenian orator was required to attend to such vocal qualities as volume and pitch if he were to succeed in being heard, let alone in being persuasive."[23]

Even in enclosed spaces, such as the Heliaia, where most jury courts took place, Johnstone argues that the noise from the crowd was enough that the orator must also maintain a high, sustained volume in order to be heard. Johnstone's ultimate point is not that these spaces were difficult for delivery—they clearly were—but that Sophists teaching rhetoric at the time understood these environmental challenges and most likely taught their students techniques of delivery in addition to other aspects of argument. Johnstone concludes that "unless they were wholly oblivious to the potential impact of physical surroundings on their effectiveness as advocates,"[24] Sophists "must have considered such elements of vocal delivery as volume, pitch, inflection, timing, and pace."[25] Delivery required a physical training of the body in order to reach other bodies in less-than-ideal environmental conditions. Demosthenes declaimed at the waves not to simply improve his voice, but to deliver against similar environmental impediments (the roar of the wind) and fellow voices (the roar of the crowd).

In the first century BCE, Roman orators had to deliver in equally acoustically poor spaces, often to crowds that could grow quite large within a city of nearly one-million people. The spaces that Romans could fill included the Circus Maximus (~250,000 capacity), the Flavian amphitheater (~50,000 capacity), the Campus Martius, and the Forum, all of which could hold tens of thousands of people.[26] Because ancient orators had no microphones, they had to develop a system to reach as many listeners as possible. As a solution, the Romans developed a relay network of heralds who would recall and repeat a speaker's message throughout the environment "to distant members of an audience."[27] Such a strategy was especially useful for speakers (usually emperors and magistrates) who might not have the best vocal projection, becoming a vocal prosthesis for the weak-voiced.

If a series of heralds could function as a machine of amplification, so too could an individual as a substitution for one's poor vocal modulation of delivery. Pliny, in a letter to Suetonius Tranquillus, explains that because he (Pliny) is a bad spoken reader, he might have a freedman read for him.[28] However, he then asks his reader if perhaps, rather than sit beside his vocal surrogate, he should provide the visual track and, while accompanying the surrogate in a low voice, provide the facial expressions and gestures. Such a move demonstrates how delivery becomes distributed among a network of actors, each performing a different track (audio/visual), "a natural development to split the tasks with each person performing the task for which he is best suited."[29]

The development of electronic delivery technologies, such as the microphone, transformed the kind of delivery environment that might be needed and moved the vocal projection from another human to machine. In addition to the performance of delivery, however, electronic delivery technologies also transformed the study of delivery, particularly the gesture. Because of the microphone, or at least neatly aligning with its introduction and widespread use for giving speeches, what had been a robust field of interest "abruptly ceases in the last decade of the nineteenth century, and there were no extended treatments of the subject at all between the 1890s and the 1980s."[30] In addition, microphones didn't just distribute sound within a space, but across spaces, particularly through speeches delivered by radio such as those by Franklin D. Roosevelt and Winston Churchill during World War II.[31] Combined with the use of the microphone in co-present oration, radio broadcasts helped to condition audiences to listen to the speaker rather than watch him, and so the typical podium-based, microphone-augmented environment for an orator becomes one that fixes his body in a single spot, "unable to move his head more than a few inches, with both his head and body concealed behind a microphone and its stand ... far removed from the image of Cicero striding freely about the rostra."[32] Thus, the microphone had an effect not only on delivering sound, but also image. A speaker standing behind a podium, limited in movement, is further made invisible by the microphone, with early models requiring a "stand to hold it near to the speaker's head."[33] Aldrete explains that the placement of microphones directly onto podiums hid even more of the body from view, and further restricted the movement of the orator from the physical location of the microphone. With the invention of the microphone, the entire delivery environment changed as well. As the speaker can now deliver her voice much farther from her particular node, she inversely cannot deliver her image, and gestures begin to disappear. A single voice, augmented, can reach an entire stadium of 100,000 people, but her body becomes diminished by scale. While modern visual equipment and television broadcasts can magnify the body, bringing it into equal measure with voice, this body is never whole, but digital, not only via the technology, but also through film logics of head shots, close ups, zooms, pans, tilts, and cuts. The body becomes cut up, and without always knowing how this will happen, the deliverer will have trouble playing to these distributed audiences.

Because of the decorum of such events, and the impossibility to respond to the orator who speaks over the radio, audiences in digital environments more resemble audiences from ancient Rome, ones that often offered competition. Roman audiences "actively and vocally reacted to the speaker's message as well as making known their own desires through shouts, clapping, and chants."[34] In addition to these sounds, multiple deliveries took place in adjacent venues so that audiences attending a trial at the Forum would have to absorb and filter "considerable background noise from other trials … people conducting business in the area, and … those passing through or simply loitering about."[35] And given that many speeches were made in outside locations, these environmental aspects of delivery become truly "environmental" since, "speakers had to contend with nature as well."[36] The interactive and instant response of modern communications, whether though tweets, Facebook posts, forum and blog comments, or simply multiple, adjacent Web browsers may provide comparative feedback systems that can disrupt or augment how one understands online text, even if this feedback is asynchronous with the initial dissemination. A comment, for instance, might respond to an author's main text, but can generate a completely new text and displace or compete with the original narrative.

To increase comprehension, orators also relied upon visual aids to augment delivery. For instance, Roman emperors and speakers would sometimes "circulate around the audience large placards on which were written the pronouncements."[37] But more commonly, gestures were used. As Aldrete notes, the rise of gesture in classical Rome most likely occurred due to several conditions on the ground. First, the Roman population increased to probably a million inhabitants by the late first century BCE, a population mass that would not achieve such numbers again until nineteenth century London. With such numbers, orators had to increasingly rely on visual communication as a way to reach the edge of the audience. As a condition of this population increase, bigger and bigger spaces were built, and the largest spaces were too big for voice alone to carry delivery. If a speaker can reasonably convey his voice 65 meters, he would not be clear to about one-third of the audience in the 100-meter Campus Martius.[38] Other spaces that did not have well-designed acoustics, such as the Forum, also required gestures to overcome auditory problems. Furthermore, much of Rome's increased population occurred not from native citizens, but from a substantial multicultural audience of travelers, slaves, servants, and others. Gesture, and the language of the body, "was a language that cut across cultural, economic, and social barriers."[39]

Although I discuss gesture more directly in the next chapter, many gestures depended upon the specifics of the delivery environment in which an orator found himself, or which he manipulated before giving a speech. One such gesture, pointing with the finger (indicating), was a gesture used frequently by Roman orators "to point at themselves, at objects and places, or at another person about whom they were speaking."[40] The Roman gesture for a "pointer" resembled our own, an extended index finger with the other fingers "folded under the thumb."[41] Among the many gestures available to a Roman orator, gestures of pointing were particularly useful to prick the emotions of the audience. However, orators also indicated and made use of the larger environment in which they delivered by pointing out "features of the physical surroundings, which were exploited to support or enhance the message of the speech."[42] These orators were imaginative in how they used the surrounding environment to image place, to produce an image of place in their own image and toward an image that they believed corresponded to the audience's mind, with the goal of integrating the audience with the larger visual environment in which the speech occurred, becoming a medium to attune the audience with this space. The speaker was a choral speaker, sifting the images located in a particular area not only toward invention, but also delivery, a group invention. A savvy speaker made use of the totality of the setting, which could be quite rich in terms of the objects available for presentation, as speakers could indicate toward the various symbolic objects and buildings in the background, so that an "orator speaking in a temple ... could simply gesture toward the cult statue to allude to virtues associated with that deity,"[43] or an orator giving a speech in the Forum, which "was a space bounded by and composed of a vast assemblage of potent visual symbols of Roman religion, culture, and history,"[44] could gesture toward a database of "statues, temples, war trophies, altars, sacred sites, monuments, buildings, and other physical objects"[45] that populated the space. "By a simple pointing motion, a speaker could use these settings to emphasize, elaborate upon, or even convey messages."[46] The speaker serves not just as a sayer, but also a shower, pointing out the visible objects within sight and bringing their attention to the audience, making them notice parts of the environment that they might otherwise overlook. The speaker connects these buildings, statues, monuments, and other objects to the psychic stream of his speech, in tandem or relay, creating a multimodal, networked presentation. The orator—while he has something to say—also has something to show, and uses the power of the images around him, calling on these visual helpers as needed to add emotional overtones (or undertones).

While modern public buildings certainly have a variety of portraits, statues, and other imagery, they do not compare to the richness of visual stimuli within buildings where Romans practiced delivery. The new senate house, the Curia Julia (which replaced the Curia Hostilia that burned down in 52 BCE), contained: a large statue of the goddess Victory; a painting of an old man leaning on a stick; a painting of a two-horse chariot; a painting of Nemea sitting on a lion while holding a palm branch; and a shield honoring Augustus. While these ornaments might not seem excessive, temples offer another spectacle worth ekphrasing. The Temple of Jupiter Optimus Maximus on the Capitoline Hill "was so stuffed with military trophies, statues, and religious offerings that at one point many of them had to be cleared out."[47] The Temple of Concord contained at least thirteen statues of deities and mythological characters, multiple paintings, gem collections, animal sculptures, and other objects.[48] The exterior had many more statues and decorations. "Such a cornucopia of potent symbols could be, and certainly was, exploited by orators such as Cicero."[49]

Speeches delivered outside in the Forum also had a rich variety of images to point toward, and this varied depending on the precise location one chose to stand while addressing the crowd. These statues and monuments are too numerous to name here, and the unofficial statues had to be cleared out at various points because they had "proliferated so much."[50] But even with these unofficial statues gone, the official statues still allowed that "nearly every historical or religious allusion in a speech could have been matched to a corresponding statue or monument."[51] Thus, while the setting might change which images were available, the images themselves might be shifted and moved. While statues, monuments, and public artwork certainly changed from emperor to emperor, the visual productions within any particular period could be shifted and modified, altering the space in which delivery occurred. While the Romans didn't have a PowerPoint-type presentation software, they effectively had a ready-made Prezi formed in a three-dimensional space that they would point to as needed. Cicero "even altered his surroundings in order to use them to advantage in his speeches,"[52] such as when he placed a new statue of Jupiter so that it was visible to a Forum audience before his third Catiline speech. During the speech, he was able to guilt the audience, who were now under the watchful guise of the statue, and thus Jupiter. "Just as a modern speaker might employ posters or slides … so Cicero ensured that he would have a visual aid available to supplement the verbal component of his performance."[53] However, Cicero's use of indication goes far beyond illustration. While visual slides, a PowerPoint, or Prezi might make a talk more informative, insightful, explanatory, or perhaps more exciting,

Cicero used his visuals to create an emotional conduit with his audience, to tap into their capacity to receive emotion, and summon the emotion he thought would affect them. He attempts to create a physical-psychic network of the very many to move his audience. He doesn't point to Jupiter to illustrate a god, but to instill fear, shame, or guilt at what this god would think of them if they fail to act in the manner Cicero prescribes.

Second only to the hands, the eyes also "reach out" to the surroundings and can direct the audience's engagement with external visual aids without directly mentioning or motioning to them. Aldrete provides the example of Marcus Hortalus, who tried to persuade Tiberius to grant his once privileged family money after they became destitute. Because his family had been famous, and had once been given money by Augustus, Hortalus gazed about the Latin Library on the Palantine, where the speech was given, and which was adorned with reminders about his family's past, looking at the medallion of his family on the wall, as well as the portrait of Augustus. Without gesturing with his arms or hands, and without indicating these visual objects with words, Hortalus used the visible environment "to recall the glorious past of his family and to remind the senate that Augustus had deemed his family worthy of being saved."[54] Cicero frequently supports this use of the gaze as a valuable rhetorical strategy, and he often explains the use of the eyes to look about a space, such as a Forum, to direct the attention of the audience and elicit emotion.

In contemporary networked environments, gazing is only just becoming an important user input, as gestures such as "winking" in Google Glass are beginning to become realistic delivery acts. But pointing with fingers is certainly commonplace. Pointing is often used in more intimate spaces, and by the audience instead of the deliverer. One points with a mouse on a computer screen, or, with touchpad interfaces, directly on a computer screen with one's finger. Heidi Rae Cooley notes how mobile devices become a key means of delivery, as a concept such as navigation "refers to an active and creative process, a 'making-in-motion' that is not a 'result' of cartography per se but a practice or action of moving toward a destination. In the context of mobile devices, navigating to a 'there' frequently involves touch (e.g., index finger upon or across a screen)."[55] This touch is not skin to screen, though, but skin to skin, echoing the skin stretched across a Shaman's drum, or more literally when considering skin residue left behind on tactile interfaces, such as keyboards and touchscreens, touching those that have touched it before. According to Cooley, citing Alexandra Schneider's assertion that the iPhone's screen is "rather like a skin," and that human skin "is the site of interface par excellence,"[56] we become a kind of co-living agent when using a touchscreen device as "Finger, hand, and wrist muscles synergistically flex and extend, abduct and adduct, in response to this tactility. Hand and device 'live' fluidly and in concert."[57] Like the Shaman and his or her drum, the two become alive, reverberating so that another world can come into being. The user may deliver oneself—in the middle voice—through navigation of physical sites and virtual sites, and participate through fingers, hands, and thumbs in active ways, although also in unconscious ways, as Sony designers aimed to have users unconsciously play and "engage the surfaces and dials of a device well after a desired function has been performed."[58]

With the audience now pointing, another kind of participation occurs that, although present in oral forms of delivery, becomes more predominant in electrate delivery. In *Participatory Composition: Video Culture, Writing, and Electracy*, Sarah Arroyo makes the connection between the uses of hands and how subjectivity and participation change in electracy. When talking about the index finger and hands, Arroyo starts out with an anecdote by Ulmer, in which he apprehends "a row of Spirit Hands, giant, oversize, pulsating ... index finger extended, inscribed GO GATORS on one side, with the logo of the university on the other ... to permit the student fans to emphasize the gesture meaning 'We're number one!'"[59] Arroyo writes that the hand reconstitutes a confusion with the I-ness of subjectivity for each student hailed by the hand's ideology. Noting Ulmer's discussion, when Ulmer employs the puncept of hand to show how it "represents the index, the signature of the subject, just like the Gator spirit hand with the school name inscribed on the index finger,"[60] Arroyo moves on to Ulmer's account of Derrida's discussion of Heidegger in "*Geschlecht II*: The Hand of Man According to Heidegger," where he explains that "Heidegger says he prefers thinking a singular hand, as in handwriting, manuscript, that is debased, depersonalized, and in which the distinctively human is lost when the writing is done with two hands, on a typewriter."[61] Arroyo picks up on Ulmer's reading of Heidegger, applying it toward a collaborative, "participatory" writing practice: "With this link of the 'one hand' to the 'distinctively human' connects the two hands (or fingers) to the 'posthuman': breaking out of the realm of the one giant hand ('I'm number one!') toward electracy, where multiple 'hands' write together."[62] Arroyo goes onto argue that video culture "merges these two images of the 'hand,'"[63] through the use of a mobile device or a computer keyboard and "bring[s] back a human element."[64] What this discussion shows for delivery is that the pointing is not done just by the subject I, but the subject we. As I'll address more in the next chapter, digital networks often require the audience to participate in order for delivery to take place, giving them not obols (although sometimes a dollar equivalent), but the desired action. The joining is not of one person's two hands, but of millions of index fingers (or thumbs) across a network.

Besides the index finger, the thumb also does important delivery work. Next to the @ (which I'll discuss in the next chapter), perhaps the most ubiquitous icon that circulates the Web is that of the "thumbs-up" to denote a Facebook "like." Clicking on the icon designates a positive feeling toward a comment, image, or other posting (or recognition of a shared negative mood). The icon mirrors the American gesture of giving a thumbs-up to indicate approval: a fairly transparent metaphor. Such icons become incorporated (in a literally figurative sense) into other pages that use Facebook plug-ins for their comments sections (another metaphor that indicates, with the thumb, the assemblage of machines).

The thumb was a powerful gesture for classical delivery, but perhaps not in the way one might expect. For delivery in the gladiatorial arena, "The thumb's prominence ... is likely linked to its perceived power, a power that is most clearly reflected in the etymological speculations concerning the word pollex,"[65] which is inherent in both "thumb" (*pollex*) and also "power" (*pollet*). The thumb is powerful not only in its unique ability over the other fingers, but also metaphorically as a synecdoche for "diverse and complex activities as spinning, lyre-playing, writing, and masturbation. No other digit performs this function with comparable frequency."[66] In the context of gladiatorial conflict, a thumb pressed flat against the fist signaled life, that a gladiator should be spared death. Such a thumb "points" at the fighter in the arena, and "arose as a means of transmitting protective powers to the fallen fighter,"[67] often appearing in goodwill gestures to deities. Such acts display a powerful thumbing of life and the spiritual, acts performed by the audience in ways similar to those brandishing Ulmer's spirit hands.

Although powerful, a "thumbs-up" was not always positive, which was the gesture for death and much different than the classic Hollywood representations (probably derived from our own culture). Anthony Corbeill discusses that in formation, the death thumb is "identical" with the gesture of the "hostile thumb" (*infestus pollex*), the thumb used in oratory.[68] Through textual analysis, Corbeill argues that while the scholarship is often conflicting, the sign for the death blow was given by a thumb pointing away from the contestant, a direction that would be up and away. Quintilian describes this gesture with some derision toward those who use it, noting that "with the head inclined toward the right shoulder the arm is stretched out from the ear and the hand is extended 'with the hostile thumb.'"[69] Whereas some scholars assume that the hostile thumb points down (as do our movies), Corbeill explains the awkwardness of such a gesture, of trying to raise the hand while pointing the thumb down, which "produces a pose that both looks clumsy and feels uncomfortable."[70] Moreover, "it is difficult to imagine why [Quintilian] would have described the accompanying hand as sublata [uplifted]. A raised hand and a downward thumb militate against each other both physiologically and culturally."[71] Either way, Quintilian found the gesture unbecoming of an orator, but if "up," the uplifted thumb takes away the power, the goodwill from the defeated gladiator, and signals his death. Ultimately, the thumb on the correct person's hand could deliver one from death, or deliver one to the underworld. Such a gesture also signals danger for SCUBA divers, who give the thumbs-up when they're having a problem and need to ascend to the surface. A thumbs-up, then, is not always a good sign, and perhaps its latent gestural history suggests unconscious associations with death and ends.

In digital environments, thumbs pan, scroll, type, and click as a gesture toward our technological devices. Thumbs produce the gaps between words, and can close gaps in a grasp. Unlike the other digits, the "thumb's power encompasses otherworldly features we would not commonly associate with individual body parts."[72] The thumb, then, as a "second hand," provides an intermediary power that is specific to delivery. The "hostile thumb" also makes the gesture of the hitchhiker, who requests a literal transportation of his or her body to another place, hailing another traveler who happens to have the power of transport. Such delivery, though now mostly illegal, often occurs safely and without difficulty. Culturally, however, much mythology has developed about the dangers of relenting to the thumb of the murdering hitchhiker who would, like the Roman emperor, call for one's spirit to be dispatched.

Gestures provided a way to indicate the visible environment surrounding an orator—who could point out relevant objects to the audience—but invisible, backstage networks also existed that the audience might be unaware of, sometimes necessarily so. In *Regendering Delivery: The Fifth Canon and Antebellum Women Rhetors*, Lindal Buchanan looks at the ways that antebellum women rhetors made use of different techniques in order to deliver their message on the public stage. In addition to considering the traditional elements of delivery, such as voice and gesture, Buchanan examines the larger social forces that affected how these women delivered speeches. According to Buchanan, delivery has been too narrowly focused on voice and gesture, and the traditional idea of a "good man speaking well," that it has developed a litany of blind spots:

> First, it makes the assumption that rhetors are male, privileged, and authorized to speak publicly, thus ignoring the concerns and constraints of those who are not. Second, it focuses solely upon the speaker's vocal and physical presentation of discourse, which is too narrow a framework to allow for a full exploration of delivery's complexities for disenfranchised rhetors. Third, it defines delivery in corporeal terms (the speaker standing and addressing the audience directly) that are off limits to many rhetors, particularly those from marginalized groups, and, therefore, elides alternative forms of rhetorical presentation. Fourth, it completely overlooks the fact that rhetorical performance is grounded in social context, which exerts itself subtly but insistently in everything leading up to and expressed at the moment of delivery.[73]

What Buchanan examines is really the overall network that both enables and prohibits women and other underprivileged groups from access to rhetoric at the level of the public sphere, the level that allows them to directly participate in democracy and affect social policy. Her argument also speaks to those with differently abled bodies that might not have access to delivery platforms and technologies because such technologies are not accessible or not designed for differently abled bodies. Although digital technologies might afford some bodies to deliver in ways they couldn't otherwise, those same technologies are often designed with a normative body in mind.

Buchanan's argument, that delivery as a practice should be opened up to all, thus applies to the context of digital delivery as well. Although, like radio and television, the Internet was first thought of as a great democratizing force, other social forces limit who has access to both reading and disseminating information online. With delivery, several factors come into play, but given Buchanan's list, we can make some generalizations: first, some online rhetors are privileged in their ability to deliver given a mastery of computer codes and can deliver information to a refined, target audience, not to mention those who are privileged enough to have computer access to being with; second, ignoring voice and gesture for the moment, composition, visual rhetoric, and digital media studies have been too quick to reduce delivery to elements of style; third, in a networked environment, where communication often happens through a screen interface, delivery cannot rely upon all corporeal functions, unless such a body is represented through video, but is even then limited; fourth, because delivery via the Internet does not usually happen from a "stage," and given that usually the author is not even present or is anonymous altogether, the network context must be looked at in addition to the social context, as well as the overall connection of technology, identity, and institution.

Buchanan shows that one of the key blockages to delivery is access, or who is allowed to deliver. For the women that Buchanan discusses, many constraints affected their delivery, not least among these were their sex and the perception of public speaking as unwomanly, as well as material considerations such as the effect of corsets upon their speaking. However, the elements that contributed most to rhetorical success were often unseen once the rhetor made the stage. Whereas antebellum women made use of a muted, more "feminine" delivery style and feminine *ethos* to avoid offending male audiences, women rhetors needed a network of social connections to reach the stage in the first place. This network ultimately worked as a collaboration that allowed the final speaker to reach her audience. Although collaboration in composition is usually associated with invention, Buchanan believes that "antebellum women collaborated extensively with their friends, families, and servants in order to achieve two objectives, resolving gender and rhetorical conflicts and reaching public platforms."[74] Antebellum women relied on their relationships to solve how gender issues might be overcome to reach the stage, and other pragmatic problems such as childcare while making a speech. To understand how such issues affect delivery, "scholars must extend their analysis from the speaker onstage to the web of backstage relationships that made her rhetorical delivery possible in the first place."[75]

Understanding these "webs of backstage relationships" ultimately helps to study how other non-privileged speakers can deliver, including those (as mentioned above) who might be differently abled and require accommodations or new delivery strategies. And whereas Buchanan's examples provide a good relay for how we can approach delivery today, as well as her desire to make our concept of delivery more complex, our "webs," although metaphoric, are much more present in our lives than the nineteenth century backstage webs that she describes; or, they are present in a different way. Delivery in the World Wide Web is always a collaboration between individuals, even if those working backstage are nonhuman algorithms and Web robots. But, as I discuss in the next sections, those backstage relations are increasingly appearing front and center.

The Digital Forum: Database Delivery

These antiquated networks function without the use of digital technologies, but still do the work of "motion" with the "very many" that Rice identifies as essential for a network rhetoric. Cicero, through his gestures, words, and other movements, put the very many images and objects of the Forum to work in motion with the very many of the crowd, putting them in motion, who in turn move Cicero, a feedback system built into this classical delivery network. Cicero's audience-as-flute was not just something to be "played" but an instrument that provided feedback (continued motion) for the delivery process. Backstage, Buchanan describes a network of the very many who helped put women orators in motion on stage in order to put into motion the front stage networks of the very many.

This "very many" can be thought of in terms of database logic. When Cicero brings attention to a statue in the Forum, it is one object of many that was either already present in the environment or placed there before a speech. This space becomes a database of symbols, memories, emotions, histories, culture, and other concepts that have the power to affect the audience. The whole of the Forum is selected from and put into motion by Cicero. Theories of digital delivery, too, must contend with how databases factor into rhetorical engagement. In the example with Cicero and the Forum, or even the concept of a memory palace, delivery has traditionally already employed the use of rudimentary, non-digital databases throughout its development. And although these databases may have functioned as actors mediating the delivery process (much as a shaman's tools), digital technologies allow databases to be even more active. To return to *Digital Detroit*, Rice explores how the networking of space both creates and reveals emerging rhetorics that can contribute to an electrate delivery. One rhetorical technique that he pinpoints is the importance of accounting for the presence and role of databases and database logic. Databases are not passive, but active participants that form "agents" when joined with a user. Together, these agents "engage in a type of communication system, one in which an agent ... attempts to understand/address/respond to another agent."[76]

Like the bits and nibbles of the schizophrenic discussed in chapter 3, the database allows for infinite combinations by the deliverer, so that any rhetorical strategy arranged by the deliverer has the potential to be a new, emerging rhetoric. A database rhetoric allows the user to "change or evoke different notions of self"[77] and for a rhetorical text "to be 'stylized' in a 'myriad' number of ways."[78] More broadly, a database rhetoric "is a way to stylize a broader concept of rhetoric and writing through one's ability to arrange many spaces at once ... it is a way to rethink how a given space ... may create various networked, rhetorical possibilities."[79] This constant emergence, the generation of the unknown from a known database, allows for a surprise, the unexpected, the kind of delivery that's often associated with the joke as either the joke's punchline or the pleasure of watching Fred Astaire dance.[80] Good delivery, it seems, also shares with networks the unexpected, the pleasure felt at being surprised. In framing network and database logic in terms of surprise, Rice uses the anecdote of going to a Bob Dylan concert to highlight the "lack of expectation"[81] as a signature feature of networks, demonstrating their ability to surprise the user with the new. Because networks are fluid, the same delivery may not emerge twice.

Although he mainly focuses on invention, and to a large extent arrangement,[82] Rice writes that databases "are generating an emerging rhetoric,"[83] and as I argue here about emerging digital technologies and delivery, a new form of rhetoric that "speaks to both new media expectations as well as traditional rhetorical concerns regarding arrangement, delivery, and place."[84] Rice does much work showing how Detroit as database creates a network in which meaning is both individually and collectively constructed through Rice's personal associations with the city. Much of this associative work is electrate in nature, drawing from Ulmer. However, while Rice chiefly sees this network doing the work of invention, it also does the work of networked delivery, of a delivery that must occur jointly.

Cicero creates networks among himself, the database available in his environment, and the audience. Rice frames this kind of co-agency as "wayfaring," an emerging rhetoric in how to map and navigate space which "frames database information delivery as exchanges among agents."[85] As Cicero moves through a speech, perhaps moving through a memory palace, he takes the audience on a tour, a journey through the speech, with each audience member establishing individual and shared connections to the words, objects, gestures, and other delivery techniques that he employs. Although the space helps create a database, delivery (as *actio*) is a movement though that space. As a rejoinder to Latour, who writes that "Network is a concept, not a thing out there,"[86] Rice offers that a network's power comes "not from the identification of certain 'things' and how they connect, but from the process of connections themselves."[87] Delivery is the act of networking, of creating that connection with the audience, not only in using a database to build possible connections with the audience, but in generating those connections with the audience as well, of not only appealing to emotion, but of generating affect. As the epigraph from Cicero at the beginning of this chapter suggests, delivery is not just channeled to the audience, but co-composed with the audience. This journey through a delivery-network allows the deliverer and audience together to make new connections, to co-invent for the issues at hand. The deliverer's hope is also that this audience will disband and extend this networking beyond the scope of the original delivery act. In other words, delivery (i.e., *actio*) needs to be remembered for its ability to move, just as a network is not primarily a thing but a mode of activity. Delivery is connecting one's ideas with those of others—the process of assembling a very many ideas toward new ones.

More than just databases of items, delivery environments, spaces, and places become produced as associations and sensations. Pointing to Deleuze and Guattari's concept of blocs, made from associations and sensations to generate meaning, a space or place can be "a complexity and possibility constructed out of, among other things, sensations."[88] Such affective engagement is what helps the deliverer form links between the database elements present in the environment and the preexisting databases of the audience. The process of delivery networks these databases together. For digital networks, or current iterations of non-digital networks, what Rice informs for delivery is the need to account for affective movement across networks. Building on Jennifer Tidwell's discussion of designing interfaces for "soft factors" such as "gut reactions, preferences, social context, beliefs, and values," Rice surmises that, "one must connect a variety of affective experiences within a specific space and cannot rely on the so-called essence a space might project."[89] Cicero used the database of his spaces to hone the affective experience of the audience, and as all environments become increasingly digital (as I touch on later) and directly manipulable, new practices and theories of delivery should be invented to account for the specifics of these spaces.

These databases can be networked in many ways, but the quickest path is to use totems or the *doxa* (commonplace knowledge) of an audience. To deliver is to adjust networks and networked spaces with the *doxa* at hand, as Randall Collins writes of intellectual and social networks: "ideas are created out of the distribution of symbols already available at a moment in time, by being reshaped for anticipated audiences."[90] These objects become a kind of interface, a way to form connections with the audience, and the concept of interface is one that theories of delivery will need to increasingly study to determine how a deliverer may connect to networks. Given that networks are increasingly turning out into the physical world (which I'll address in the next section), interfaces may trend toward something like Paul Dourish's definition of "direct manipulation" in which the "fundamental principle ... is to represent explicitly the objects that users will deal with and to allow users to operate on these objects directly."[91] Rather than the deliverer holding up or pointing to an object, the deliverer presents the object, or interface, to the audience for them to manipulate themselves. Again, delivery becomes the work of the audience as much as the deliverer, and the interface becomes the instrument, the flute, that does the bulk of the work for the deliverer (the flute is not sound, but provides the interface—or interhand or intermouth—to make sound). The interface, like the shaman to audience, or spirit-helper to shaman, "connects; it does not act only as a conduit between user and information."[92] Or as Ulmer considers more broadly, "Another name for 'rhetoric' in a computer context is 'interface.'"[93] However, it could be that rhetoric is too broad a term to conflate wholly with interface, and a smaller term, such as delivery, fits better. If the shaman was the interface between an audience and the spirit world, and the deliverer the interface between rhetoric/argument/affect and an audience, or the delivery environment an interface between the deliverer and audience, then this act of delivery is an act of interfacing, and the two might be coterminous, with—in Ulmer's case—interface providing a better metaphor for a digital delivery that users can manipulate directly and use to self-deliver. As I discuss in the next chapter, digital technologies provide the opportunity for the audiences to more directly participate in the manipulation of those spaces, of reorienting the interface, a feature that the deliverer must anticipate in ways similar to those advocated by DeVoss and Ridolfo through their concept of rhetorical velocity.

If, as discussed in chapter 1, an older concept of delivery posited a single deliverer before an audience of many, or a Pony Express rider making a linear route from node to node, then delivering in a network is a disjointed delivery, not necessarily in the sense of avoiding a direct path, but a kind of digital cryptography that needs indirectness in order to deliver. "The secret of the network is the way messages are routed, or not routed, from one node to another."[94] Such routing often "involves following disjointed paths as much as it involves following carefully ordered and routed paths."[95] I don't know that a logic for this kind of delivery has yet been developed, but if, as Rice argues, the logic of a network is full of twists and turns, then a polytropic delivery logic should be worked out to make use of it. But part of the problem of working this out is the complexity of networks, particularly its unknowableness, which connects back to the ability of the network to surprise. Rice takes issue with the view that complexity can be "based on a *known* and not a secret" for "it is not a known variable," especially in networks: "while it is possible to trace the connections and how they form relationships, a fundamental feature of the network is its randomness, its dependence on unknown variables."[96] A deliverer cannot know every audience's secrets, how each one is "routed," for as psychoanalysis tells us, even they may not know how. Part of the delivery process is to attempt to reveal the unknown, which may remain unspeakable affective sensations, but also realizing that part of the process is dealing with these unknown complexities, and in fact, embracing them as part of a delivery strategy. The approach that Rice picks up on is clustering, "the process of gathering connections together."[97] Part of the logic of clustering is selecting from a database, of putting these ideas or objects into a shared space, and networking them together. This is the known part of the process. However, the "secret … is not always knowing how connections form or will form."[98]

While this process sounds great for generating ideas, for invention, how could such a haphazard result be good for delivery? Perhaps part of the point is to break out of an old view of delivery as a transitive distribution of information from one node to many, from a known to a known, and to rethink it as a process whereby multiple participants gather and help to form a group decision, working from a known problem and making known an unknown solution (or revealing an unknown problem).

To demonstrate the complexity and unknowableness of the network, one of the examples that Rice highlights is that of packet switching. Conceived independently by Paul Baran at the RAND Corporation and Donald Davies at the National Physics Laboratory, packet switching was used in the original ARPANET, the current iteration of the Internet, and most local area networks in order to speed up the efficiency of the network. A packet usually consists of a header, which tells the network where the packet should be delivered, and a payload, or the information that is extracted and used by another software application. The total size of the packet is usually a fixed amount, dividing a larger set of data into smaller units. In some cases, the network may allow out-of-order delivery, so that the order is rearranged into the proper order upon delivery, while some networks require in-order delivery, sending packets sequentially. One of the analogies sometimes used to describe this process is that of postal delivery, where the header is the envelope and the payload the letter. If the letter is too long, the content may be broken up and sent as multiple deliveries, requiring the receiver to reorder the information upon delivery. Of course, network protocols do this for us with digital packets.

Rice finds the packet switching metaphor important because it "teaches literacy conventions to not begin with already-structured and distinct sequences (set blocks), but to work with unassembled sets of meaning (broken blocks)."[99] Packet switching is disjointed. Rather than printed materials, which provide the entire, pre-arranged structure of the message in total, "from the beginning," the logic of packet switching offers a kind of delivery out-of-sequence, a non-linear wayfaring through the network, and with "the proliferation of disjointed delivery comes noninstrumental reasoning regarding space."[100] As an anachronistic application, a kind of packet-switching logic allows Cicero to move through the Forum via many twists and turns, moving the audience through this space so that they collaboratively network a delivery; even if Cicero had preplanned many of the routes, the audience may demand he take others. Although delivery-machines—whether Demosthenes's delivery-machines or digital, networked-machines—have an instrumentalism to them (they perform practical functions), what is delivered need not be instrumental, or not instrumental in the ordered, linear, regimented logic that Ong or McLuhan would ascribe to print. What Rice shows us with packet switching is that delivery need not simply be about getting logical, linear information to an audience, but that there's an affective aspect that (which in many ways is instrumental) is not instrumental in terms of literate information. In addition to the loss of the body, this is another reason why delivery effectively dies with the rise of print, which has difficulty supporting this degree of networked delivery.

In many ways, it's ironic that what gives Gracchus the noninstrumental elements of pitch is instrumental, a flute, but that this instrument is itself noninstrumental in that it should get left at home when delivery is to occur (at least, as Cicero advocates). One way to frame this noninstrumental element is in terms of "cool." The cool is often considered extraneous, nonessential to delivering a message, merely affective ostentation that, albeit attractive, is unnecessary to the message of a document and thus even sometimes distracting. Echoes of Edward Tufte's arguments against chart junk enter this conversation, unnecessary elements placed on charts, graphs, maps, and other informational designs that do not directly aid the understanding of the graphic's information or argument. However, the cool is an important interface of participation, a means of electrate delivery.

In *Understanding Media*, McLuhan identifies forms of media such as television and radio as "cool," media that lack details and require audience participation to fill in the gaps. Unlike hot media, which provide all the necessary information, such as a book or highly-detailed HD image, cool media provide just enough information to get the audience involved, a kind of enthymematic operation. But this lack, this hole provides an entry-point for the audience. Going back to Rice, who wrote the book on rhetoric and cool,[101] cool media "are not literal representations; they leave open details for further participation and involvement."[102] It's the essential-nonessential, noninstrumental elements (in terms of literal representation) that do the work of cool media and cool delivery and actualize such participation. "One has to fill in the details. One has to participate."[103] And this participation, as Rice points back to McLuhan, is not based in logical reason, but affect, sensation: "This feeling does not have its basis in concepts or ideas, but seems to creep in uninvited and unexplained."[104] But what really makes the concept of cool important for delivery is that, as I've argued about delivery, it is not meant to put an end to discussion, to find a final solution to a problem, but to spur group invention: "To put such thinking into a cool interface would be to look for a response other than that of closure."[105]

Ultimately, delivery occurs in an open environment, across multiple databases, multiple networks, all in motion. Sometimes, attempts are made to constrain and control such environments, either through the physical construction of spaces, such as the modifications of the open Pnyx I to the closed, delimited space of the Pnyx II, or by limiting the protocols, procedures, and expectations for who can deliver, such as the issues Buchanan describes that faced antebellum women orators. But such spaces are always subject to change, either directly—as Cicero did—or indirectly through gradual evolutions. Delivery must be attuned to such spaces and how they might—or might not—be malleable toward rhetorical effect. And when delivery environments do change, offering possibilities for new delivery-networks, then deliverers must make use of such changes. The next section discusses one such potential shift, the eversion of the Internet, and the ramifications for developing a digital delivery.

Everted Delivery

Digital networks, such as the Internet, have traditionally been visualized as inner-spaces. From the term and description of "cyberspace" by William Gibson,[106] to movies like *Tron* and the *Matrix* trilogy, digital spaces have been imagined as spaces that one goes into, often by plugging in the physical body and uploading one's consciousness. However, this older model is beginning to outlive its usefulness as networked technologies change, and in his 2007 novel *Spook Country*, Gibson rethinks networked spaces from inverted forms such as cyberspace to everted spaces in which the Internet overflows into everyday physical environments. If cyberspace were once separate, a thing that humans go into, the paradigm has shifted as external things become "smart." If, as James Bridle writes, the network "is not space (notional, cyber or otherwise) and it's not time (while it is embedded in it at an odd angle), it is some other dimension entirely,"[107] then the cyberspace metaphor, in its early iterations, made sense. However, as new technologies develop, this network dimension becomes more porous, allowing more spirits to seep out as the boundaries between dimensions collapse, allowing new agents to participate in the physical, everyday world. Indeed, David Rose has called such networked objects "enchanted objects."[108] As Steven Jones writes,

> Nowadays, it feels as though the digital network is breaking through to the physical world, to the everyday physical dimension in which we live, as if through cracks that have opened in the fabric we once believed separated the mundane world from cyberspace. The result is irruption, eversion, a new mixed reality in progress, still haunted by the earlier metaphor of different dimensions.[109]

To extend Mitchell's discussion of "what do images want," we may now have to ask, "what do things want?" or "what does the database want?" The shamanic worldview helps provide precedence for how to navigate such a world, not taking account of the old spirits, but the new ones—algorithms, Web robots, trolls, and other actors that must be accounted for in the delivery process, the delivery feed.

Of course, although the shamanistic spirit world haunted these communities' daily life, it was still a metaphysical fiction to help make sense of their world, to help make decisions on practical matters—a delivery apparatus. And although the metaphors we create for the network (itself a metaphor) are myths themselves, and are made up of various fictions, these fictions have real implications, perhaps more so than in shamanic cultures. "Thanks to the vast hardware and software and communication infrastructure of orbiting satellites, monitoring stations, fiber-optic cables, cell towers, networked servers, and portable devices, a fictional world can be made to augment or haunt the real physical world."[110] Digital prosthetics help to make sensible this otherwise insensible world, primarily what Interactive Design Professor Anthony Dunne identifies as the "extrasensory nature of electromagnetic radiation."[111] Dunne feels that this world's physicality is often treated as conceptual rather than something real, immaterial rather than material, a common misconception about the materiality of digital technologies and digital information. Yet, Dunne argues that "We are experiencing a new kind of connection to our artificial environment. The electronic object is spread over many frequencies of the electromagnetic spectrum, partly visible, partly not. Sense organs function as transducers, converting environmental energy into neural signals."[112] Jones sees this metaphor of "transducers" as useful for thinking about the everting network, as "gateways for transformation, portals between realms," for they are "precisely what's most important."[113] Transducers, then, as technologies that literally "lead across," are important delivery technologies that can be employed by a digital deliverer, transforming one kind of signal into another, even if (or, especially when) that technology can do so at distance from the deliverer.

This transduction does not just occur at the lateral level, but also up and down. Transduction as delivery, then, can also refer to hypoduction, a leading down, working not just upon the unseen electrical, magnetic, and radiation waves, but also upon affective waves that traverse across spaces and individuals (more akin to Rice's networks). If transduction is, as William Turkel defines it, "the conversion of energy from one form to another,"[114] delivery as transduction is as much about converting digital energy (in whatever form) to affective energy (or the other psychic levels of feeling and emotion), and vice versa.

One film that offers this alternative vision of networked space is *Minority Report*, often hailed as a prescient look into how technologies such as augmented reality will shape our future interactions with people, spaces, and information. In the film, each individual receives custom messages—such as advertisements, notices, and other information—based on sensors that scan one's retinas when passing through a ubiquitously networked environment. Nearly every surface or object is "smart" and can adjust to deliver information specific to that person's history, culture, or state of mind. For instance, as the main character John Anderton (Tom Cruise) runs from the police (he's accused of a murder that he will commit in the future), these scanners sense his heightened, adrenaline-laced emotional state and offer him ads for alcohol and vacations. Unfortunately, Anderton doesn't have time for a drink.

This networked space shows an eversion of the network in which a user doesn't go into the Internet to access information, even if from a terminal such as a Web browser, but that the network and information come to the user, a kind of ultra-specific, micro-delivery. Although contemporary environments do not yet approach this level of smartness, such specificity has been a project for advertising via Google AdSense and other tracking-based advertising platforms. But this is only one kind of delivery to consider, and although important, less interesting to me than the larger implications that an everted digital network has for delivery as a whole. Again, Gracchus's flute seems prescient here, for if an appliance such as the refrigerator reminds us to fetch milk (a memory aid to foster delivery), then networked, smart environments have the potential to also serve as delivery-networks, not just for milk (which, of course, is rife with delivery problems as an industry), but for other kinds of information to aid all kinds of delivery.

Like other facets of delivery that I've discussed, the everting of the network actually harkens back to pre-print logics of delivery. Certainly, Cicero's database was always everted, outside and visible for the audience to see. One of the implicit points in Rice's description of databases and networks is that the database is increasingly outside of digital servers as digital technologies per se are not necessary for the activity of a network. But if ever there was a physical realization of the shamanic metaphor, it might be found in the concept of Internet of Things (IoT), whereby everyone with the digital tools and knowhow can make digital information appear within a particular space. Such DIY ethos is at the heart of fiction that imagines a total network eversion, such as Vernor Vinge's novel *Rainbows End* or Tim Maughan's short story "Paintwork," in which graffiti artists employ QR codes in order to deliver their art. Although QR codes have mostly gone out of fashion (if they were ever *in* fashion), they present an important moment in which portals to the digital world are posted alongside traditional forms of print media. As Jones writes, "QR codes *encode* in more than one sense—they stand as signs for an unspoken idea, the idea that the network and its data are connected to the grid of the physical world, and that those connections can be revealed by way of readily available, cheap, and ubiquitous acts of dimensional translation."[115] The problem, according to Jones and most likely noticed by anyone tracking a QR code's engagement, is that it is difficult to get the audience to point their device at a code and summon the digital dimension. In other words, it's difficult to get the audience to become shaman and participate in the act of delivery.

Jones sees such audience participation as a larger problem for all mixed-reality environments, particularly augmented reality and other media that must be actively participated in, at least until retina-scanning becomes commonplace. Although some smart environments do respond to users automatically through GPS tracking or Bluetooth-to-beacon technologies—making the audience a more passive participant—some digital technologies still require more direct engagement: "You have to do something to reveal the data, so you're already at least minimally engaged. And what you're doing is triggering a translation from one code to another, and then to another, practicing the process, exploring the possibilities of such acts of decoding and encoding in today's mixed-reality environment."[116] But returning to delivery environments more broadly, such spaces were already mixed, already databases, already needing the audience to engage in the process of decoding from one medium into another in order to process the deliverer's presentation in a co-act of delivery. Going back to Latour, what Jones is really showing us is that the environment is itself a mediator of delivery, a participant just as a shaman's environment and the "things" within it. If the deliverer is not the sole mediator, we might say she is the meta-mediator. And even though this participation might be difficult to induce, Jones implies that such delivery "wants" to happen—such environments gesture for a happening. If we take a QR code to stand in for any object that summons interaction, whether the augmented reality company Layar's "call to action" graphic, a billboard that asks us to visit a website, or even a statue in a public square that is referenced by a speaker, all of these objects perform a different kind of gesture than the deliverer, but an important gesture of delivery nonetheless. Although the speaker gestures with something visible (a hand/finger/thumb) or toward something visible (an object), these objects themselves gesture to the unseen, the unspoken, but about which they refer (the R of QR). As Jones submits:

> QR codes *are* an interesting phenomenon, in part because they're so basic, because they so nakedly reveal the gesture of connecting data with the physical world, in fact reveal *the cultural desire to make* that gesture ... QR codes make more sense if we interpret them as a cultural symptom—mundane signs that someone is trying to communicate with invisible, unknown intelligences out there somewhere in the ether—in 'the digital realm.'[117]

Delivery requires, in part, delivering desire, the desire to deliver, and the desire to participate in the delivery process so that affect can flow.

Instead of focusing further on QR codes, however, I want to turn to augmented reality (AR), which presents a more promising technology for theorizing delivery. Sometimes called "mixed reality," AR overlays digital data upon the physical world in some way, either as text, image, video, sound, or other sensory data. Unlike virtual reality, AR must be integrated into the already existing and sensed environment, rather than as a part of a completely constructed digital environment in which a person enters and immerses their body. Again, AR is a technology of eversion, flowing out into physical spaces in which we already dwell.

Although trending in recent years as a technology topic with the introduction of Google Glass and Microsoft's HoloLens, AR has actually been around for several decades with many robust, current uses. The aeronautic company Boeing first began using AR for location-based instruction manuals in the mid-1990s, a method currently used for military vehicle repair and newly developed by the Osterhout Design Group as a form of headwear to provide astronauts with detailed repair instructions during space walks, allowing them to see information overlaid directly upon equipment. AR is also used as a pedagogical aid in medical fields, a sensory prosthetic for firefighters when engaged in fire rescue (allowing them, among other things, to "see" in smoke-filled rooms), and has been used for years in military targeting systems. Moreover, commerce and gaming have taken an increased interest in AR technologies, developing new ways to sell products and new ways to construct games. These are all examples of how augmented reality, technically, can change the delivery of information. It's easy to understand how digital information overlaid upon a spacecraft is much more efficient and safe than trying to sort through an instruction booklet during a spacewalk, or rely upon audio instructions delivered over a radio headset.

But this technical delivery is only a part of what AR tells us about delivery and digital technologies. Indeed, there are some clear potential benefits for AR, everting digital, technical information into a live, physical environment in useful and efficient ways. For although technologies such as Microsoft HoloLens offer one version of a hands-free, more immersive AR experience, most current AR is done with a mobile device, such as a smart phone, using the phone's camera to detect the physical environment and the presence of triggers that indicate where and what augmentation should appear on the screen. Again, this augmentation may be text, image, video, 3D object, or anything that can be rendered into a computer file. To summon this data, the trigger requires the user to make a gesture with the mobile device, to point the device's camera at the trigger and view the augmentation on the screen. Such technologies bring up important questions about the embodiment of users who would seek to deliver (or auto-deliver) and the kinds of environments needed to support such everted delivery.

Mobile delivery technologies require a certain amount of embodiment and most interactions with AR require some sort of performance in order to trigger another action, mainly a prior action of moving through an environment, touching an object, or scanning a code or image. When viewing AR through a handheld mobile device, the audience holds a screen up to the world, performing an initial gesture of abduction that enacts this delivery process. In this way, it's not only images that make the body present again for a post-print delivery, but also actual bodies as users have to engage with texts in new somatic ways. But in addition to how bodies must interact and adapt to new delivery environments, this embodiment also brings up the question of who can participate. As I mention in the introduction, studies of delivery must contend with disability studies more robustly than they do now (or than I do here), and account for differently abled embodiment. Not every body can perform the gestures needed to trigger a placed-based augmentation, nor perhaps sense the digital data delivered via a device, at least a device not already set to accommodate the user's needs.

Some developers of AR technologies have begun to consider such complications of a re-embodied delivery and how AR can be used to deliver information to differently abled bodies. Although some contingents of deaf culture might not readily accept such technology, AR can be used for speech recognition to make the whole world closed captioned. In addition, although Google Glass isn't particularly good at AR, it can allow some deaf persons to perceive sounds since it transmits sonic vibrations primarily through bone conduction. David Trahan, a digital marketer who is deaf in his right ear, now makes Glass part of his daily life.[118] AR can also be used to augment the environment with sounds for the blind, warning the user, for instance, if he or she might come into contact with a person, vehicle, sign, or other object. "Sight-Finder," one such app, is being developed by Nippon Telegraph and Telephone Corporation. Text-to-speech apps could provide more audible augmentations by reading text for the blind when braille isn't available. And whereas social apps like FourSquare help locate one's friends, apps such as Mapability help disabled persons locate the nearest wheelchair-accessible venues.[119]

AR apps are also used to help treat cognitive impairments, learning disabilities, and emotional trauma. Helen Papagiannis, an AR researcher, has written an AR pop-up book to help those suffering from phobias to directly encounter their fears. Her book *Who's Afraid of Bugs* includes various insects that appear to come alive through the companion AR app. As she states, "It was inspired by AR psychotherapy studies for the treatment of phobias such as arachnophobia. AR provides a safe, controlled environment to conduct exposure therapy within a patient's physical surroundings."[120] Papagiannis's work is an interesting example of how AR integrates print and digital technologies to account for one's environment and emotional state.

Of course, AR poses many risks to bodies, as delivery has always threatened. Not only are there health issues associated with using AR, such as eye strain, blunt trauma, motion sickness, skin irritation, cancer, and retinal projection, there are many usage risks such as automotive use, distraction from the immediate physical environment, and probably others that have yet to emerge, but as Paul Virilio warns, are invented along with the technology.[121] For instance, architect Rana Abboud, who has studied AR's potential for construction trades, notes that

> In some places I went to, the marketing around it was really glossy and amazing. But you actually tried the application and things didn't quite work as planned. For instance, the Museum of Vancouver put out an app that we trialed and the tracking was not quite there, and things would disappear on you and then re-appear. It wasn't stable enough.[122]

Because most AR apps rely upon either GPS or computer vision, the accuracy of AR registration may be misaligned or jerky, which can create navigational hazards. As one of the first lawyers working with AR and the law, Brian D. Wassom argues that either one of these errors can create an injury risk for those using the technology, and "If a court later determines that it was objectively reasonable for the injured party to have relied on the location data, the creator of the AR experience may be found liable for the injury."[123]

Such examples show just how networked bodies, environments, and digital technologies have or may become. Any consideration of embodiment should be thought of both in terms of the technological device as well as the delivery environment. More rhetorically, technologies such as AR require the deliverer, as was required of Cicero, to consider how the environment may be reconstituted to best suit delivery, or designed anew altogether. Toward this question, or prompting for this question to be asked, Lev Manovich argues that we must develop a poetics for AR spaces. In "The Poetics of Augmented Space: Learning from Prada," Manovich seeks to "re-conceptualize augmentation as an idea and cultural and aesthetic practice rather than as technology,"[124] away from viewing AR as primarily a digital technology and instead an everyday practice, a move similar to the one Rice makes regarding networks as technology and networks as a practice. Toward this shift, Manovich has to create his own taxonomy and makes an initially useful distinction between how spaces have been augmented in the past by previous forms of media and how this relationship changes as the media themselves become dynamic and often localized to an individual user who carries around a portable device capable of filling any space with new information flows. For instance, although spaces have always been augmented by art, architecture, informational signs, or other visual elements to help one navigate or aesthetically enjoy a space (or to deliver), AR can provide continually shifting and individualized enhancements and augmentations not previously possible. Architects must now consider how cell reception and radio waves might bounce around their designs, and artists must consider more than just the space of the gallery for their artwork.

Another important aspect that Manovich explores is that the user in an AR environment not only receives data, but becomes and transmits data through video and location-based surveillance, building his claim that "*augmented space is also monitored space*."[125] In the current technology of individually specific targeted ads, presented to us via Web robots that gather our user habits, this may not seem very shocking and we might conclude that, as Guy Debord states about the society of the spectacle, such self-surveillance is only indicative of a choice we've already made, something we do to ourselves. Manovich feels that unlike previous forms of architecture and art that dominate a society, ones that were more difficult for the average citizen to change (at least legally), then "today's electronic dynamic interactive displays make it possible for these messages to change continuously; making the information surface a potential space of contestation and dialog, which functions as the material manifestation of the often invisible public sphere."[126] Ultimately, Manovich argues that many of the questions associated with AR manifest in the interaction of data with the spaces through which data flows:

> In short, I suggest that the design of electronically augmented space can be approached as an architectural problem. In other words, architects

along with artists can take the next logical step to consider the 'invisible' space of electronic data flows as *substance* rather than just as void—something that needs a structure, a politics, and a poetics.[127]

These are not just artistic and design problems, but rhetorical problems (if the three are separable), and a deliverer needs to be attuned to how such spaces affect delivery, and/or how they might be modified to foster delivery. If a digital Pnyx were to be constructed, what would it look like, and how would it function? Perhaps part of the point is that, as John Tinnell has described,[128] all the world's a link for possible augmentation, and thereby possible delivery. Delivery is not invested in any one location, such as an amphitheater or forum, but in all spaces in which networking can occur.

In this way, AR artists have been using AR for delivery purposes for several years now. As a piece of activist art, Mark Skwarek has developed the logo hacking-based AR app "The Leak in Your Hometown" after the BP oil spill in order to better connect the everyday purchases of BP gasoline with the disaster in the Gulf of Mexico, networking how an event in one space is actually occurring, or in some sense caused by, many other locations. Any occurrence of BP's "Helios" logo may be used by the app to trigger the AR overlay in order to "target corrupt corporations and expose their misdeeds by generating subversive messages on the corporation's own logo or advertisements. This turns the corporation's own logo against them; countless logos now act as billboards for the activist cause."[129] This app, which overlays the logo with a 3D animation of a broken oil pipe, gushing oil, shows how AR might be used to take an existing space, network it with a digital database, and deliver content in physical locations to make a rhetorical point or evoke an emotional response (or both). Of course, the audience must download and participate in this delivery, going back to the problem posed by Jones. But once they do, this app also recalls Rice's point about the unexpected, that an AR app might summon an item from the database that a viewer didn't expect, delivering a shock upon seeing it.

Similarly, the artist Conor McGarrigle seeks to publically deliver data that would otherwise be hidden. In his AR mobile app *NAMAland*, McGarrigle uncovers data about bailout money used by the National Assets Management Agency (NAMA), an Irish Government Agency established in December 2009 to help Irish banks by purchasing €40 billion in bad loans, thus removing them from the balance sheets. This strategy failed, however, and Ireland was forced to enter into an IMF/EU bailout program the following year. As McGarrigle writes, "Despite … its pivotal role in the financial collapse NAMA was very secretive in its workings. Legally exempted from Freedom of Information requirements, the agency was intent on shielding its property portfolio, and the individuals and corporations involved, from public scrutiny under the guise of 'commercial sensitivity.'"[130] McGarrigle created *NAMAland* to make this information widely available instead of being kept secret, to allow individuals to access the data in the physical

locations of Dublin by geotagging and mapping where the information per-
tained (i.e., banks and buildings), and to augment those spaces with the
financial data. Thus, McGarrigle created a kind of wayfaring app, delivering data to users in the affected spaces. Through *NAMAland*, McGarrigle
seeks to

> visualize this one aspect of the Irish financial collapse by overlay-
> ing an augmented layer of NAMA property data over the physical
> space of Dublin. This serves to make concrete what has become an
> abstract account of financial transactions by associating it with real
> buildings and lands which can be interrogated in real space on any
> smartphone.[131]

As such, *NAMAland* garnered coverage in other networks, such as television
and social media coverage, and the use of the app became a popular walking
tour. But what McGarrigle is really tapping into is a general sensation felt
by many of his fellow citizens about the role that NAMA and the banks
played in the bailout, themselves seeking a way to participate in this debate
and continue the question of how to solve it. Doing so requires delivering
the invisible, tapping into a database and networking it with other agents.

Finally, AR shows the necessarily collaborative nature of delivery, one
that might only be available to the audience who, through a final gesture,
puts the whole package together. Considering the nature of computational
and physical spaces in dance, specifically working against a concept of digital dualism in which physical and digital works are separate, Vincs *et al.* discuss the dance performances *The Crack Up* and *Recognition*, which feature
digitized, augmented partners and interactive overlays on stage with live,
human dancers. As the dancers perform, the computer elements respond and
perform. However, although the audience can see the whole performance,
the human dancers are usually working without the whole picture, "everting" the usual relationship in which the dancers know the whole routine
ahead of time, causing some dancers to express "concern about the potential
'disembodiment' of the art form through the introduction of digital technology" because of a perceived "incompatibility" between human and digital
bodies.[132] As Vincs *et al.* describe this new dance relationship,

> The audience is privy to the dancer operating within their environ-
> ment, inclusive of digital layers, and is able to construct meaning con-
> stituted from all the available elements. The dancer may have their
> own internalised view of the environment, however, it is the audience
> member who is in a position to evaluate the elements as a single real-
> ity, not as completely separate physical and digital experiences ... The
> embodied experience that is fundamental to dance practice is normally
> understood first from within the dancer's own body and then shared
> with others through performance. Augmented reality, in the sense that

we describe it here as a means of integrating physical and digital experiences, reverses this premise since the full experience is only available to the audience.[133]

Although Cicero casts the orator as the flute player and the audience in the role of the flute, this scenario seems to reverse these roles so that the audience is the one viewing, selecting, and conscious of delivery as a whole. In digital delivery, perhaps this is the dance that is performed, where the audience member has the best view of how all the components of author, robots, algorithms, environment, and databases come together as a delivery-network for the final delivery, given that such delivery only spurs more delivery, creating more flutes, flute players, and blind spots.

What these examples also show is the importance of the delivery environment for delivery. Even if technologies such as AR don't develop more fully, such location-based practices that require an everted network will still find use in whatever technology comes next, so long as it is networked and database driven, which has really been the case for delivery all along. To a certain extent, time was and is important for delivery. Rhythm still pertains. But digital delivery requires as much integration with space as with time, if not more, so that a space is always delivering, Gracchus's flute made "smart." While some spaces already have such delivery networks through various media, digital technologies via databases and visualizing technologies such as AR allow more precise, rhetorical integration of information into a space and network with any or all objects within that space. As G.A. Rhodes writes of AR, "it is an art of apparatus but not of the objects themselves, instead the objects are plugged into each other, broadcasting to each other and constantly looping in real live time … We are no longer seeking to grapple with mediation, but have embodied it. We are, instead, grappling with our relationship to the interface and machine."[134] If Cicero tailored the space to fit his speech, one can now tailor a speech and environment to fit each other, program the objects to give the speech themselves, or get the audience to manipulate the objects instead, performing delivery themselves and without the deliverer being present. If one wants to know how to deliver, they must learn how to network databases for specific places and audiences; they must learn how to turn this into an interface. Moreover, they must become attuned to the audience through such interfaces, specifically delivery-networks and posthuman interfaces, the subject of the next chapter.

Notes

1. Jeff Rice, *Digital Detroit: Rhetoric and Space in the Age of the Network* (Carbondale, IL: Southern Illinois University Press, 2014), 9.
2. Steven E. Jones, *The Emergence of the Digital Humanities* (New York: Routledge, 2014), 70.
3. Cicero, *On the Ideal Orator (De Oratore)*, trans. James M. May and Jakob Wisse (New York: Oxford University Press, 2001), II.338.

4. Rice, 5.
5. Rice, 10.
6. Ibid.
7. Ibid.
8. Bruno Latour, *Reassembling the Social: An Introduction to Actor-Network-Theory* (New York: Oxford University Press, 2005, 128).
9. Ibid., 46.
10. Ibid., 210.
11. Ibid., 128.
12. Rice, 6.
13. The word Pnyx is derived from πυκνός, which takes this meaning; Henry George Liddell and Robert Scott, *Greek-English Lexicon* (Oxford, UK: Oxford University Press, 1935), s.v. "πυκνός."
14. Mogens Herman Hansen, *The Athenian Ecclesia II: A Collection of Articles, 1983–1989* (Copenhagen: Museum Tusculanum Press, 1989), 89.
15. Ibid., 92.
16. Ibid., 28.
17. Gregory S. Aldrete, *Gestures and Acclamations in Ancient Rome* (Baltimore, MD: Johns Hopkins University Press, 1999), 77.
18. Quintilian, *The Orator's Education*, Vol. 5, ed. and trans. Donald A. Russell (Cambridge, MA: Harvard University Press, 2001), XI.3.27.
19. Christopher Lyle Johnstone, "Communicating in Classical Contexts: The Centrality of Delivery," *Quarterly Journal of Speech* 87, no. 2 (2001): 127.
20. Ibid., 128.
21. Ibid.
22. Ibid., 131.
23. Ibid.
24. Ibid., 138.
25. Ibid.
26. Aldrete, 78.
27. Ibid., 78–79.
28. Pliny, *The Letters of the Younger Pliny*, trans. Betty Radice (London: Penguin Classics, 1963), IX:34.1–2.
29. Aldrete, 79.
30. Ibid., 75.
31. Ibid.
32. Ibid., 75–76.
33. Ibid., 75.
34. Ibid., 77.
35. Ibid.
36. Ibid.
37. Ibid., 79.
38. Ibid., 81.
39. Ibid., 83.
40. Ibid., 17.
41. Ibid., 18.
42. Ibid.
43. Ibid., 19–20.
44. Ibid.

45. Ibid.
46. Ibid.
47. Ibid., 21.
48. Ibid.
49. Ibid., 21–22.
50. Ibid., 24.
51. Ibid.
52. Ibid., 25.
53. Ibid., 26.
54. Ibid., 32.
55. Heidi Rae Cooley, *Finding Augusta: Habits of Mobility and Governance in the Digital Era* (Lebanon, NH: Dartmouth College Press, 2014), xxvii.
56. Ibid., 36.
57. Ibid., 37.
58. Ibid., 36.
59. Gregory L. Ulmer, "The Spirit Hand: On the Index of Pedagogy and Propaganda," in *Theory/Pedagogy/Politics: Texts for Change*, ed. Donald Morton and Mas'ud Zavarzadeh (Urbana, IL: University of Illinois Press, 1991), 142.
60. Sarah J. Arroyo, *Participatory Composition: Video Culture, Writing, and Electracy* (Carbondale, IL: Southern Illinois University Press, 2013), 36.
61. Ulmer, "Spirit Hand," 148.
62. Arroyo, 36.
63. Ibid.
64. Ibid.
65. Anthony Corbeill, *Nature Embodied: Gesture in Ancient Rome* (Princeton, NJ: Princeton University Press, 2004), 61.
66. Ibid., 43.
67. Ibid., 62.
68. Ibid., 47.
69. Ibid.
70. Ibid., 48.
71. Ibid.
72. Ibid., 44.
73. Lindal Buchanan, *Regendering Delivery: The Fifth Canon and Antebellum Women Rhetors* (Carbondale, IL: Southern Illinois University Press, 2005), 129.
74. Ibid., 133.
75. Ibid.
76. Rice, 27.
77. Ibid., 37.
78. Ibid.
79. Ibid.
80. See chapter 1, this volume.
81. Rice, 10.
82. Rice rightly notes that invention and arrangement are networked, and I would also offer that they are also networked with memory and delivery.
83. Rice, 31.
84. Ibid., 29.
85. Ibid., 28.
86. Latour, 131.

87. Rice, 44.
88. Ibid., 53.
89. Ibid., 113.
90. Randall Collins, *Interaction Ritual Chains* (Princeton, NJ: Princeton University Press, 2004), 190.
91. Paul Dourish, *Where the Action Is: The Foundations of Embodied Interaction* (Cambridge, MA: MIT Press, 2004), 13.
92. Rice, 114.
93. Gregory L. Ulmer, *Heuretics: The Logic of Invention* (Baltimore, MD: Johns Hopkins University Press, 1994), 28.
94. Rice, 127.
95. Ibid.
96. Ibid., 125.
97. Ibid., 126.
98. Ibid.
99. Ibid., 130.
100. Ibid.
101. See Jeff Rice, *The Rhetoric of Cool: Composition Studies and New Media* (Carbondale, IL: Southern Illinois University Press, 2007).
102. Rice, 133.
103. Ibid., 134.
104. Marshall McLuhan, *Understanding Media: The Extensions of Man* (Cambridge, MA: MIT Press, 1994), 336.
105. Rice, 133.
106. The term *cyberspace* was first coined by William Gibson in his short story "Burning Chrome," *Omni Magazine*, July 1982.
107. James Bridle, "#sxaesthetic," BookTwo blog, March 15, 2012, http://booktwo.org/notebook/sxaesthetic.
108. See David Rose, *Enchanted Objects: Design, Human Desire, and the Internet of Things* (New York: Scribner, 2014).
109. Jones, 48.
110. Ibid., 120.
111. Anthony Dunne, *Hertzian Tales: Electronic Products, Aesthetic Experience, and Critical Design* (Cambridge, MA: MIT Press, 2006), 102.
112. Dunne, 107.
113. Jones, 135.
114. William J. Turkel, "Intervention: Hacking History, From Analogue to Digital and Back Again," *Rethinking History* 15, no. 2 (June 2011): 291.
115. Jones, 44; emphasis in original.
116. Ibid., 45.
117. Ibid., 46; emphasis in original.
118. Andy Meek, "Voices In Your Head: How Google Glass Lets a Half-Deaf Person Hear," Fast Company, August 15, 2013, accessed July 21, 2015, http://www.fastcompany.com/3015749/voices-in-your-head-how-google-glass-lets-a-half-deaf-person-hear.
119. Brian D. Wassom, *Augmented Reality Law, Privacy, and Ethics: Law, Society, and Emerging AR Technologies* (Waltham, MA: Syngress, 2015), 243–258.
120. Helen Papagiannis, "New Work: First AR Pop-up Book for iPad 2 and iPhone 4 Using Image Recognition," Augmented Stories, June 27, 2011, accessed July

21, 2015, http://augmentedstories.com/2011/06/27/new-work-first-ar-pop-up-book-for-ipad-2-and-iphone-4-using-image-recognition.

121. Wassom, 175–208.

122. Quoted in Andrew Heaton, "Major Obstacles for AR on Construction Sites," Sourceable, April 8, 2014, accessed July 21, 2015, https://sourceable.net/major-obstacles-for-ar-on-construction-sites.

123. Wassom, 193.

124. Lev Manovich, "The Poetics of Augmented Space," *Visual Communication 5*, no. 2 (2006): 220.

125. Ibid., 223; emphasis in original.

126. Ibid., 232.

127. Ibid., 237; emphasis in original.

128. See John Tinnell, "All the World's a Link: The Global Theater of Mobile World Browsers," *Enculturation*, December 14, 2011, accessed July 24, 2014, http://enculturation.net/all-the-worlds-a-link.

129. Mark Skwarek, "Augmented Reality Activism," in *Augmented Reality Art: From an Emerging Technology to a Novel Creative Medium*, ed. Vladimir Geroimenko (Heidelberg: Springer 2014), 8–9.

130. Conor McGarrigle, "Augmented Interventions: Re-defining Urban Interventions with AR and Open Data," in *Augmented Reality Art: From an Emerging Technology to a Novel Creative Medium*, ed. Vladimir Geroimenko (Heidelberg: Springer 2014), 86.

131. Conor McGarrigle, "NAMAland," in *Augmented Reality: Innovative Perspectives across Art, Industry, and the Humanities*, ed. Sean Morey and John Tinnell (Anderson, SC: Parlor Press, forthcoming).

132. Kim Vincs, Alison Bennett, John McCormick, Jordan Beth Vincent, and Stephanie Hutchinson, "Skin to Skin: Performing Augmented Reality," in *Augmented Reality Art: From an Emerging Technology to a Novel Creative Medium*, ed. Vladimir Geroimenko (Heidelberg: Springer 2014), 164.

133. Ibid., 172–173.

134. Geoffrey Alan Rhodes, "Augmented Reality in Art: Aesthetics and Material for Expression," in *Augmented Reality Art: From an Emerging Technology to a Novel Creative Medium*, ed. Vladimir Geroimenko (Heidelberg: Springer 2014), 133.

Bibliography

Aldrete, Gregory S. *Gestures and Acclamations in Ancient Rome*. Baltimore, MD: Johns Hopkins University Press, 1999.

Arroyo, Sarah J. *Participatory Composition: Video Culture, Writing, and Electracy*. Carbondale, IL: Southern Illinois University Press, 2013.

Bridle, James. "#sxaesthetic." BookTwo blog. March 15, 2012. Accessed April 16, 2015. http://booktwo.org/notebook/sxaesthetic.

Buchanan, Lindal. *Regendering Delivery: The Fifth Canon and Antebellum Women Rhetors*. Carbondale, IL: Southern Illinois University Press, 2005.

Cicero. *On the Ideal Orator (De Oratore)*. Translated by James M. May and Jakob Wisse. New York: Oxford University Press, 2001.

Collins, Randall. *Interaction Ritual Chains*. Princeton, NJ: Princeton University Press, 2004.

Cooley, Heidi Rae. *Finding Augusta: Habits of Mobility and Governance in the Digital Era*. Lebanon, NH: Dartmouth College Press, 2014.

Corbeill, Anthony. *Nature Embodied: Gesture in Ancient Rome*. Princeton, NJ: Princeton University Press, 2004.

Dourish, Paul. *Where the Action Is: The Foundations of Embodied Interaction*. Cambridge, MA: MIT Press, 2004.

Dunne, Anthony. *Hertzian Tales: Electronic Products, Aesthetic Experience, and Critical Design*. Cambridge, MA: MIT Press, 2006.

Harding, Phillip. "Demosthenes in the Underworld: A Chapter in the *Nachleben* of a *Rhētōr*." In *Demosthenes: Statesman and Orator*, edited by Ian Worthington, 246–271. New York: Routledge, 2000.

Hansen, Mogens Herman. *The Athenian Ecclesia II: A Collection of Articles, 1983–1989*. Copenhagen: Museum Tusculanum Press, 1989.

Heaton, Andrew. "Major Obstacles for AR on Construction Sites." Sourceable, April 8, 2014. Accessed July 21, 2015. https://sourceable.net/major-obstacles-for-ar-on-construction-sites.

Johnstone, Christopher Lyle. "Communicating in Classical Contexts: The Centrality of Delivery." *Quarterly Journal of Speech* 87, no. 2 (2001): 121–143.

Jones, Steven E. *The Emergence of the Digital Humanities*. New York: Routledge, 2014.

Latour, Bruno. *Reassembling the Social: An Introduction to Actor-Network-Theory*. New York: Oxford University Press, 2005.

Lev Manovich, "The Poetics of Augmented Space," *Visual Communication* 5, no. 2 (2006): 219–240.

McGarrigle, Conor. "Augmented Interventions: Re-defining Urban Interventions with AR and Open Data." In *Augmented Reality Art: From an Emerging Technology to a Novel Creative Medium*, edited by Vladimir Geroimenko, 81–95. Heidelberg: Springer 2014.

———. "NAMAland." In *Augmented Reality: Innovative Perspectives across Art, Industry, and the Humanities*, edited by Sean Morey and John Tinnell. Anderson, SC: Parlor Press, forthcoming.

McLuhan, Marshall. *Understanding Media: The Extensions of Man*. Cambridge, MA: MIT Press, 1994.

Papagiannis, Helen. "New Work: First AR Pop-up Book for iPad 2 and iPhone 4 Using Image Recognition." Augmented Stories. June 27, 2011. Accessed July 21, 2015. http://augmentedstories.com/2011/06/27/new-work-first-ar-pop-up-book-for-ipad-2-and-iphone-4-using-image-recognition.

Pliny. *The Letters of the Younger Pliny*. Translated by Betty Radice. London: Penguin Classics, 1963.

Quintilian. *The Orator's Education*. Vol. 5. Edited and Translated by Donald A. Russell. Cambridge, MA: Harvard University Press, 2001.

Rhodes, Geoffrey Alan. "Augmented Reality in Art: Aesthetics and Material for Expression." In *Augmented Reality Art: From an Emerging Technology to a Novel Creative Medium*, edited by Vladimir Geroimenko, 127–147. Heidelberg: Springer 2014.

Rice, Jeff. *Digital Detroit: Rhetoric and Space in the Age of the Network*. Carbondale, IL: Southern Illinois University Press, 2014.

Skwarek, Mark. "Augmented Reality Activism." In *Augmented Reality Art: From an Emerging Technology to a Novel Creative Medium*, edited by Vladimir Geroimenko, 3–29. Heidelberg: Springer 2014.

Turkel, William J. "Intervention: Hacking History, From Analogue to Digital and Back Again." *Rethinking History* 15, no. 2 (June 2011): 287–96.

Ulmer, Gregory L. *Heuretics: The Logic of Invention*. Baltimore, MD: Johns Hopkins University Press, 1994.

———. "The Spirit Hand: On the Index of Pedagogy and Propaganda." In *Theory/Pedagogy/Politics: Texts for Change*, edited by Donald Morton and Mas'ud Zavarzadeh, 136–151. Urbana, IL: University of Illinois Press, 1991.

Vincs, Kim, Alison Bennett, John McCormick, Jordan Beth Vincent, and Stephanie Hutchinson. "Skin to Skin: Performing Augmented Reality." In *Augmented Reality Art: From an Emerging Technology to a Novel Creative Medium*, edited by Vladimir Geroimenko, 161–174. Heidelberg: Springer 2014.

Wassom, Brian D. *Augmented Reality Law, Privacy, and Ethics: Law, Society, and Emerging AR Technologies*. Waltham, MA: Syngress, 2015.

6 Posthuman Gestures and Electrate Attunements

> Any extension, whether of skin, hand, or foot, affects the whole psychic and social complex.
>
> —Marshall McLuhan, *Understanding Media*[1]

> The body is in constant motion with no point of reference: the body, therefore, *is* motion.
>
> —James Elkins, *The Object Stares Back*[2]

> Your wagging finger made me tremble with emotion.
>
> —Cicero[3]

Gestures have provided an important visual element to classical delivery. If one didn't use gestures, supplementing the aural track with a visual one, not only did the orator risk failure to produce emotions within an audience, but also risked failure of imparting emotions into himself, for "not to gesticulate enough indicated a lack of emotional engagement ... and was seen as a grave error."[4] Although spaces like the Pnyx required extensive vocal training in order to reach the audience's ears, sometimes gestures could better reach the eyes of those in the back rows. As Aldrete notes, many knew of Demosthenes's use of declaiming with a mouth full of pebbles, but "he also practiced all of his speeches before a full-length mirror because he realized that what his body said was as important as his words."[5]

But a gesture was not just a head, arm, or leg movement used to express feeling. As the term originally derives from *gerēre*, to carry, gesturing is the "manner of carrying" the whole body.[6] In this carrying, it is also the "manner of placing the body; position, posture, attitude."[7] The act of gesture is an act of delivery in which the deliverer positions herself in relation to other bodies, in relation to the larger environment and network. Even in classical delivery, gestures do much of the work of keeping the network together by tuning the speaker with the audience. Cicero, in *De Oratore*, discusses how gestures create visual attunement between speaker and audience, comparing the human body to a lyre. As the player evokes emotions in the audience with certain notes, so the orator—using his own body as instrument—can play the body's different components as the strings, so that different combinations of "notes" are produced from gestures and other movements that create specific affective sensations in the audience.[8] Although Cicero advises one to "play" one's own body in order to arouse the feelings in the audience, we might revise this metaphor and suggest that while an orator should "play themselves,"[9] they play themselves as a musician playing the audience as instrument, or perhaps, orchestra.

The orator attempts to reach beyond the gap between bodies, integrating his machine with others to produce an assemblage and create a single machine. And when the machine goes out of tune, delivery goes badly. As Cicero admonishes Marcus Calidius about his poor gesturing, there was "no hint of agitation in you, neither of mind nor of body! Did you smite your brow, slap your thigh, or at least stamp your foot? No. In fact, so far from touching my feelings, I could scarcely refrain from going to sleep then and there."[10] Such a statement points not toward just any emotions, but those of distress, excitement, arousal, interest, anything that might keep Cicero from falling asleep. Boredom, it seems, is not the mood one wishes to evoke with delivery, and so only certain kinds of emotions seem appropriate. When one becomes bored, one disengages from the larger collective that the orator is trying to assemble, and we might speculate that as soon as one audience member disengages from the assemblage, then the potential exists for a chain-reaction to take effect. Should one cry out at this point, admonishing the speaker for their boredom, then a counter-effect would occur, creating a group not integrated with the speaker, but in opposition. Or, the audience disintegrates one-by-one, as decorum is bored away and one listener speaks to his neighbor, which then spreads to the next, and so on, until there are many conversations going on at once. While this may actually help the deliverer, should such conversations stay on topic, the probability is that other matters come into private circulations.

Of course, a sustained level of a specific emotional intensity can have the same boring effect, just as a monotonous style can lull a reader to sleep in alphabetic writing. To this extent, delivery and style become linked, and we might say that style is put at the service of delivery, a style of performance. As we vary style through the use of synonyms, several gestures might convey the same emotion, and the variation in these gestures creates a variation in emotional intensity. An orator had to select from the database of possible word-gesture combinations and select the right ones that, "not only expressed just the appropriate feeling, but also denoted the desired nuance of emotional intensity."[11] The system of gesture—at least the system that was developed and used by Roman orators—was thus complex and varied, tied to form, movement, and timing because "of the perceived link between gesture and emotion,"[12] and thus it provided another available means of persuasion. As Aldrete makes clear, "gesture provided a direct path for the speaker to work on the emotions of his audience."[13] However, the bodies that delivered these gestures did so in another apparatus (orality), but toward the same purpose as that of an electrate deliverer—affective attunement with the audience. For a digital context, the body that the deliverer gestures with needs to be thought of more thoroughly than just a body on a stage and account for how a networking of other bodies and technologies helps construct a posthuman deliverer.

If there is a dominant motif of the posthuman, electracy, and contemporary digital technologies, it would seem that it would be that of augmentation. Often, these augmentations are depicted as technologies grafted onto human bodies, whether such augmentation is simply psychic and conceptual in nature, or whether actually "interpenetrating," to use Katherine Hayles's term. These interconnected human/machine bodies may also be cast in terms of prosthetics, a term that Ulmer—in describing electracy more broadly—often references when arguing for the need to develop digital machines, devices, and aids that can help support a capacity for judgment necessary in an Internet age. Although he sees the strength of technology in facilitating such a prosthetic, what Ulmer primarily argues for is a logic system that can make full use of digital technologies, to do for the Internet what the Greeks did for the alphabet (literacy), something I detail more in the postscript. As discussed in the previous chapter, the technologies of networks augment the body; as a network is always a motion of the very many, a body augmented by a network is a body always in motion, always augmented not just by the digital technology, but also by other bodies. James Elkins argues that the body itself is like a network, always in motion. In many ways, then, the previous chapter might be conflated with this one, as both discuss that what we augment with, both technologically and logically, are primarily networks.[14] However, here I want to break this down a bit more.

To face the assembly, Demosthenes relied upon augmentation through different kinds of technologies, as I've repeatedly discussed, machines that range from sound to image to haptic. Demosthenes needed to couple with these various machines to enact a process that will eventually produce another process. The difference between this Demosthenes and a digital counterpart, however, is that these delivery-machines didn't augment his speech at the time of its delivery; they augmented him and were necessary to the larger delivery process and performance prior to the final delivery act. Instead, a posthuman body performs the operations of delivery on behalf of the deliverer (leaving the deliverer at home), or beside the deliverer, simultaneously on the stage with her. Instead of posthuman then, we might take Brian Rotman's term *para-human*, "since the condition in question is one of horizontal movement, not upwards or forwards but sideways; not linear or sequential but dispersive and parallel; not going beyond but an expansion, a multiplication, and intensification of what was always there; a new realization of the past and its futures."[15] Even if *hypokrisis* works from above to below, the realization of this movement is horizontal, moving and being moved across networks that perform this work of realization, of delivery, of making the unknown known. The posthuman, then, is a branching out, like the shaman, using the tools of delivery to construct a network, a delivery-machine, which creates an affective attunement with the audience.

One way that delivery attunes through a network is through *hypokrisis*, by getting under the skin. With oral delivery, this happens through gestures and with speech. As Ong might put it, this feature of oral delivery, of *hypokrisis*, is psychodynamic and taps into a shared emotional state of the audience that print (pre-hypertext) cannot match. Unlike writing (or print), an oral delivery as a "physical constitution of sound ... proceeds from the human interior and manifests human beings to one another as conscious interiors, as persons, the spoken word forms human beings into close-knit groups. When a speaker is addressing an audience, the members of the audience normally become a unity, with themselves and with the speaker."[16] If instead, according to Ong, the speaker were to pass out written text for them to read, they would then begin to enter into their own interior world with the text and the audience would become "shattered, to be re-established only when oral speech begins again."[17] For Ong, "readership" is an abstraction of individuals spread across vast distances, perhaps reading the same writing, but at different times, in different contexts, and in isolation, without the ability to respond to the writer or with each other. Such is not a defense of Plato's critique about writing in the *Phaedrus*, but simply a difference in the effect writing has on an audience.

While writing as a delivery technology may indeed create emotional connections, may use effective language, voice, style, or arrangement to effect *pathos*, oral delivery (at this point, sticking with pre-hypertext modalities), has a better chance of injecting affect and is the most probable (if not possible) way to do so at the group level. This, perhaps, is one reason that Ong considers the "interiorizing force of the oral word" as especially sacral, "to the ultimate concerns of existence."[18] Of course, apparatus theory via Ulmer tells us that the two are intimately connected simply because sacral institutions developed the ritualistic practices of orality. However, Ong derives from this the power that words have to effect action as a kind of speech act: "The Hebrew *dabar*, which means word, also means event and thus refers directly to the spoken word. The spoken word is always an event, a movement in time, completely lacking in the thing-like repose of the written or printed word."[19] Action, implied in two of the terms for delivery, *hypokrisis* (as acting) and *actio*, work toward this logic that effective delivery produces some sort of action, not only in the original motion, but a co-motion that keeps going as the audience is required to act as well.

Rotman also finds problems in affective transfer through print, and why it makes a bad delivery system, at least in terms of *hypokrisis*. He describes the alphabet's "reductive relation to the corporeal dimension of utterance, to speech's embodiment."[20] Because the alphabet's letters are "in no way iconic" (i.e., they don't look like human bodies or reference human body sounds), and because each letter's sounds are "meaningless monads, minimal hearable fragments of speech absent any trace of the sense-making apparatus of the body producing them,"[21] letters and the bodies that produce them are significantly separated beyond the simple material forms of paper and flesh. As James Elkins writes regarding faces, "Words don't give us faces, I think; the best they can do is recall for us what it is like to try to remember a face. If I read a close description of a face and attend to it very carefully and try to construct it in my mind, I end up with something monstrous."[22] Almost totally, the alphabet (and by extension, print) completely remove what's important for the body regarding delivery, and what's important for delivery regarding the body: a delivery of affect.

> For what the alphabet eliminates is the body's inner and outer gestures which extend over speech segments beyond individual words. Both those visually observable movements that accompany and punctuate speech (which was never its function to inscribe) and, more to the point, those inside speech, the gestures which constitute the voice itself—the tone, the rhythm, the variation of emphasis, the loudness, the changes of pitch, the mode of attack, discontinuities, repetitions, gaps and elisions, and the never absent play and musicality of utterance that makes human song possible. In short, the alphabet omits all the prosody of utterance and with it the multitude of bodily effects of force, significance, emotion, and affect that it conveys.[23]

A study of delivery should reconsider how gestures pertain not to traditional oral delivery, but to a digital, networked, electrate delivery. What is the gesture for us? As Rotman goes on to write, digital technologies, including video and motion-capture technology, allow us to record, study, and write with the body as never before. Even GPS tracking of bodies allows one with the data to track how bodies move through space and design delivery environments that gesture to the passersby, as seen in *Minority Report*. However, the body can exist in other ways, integrated with digital technologies that can do the gesturing for the body, without the body present. In a way much more sophisticated than the alphabet, new interfaces of the body are possible that can travel through networks and network simultaneously. Beyond mediums of paper or codex on which print is pressed, the interface of print does not move—in fact, its best quality is that it does not move even as it circulates from writer to reader. Print is still useful for this static quality. But when it comes to electracy, a digital delivery needs to move again.

Rice makes similar moves toward attunement. As I discussed in the last chapter, the network theory that Rice produces primarily works toward invention, arrangement, and memory, although he does at times bring up the term "delivery." Though unexplored, I find a logic of networked, digital delivery implicit in *Digital Detroit*, particularly as Rice begins to define how the process of decision making might lead toward a concept of *satisficing*, or settling upon a good enough decision rather than one that is resolute and finished; in other words, a satisficing, good enough decision is left open for revision, a kind of decision making that fluid networks demand. As found with the schizo, the shaman, and now with a deliverer working with digital technologies, "collecting attachments" and forming assemblages is not the end toward resolutions,[24] but a process toward becoming, toward "further decisions. What we don't need are declarations or promises, but collections of information, databases, we navigate within."[25] Therefore, "networks are not revolutionary gestures."[26] The collection of these attachments is the process of attunement, the process of networking, the process of delivery, which, as I have argued throughout this book, is the process of group invention, collective decision making. In the case of networked rhetoric, it could be that the audience is not always aware that delivery is happening. Of course, it might have been the case that an audience member in classical Greece or Rome didn't know delivery was taking place, or was continuing to take place outside the Forum, a kind of inverse of Burke's parlor. Or, what the audience member thought was delivery, the content of the speech's ideas, was far from the important element actually delivered, the affective sensation felt by the body upon witnessing the delivery. Perhaps a networked, digital delivery is not much different from classical delivery. Or maybe it's very different but still trying to operate in the classical guise in the form of trial setting deliveries that "constitute a final pay-off of a verdict's settlement on proof or argument."[27] This is not the schizo's both/ and, but the "opposite gesture of the additive,"[28] for Rice, the "'this' and 'this' and 'this' of satisficing."[29] An electrate delivery, then, would focus on Rice's concept of satisficing as a means of keeping connections going, of building the delivery-network, of working toward more decisions, but also more collective invention.

Through this integration of deliverer and machine into network, producing augmentations, the deliverer is no longer human, but posthuman. As an augmented, enhanced being, traditional aspects of delivery such as tone, gesture, clothing, facial expressions, and the other unspeakable elements assume new meanings, implications, and positions. Moreover, as McLuhan might argue, these "extensions" expand not our bodies *per se*, but our central nervous system, the range of not only one's abilities to deliver across networks, but the audience's ability to participate in the delivery process, to join and form networks as part of the delivery process. Thus, a posthuman Demosthenes delivering within an invisible space with an invisible audience, one that she cannot speak to, complicates how delivery occurs—how affect might be delivered in hyper-complex networks of circulation. Gestures, tonality, and expression can now be made not just with the body alone, not just with machines that are immediately present, but with a range of teletechnologies and telemedia. The posthuman deliverer must also contend with the nonhuman, such as Web robots (algorithms) and posthuman audiences. Those who best represent this potential for posthuman delivery are artists who are working with such technologies in order to create new kinds of digital, posthuman gestures. For example, Eduardo Kac creates networked, bio-engineered artworks from which digital delivery-networks might be constructed. As an artist who makes "gestures," Kac does so by constructing delivery-machines, providing new networked relationships that question what a gesture means within delivery. Kac uses digital media installations to gesture toward both the invisible spirits with which he integrates, and an audience who is unconscious to such forces. In his role as an artist, especially one constructing digital networks, Kac serves as a shamanic mediator between the two realms. But as the deliverer is different, so is the audience. Although the classical idea of delivery involves an orator addressing a crowd, usually arranged in a structure made for such gatherings, an electrate delivery requires not only the audience to gather around the deliverer, but also the deliverer to gather around the audience. The assemblage of the deliverer does not just stop with his or her integration with digital technologies, but extends to the audience within/throughout a rhizomatic structure. Digital delivery requires not just a performance of the deliverer, but it requires the audience to perform and take a role in the delivery process.

Before looking at Kac's work, and perhaps a bit belatedly, I should note how I work with "posthuman" in this chapter. As Cary Wolfe writes in *What is Posthumanism?*, the term "posthuman" produces "different and even irreconcilable definitions."[30] Rather than account for all of these definitions, this chapter begins with two. The first, a common perception of posthuman that occurs when the "natural" human body integrates with other machines, substances, and "prosthetics" that lead to something other than human, either cyborg or an augmented human. The kind of posthuman I'm thinking of here permeates the work of Donna Haraway and the singularity theory of Ray Kurzweil, who offers that humans will reach an event horizon of machine integration where the two can no longer be pulled apart. While Kurzweil might be identified as a transhumanist, viewing technology as a means to improve the human toward a kind of liberal human transcendence (addressed by N. Katherine Hayles in *How We Became Posthuman*), my use of posthuman more aligns with Wolfe's: "posthumanism in my sense isn't posthuman at all—in the sense of being 'after' our embodiment has been transcended—but only posthuman*ist*, in the sense that it opposes the fantasies of disembodiment and autonomy, inherited from humanism itself, that Hayles rightly criticizes."[31] Delivery doesn't transcend the body, but requires the body, however that body might be formed. Although this chapter contends with the embodiment of the posthuman, rather than focusing on a techno-integration my concern is with the kind of thinking (from intellect to affect) that such integration makes possible or necessary for a posthuman organism to survive and thrive according to her own desires, and therefore the kind of thinking necessary for delivery.

Whereas I offer this initial description, again, I also don't want to close down a definition or understanding of posthuman or posthumanism. I think the many contested interpretations of what a posthuman present or future might look like, or various movements of posthumanism, all might produce different possibilities for delivery, and each should be explored. For now, like Sid Dobrin's arguments about the posthuman and writing studies in *Postcomposition*, my own argument "regarding posthumanism and subjectivity revolves around the idea that the shift to the posthuman is not a matter of choice—though some may choose to transform more directly—but instead a phenomenon of the current conditions of networked societies."[32] So a "posthuman gesture" asks both what a posthuman gesture might look like, what kinds of networked bodies might be constructed to perform the gesture, as well as a gesture toward the posthuman, to imagine the good enough body or gesture for a good enough delivery, a post-delivery. As Hayles has argued, the posthuman does not signal the end of the human. Instead, "What is lethal is not the posthuman as such but the grafting of the posthuman onto a liberal humanist view of the self."[33] This warning beckons not just toward considering new kinds of delivery that disrupt the traditional ways that delivery has been considered, but developing new theories about what kinds of actors deliver and the kinds of networked subjectivities such a delivery entails. While I have considered classical orators and shamanic figures, these are simply relays to consider newer, networked conditions that demand asking what a post-deliverer might be like.

One last interpretation of posthuman that I use here refers to the human that we have left behind, specifically the tail we no longer have, a tail that is posthuman as it disappears prior to delivery. That is, what is the prehuman that the human posts, that eventually leads to the posthuman? Regarding tails, what is this post of the human, and what can it teach us about how to use and incorporate (literally) writing technologies that might require thinking with the post rather than the head? These two concepts of posthuman dominate much of this chapter, although the term could and should be read with other meanings in mind; I hope that what follows will eventually lead to a consideration of other definitions of posthumanism and how the concept affects theories of delivery—ones that might involve postspecies, postgender, postrace, postbody, and many others—by invoking the possibilities that a t@il augmentation might hold.

Becoming T@iled[34]

As Hayles explains in *My Mother Was a Computer*, 1930s and 1940s computers required human beings to do most of the "thinking" and that interpretations of *computer* "from World War II to the end of the twentieth century mark a shift from a society in which the intelligence required for calculations was primarily associated with humans to the increasing degradation of these labors to computational machines."[35] Before computers became "intelligent" so that they could think for us, humans had to do the thinking for them. Although this example should not be construed as providing an etiological anecdote for a transition into posthumanism, it does highlight one attitude toward a particular relationship between posthumans and computers: the prosthetic function that we often assume of computers is one of calculations, of performing mathematical-based utilities that augment the processing speed of the human brain, making a posthuman mind. Perhaps because of this preoccupation with the cerebral, the "brain" or "mind" becomes an iconic location of where the prosthetic connection occurs. Going back to a pre-everting Internet, one only has to think of the science fiction fantasy motif of uploading one's consciousness into a machine and leaving the body behind, as in *The Matrix* where the "mind" is inserted into a virtual environment—a prosthetic space—and the manipulation of such an environment is one of manipulating codes: the savviest posthuman is one that never loses her ability to compute. Instead of leaving the body behind, though, what about the body's "behind"? Instead of focusing on the head of the posthuman, what if we focus on the "post" of the posthuman—the tail?

In the womb, we all have tails. The human embryo continues to grow its tail until the fourth or fifth week, but around the seventh week of development the tail begins to disappear. The tail is never something that any animal gains, but a body part that humans in particular lose. The human embryo grows out of a tail, which disappears as the embryo continues to develop. However, although we lose most of its physical aspects, except for the few vertebrae that compose the coccyx, do we lose all of the psychological ones? What parts of our psychic tails remain? Do we still try to use our latent tails, or unconsciously sense that we have phantom tails? For those animals with tails remaining, what functions do the tail allow for that become missing for us? We are all conceived with tails, but what kind of conceiving would tails permit? What kind of gesture would a tail perform?

Other animals have found many uses for their tails. Fish use tails for hydrodynamic propulsion, and the thresher shark uses its tail to also stun prey. A lizard can use its tail to deceive, fooling a predator into attacking their detachable appendage so that it may escape. The rubber boa also deceives with its tail, using "short, blunt tails that look almost identical to the head. When threatened by a predator, this snake arranges its body in such a manner that the tail is exposed while the head is hidden safely beneath the snake."[36] Birds may use their tails as a rudder, but also ostentatiously to attract, such as the elaborate tail displays of peacocks. Squirrels use their tails for balance as they prance around trees limbs, to help regulate and store body heat, and, like the bird, as a rudder when jumping.[37] Horses and cows swat flies away from their rears; the hippopotamus swats dung. Larger tails store fat in addition to their other functions. One of the main points to take from the tail, then, is that they most often have multiple uses, and besides providing attunement for balance, motion, temperature, and hunting, tails provide a means of telling—tails can become tales. Such tales are most commonly observed in the dog or the cat.

Figure 6.1 depicts various tails/tales of the cat. The cat can use its tail to communicate commands/requests, but what the tail primarily delivers is mood. The cat tail is rhetorical and becomes a means to deliver, through a visible signal, what the animal cannot (or chooses not to) express audibly. The cat's tail gestures, and what it gestures is a state of mind. Toward electrate attunements, Ulmer argues that one needs to "do your duty, shake

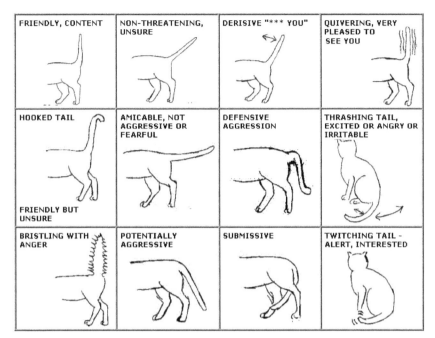

FRIENDLY, CONTENT	NON-THREATENING, UNSURE	DERISIVE "*** YOU"	QUIVERING, VERY PLEASED TO SEE YOU
HOOKED TAIL / FRIENDLY BUT UNSURE	AMICABLE, NOT AGGRESSIVE OR FEARFUL	DEFENSIVE AGGRESSION	THRASHING TAIL, EXCITED OR ANGRY OR IRRITABLE
BRISTLING WITH ANGER	POTENTIALLY AGGRESSIVE	SUBMISSIVE	TWITCHING TAIL - ALERT, INTERESTED

Figure 6.1 Cat communication through its tail, courtesy Sarah Hartwell/ *Messybeast.com.* Used by permission.

your booty."[38] What a posthuman tail might afford is a way to interface this "post" and connect to delivery-networks to account for and deliver affect, which becomes an aesthetic action already apparent through Roland Barthes's image logic of the *punctum*, which injects (*hypokrisis*) an aesthetic experience like a scorpion's tail. We might consider the need to construct our own prosthetic tails to give us similar powers. We might consider what it would mean to re-tail ourselves.

One tail that we have already begun to adopt is the @, sometimes referred to as "the monkey's tail." The @ appears nearly ubiquitously in online environments, and provides one kind of code that we commonly write with. However, because of its ubiquity, we often overlook its function as a code, that it instructs our "intelligent" computers to enact a certain command, or that it changes the way that we write/think in other kinds of environments. We write everyday with the @, yet it remains transparent to our thinking prosthetics. The @ as a monkey's tail, however, does more than just instruct our posthuman parts toward some specific function: it becomes prosthetic as a posthuman tail, and serves a different kind of prosthetic function than one of "thinking." As such, the @ needs to be theorized both inside and outside current conversations of how posthuman bodies and codes interact. We need to theorize what it means to both "write" a prosthesis such as a t@il, what that t@il looks like once written, and how it performs as a function of delivery at the level of code.[39]

Other digital appendices have already been tested for their integration with the posthuman. Dobromir G. Dotov, Lin Nie, and Anthony Chemero have demonstrated how easily the hand-mouse circuit becomes "natural" when using it to operate (assemble with) a computer. As Chemero states, "The person and the various parts of their brain and the mouse and the [computer] monitor are so tightly intertwined that they're just one thing ... The tool isn't separate from you. It's part of you."[40] Dotov, Nie, and Chemero attempt to test Heidegger's "ready-to-hand" theory and determine if we normally overlook the mouse and monitor. By purposefully disrupting the hand-mouse circuit, the team creates a cognitive dissonance in the users, effectively creating Heidegger's "unreadiness-at-hand." The malfunction breaks the circuit, cuts the human from his or her cyborg infrastructure, but also from a prosthesis that aids in thinking (and acting) in the network. As Chemero further conjectures, "The thing that does the thinking is bigger than your biological body ... You're so tightly coupled to the tools you use that they're literally part of you as a thinking, behaving thing."[41] If we remove the hand-mouse and break this version of a posthuman machinic assemblage, then what occurs when we add (or cut off) the tail? What is the cognitive malfunction that would occur if one had (or no longer had) access to the @ and all that the @ affords? Is the @ already so "invisible" that we've incorporated it into our cognitive process? Or, another question: what does the @ give us access to in the first place?

What is the natural history of this m@rk? While many debate the origins of @, some competing theories are worth mentioning. Like proto-alphabetic writing in general, the @ begins in economics as a way to account for goods and currency. Berthold Louis Ullman claims that the @ might have been a ligature "which is really for *ad*, with an exaggerated uncial *d*,"[42] perhaps used by medieval monks to save labor and space. Likewise, it may also represent an "a" inside of an "e" to signify "each," as in the accounting discourse, "each at $10," not unlike modern day accounting usage where @ means "at the rate of" (or short-hand for the Greek ἀνά which has the same meaning). Its evolution of design may have arisen from the Norman French by altering the grave-accentuated *à*—which is used similarly as "at" or "each" when referring to accounting—so that the writer can make the mark without raising the writing instrument. This practice is first documented in the writings of the Italian merchant Francesco Lapi, whose use of the @ within a letter is "the first recorded use of the 'at' sign outside a monastery" as discovered by Giorgio Stabile.[43] Figure 6.2 renders this possible evolution.

Figure 6.2 Possible evolution of the @ symbol, created by author.

For the Portuguese, the @ historically stood as a symbol for a unit of specific weight (16 liters of liquid), as in the weight of goods contained in an *arroba*, a kind of jar derived from the Greek *amphora*.[44] Italians may also have adopted this usage as their @-term *anfora*, so that one @ equals one *anfora*. But besides a jar, an accounting symbol, or its other uses, the @ has a variety of epithets given by different cultures. For the Russians, the @ is a *sobachka*, or little dog. Koreans may refer to it as a snail (*dalphaengi*). The @ is sometimes referred to as an "ear" of a variety of species, from pigs to elephants (one of the sense organs for delivery). But in a variety of languages, the @ is referred to as a tail—sometimes a mouse's, pig's, or cat's—but often a monkey's tail, where the tail section is that which wraps around the indefinite article. Many languages derive their tails from the German term *Klammeraffe*, which refers specifically to the spider monkey and the prehensile use of its tale in New World arboreal habitats.[45] The spider monkey, like many monkeys, uses its tail as another hand with which to grasp branches or other objects as it climbs about the rainforest. This tail becomes a tool for movement (which we know from Rice is necessary for a network), for reaching places its other limbs might not find accessible, and for ascending into the arboreal habitat, leaving many of the dangers of the ground below. The tail of the spider monkey is transcendent and deliverant.

The @ takes up a transcendent quality as well, in multiple ways. One way is through the lengthening of the tail—as shown in figure 6.2—which created a new typographical mark eventually transcending the symbol itself to that of art. As used in Twitter, the @ serves to gain one's attention—@seanmorey—as a peacock might spread its tail feathers and attract a mate: the @ becomes aesthetic, despite (or perhaps because of) its use as a functional code. In 2010, the Museum of Modern Art (MoMA) included the @ in its architecture and design collection; what makes the @ aesthetic in MoMA's eyes? Alice Rawsthorn explains that the acquisition committee determines each piece according to questions such as its form and function, design principles that MoMA favors such as clarity, honesty, and simplicity, societal and cultural impact, innovation, and finally, according to Paola Antonelli, the senior curator of architecture and design at the time of the @'s inclusion, "If this object had never been designed or manufactured, would the world miss out. ... Even just a bit?"[46] The @ met such criteria, as an old accountancy symbol was developed—without modification of form or meaning—toward a new, digital function. Furthermore, Antonelli views its many names as "proof of its importance, because we care so much about the @ that we've started to mythologize it."[47] The @ develops so many pseudonyms/epithets but has never developed an official English name, and the Oxford English Dictionary simply includes it as the "at sign."

Although the @ has not lost its original meaning, it takes on new ones. The @ symbol becomes a floating signifier, an open work of art, which can take on many meanings. The @ is an open sign, both figuratively and literally. Rawsthorn observes that the @ still looks the same after several hundred years despite not existing as a physical object such as furniture, vehicles, or other more material museum pieces. This permanence, despite its lack of "physicality," is one reason that MoMA chose the @: "both the old and new @ fulfill the same function of simplifying and clarifying something that's fiendishly complicated to make and interpret: handwritten script and computer code respectively"[48] which Antonelli views as "an act of design of extraordinary elegance and economy."[49]

The "new @" referred to by Rawsthorn and Antonelli is the @ "economically" borrowed by Raymond Tomlinson, historically noted to have sent the first email message. Tomlinson chose the @—a character not widely used for anything else but accounting, yet still on computer keyboards since it featured on the American Underwood typewriter in 1885—to serve as the bridge between the human and the network. The user is located @ a particular computer server. The "elegance and economy" shown by this choice are qualities both "prized by MoMA, especially 'economy' in a time of recession and environmental crisis, when reinventing something that's under-used seems much smarter than designing something new."[50] So, we're back to economy after all. But its "under-use" within an economy of symbols is what allows it to function as a floating signifier, which is why Tomlinson was able to borrow it for email in the first place. So while the @ has only limited functions as a computer code, it's filled with many particular meanings, becoming many varieties of t@ils. Thus, the very character that we use in this transformational way, to create a variety of aesthetic designs via the programs that feature @, is itself an aesthetic glyph of writing ourselves a posthuman tail in order to further write our posthuman selves and offer posthuman gestures. In the economy of the @, its value is not (only) money, but how it might be used in multiple ways by a variety of desires, including as a means of delivery. MoMA considered this potential variety of @s as well, selecting a display of many @s in a variety of typefaces and sizes.[51] Each of the individual uses of @ takes on a unique performance as we t@il ourselves, eventually creating a long t@il that extends throughout networks.

Another aesthetic consideration: in *A Thousand Plateaus*, Deleuze and Guattari begin the chapter "1837: Of the Refrain" with a plate of a painting by Paul Klee entitled *Twittering Machine* (*Die Zwitscher-Maschine*, 1922; also in the MoMA collection). In the painting, four birds perch on a hand crank, perhaps chained to it. Birds sing for many reasons, such as to mark their territory, or to express their desire for a mate. These birds, in particular, have become territorialized and make up a twittering machine with the instrument on which they've become attached; and they don't sing, they twitter. At least, the integration with the hand crank creates a twittering machine, and not a singing machine. But what exactly is a twitter? Of a bird, to twitter is an intransitive verb that means "to utter a succession of light tremulous notes; to chirp continuously with a tremulous effect."[52] It also means "to spin or twist unevenly, to make 'twitty.'"[53] As a noun, a twitter is implicated with desire, and so twittering delivers a performance of desire:

"a condition of twittering or tremulous excitement (from eager desire, fear, etc.)."[54] However, a twitter is also "an entanglement; a complication."[55] To twitter is to network, and like the birds in Klee's painting, one cannot twitter without also becoming ensnared.

The microblogging site Twitter contains all of these definitional aspects of "twitter." The service prompts for spontaneous updates of excitement; the @ (which serves as a method of making responses to others public) and hyperlinks create a twitty, and even the nature of the short (140 characters or less), regular posts mimic the short, repeated "tweet tweet" of a bird's tune or the shaman's drum.[56] And this rhythm is carried across by the @. Deleuze and Guattari indicate that the formal feature of language that best represents the way that their assemblages connect is the "and" and the indefinite article. The "and" and "a" provide a method toward linking machines together, to move from break to break in various flows. As an image, these words may be quickly represented by the character @. In the digital Internet, the @ provides one of the many points of connection for making assemblages, and integrating the post@human via the t@il, of which the @ is always necessary for (email) posting in general. It is not just that the @ serves as the link between sender-receiver, between the sender, recipient, and the conduits (email address domains) making such a connection possible, but that it provides the conductor of desire itself, as if it were the indefinite article: "the indefinite article does not lack anything ... but expresses the pure determination of intensity, intensive difference. The indefinite article is the conductor of desire."[57]

This kind of linking, with the "@" as an "an" and as an "and," not only provides a way of connecting, but also one with a vector, projecting a line of flight. We might say the @ gives direction with purpose, if purpose can be taken to mean the striving toward a desire, Spinoza's *con@tus*. Lacan tells us that the desire expressed by the *objet petit a*, from where the theoretical functioning of the @ derives for Ulmer, can never be reached. Yet we strive for it. We should also consider multiple @s at the same time, and include the @'s accounting meaning of "at the rate of." This origin refers to actual money, and fits nicely with Deleuze and Guattari's theories of how capitalism affects the socius and leads to schizophrenic coping mechanisms (the logic of and ... and ... and); for if capitalism requires the constant attainment of flow, puncept intended, then Lacan's *objet petit a* is indeed unreachable. A million @s will never be enough.

But rather than focus on the @s themselves, their function as the link between the human@post provides an aesthetic line of flight. Toward its function as art, as an image, the Portuguese's use of the @ to resemble an amphora lends credence to the potential of the @ image to serve as an image category for a means of connection, a way of gathering. While typically only two kinds of categories cluster about the current use of @—as the sender/receiver signifier and a signal of presence in the form of a domain address—is it possible that the @ could cluster many other machines around it as well, becoming a kind of Body without Organs, assembling different paths of desire, serving as a gathering place? Ulmer's chora—a digital collage space of gathering and invention—might be thought of as chor@, where @ is the non-place, a space that allows a gathering and sifting to occur. The @, then, becomes a point of departure (or arrival) for thinking about how to construct a t@il for the human@post of the posthuman, not in the limited sense that such a symbol is used to send emails or link usernames on Twitter, but as an important networking component that might be expanded upon, opening the @ further for delivery than even its current uses.

Ulmer theorizes the @ as the *objet petit a* for electracy, which might potentially foster posthuman group identity formation: "The object @, joining letter and signifier, preserving a piece of the Real in the Symbolic (discourse). The implication for individual and collective identity formation, in the context of the apparatus, is profound. The electrate category emerges at the opposite pole of the literate one. It is not universal, but is a *sinthome*, a non-sense letter sported by a particular body."[58] The @ is performed by the posthuman, twitched about like the cat's tail, and as a non-sense letter is a remainder that requires a body to which it desires, or creates desire, for the assemblage with a body. Toward this, the space at the center of the @ provides the hole of the unconscious, a black hole that spirals into the singularity.[59] However, Deleuze and Guattari read a black hole differently and not always as a collapse into the singularity. They point to Klee's figure of the black hole (what Klee calls a "gray point") which begins as

> nonlocalizable, nondimensional chaos, the force of chaos, a tangled bundle of aberrant lines. Then the point "jumps over itself" and radiates a dimensional space with horizontal layers, vertical cross sections, unwritten customary lines, a whole terrestrial interior force ... The gray point (black hole) has thus jumped from one state to another, and no longer represents chaos but the abode or home. Finally, the point launches out of itself, impelled by the wandering centrifugal forces that fan out to the sphere of the cosmos.[60]

The @ is not only an unconscious that spirals inward, but outward, producing gr@y spots throughout. These gr@y spots works toward creating an unconscious state to unify desire/body/machine, spiraling outward and gathering parts, networking. And although not universal for every body, the @ is also Lacan's empty universal joined to particular bodies and filled with particular desires. The @ contains its own remainder, subverting its simple use as code: "the @ marks the object (a), the expressible standing in for the inexpressible."[61] If the @ becomes the expressible image for the inexpressible which is the unconscious (hole), the @ provides a hole, a point of attachment, in which to insert a new machine, a prosthesis for something lost.

In the movie *Avatar*, the Na'vi people network with the ecology of their planet Pandora through their ponytails, which might inform how we consider our own t@ils as a means to connect with our own networked ecologies and gain access to our own avatars.[62] As Ulmer explains, the term avatar (as a category for the online personas that a user may adopt) was borrowed from the original Sanskrit *avatara*, a term that specified the incarnation of a deity in Hindu mythology.[63] A digital avatar does not represent any single element of the online persona, but all avatars across all online platforms, those we use on Facebook, Twitter, email, online gaming—all of these together form one's avatar, one's online identity: "'Avatar,' then, is a practical point of entry for theorizing the emergence of the new identity experience of electracy, that is supplementing and displacing 'selfhood,' the identity formation of literacy."[64] We construct t@ils and deliver to others via the @, either through email, Twitter, or other platforms, and create online presences becoming avatar. As Ulmer further explains, the etymology of *avatara* includes "*ava*, down + *tarati*, he crosses over."[65] The avatar via the @ provides a crossing down, a descending movement, a movement opposite of the traditional ascendant direction of transcendence, not into the cloud, into a heaven, but down into the machine, a movement toward the tail, a networked gesture toward *hypokrisis*. In addition, punceptually enough, the *ava* (down) in Sanskrit and the ává (rate) in Greek can both be expressed by the @, which, through the avatar also links the individual with the collective via the process of identity formation: "The third dimension of a language apparatus (after technology and institutional practices) is identity formation, individual and collective. The term covering the site of new identity experience in electracy is avatar."[66] As in the film, one's avatar joins the individual and collective toward a group connected by a new kind of economy of t@ils. Avatar, like interface and as interface, but as intert@il, may be a new category for delivery.

The avatar, to the extent that it contains all the components of one's online persona, might be better stated here as @v@t@r, since unlike the t@il in Twitter alone, the @v@t@r necessarily contains many t@ils.[67] The @v@t@r contains multiple t@ils, multiple lines of flight. However, each t@il of the @v@t@r, or the total number of t@ils it contains, can be long or short, many or few. In *The Long Tail*, Chris Anderson describes a business model for Internet retail sales that entails selling less of any particular good and instead offering more types of products (an economy of the very many). As Anderson differentiates between "old" media and new media, the former "can bring one show to millions of people with unmatched efficiency. But it can't do the opposite—bring a million shows to one person each. Yet that is exactly what the internet can do so well."[68] The Internet can deliver the "everything else," the non-hits that typical broadcast media and brick-and-mortar stores can't because of economics: "The simple picture of the few hits that mattered and the everything else that didn't is now becoming a confusing mosaic of a million mini-markets and micro-stars. Increasingly, the mass market is turning into a mass of niches."[69] Micromolarities are becoming the norm. And these micromolarities cluster together to form what Anderson calls the "Long Tail," which, although they don't sell as many quantities as the "hits" that make up the head, in aggregate can potentially add up to a greater mass: "The onesies and twosies were still only selling in small numbers, but there were so *many* of them that in aggregate they added up to a big business."[70] The Long Tail, by adding this prosthesis to the head, allows a way to make the invisible visible: "Many of these kinds of products have always been there, just not visible or easy to find ... Now they're available, via Netflix, iTunes, Amazon, or just some random place Google turned up. The invisible market has turned visible."[71] The Long Tail aggregates, for it is an aggregate, and in doing so makes the formerly microscopic noticeable.

Connecting to the market/economic implications of the Long Tail, the form of "tail" in words such as "detail" and "retail" refers to its meaning of "cut," specifically to cut up into pieces. In contrast to wholesale, mass produced goods become cut up and distributed to smaller retail outlets. With schizophrenic logic, we often construct our avatars like Deleuze and Guattari's schizo, building an overall avatar through assemblages of multiple @'s, cutting off pieces from one flow and directing them into another. The avatar engineer schizzes digital technologies and codes and assembles those cut pieces into her t@il, or creates a long t@il that grants access to an @v@t@r. Rather than shouting at the surf to build a body for delivery, we should now cut and paste. One delivers herself, crosses over into the Internet in small quantities, re-tails herself, not (always) as a whole body, but as organs, as micromolarities of the whole.

Implicated in this schizophrenic logic of the cut, of biting off bits and reattaching them, is desire. Our missing tail that we lose in the womb becomes the fetish object that within the domain of the Internet becomes totemic. The Long Tail is also the long(ed for) tail, and this t@il can be very long: "What's truly amazing about the Long Tail is the sheer size of it. Again, if you combine enough of the non-hits, you've actually established a market that rivals the hits."[72] So long, in fact, that it extends to infinity. As mentioned earlier, *Klammeraffe* derives from the German name for a spider monkey; its scientific genus, *ateles* (*a* + *telos*) translates to "without end." The linking of various social network sites, logos, email signatures, brands, images, codes, and other traces all add up and create a long tail(s) for the @v@t@r, which makes distributing that persona more efficient, and once that persona is distributed, the ability to deliver via the network. Becoming @v@t@r is simply becoming a digital sh@m@n, who used a long tail of tools such as drums, fringe, costumes, amulets, and other items for delivery. To deliver one's @v@t@r, one assembles it in the form of a long t@il, consciously or not.

Toward this @v@t@r, the t@il becomes the primary means of circling around the user's unconscious desires and appears as a m@sk, an alt identity, forming a loop that iconically resembles what it performs. Noting that one source of inspiration for Tomlinson's choice of the @ might have been an image of the title character in Alfred Jarry's play *Ubu Roi*, Daniel Soar writes that, as an obese, "greedy slob ... who seeks instant gratification,"[73] the "spiral *gidouille* ... is meant to symbolise the tyrant's intestines."[74] Through the puncept, the word *gidouille* conducts "a gross combination of *Gribouille, grenouille, andouille, couille, gargouille*: gargoyles, testicles, tripe, frogs, power-hungry fiends."[75] From this chain of associations, Soar observes that the @ "turns out to be engorged with potential meanings," which even better symbolizes the variety of becomings available to Twitter users, who can become "anyone, and in 140 characters or fewer can produce a digested version of whatever personality they choose."[76] In this image of Père Ubu (figure 6.3) we see the anonymous @ user, shrouded in anonymity (even when one's name is exposed) with his hooded mask, bulging from the gut. But bulging from what? A diarrhea relieved by tweets? An urge to spill one's guts, easier to do when one has taken an avatar and is not to be accountable for the mess?

At *Ubu Roi*'s 1896 Parisian premiere, Jarry opened the play with a lengthy introduction in which he explained that such anonymity would be used in the play: "Our actors have been willing to depersonalise themselves for two evenings, and to act behind masks, in order to express more perfectly the inner man, the soul of these overgrown puppets you are about to see."[77] Actors playing characters that are playing puppets provide an important correlate with the practice of playing a character that is disguised as a puppet (avatar) online. Like Ulmer's description of the object @, the mark itself is not as important as the unconscious desires that seek to pass through it. The avatar becomes the online body (or in the case of Père Ubu, onstage) into which the soul may descend, protected by the m@sk that the spiraling @ affords.

Figure 6.3 Wood cut of Père Ubu by Alfred Jarry, *Ubu Roi*, public domain.

Furthermore, Jarry's introduction details the de-tails, that is, the bits and pieces that he, for one reason or another, wasn't able to include (or purposely cut):

> The play having been put on prematurely, and with more enthusiasm than anything else, Ubu hasn't had time to get his real mask ... It seemed very important if we were to be quite like puppets—*Ubu Roi* is a play that was never written for puppets, but for actors pretending to be puppets, which is not the same thing—for us to have carnival music, and the orchestral parts have been allotted to various brasses, gongs and speaking-trumpet horns that we haven't had time to collect ... here you must accept doors that open out on plains covered with snow falling from a clear sky, chimneys adorned with clocks splitting to serve as doors, and palm-trees growing at the foot of bedsteads for little elephants sitting on shelves to munch on. As to our orchestra that isn't here, we'll miss only its brilliance and tone. The themes for *Ubu* will be performed offstage by various pianos and drums.[78]

Jarry prefaces a play that appears not only absurd, but also stripped-down, reduced to the bare essentials that can stand-in for more extravagant sets, or more robust music. And yet, the description of the cuts (cuts which also include/exclude whole acts) provides a variety of rich images that, would they have been included, seem like Deleuze and Guattari's schizophrenic table, or a shaman's instruments, rather than a traditional mise-en-scène.

If we were to read Jarry's introduction according to Soar's thoughts on the @, then we can see the same spontaneity and "enthusiasm" in this introduction in the typical approach to Twitter. Every idea gets included and broadcast, but without much detail and explanation, spurred by desire and affect rather than careful planning and reason, so that each tweet is a reactionary outburst rather than a thoughtful, full-fledged account. Beyond Twitter, instant and text messaging in general make cuts by adopting short message system acronyms and shorthand. But one aspect of the play that Soar neglects to mention is *Ubu Roi* as a harbinger of the Theatre of the Absurd. If we accept a general definition that posits this movement has having "in common the basic belief that man's life is essentially without meaning or purpose ... that human beings cannot communicate,"[79] which leads to "the futility of existence being conveyed by illogical and meaningless speeches and ultimately by complete silence,"[80] then communication in the Twitter-verse, to Soar at least, seems to be the precursor to "silence." Thus, the @, which seemed like it served a logical function in accounting and email, has become @bsurd thanks to Twitter, at least according to Soar, who feels that Twitter is too individualized, too loud, too messy. As he explains, the original name for Twitter was just "twttr, in evident homage to the first word of *Ubu Roi* ('Merdre!', usually translated as 'Shittr!')."[81] While in email the @ is "all about precision and privacy,"[82] the routing of a message to one user at one Internet domain, Twitter "makes @ a tool for sending a message to an individual … that anyone who chooses to can overhear,"[83] inverting this relationship so that the many can now participate in a message to the one. Soar hears the @ in twitter as moving from a whisper to a shout by users who too freely broadcast their immediate thoughts and actions. Through its abuse in Twitter, Soar argues that the "@ has got out of control."[84]

Soar is thinking of communication in an instrumental way, a way that is not necessary for networks to form, for delivery to occur. The @ is @bsurd, but not because the r@te at which it is used, but the holes that it opens for desire to link with, for affect to flow. The @ isn't so much the signifier of all these potential meanings (although, of course, it could serve that function just as any symbol) but rather the link that makes such meanings and @ssemblages possible. The @ is the point of attachment, and like other tails, the t@il provides multiple uses, functionally and aesthetically, whether used for private messages via email, or broadcasts via other outlets. But in either case, the @ provides this outlet, not just computationally, but psychically and affectively as well. The t@il provides the potential for rebirth into any desirous avatar one pleases, so that in cyberspace or cyberspace everted, we are delivered into the world tail first, even in the simplest form of email, where the @ appears on the tail-end of our usernames, opening a wormhole for telepresence.[85] Through this hole—the @ referred to by Ulmer's theory of the object @—we are offered rebirth—several times over—and we are reborn through our tail. This tail of the @, the *Klammeraffe*, grasps the unconscious hole in the middle, providing a shield to hide the hole in the "a," but also to offer a secret point of entry, a cyclical maze or crypt-like structure that opens the possibility for discovery. Or, if a gr@y spot, a secret point of escape after the tail has created the pathway. The process of attaching a prosthetic t@il does not involve starting at the hole, but with the t@il itself, working toward the unexpressible, working down via *hypokrisis*.

McLuhan's quote at the beginning of this chapter is not meant to suggest a technological determinism regarding the t@il, but instead prompt questions of how the psychic and social complex responds to having a t@il, and what delivery practices might develop around this posthuman feature that integrates one with the machine at the symbolic level. Having a t@il can be good or bad, depending on how we use it and the kinds of gestures made with it. The conversation about this use has barely begun, regarding both the history of the @ itself, and how we have built practices around its use, transforming it from writing to print to screen. As Neil Verma observes:

> Notice that @ begins as a unit of denomination (*x* @'s of wine), then becomes an operator indicating a relationship *between* denominations (*x* casks of wine @ *y* euros). Then, notice that @ simulates the image of a person in a physical location (so-and-so@someplace), then it *conflates* place and person (@so-and-so-*as*-someplace).

While these two lines of etymological evolution seem separate, they obey a homologous principle. In both cases, the *arobase* gradually refuses to designate objects or to coordinate them between one another—instead, it wants to *transform* objects. Thus, the mystical character of the glyph lies less in its prodigiously engorged organ of meaning than in the promethean transformations undergone within its coil.[86]

Verma—perhaps unwittingly—suggests that while we have transformed the @, it has a certain agency as well, transforming both itself and those who use it. Because such agency and transformation is undertheorized, perhaps we have not sufficiently considered the potential (dangers) of the @. If we have created a t@il for ourselves, or if that t@il has grafted itself onto our human posts, then we might further consider how this occurs, why we construct such t@ils, and what they offer our posthuman beings, in whichever way one considers such a being. For while the @ provides an aesthetic symbol that transcends its simple function as code, the birds in Klee's *Twittering Machine* have become ensnared with the machine's hand crank, and Père Ubu's bloated gut onto which the @ is inscribed suggests the symbol's nasty *hypokritical* underside (which may, in fact, be our own), one we need to learn how to reason with and deliver from underneath.

Teleporting an Unknown State: Invisible Subjects, Invisible Audiences

Through his artistic gestures, Eduardo Kac assembles in a more material way the construct of a delivery-machine. In *Time Capsule* (1997), he was the first human to implant a microchip into his own body, literally putting information under his skin. The location was meant to further implant affective responses as Kac chose to embed the chip into his left ankle, an area of the body where slaves were typically branded. In more ways than one, Kac created his own digital brand, a branding reminiscent of his Jewish ancestry and the tattoo serialization and processing by the Nazis. After implanting the chip, he entered himself into the animal surveillance database (the typical use for such microchips) and recorded his tracking information, listing himself as both animal and owner. However, the implantation of memory has other implications for both digital delivery and digital memory. Kac explains that in 1997, after the "digital revolution" which saw the "rise of cell phones ... the popularization of the digital networks,"[87] things were beginning to move into a "post-digital paradigm,"[88] which also corresponded to a "cultural shift ... in relation to memory." The chip implantation was an attempt to work with memory, those "we inherited from the past, but also projected it into the future."[89] After loading some sepia tone photographs of his family onto the chip, Kac self-implanted the chip into his leg with a live feed broadcasting to both television and the Internet.

So what's the relationship between these two elements? One is the memory of the past that gets externalized and through a slow process of identity formation, cultural debate, you internalize those memories. On the other hand, and quite literally, on the hand, I had the microchip. In a few seconds, with no historical context, with no tradition, with no identity formation, with nothing, with just a gesture of injection ... boom, the microchip goes into the body. It's a memory microchip, it's a microchip that stores memories, digital information. So, what's the relationship between the complex, subjective, processural, internalization of those photographs and the abrupt internalization of digital memory? And the body, in this case my body, becomes the interface where these two questions come together.[90]

Simply, the microchip contains digital information and serves as a prosthetic for memory. However, Kac and his body play a shamanic role in how the questions raised by this prosthesis rise to the surface as the memory chip becomes implanted beneath. From the perspective of grammatology in general and electracy in particular, Kac expresses the need to develop the practices, identities, and institutions that circulate around the technology and effects of digital technologies. Through the integration of a machine, Kac combines digital and biological codes, and can now use both to store information. In this case, memory, as an idea, helps to facilitate Kac's delivery, but delivery is also used to deliver, quite literally, memory. Kac engages directly in *hypokrisis*, for he puts a kind of knowing underneath the skin using a hypodermic syringe, with the gesture revealing unexplored sensations in reaction to the gesture. These are memories he cannot access directly; he requires another machine, a scanning device, to read the chip's buried, digital codes.

By integrating these various codes, Kac has developed an aesthetic logic of the bite within digital media throughout his many artworks. Whether he tears away the genes of one animal and puts them in another, or takes a bit(e) from one digital code and implants it into himself, he becomes a digital shaman that does for digital codes what the traditional shaman did for her own community. Toward a biological form of networking, he often mixes the codes that drive various bodies. If Kac has a totem animal, it would have to be from his most famous bioartwork, *GFP Bunny* (aka Alba), a rabbit who's DNA he crossed with a bioluminescent jellyfish. Under a black light, Alba glows in a fluorescent green, and is the first larger mammalian animal to undergo transgenic modification. In almost a literal cut-and-paste way, Kac combined different genes, different bits of information, to deliver a new creature. In many ways, Kac out shamans the shamans, by taking certain "spirits" from other animals (the spirit that gives the jellyfish the power to glow) and giving it to another. In doing so, Kac makes the invisible spirit visible within a different context. But whereas he delivers one bit of code into another body, himself the medium that facilitates that exchange, he also unconceals the cultural and psychological anxieties that this kind of practice often induces, bringing to the surface fears of mutants and monsters run amok. In a very material way, Kac delivers the unconscious, an unconscious that glows in the dark, but is otherwise invisible within the "illuminated" light of consciousness.

Kac also shows us one way in which we might perform the delivery technique of the gesture through digital technologies. He often describes his art works and practices as a form of gesture, and while his metaphor derives from painting, the tele-nature of his works, that they can themselves gesture, offers broader possibilities (if the artistic gesture were not enough). In answering a question about his creation of new life, of making the chimeras of legends become reality, Kac responds and shows that the gesture opens questions rather than closing off possibilities. In equating asking a question with making a gesture, he states: "I say gesture like a painter would make a gesture on a canvas that expresses an idea. In my case it's a physical as well as a psychological gesture."[91] Whereas commercial art, such as advertisements, gestures to close decision making, offering a pre-made solution, Kac's art (as art does in general) gestures to open it again, not only at the level of the individual, but also the collective. In other words, rather than being persuasive toward a particular outcome, Kac attempts to provide more options, echoing Rice's decision-making strategy of satisficing to deliver a kind of creativity that fosters creative delivery.

But no matter how Kac "gestures," he does so to facilitate delivery rhetorically, as rhetoricians might understand it, but which he discusses in terms of communication, a vague term but one used in a specific way. Kac's notion of communication doesn't simply revolve around a one-way communication—the way that mass media typically operates, and the direction of a spirit-human relationship without the powers of a shaman—but is always dialogical. Kac reveals that his interest in networked art, art that can communicate, is mystorical, grounded in his own shamanic initiation (but without the skin flailing), particularly through conversations with his grandmother who would create a dialogue and explain to him blind obedience vs. dialogic communication, prompting him to become "interested in Bouber and Bahktin and other philosophers who also dealt with philosophy of dialogue. And, many years later, without thinking about it ... I started to work with communication as the core aesthetic element of my work."[92]

This dialogue, this communication, isn't meant to *persuade* someone of one's own point of view (necessarily) but to *understand* the other's point of view, to, as Kac says, transport one into another's mind, "to be able to transport myself to another space, to another time ... to be able to enter that world and have different feelings."[93] The shaman's spirit leaves his body and travels to other realms, to gain knowledge of other's situations, and thus one's own—and one's community's—situation. The shaman wayfares, networks. This kind of content delivery becomes an auto-delivery, but, ideally, for both (all) parties involved. It is not just a question of making something appear to the eye, but to create the "feeling" that exists between the gaps of space and time. The shaman's spirits exist in the same time, and the same place, yet are invisible. Kac's grandmother experienced events in a different space and time, but yet can be felt by Kac because of the empathy, or the telepathos, that he was able to create. This telepathos, a networked *pathos*, resembles Guattari's pathic logic, "which is the sort operating in group subjects,"[94] to cluster an audience and think through/with the cluster's pathic elements. What Kac attempts to do is to create a system, a practice for making that telepathos function as a logic system, and what Kac tries to deliver via this logic are those spirits that lie within our unconscious: "More than making visible the invisible, art needs to raise our awareness of what firmly remains beyond our visual reach but, nonetheless, affects us directly."[95]

Kac's work achieves this through its digital coding, but not in a computational mode. Rather, the coding Kac uses enacts a feedback loop, a dialogue, between the artwork and the audience, so that the coding of the audience becomes a coding of the artwork, and vice versa. Cary Wolfe points out that "Wieczorek finds a precursor to this new work of Kac's that links the parallels between art and scientific theory in minimalism, with its 'potentially endless sequence of repeated shapes,'"[96] as well as minimalistic interaction with the viewer, which creates "ever-shifting viewpoints over time, through a kind of feedback loop."[97] Wolfe argues that these feedback loops resemble "a similar emphasis in systems theory … on the autopoiesis … of the observing system"[98] which Wolfe claims "Kac's work insist[s] on again and again, most obviously in his inclusion in the work itself of remote, Internet-based observer-participants."[99] Rather than become a regressive reflexity, which is Wieczorek's perspective, Wolfe thinks of this observer/participant interaction as "*recursive*—it uses its own outputs as inputs, as Luhmann defines it. It is only on the basis of that recursivity—a dynamic process that takes *time*—that reflexivity becomes *productive* and not an endlessly repeating, proverbial hall of mirrors associated with the most clichéd aspects of postmodernity."[100] It is this process, this repetition that provides a salient aspect of delivery, and it has already been established once by the shaman's drum. This dialogue, communication, feedback loop—however you name it—all require a rhythm, a regular—but discontinuous—beat which provides the loop along which feedback may travel, so that the byte taken may be regurgitated and fedforward down the line: communication is a biting together, sharing a meal. In some ways, this trajectory resembles Ridolfo and DeVoss's concept of rhetorical velocity. However, this velocity requires rhythm, not to become the "hall of mirrors," but to become recursive, revisable, and eventually deliverable. The only snag, as Wolfe says, is that this often "takes time." Delivery, also, takes time. This is time that Ulmer, through his admonition against the general accident of the Internet, has already made clear we don't have.[101] Although velocity is simply speed with direction, we need to make sure that the speed is that of a flash, Ulmer's *reasoneon*, and that an electrate delivery is an instant one.

Kac's work bypasses the delay in traditional delivery by harnessing the speed and ubiquity of digital networks and creating conversations that could not occur across space otherwise. In his work *Essay Concerning Human Understanding* (1994), Kac uses a simple phone line to link a canary and a plant six-hundred miles apart, showing "our own longing for interaction, our desire to reach out and stay in touch."[102] By observing the plant or the bird, the audience changes each species' behavior and thus the conversation. However, Kac's Web-based installations afford the audience even more direct participation. In *Teleporting an Unknown State* (1994–1996), Kac "combined biological growth with (remote) Internet activity"[103] by placing a seed and substrate in a dark room and making the audience responsible for giving the seed light for development: "Remote individuals responded to email announcements and sent light via the Internet to enable this seed to photosynthesize and grow in total darkness. The installation created the experience of the Internet as a life-supporting system."[104] By pointing their digital cameras to the sky, these remote individuals caused light to shine down from a projector onto the plant. As feedback, the "slow process of growth of the plant was transmitted live to the world via the Internet as long as the exhibition was up. All participants were able to see the process of growth via the Internet."[105] This piece reverses, in many ways, the typical direction of delivery, or if not reverse, at least recycles. Instead of the artist/ installation delivering a message, it requires the audience to make the delivery instead. Or, rather, the artwork demonstrates the larger circulation, the larger ecology necessary for delivery, but in doing so, focuses on the audience's responsibility in the process. For if the audience does not answer the call, does not participate, then the plant dies and all delivery stops. According to Kac,

> The poetics of this piece's network topology operated a dramatic reversal of the regulated unidirectional model imposed by broadcasting standards and the communications industry. Rather than transmitting a specific message from one point to many passive receivers, *Teleporting an Unknown State* created a new situation in which several individuals in remote countries transmitted light to a single point in the Contemporary Art Center, in New Orleans. The ethics of Internet ecology and network community were made evident in a distributed and collaborative effort.[106]

Demosthenes did not deliver in the mode of broadcasting, but relied upon his own kind of ecology of the assembly, and required his audience's participation. However, he was still responsible for delivering his argument and making his audience aware. Kac shows us that while the deliverer might set up a delivery-machine, the audience must, at least in some part, become responsible for the rest of delivery. The trick for the deliverer, then, is to deliver the desire that makes the audience willing and wanting, the problem noticed by Jones with QR codes in the previous chapter. The unknown state that becomes teleported is not the state of the seed, but the unknown state of unconsciousness that influences participation.

Kac's *Genesis* project (1998–1999) extends this audience participation through a piece that not only becomes networked, but also incorporates his interest in transgenic art. Kac's creation of the installation shows how the Internet becomes a thinking prosthesis and an aid for making art. Kac took a Biblical verse from the book of *Genesis* ("Let man have dominion over the fish of the sea, and over the fowl of the air, and over every living thing that moves upon the earth") and converted it into Morse code. Because he did not own a Bible, he copied the text from an edition on the Internet, integrating hypertext from the start of the project. Kac also "used a Web site to create the Morse translation."[107] Kac created his own conversion from Morse to the four nucleobases of DNA—cytosine (DOT), thymine (DASH), guanine (LETTER SPACE), and adenine (WORD SPACE)—and sent his DNA sequence to a company that synthesizes DNA. After he received the DNA, Kac inserted the gene into its context: "The context of the gene is the body of an organism, and the context of the organism is its environment. In the case of my *Genesis*, the organisms are bacteria … and their environment is at once their dish, the gallery, and the Internet."[108] To network the bacteria, Kac placed a microvideo camera and a UV lightbox above the Petri dish, which housed the bacteria. As the bacteria grow and reproduce, "Remote participants on the Web interfere with the process by turning the UV light on … The energy impact of the UV light on the bacteria is such that it disrupts the *Genesis* DNA sequence, accelerating the mutation rate."[109] The Web participants directly change the content of the exhibit, and participate in how the art delivers. Kac, again, describes this process as a gesture: "In the context of the work, the ability to change the sentence is a symbolic gesture: it means that we do not accept its meaning in the form we inherited it and that new meanings emerge as we seek to change it."[110] The audience participates in the art work by performing a gesture that creates mutation, and this gesture is "the smallest gesture of the on-line world—the click."[111] In a feedback loop, the interaction between installation and audience demonstrates an attitude by the audience to the meaning of the Biblical scripture:

> To click or not to click is not only an ethical decision but also a symbolic one. If the participant does not click, he allows the Biblical sentence to remain intact, preserving its meaning of dominion. If he clicks, he changes the sentence and its meaning but does not know what new versions might emerge. In either case, the participant faces an ethical dilemma and is implicated in the process.[112]

W. J. T. Mitchell heeds caution regarding this kind of participation, and writes of Kac's work that "Perhaps the most disturbing and provocative sort of biocybernetic art, however, is work that does not attempt to represent the genetic revolution, but to participate in it."[113] This participation, which can seem unethical and grotesque to some, is precisely the kind of delivery necessary for an audience which cannot always be seen. The major point is not that the artist participates in debate, and creates art that participates in the debate (Kac makes his own spirits), but that the art installations require the audience to participate, making them, in part, responsible for delivery.

Mitchell points out a potential problem with a delivery method based on Kac's works: "Kac's work dramatizes the difficulty biocybernetic art has in making its object or model visible. In looking at the *Genesis* installation, or hearing about the synthetic rabbit, one takes it on faith that the work exists and is doing what it is reported to be doing. There is, in a very real sense, nothing to see in the work, only documents, gadgets, black boxes, and rumors of mutations and monsters."[114] But this, of course, is no different than a classical notion of delivery, or any kind of cognitive research of writing, where the "mind" of the audience cannot be represented as anything other than a black box, and measurements can only come from later actions (be it responses or writing practices).[115] That is, although delivery may be real, it mostly works in the virtual. "Affect, we learn, is a virtual experience ... it is a potential, a nonfixed intensity that moves as soon as it occurs."[116] Even though medical instruments afford us the ability to see what regions of the brain might be at work when the subject is writing/reading/listening/communicating, this still does not tell us exactly what happens in the mind when one engages in these activities. The body as a black box, that the deliverer cannot know what his audience is feeling or experiencing during delivery, only shows to what extent an audience's body is a BwO onto which the deliverer must attune and attach, or depending on the method, provide machines that the audience attaches to themselves, constantly changing these arrangements to account for the unknowable. This uncertainty of effect/affect has always been a part of rhetoric at all levels, which is why rhetoric is an art. And, as Mitchell goes on,

> Perhaps this is the point ... The object of mimesis here is really the invisibility of the genetic revolution, its inaccessibility to representation. The real subject matter, then, becomes the idea of the work and the critical debate that surrounds it as much as its material realization. In response to the predictable objection that the work is a kind of irresponsible "playing" with genetic technologies, Kac's equally predictable response is that purposeless play is at the heart of the aesthetic gesture as such.[117]

In this play, Kac's work takes on another meaning of delivery, that of giving birth to a new species that has become genetically modified. Such mixing of codes provides new kinds of beings, new ways of becoming that did not exist before. Rhetorically, the act of delivery offered the same potential to the Greeks, for as an orator made his case, and mixed affect with *logos* in different quantities, the collective experience of the speaker/audience birthed a response to a choice—they chose one solution among many to solve a particular problem. They chose a particular way of being in the world. Delivery becomes becoming, and leads toward this being. In a delivery-network, however, decision making is all becoming. Kac's work allows the invisible to become visible, and produces debate about questions and problems that did not exist before the gesture was made. Kac's work delivers both the problem, as well as a way for the audience to participate in the debate about the problem. In other words, Kac's works spur invention at the group level, which is nothing other than delivery.

Notes

1. Marshall McLuhan, *Understanding Media: The Extensions of Man* (Cambridge, MA: MIT Press, 1994), 4.
2. James Elkins, *The Object Stares Back: On the Nature of Seeing* (New York: Harcourt, 1996), 135.
3. Cicero, *On the Ideal Orator (De Oratore)*, trans. James M. May and Jakob Wisse (New York: Oxford University Press, 2001), II.188.
4. Gregory S. Aldrete, *Gestures and Acclamations in Ancient Rome* (Baltimore, MD: Johns Hopkins University Press, 1999), 15.
5. Ibid., 5.
6. *Oxford English Dictionary*, 2nd ed., s.v. "Gesture."
7. Ibid.
8. Cicero, *De Oratore*, III.216.
9. Although, given the *hypokritical* nature of delivery, the orator also plays someone else, or, looks like they're playing themselves while playing someone else (i.e., acting).
10. Cicero, *Brutus, Orator*, trans. G. L. Hendrickson and H. M. Hubbell (Cambridge, MA: Harvard University Press, 1939), 278.
11. Aldrete, 15–17.
12. Ibid., 17.
13. Ibid.
14. Even if the individual technologies change, they all support networking of one form or another.
15. Brian Rotman, *Becoming Beside Ourselves: The Alphabet, Ghosts, and Distributed Human Being* (Durham, NC: Duke University Press, 2008), 103.
16. Walter Ong, *Orality and Literacy: The Technologizing of the Word* (New York: Routledge, 2002), 73.
17. Ibid.
18. Ibid., 74.
19. Ibid.
20. Rotman, 3.
21. Ibid.
22. Elkins, 163.
23. Rotman, 3.
24. Jeff Rice, *Digital Detroit: Rhetoric and Space in the Age of the Network* (Carbondale, IL: Southern Illinois University Press, 2014), 227.

25. Ibid.
26. Ibid., 217.
27. Ibid., 220.
28. Ibid., 217.
29. Ibid., 217.
30. Cary Wolfe, *What is Posthumanism?* (Minneapolis, MN: University of Minnesota Press, 2010), xi.
31. Ibid., xv; emphasis in original.
32. Sidney I. Dobrin, *Postcomposition* (Carbondale, IL: Southern Illinois University Press, 2011), 66.
33. N. Katherine Hayles, *How We Became Posthuman: Virtual Bodies in Cybernetics, Literature, and Informatics* (Chicago, IL: University of Chicago Press, 1999), 286.
34. This section was previously published by the author as the essay "Becoming T@iled" From *Writing Posthumanism, Posthuman Writing* (c) 2015 by Parlor Press. Used by permission.
35. N. Katherine Hayles, *My Mother Was a Computer: Digital Subjects and Literary Texts* (Chicago, IL: University of Chicago Press, 2005), 1.
36. Whit Gibbons, "All Reptiles Have Tails with Many Uses for Them," *Aiken Standard*, March 6, 2010, accessed April 16, 2014, http://www.aikenstandard.com/article/20100306/AIK0101/303069991.
37. In the sense that "cybernetics" derives from the Greek word for "steersman," the tail provides a cybernetic function.
38. Gregory L. Ulmer, *Internet Invention: From Literacy to Electracy* (New York: Longman, 2002), 299.
39. The use of "t@il" is meant to show the connected nature of the "tail" with "tale," but also its connection with networked ways of tailing/telling. Any other words with @ embedded within are similarly meant to convey a networked sense of the word, as well as all the other senses of @ as theorized in this book. Similarly, although the usage of @ will at times refer to the "at-sign" properly, it should not always be "heard" as "at," but sometimes an unpronounceable symbol to be "seen" rather than "said."
40. From an interview with Brandon Keim, "Your Computer is a Part of You," *Wired*, March 9, 2010, accessed July 18, 2015, http://www.wired.com/2010/03/heidegger-tools/; also, see Dobromir G. Dotov, Lin Nie, and Anthony Chemero, "A Demonstration of the Transition from Ready-to-Hand to Unready-to-Hand," *PLoS ONE* 5.3 (2010): doi: 10.1371/journal.pone.0009433.
41. Ibid.
42. Berthold L. Ullman, *Ancient Writing and Its Influence* (Toronto: University of Toronto Press, 1980), 187.
43. Tony Long, "May 4, 1536: C U @ the Piazza," *Wired*, May 4, 2009, accessed September 20, 2011, http://www.wired.com/2009/05/dayintech_0504/; also see Giorgio Stabile, "L'icon@ dei mercanti," Trecanni.it. Rome: Istituto della Enciclopedia Italiana, 2005, accessed September 20, 2011, http://web.archive.org/web/20080609015621/http://www.treccani.it/iniziative/eventi_icona.htm.
44. In a personal communication with the author, Rui Coelho and Joana Fernandez de Carvalho, Portuguese ichthyologists formerly at the Florida Museum of Natural History, stated that the term *arroba* now refers to the @ in Portuguese vernacular.

45. Karen S. Chung, "Summary: The @ symbol," *The Linguist List*, Ypsilanti, Michigan: Institute for Language Information and Technology, July 2, 1996, accessed September 20, 2011, https://linguistlist.org/issues/7/7-968.html.

46. Quoted in Alice Rawsthorn, "Why @ Is Held in Such High Design Esteem," *The New York Times on the Web*, New York Times, March 21, 2010, accessed September 20, 2011, http://www.nytimes.com/2010/03/22/arts/design/22iht-design22.html.

47. Ibid.

48. Ibid.

49. Ibid.

50. Ibid.

51. Ibid.

52. *Oxford English Dictionary*, 2nd ed., s.v. "Twitter, v.1."

53. *Oxford English Dictionary*, 2nd ed., s.v. "Twitter, v.2."

54. *Oxford English Dictionary*, 2nd ed., s.v. "Twitter, n.1."

55. *Oxford English Dictionary*, 2nd ed., s.v. "Twitter, n.3.c."

56. Given the many *twitters* that many celebrity Twitter users and others find themselves in after an ill-advised tweet, we might also consider the sn@res that one's t@il might get caught in.

57. Gilles Deleuze and Félix Guattari, *A Thousand Plateaus: Capitalism and Schizophrenia*, trans. Brian Massumi (Minneapolis, MN: University of Minnesota Press, 1987), 164.

58. Gregory L. Ulmer, *Avatar Emergency* (Anderson, SC: Parlor Press, 2012), 171.

59. "Black hole" is another one of @'s many epithets.

60. Deleuze and Guattari, 312.

61. Gregory L. Ulmer, "Corridor Window @ Shands Hospital," *Heuretics: Inventing Electracy*, June 2, 2008, accessed February 20, 2010, https://heuretics.wordpress.com/2008/06/02/corridor-window-shands-hospital.

62. *Avatar*, DVD, directed by James Cameron (2009; Los Angeles, CA: Twentieth Century Fox, 2012).

63. Gregory L. Ulmer, "Avatar," *Heuretics: Inventing Electracy*, December 1, 2008, accessed February 20, 2010, https://heuretics.wordpress.com/avatar-2.

64. Ibid.

65. Ibid.

66. Ibid.

67. If we use the full Sanskrit version, avatara, then the tail letter becomes another t@il: @v@t@r@.

68. Chris Anderson, *The Long Tail: Why the Future of Business Is Selling Less of More* (New York: Hyperion, 2006), 5.

69. Ibid.

70. Ibid., 9.

71. Ibid., 6.

72. Ibid., 22–23.

73. Daniel Soar, "Short Cuts," *London Review of Books* 31, no. 10 (2009): 18.

74. Ibid.

75. Ibid.

76. Ibid.

77. Alfred Jarry, *Ubu Roi*, trans. Beverly Keith and Gershon Legman (Mineola, NY: Dover, 2003), 1–2.

78. Ibid., 2–3.
79. "Absurd, Theatre of the," Phyllis Hartnoll and Peter Found, eds., *The Concise Oxford Companion to the Theatre* (Oxford, UK: Oxford University Press, 1996).
80. Ibid.
81. Soar.
82. Ibid.
83. Ibid.
84. Ibid.
85. "Wormhole" is yet another one of @'s many epithets.
86. Neil Verma, "Glyphs Gone Wild," quoted in Sean Morey, "Becoming T@iled," *Writing Posthumanism, Posthuman Writing*, ed. Sidney I. Dobrin (Anderson, SC: Parlor Press, 2015), 150–151; emphasis in original.
87. "One on One – Eduardo Kac – 23 Feb 08 – Part 1," YouTube video, 11:44, posted by "Al Jazeera English," February 17, 2008, https://www.youtube.com/watch?v=evxlR3zJ11o.
88. Ibid.
89. Ibid.
90. Ibid.
91. "One on One – Eduardo Kac – 23 Feb 08 – Part 2," YouTube video, 10:25, posted by "Al Jazeera English," February 17, 2008, https://www.youtube.com/watch?v=T6Y48s8edsE.
92. "One on One – Eduardo Kac – 23 Feb 08 – Part 1."
93. Ibid.
94. Gregory L. Ulmer, *Electronic Monuments* (Minneapolis, MN: University of Minnesota Press, 2005), 16.
95. Eduardo Kac, *Telepresence and Bio Art: Networking Humans, Rabbits, and Robots* (Ann Arbor, MI: University of Michigan Press, 2005), 236.
96. Wolfe, 161.
97. Marek Wieczorek, "Playing with Life: Art and Human Genomics," *Art Journal* 59, no. 3 (Fall 2000): 59.
98. Wolfe, 161.
99. Ibid.
100. Wolfe, 161–162; emphasis in original.
101. Gregory L. Ulmer, *Avatar Emergency*, ix.
102. Kac, 219.
103. Ibid., 221.
104. Ibid., 223.
105. Ibid.
106. Ibid., 223–224.
107. Ibid., 251.
108. Ibid.
109. Ibid.
110. Ibid., 251–252.
111. Ibid., 252.
112. Ibid.
113. W. J. T. Mitchell, "The Work of Art in the Age of Biocybernetic Reproduction," *Modernism/Modernity* 10, no. 3 (2003): 494.
114. Ibid., 495.

115. The black box also becomes a metaphor for memory, specifically "accurate" and "truthful" memory such as that which comes from the "black box" of an airplane. This information records the memory of a crash or other incident that in turn becomes a post-traumatic delivery-machine.
116. Rice, 137.
117. Mitchell, 495.

Bibliography

"Absurd, Theatre of the." *The Concise Oxford Companion to the Theatre.* Edited by Phyllis Hartnoll and Peter Found. Oxford, UK: Oxford University Press, 1996.

Aldrete, Gregory S. *Gestures and Acclamations in Ancient Rome.* Baltimore, MD: Johns Hopkins University Press, 1999.

Anderson, Chris. *The Long Tail: Why the Future of Business Is Selling Less of More.* New York: Hyperion, 2006. Print.

Chung, Karen S. "Summary: The @ symbol." *The Linguist List.* Ypsilanti, Michigan: Institute for Language Information and Technology. July 2, 1996. Accessed September 20, 2011. https://linguistlist.org/issues/7/7–968.html.

Cicero. *Brutus. Orator.* Translated by G. L. Hendrickson, H. M. Hubbell. Cambridge, MA: Harvard University Press, 1939.

———. *On the Ideal Orator (De Oratore).* Translated by James M. May and Jakob Wisse. New York: Oxford University Press, 2001.

Deleuze, Gilles and Félix Guattari. *A Thousand Plateaus: Capitalism and Schizophrenia.* Translated by Brian Massumi. Minneapolis, MN: University of Minnesota Press, 1987.

Dobrin, Sidney I. *Postcomposition.* Carbondale, IL: Southern Illinois University Press, 2011.

Elkins, James. *The Object Stares Back: On the Nature of Seeing.* New York: Harcourt, 1996.

Gibbons, Whit. "All Reptiles Have Tails with Many Uses for Them." *Aiken Standard.* March 6, 2010. Accessed April 16, 2014. http://www.aikenstandard.com/article/20100306/AIK0101/303069991.

Hayles, N. Katherine. *How We Became Posthuman: Virtual Bodies in Cybernetics, Literature, and Informatics.* Chicago, IL: University of Chicago Press, 1999.

———. *My Mother Was a Computer: Digital Subjects and Literary Texts.* Chicago, IL: University of Chicago Press, 2005.

Jarry, Alfred. *Ubu Roi.* Translated by Beverly Keith and Gershon Legman. Mineola, NY: Dover, 2003.

Kac, Eduardo. *Telepresence and Bio Art: Networking Humans, Rabbits, and Robots.* Ann Arbor, MI: University of Michigan Press, 2005.

Keim, Brandon. "Your Computer is a Part of You." *Wired,* March 9, 2010. Accessed July 18, 2015. http://www.wired.com/2010/03/heidegger-tools.

Long, Tony. "May 4, 1536: C U @ the Piazza." *Wired.* May 4, 2009. Accessed September 20, 2011. http://www.wired.com/2009/05/dayintech_0504/.

McLuhan, Marshall. *Understanding Media: The Extensions of Man.* Cambridge, MA: MIT Press, 1994.

Mitchell, W. J. T. "The Work of Art in the Age of Biocybernetic Reproduction." *Modernism/Modernity* 10, no. 3 (2003): 481–500.

Morey, Sean. "Becoming T@iled." *Writing Posthumanism, Posthuman Writing*, ed. Sidney I. Dobrin, 133–154. Anderson, SC: Parlor Press, 2015.

"One on One – Eduardo Kac – 23 Feb 08 – Part 1." YouTube video, 11:44. Posted by "Al Jazeera English," February 17, 2008. https://www.youtube.com/watch?v=evxlR3zJ11o.

"One on One – Eduardo Kac – 23 Feb 08 – Part 2." YouTube video, 10:25. Posted by "Al Jazeera English," February 17, 2008. https://www.youtube.com/watch?v=T6Y48s8edsE.

Ong, Walter. *Orality and Literacy: The Technologizing of the Word*. New York: Routledge, 2002.

Rawsthorn, Alice. "Why @ Is Held in Such High Design Esteem." *The New York Times on the Web*. New York Times. March 21, 2010. Accessed September 20, 2011. http://www.nytimes.com/2010/03/22/arts/design/22iht-design22.html.

Rice, Jeff. *Digital Detroit: Rhetoric and Space in the Age of the Network*. Carbondale, IL: Southern Illinois University Press, 2014.

Rotman, Brian. *Becoming Beside Ourselves: The Alphabet, Ghosts, and Distributed Human Being*. Durham, NC: Duke University Press, 2008.

Soar, Daniel. "Short Cuts." *London Review of Books* 31, no. 10 (2009): 18.

Stabile, Giorgio. "L'icon@ dei mercanti." Trecanni.it. Rome: Istituto della Enciclopedia Italiana. 2005. Accessed September 20, 2011. http://web.archive.org/web/20080609015621/http://www.treccani.it/iniziative/eventi_icona.htm.

Ullman, Barthold Louis. *Ancient Writing and Its Influence*. Toronto: University of Toronto Press, 1980.

Ulmer, Gregory L. "Avatar." *Heuretics: Inventing Electracy*. December 1, 2008. Accessed February 20, 2010. https://heuretics.wordpress.com/avatar-2.

———. *Avatar Emergency*. Anderson, SC: Parlor Press, 2012.

———. "Corridor Window @ Shands Hospital." *Heuretics: Inventing Electracy*. June 2, 2008. Accessed February 20, 2010. https://heuretics.wordpress.com/2008/06/02/corridor-window-shands-hospital.

———. *Electronic Monuments*. Minneapolis, MN: University of Minnesota Press, 2005.

———. *Internet Invention: From Literacy to Electracy*. New York: Longman, 2002.

Wieczorek, Marek. "Playing with Life: Art and Human Genomics." *Art Journal 59*, no. 3 (Fall 2000): 59–60.

Wolfe, Cary. *What is Posthumanism?* Minneapolis, MN: University of Minnesota Press, 2010.

Postscript
The Death of Delivery (and Other Transitions)

Ends and deaths are merely moments of new formations, hybrids, and mutations. One category may appear to end, but its components move on in new formations.

—Sidney I. Dobrin, *Postcomposition*[1]

Wanted—young, skinny, wiry fellows, not over eighteen. Must be expert riders, willing to risk death daily. Orphans preferred.

—California newspaper help-wanted ad for the Pony Express, 1860[2]

The best moments can't be preconceived. I've spent a lot of time in editing rooms, and a scene can be technically perfect, with perfect delivery and facial expression and timing, and you remember all your lines, and it is dead. When you're feeling something, dialogue is irrelevant.

—Brad Pitt[3]

Having run from the Battle of Marathon to Athens, 26.2 miles, to tell the Athenians of the victory over the Persians, Pheidippides delivered his message—*nikomen* ("we have won")—and collapsed in death. Pheidippides was a *hemerodrome*, a kind of herald translated as "day-runner"[4] or "professional-running courier."[5] As a professional deliverer, his body was well-conditioned to make the run, as he had previously covered 150 miles from Athens to Sparta, in two days, to request aid for the battle. Given some dispute between accounts (if any are true), it was probably this longer distance, although still manageable, as the more likely factor that contributed to Pheidippides's mythic death.

Regardless of whether such stories are truth or fiction, delivery and death have always run together, from cradle to grave, delivery to deliverance. Delivery is dangerous, even for those who do it in a "safe" environment, for if the wrong tune is struck with an audience, disaster can occur. Failure to deliver has consequences, and delivery is dangerous no matter the technology. As Dennis Baron writes, "Communication technology, while generally less dangerous than other sorts of technological development (enriched uranium, asbestos, the automobile), always brings with it a certain amount of risk."[6] To rephrase Virilio, when we invent the delivery technology, we invent the delivery accident. Considering phones, for example, Baron notes that Hitchcock's *Dial M for Murder* (1954) "may be the most famous fictional example of a telephone triggering a death ... but more recently we've seen that real-life terrorists who prefer not to martyr themselves can use cell phones to set off the bombs they leave by the roadside, at the mall, or on a crowded bus."[7] We also witness death from talking or texting on smart phones, and can only imagine what other dangers might develop from emerging and everting networked technologies, including smart environments and the Internet of Things.

Besides Pheidippides as dead-man-delivering, we have to include Demosthenes and conclude with the denouement of the film. Through his engagement with Philip of Macedonia and a whole network of connections and storylines that are actually too complex to depict in a film, Demosthenes made a few fatal enemies and ends up in exile in the Temple of Poseidon on the island of Calaueria after Athens engages with and loses a brief war with Macedon, which he supported. Suffice to say, as Phillip Harding writes, "when Demosthenes went down to the underworld, he carried with him some heavy baggage in the form of Aeschines, Harpalus and Philip of Macedon."[8] The final scenes depict Demosthenes escaping Athens to Calaueria, in which he engages with Archias—a former theatrical actor and agent for Antipater, sent to deliver Demosthenes back to Athens for, most likely, his execution. The scene starts with Archias, accompanied by a group of Thracian spearmen, attempting to coax Demosthenes from the Temple of Poseidon. The scene, based on Plutarch's history, unfolds as such:

FADE IN:

EXT. THE TEMPLE OF POSEIDON ON CALAUERIA – EVENING

ARCHIAS and his Thracian SPEARMEN approach, surround, and survey the temple. Archias approaches the altar, but does not cross it.

> ARCHIAS
> Come out Demosthenes. Go back with me to Athens. I promise, you'll suffer no harsh treatment.

DEMOSTHENES appears from the entrance to the temple, straddles the entryway, and calmly addresses Archias.

> DEMOSTHENES
> I chanced to dream strangely last night. We were both acting in a tragedy, *Antigone* I think, competing for a prize. I had won the favor of the audience, who adorned me with the sweetest praise, but yet I had no stage decorations, no costumes, just my bare body and instinct, and so my victory from the jury was lost.

> ARCHIAS
> (sweetly, to garner favor)
> I have no doubt, as you have always been the greatest orator. You should have won with voice alone, if not in dreams, then in life. But come with me, we will go back to Athens, and we can test your dream upon the stage.

DEMOSTHENES

(derisively)

O Archias, you never did convince me by your acting, nor will you now convince me by your promises.

Archias becomes frustrated by Demosthenes's derisive tone, insult, and refusal to cooperate.

ARCHIAS

Damn you Demosthenes, I will cross this altar and bring you out by force!

DEMOSTHENES

Ah. Now you utter the language of the Macedonian oracle, you puppet of Antipater. A moment ago you were acting a part. So be it, hypocrite. But wait one moment, and I will write a final message to my family, which I hope you will deliver to them.

CUT TO:

INT. THE TEMPLE OF POSEIDON – EVENING

With these words, Demosthenes retires into the temple, and taking a scroll, as if about to write, puts his pen to his mouth and bites it, as if he were placing it there while thinking of what to write, a gesture of thought. He keeps it there longer than what would be expected, and then covers his head, huddling over the writing desk. The Thracian spearmen laugh and mock him for this gesture.

CUT TO:

EXT. THE TEMPLE OF POSEIDON – EVENING

SPEARMEN

Look at that weak coward.
Some great statesman.
Who's the real hypocrite, Demosthenes?
Behold the part he plays now!

ARCHIAS

Rise up Demosthenes, please! Come now and they'll be no harm to you. I swear.

CUT TO:

INT. THE TEMPLE OF POSEIDON – EVENING

Demosthenes, now feeling below his skin that the poison he took from the pen is affecting and overpowering him, uncovers his head, turns, and fixes his eyes upon Archias.

CUT TO:

EXT. THE TEMPLE OF POSEIDON – EVENING

Still barely composed, Demosthenes begins to exit the temple, and we seem him appear to Archias, emerging from the entrance toward the altar.

DEMOSTHENES

You now try to play the part of Creon as in our tragedy last night. Do it. Cast this body out without burial. But I, O beloved Poseidon, will depart from your sanctuary while I am still alive; I will not let Antipater and the Macedonians leave your temple defiled.[9]

Plutarch's own summary bests finishes the final directions: "So speaking, and bidding someone support him, since he was now trembling and tottering, he had no sooner gone forth and passed by the altar than he fell, and with a groan gave up the ghost."[10] This death scene depicts some interesting themes this book has been working with: the conflation of acting with delivery, but also the separation of delivery from acting; the difference between *hypokrisis* and a hypocrite; the need for environment and fringe (costume, decorations) when delivering; the transition between one communication apparatus (orality) and another (literacy). Demosthenes offers his last breath not in support of Athenian democracy (a system that requires literacy), which he worked his whole career to sustain, but an older, oral apparatus of religion. He exists and exits in a moment, the transition between orality and literacy, a transition that would last for several hundred years but which is analogized in him taking poison from his pen into his mouth, the killing of one mode of delivery with another.

To a certain extent, Demosthenes overcame his baggage, and was one of the most assigned authors up until the World Wars of the twentieth century. But even this prestige has begun to die out: "among the classical authors Demosthenes has suffered a worse reversal of fortune than most. From being one of the top four and mandatory reading for all students in the field, he has fallen into almost total neglect."[11] Demosthenes is certainly a symbol for delivery, at least oral delivery, and as I hope I have shown, a proto-digital delivery in a certain sense. But he is also a symbol for this relationship between delivery and death.

This relationship, of course, predates Demosthenes. Myths of Hermes depict him as providing important delivery functions via his role as the personal herald of Zeus, a mediator between humans and the gods. But he also oversaw other kinds of delivery, such as animal husbandry, roads, travel, language, writing, translation, animal omens, divination, and dreams. His visage and iconography (winged shoes, winged traveler's cap) are often appropriated into logos for modern delivery companies. Besides being winged, his cap also made him invisible, able to play the unseen spirit that delivered messages to one who seemed to hear voices from thin air.

However, Hermes delivered not only for Zeus, but also for the dead, as he held dual roles of deliverer for the gods and psychopomp, one who delivers departed spirits to the underworld. Hermes is also the god of merchandise (mercury=merchant), and delivery exacts a toll. Certainly, for many Greeks, bribes became a useful way to secure favorable delivery, an image Demosthenes attempted to work against. But in terms of the underworld, when Hermes delivers souls to the River Styx, he delivers them to Charon, the ferryman, who in turn demands coin for delivery to the underworld proper on the other shore. This payment for delivery was important for the ancient Greeks, as David George explains:

> There is no doubt that the ancients took this seriously. Many states had laws that punished people who did not fulfill their duties to bury the dead [and include a coin under the dead's tongue or on the eyelids for Charon's payment]. The family had obligations to make sure that the dead were cut off from this world and sent to the next. Because if they didn't, the dead would be ghosts in this world, and that affected everyone.[12]

Although delivery relies on surfaces (water, bodies, images, pages) it also requires the depth of the underworld, the depth of the ocean (to create surf for Demosthenes), and the depth of the unconscious. The Greeks sought to bury their souls in another realm; the shamans sought to contend with the invisible on an ongoing basis. For a while, digital information was confined to cyberspace, but now these spirits are breaking out, making everyday objects "enchanted." A new delivery is needed to learn how to contend with such a metaphysics.

Death becomes an important moment for delivery to occur, a transitional opportunity for decision making. One of the ways that we deliver from death is through the process of monumentality. The visual structures of mourning provide an official, approved way to consider death, ways that make visible the values that a society recognizes and shares. Whereas traditional monuments have been made of physical structures of stone, metal, and other materials, monumentality can be digital as well, and in the everting network, a hybrid of the two.

Before Gibson implicitly declared the death of cyberspace in *Spook Country*, Ulmer revisits his concept of the MEmorial in *Electronic Monuments*.[13] Much of Ulmer's work—from *Heuretics* through *Internet Invention*, and more recently, *Avatar Emergency*—considers how the structures of networks might be developed into a poetics of invention (heavily relying upon memory). Although he pitches *Electronic Monuments* in a similar way, as a mode to invent solutions toward problem solving and decision making (as Rice later does in *Digital Detroit*), I find this work to also offer a mode of electrate delivery, a method for delivering affective information to a larger group, and then through that networking, a method for making decisions (or at least for becoming aware that a decision needs to be made, or has already been made, prompting a forensic deliberation).

Although Ulmer's other practices—such as the mystory—use the networks formed through personal experience to make individual decisions, electronic monuments tap into the collective unconscious and deliver, *hypokritically*, to both groups and the individual who create them. As Ulmer discusses, underneath the "official" values portrayed by a monument are the abject values that remain in the collective unconscious. The digital Internet provides the possibility for a distributed monumentality that allows for these abject sacrifices to rise to the surface, a type of distributed *hypokrisis*. One no longer has to go to a particular monument, but can access and participate in monuments remotely. Such distributed practices of monumentality affect how we collectively read problems connected to whatever death the memorial is meant to remind us of, whatever memories it is meant to deliver. But besides just electronic networks, electronic monuments link seemingly unrelated databases to enable delivery, allowing sub-surface traces to appear and be read.

In *Teletheory*, Ulmer begins to lay the foundations for the electronic monument (via its other name, MEmorial), particularly its function toward problem solving (or, at least, problem identification). The solution that the electronic monument provides is not instrumental in the typical consulting sense, but instead consults through analogy, particularly the puncept, which has the economy and speed to think within an age of rapid information circulation and accumulation:

> One of the obstacles to problem-solving in the information age is the knowledge explosion itself. We are buried in data which by its sheer quantity impedes comprehension. Moreover, having tended to concentrate more on data processing than on understanding, we are in need of some new ideas (*moiras*). Speed is essential, but not only the algorithmic speed of calculation. The history of invention suggests that however valuable the analytical model may be for exploiting discoveries, the discovery process itself works with the poetic devices of analogy—with the association of elements previously unrelated (as in the surprise editing of the joke).[14]

This information explosion is one of the problems for delivery, not only in the collection of information into databases, of "big data," but also as this information is moving out of database servers into the Internet of Things. Information need not be contained and safely accessed from a computer terminal, but encountered out on the street. While the possibility may have existed for delivery to occur in any location, this is now becoming a probability, especially as delivery can now be instantly *kairotic*, being networked to the very geographical location that demands discussion, nearly instantaneously.

Ulmer claims that the need for this new genre, besides technological, is affective, and related to what I outline in chapter 3. In general, the body has become affectively dumb and requires a new prosthetic in order to combat what he identifies as compassion fatigue. To counter this trend, an electronic monument relies on a performative method, and Ulmer lays out specific instructions for how to construct one's own electronic monument and constructs his own, the Chora Mirror (Upsilon Alarm), a memorial that acknowledges the abject sacrifices made through child abuse that permit the freedom to have and raise one's own children (as opposed to state-controlled child rearing). One of the first steps begins with viewing the spectacle (the general information sphere), but then bringing this information back to the individual level, trying to use it as an irritant under one's own skin (a gesture similar to Kac's). Electronic monuments are not just about the public, but also about oneself—they require auto-delivery. The electronic monument provides an extimate mapping of the world to the viewer, to help make her aware of her particular situation. As an overarching example, and also an example of how a performative memorializing might work, Ulmer notices the news story of Bradley McGee, a two-year-old who was a victim of child abuse when his father "repeatedly rammed [his] head into the toilet like a plunger, angered that the toddler had soiled his pants."[15]

Traditional consulting involves using literate logic to try and solve problems. For instance, given an individual case of child abuse, the state agencies that oversee child protection may attempt to analyze the case and make laws that will prevent this kind of abuse from happening to other children. But this kind of instrumental approach can only work if we allow the state to take complete control of child-rearing so that no possibility exists for parents to mistreat their children. Otherwise, as we continually witness through the media, child abuse will persist. The value of freedom overrides total surveillance as a possibility, and the state is unable to see this as a necessary aporia: "Conventional consultants try to isolate the aberration as exception, unaware of the logic of bare life. They are unable to conceive of America as we-who-abuse-children."[16] Delivery, at an affective level, fails to occur. If we continue to look at problems using literate logic, a blind spot will necessarily persist in our self-knowledge, especially at the level of values. Ulmer writes that we value freedom, and so behave accordingly, not realizing that child abuse is a necessary sacrifice for the part of that freedom which we understand as a parent's right to have and raise children: "until the abuse is acknowledged as the symptom of a value (until it is given the collective recognition as such) there is no hope of altering the behavior."[17] To produce this collective recognition, one filtered through his own experiences, Ulmer constructs the electronic monument as a form of "allegory, a figure of thought. I juxtapose some documents from two domains (my life, public problem), and the human sensorium does the rest. If a correspondence exists, the feeling occurs as an event."[18] Ulmer sorts through a database of affective sensations in order to link different databases and create his own network, a network that may then spread and deliver to others. If Rice attempts to produce a digital Detroit, Ulmer attempts to produce a digital death, which may then be felt, with this feeling delivered and applied through and among networks.

To deliver in this way is to perform the electronic monument, through which the deliverer becomes attuned to the information sphere until she notices a sting, theorized as Roland Barthes's *punctum*, a sensation under the skin. When the deliverer notices this feeling—produced by an image, news story, or other "thing"—the deliverer explores that feeling in order to produce an image category that can capture the mood. In this active exploration, the deliverer is not looking to solve the problem, but to understand her relationship to the problem and how that problem manifests inside of her. Ulmer's slogan for his consulting group, the EmerAgency, is "Problems B Us," which is to say that these problems are internalized in us, they are *hypokritical*. Examining the outside situation can help us understand our own situation and provide necessary self-knowledge from which to participate more intelligently (affectively smart) in public policy. We might identify the middle part of this delivery as invention, or recognize that these distinctions are increasingly dying.

Rather than deliver a sensation via *hypokrisis* into the body, the kind of *hypokrisis* that an electronic monument performs extracts information, affect, from under the skin as it attempts to reveal the blind spot through a connection based on mood. It seeks to extract what has already been placed there. Electronic monuments expose the personal and collective *ATH*, that is, the blindness or foolishness that causes us to behave in a certain way according to certain values.[19] As the example of child abuse shows, society displays "dumbness" about freedom at the level of child rearing. Electronic monuments would help to map this blindness. Because the image stings at the level of emotion, the gathering (Rice's clustering) device that helps to eliminate compassion fatigue is not the literate concept, but mood: "The MEmorial does not define (analyze) the disaster but discovers its mood ... Through attunement the disaster matters to me."[20]

Once this feeling is mapped, the deliverer can plan the delivery-machine, the physical construction of the monument. Because they demonstrate an abject value, electronic monuments should be peripheral monuments to official memorials that portray the professed, conscious values of the society, thereby establishing a connection between the official sacrifices and the abject sacrifices overlooked through their juxtaposition. Ulmer instructs that the electronic monument for Bradley McGee be attached to the *Space Mirror*, which is the Astronaut Memorial at Kennedy Space Center, Florida, since the peripheral nature of the electronic monument must be attached to an established, existing memorial that honors an "acknowledged sacrifice, so that the juxtaposition establishes the public and collective nature of the abject sacrifice."[21] The Space Mirror is a 42.5-foot-high by 50-foot-wide slab of black granite with twenty-one total names engraved, the names of those who have given their lives to space exploration. We acknowledge these sacrifices on behalf of a collective value. However, we don't acknowledge children, such as Bradley McGee, who become sacrificed for other, less explicit values. Ulmer's add-on (networked) Chora Mirror ("an electronic panel substituted for just one of the ninety-three granite panels"[22]) is meant to link these two values, to use the former to illuminate the latter, to allow a bit of its black light to reflect and let the abject be recognized for at least the interval of a solar eclipse, during which the name of one abused child flashes every second for as long as the eclipse lasts, and "while the heroes' names are invisible."[23]

As Craig Stroupe notes, such works participate in the "rhetoric of irritation," the juxtaposition of "'inappropriately' opposed categories into a constitutive whole."[24] Stroupe explains that "Ulmer combines images and words by enacting a dialogue between academic and promotional intentions, a dialogue made possible by his blithely ignoring the appropriate distinctions between their purposes and contexts,"[25] and the combination of these images and words "illustrate and enact the dialogical tug-and-pull between these cultural tensions and identities, words and images essentially riffing off the same theme."[26] One of the logics at play for delivery is a disjuncture between the visual and verbal tracks. If a body in an oral apparatus attempted to sync or coordinate between speech and gestures—the audible and visual tracks—an electrate delivery would attempt to skew these tracks, to put them out of sync and irritate the audience, shock them out of a numb compassion fatigue, to get them to take notice of delivery and participate. Delivery works best with multiple tracks, but an electrate delivery would make their juxtaposition inappropriate. For Ulmer's case, he juxtaposes the values of manifest destiny (applied to space) with child abuse to deliver an alarm, one that, he hopes, will affect public policy by attending to the "details of the conditions sustaining abuse by the promise of divination: the problem explains the consultant ... Problems B Us."[27] As with any kind of divination, the one constructing the electronic monument asks a "burning question" which is then applied to the public issue. "A side effect is the exposure to public attention of a situation, the configuration of the lifeworld sustained by this sacrifice (regardless of what my personal dilemma might have been)."[28] The electronic monument affects public policy by bringing into relation these two values, one explicit and one abject. It allows the deliverer who constructs it to notice the "conditions sustaining the abuse by the promise of divination: the problem explains the consultant."[29] On the collective level, it reveals the price we pay for childrearing. However, the individual level produces a more specific result, as delivery is inverted toward invention. The electronic monument allows for composition written in the middle voice. It does not (only) address an external audience, an I-Them communication, but primarily an I-I communication: electronic monuments are "self-addressed ... in the middle voice," and then "extended through a networked environment to become a group subject."[30] What was Ulmer's testimony? How did he, to himself, bear witness to the sacrifice of Bradley McGee and other abused children? By witnessing the conditions that make child abuse possible and how he benefits from these conditions: "I am a parent; a father of two sons. My right to have children and raise them in my own way was paid for by Bradley McGee (and all the others)."[31]

In some ways, this process might seem to undercut what I've been saying all along about delivery, that it necessarily brings about group invention. But this individual invention is put toward this purpose, or it proves the principle, as the everted network delivers—as an agent—to the audience, who is in this case the deliverer making the electronic monument. Perhaps delivery is dead, and it's all invention, or invention is dead, and it's all delivery. However the individual creates the monument and asks the question, the question is delivered to (and answered by) the larger audience once that memorial is networked with the general public. As a node in the network, Ulmer is always connected to it, and so may self-deliver from it (invention), or, after invention has occurred, foster group invention (delivery), working toward delivering an affective response to an unnoticed (invisible) value and problem. Ultimately, electronic monuments can become linked together at the level of a group subject, and *ATH* can be delivered; ultimately, this is how Ulmer views a network of electronic monuments: "The goal of cumulative MEmorials is collective self-knowledge."[32] This opens memorializing to a networked, democratic process, one that does not deliver a final solution, but ongoing invention. Because of an electronic monument's broad and specific applicability, its range is open to all problems, be they social, environmental, biological, economic, educational, and others. Thus, an electronic monument can serve as a general practice for an electrate citizenry, allowing anyone to deliver with it, just as the definition, within a literate apparatus, can be used to find the essence of any "thing."

Taking in a syncretic view, it should be noted that the 2006 *Time Magazine* person of the year—the year *Electronic Monuments* was published—was "YOU," or the many users who generate content on the Internet. We are already gathering into collectives to address problems via digital technologies, but our practices mainly derive from the entertainment industries. What Ulmer gives us is a specific method for not just putting ourselves into the Internet, but also seeing what an electrate culture, made ubiquitous by the Internet, puts into us. In other terms, how the network, broadly construed, delivers *hypokrisis*. The Latin root for monument comes from *monēre*, which can be translated as "to remind." As a gesture, monuments remind us, commemorate, serve as places of memory, so that events, persons, and those values that society wants us to emulate may be embedded/embodied. They are tools for delivery. However, *monēre* can also be translated as "to warn." An electronic monument gets more at this latter definition, helping to deliver warnings both individually and collectively that one's professed values might be out of tune with one's best interest, and that there is always an abject sacrifice that must be paid in order to sustain them. Demosthenes was an abject sacrifice to maintain Macedonian rule. The question that an electronic monument will have to answer, as Ulmer frames it, is whether the "Internet prosthesis" can enable the "group subject to awaken, to kill its own dumbness in a revelation of its freedom ... its power to choose a course of action other than the one dictated by material nature or ideological habit?"[33] In the Internet prosthesis, is there a practice of delivery that can support such awakening? Rice's satisficing and Ulmer's electronic monuments are a start, but we need more models, we need a digital Demosthenes to demonstrate the possibilities.

As my final gesture, I offer that Ulmer's concept of avatar, discussed in the previous chapter, may also be as much a concept of delivery as for invention. In *Avatar Emergency*, Ulmer describes avatar as a wisdom that descends to terrestrial earth during a time of crisis (*krinein*, judgment). "The function of avatar is counsel in a situation of emergency requiring decision ... Through avatar you go beyond the limits of 'self' to understand action from the position of communal well-being."[34] A crisis is a crisis because a decision must be made in order to restore measure, but this judgment cannot happen with higher faculties alone (reason) and requires an embodiment, which is why avatar (the descent of a deity to the lower (*hypo*) world) becomes necessary. Avatar's counsel is a judgment that happens below, embodied, just as *hypokrisis*, delivery, is one that happens not with reason (alone), but from and in the body, the gut, an affect that affects not just the mind but the whole being, and networks of beings. A delivery of avatar is also one of "flash reason" which "separates out and adds 'affect' to concept and percept,"[35] a dromodelivery needed in the age of the network. Pheidippides has as much to teach us about delivery as Demosthenes. In addition, although an individual has an avatar, that avatar is delivered to them from the network, complicating the way we typically perceive the direction and agency of delivery: "The electrate equivalent of 'voice' is not just 'image' but 'avatar,' with the difference being that avatar is an expression you receive, not one that you send."[36] Perhaps avatar—and electronic monuments—are the best models of what I mean by a "flute" that leaves the flute player at home and delivers on his or her behalf.

So far, the attempt to reimagine delivery through its engagement with digital technologies has produced some useful theories, but has remained relatively stagnant about how we understand delivery and how we understand the canons of rhetoric. Although Brooke, Porter, Ridolfo, DeVoss, and others have made moves to divest some of the traditional notions of delivery and its related canons, it is still frequently posited as the final step in a rhetorical process, as the fifth of the five canons, and even here, as the "tail," a telos. But we should kill this notion. Death and delivery is a cycle, invention is delivered as much as delivery is invented. Like the monkey's t@il, the process is ateleological. Delivery, as death, is merely a transition toward another rhetorical beginning. Delivery should not be abandoned as a theoretical question, but should instead be substantially rethought, beyond what anyone might identify as delivery, changing it into, as Dobrin offers, "new formations, hybrids, and mutations." Delivery as a category may die, must die, even as some of its components continue to find use in new formations.

Notes

1. Sidney I. Dobrin, *Postcomposition* (Carbondale, IL: Southern Illinois University Press, 2011), 1.
2. Christopher Corbett, *Orphans Preferred: The Twisted Truth and Lasting Legend of the Pony Express* (New York: Broadway Books, 2014), 84.
3. Brad Pitt quoted in Ann Hornaday, "Ann Hornaday Interviews Brad Pitt about His Legacy as a Father, and 'The Tree Of Life,'" *The Washington Post*, May 28, 2011, accessed July 23, 2015, http://www.washingtonpost.com/entertainment/movies/ann-hornaday-interviews-brad-pitt-about-his-legacy-as-a-father-and-the-tree-of-life/2011/05/25/AGJVeFCH_story.html.
4. Donald G. Kyle, *Sport and Spectacle in the Ancient World* (Oxford, UK: Blackwell, 2007), 100.
5. See Edward S. Sears, *Running Through the Ages* (Jefferson, NC: McFarland, 2008).
6. Dennis Baron, *A Better Pencil: Readers, Writers, and the Digital Revolution* (New York: Oxford University Press, 2009), 147.
7. Ibid.
8. Phillip Harding, "Demosthenes in the Underworld: A Chapter in the *Nachleben* of a *Rhētōr*," in *Demosthenes: Statesman and Orator*, ed. Ian Worthington (New York: Routledge, 2000), 248.
9. Adaptation based on Plutarch, *Lives*, Vol. VII, trans. Bernadotte Perrin (Cambridge, MA: Harvard University Press, 1919), *Life of Demosthenes* 29.1–5.
10. Plutarch, 29.5.
11. Harding, 265.
12. David George, "Hades," *Clash of the Gods*, season 1, episode 3, directed by Jessica Conway, aired August 17, 2009 (New York: A&E Home Video, 2010), DVD.
13. One of the subplots of *Spook Country* features AR artists layering digital scenes of famous celebrity deaths in the actual locations of these death scenes.
14. Gregory L. Ulmer, *Teletheory* (New York: Atropos, 2004), 204.
15. Gregory L. Ulmer, *Electronic Monuments* (Minneapolis, MN: University of Minnesota Press, 2005), 118.
16. Ibid., 157.
17. Ibid., 140.
18. Ibid., 147.
19. Ibid., xxiv; Ulmer develops *ATH* from its Greek roots where this blindness in the individual becomes "'calamity' and 'disaster' in a collectivity" (xxiv). The Greek example Ulmer gives to demonstrate *ATH* is that of Plato's *Euthyphro*. In this text, Socrates uses the definition (a new device of literacy) to show that Euthyphro's reasons for wanting to prosecute his father for murder involved a contradiction based on the definitions of piety and impiety. These terms turned out to be different in different contexts. Euthyphro did not appreciate having this contradiction pointed out.

20. Ibid., 154.
21. Ibid., 175.
22. Ibid.
23. Ibid.
24. Craig Stroupe, "The Rhetoric of Irritation: Inappropriateness as Visual/Literate Practice," in *Defining Visual Rhetorics*, ed. Charles A. Hill and Marguerite Helmers (New York: Routledge, 2012), 245.
25. Ibid.
26. Ibid.
27. Ulmer, *Electronic Monuments*, 175.
28. Ibid.
29. Ibid.
30. Ibid., 171.
31. Ibid., 174–175.
32. Ibid., 140.
33. Ibid., 149.
34. Gregory L. Ulmer, *Avatar Emergency* (Anderson, SC: Parlor Press, 2012), 77.
35. Ibid., xix.
36. Ibid., xi.

Bibliography

Baron, Dennis. *A Better Pencil: Readers, Writers, and the Digital Revolution*. New York: Oxford University Press, 2009.

Corbett, Christopher. *Orphans Preferred: The Twisted Truth and Lasting Legend of the Pony Express*. New York: Broadway Books, 2014.

Dobrin, Sidney I. *Postcomposition*. Carbondale, IL: Southern Illinois University Press, 2011.

George, David. "Hades." *Clash of the Gods*. Season 1, episode 3. Directed by Jessica Conway. Aired August 17, 2009. New York: A&E Home Video, 2010. DVD.

Harding, Phillip. "Demosthenes in the Underworld: A Chapter in the *Nachleben* of a *Rhētōr*." In *Demosthenes: Statesman and Orator*, edited by Ian Worthington, 246–271. New York: Routledge, 2000.

Hornaday, Ann. "Ann Hornaday Interviews Brad Pitt about His Legacy as a Father, and 'The Tree Of Life.'" *The Washington Post*. May 28, 2011. Accessed July 23, 2015. http://www.washingtonpost.com/entertainment/movies/ann-hornaday-interviews-brad-pitt-about-his-legacy-as-a-father-and-the-tree-of-life/2011/05/25/AGJVeFCH_story.html.

Kyle, Donald G. *Sport and Spectacle in the Ancient World*. Oxford, UK: Blackwell, 2007.

Plutarch. *Lives*. Vol. VII. Translated by Bernadotte Perrin. Cambridge, MA: Harvard University Press, 1919.

Stroupe, Craig. "The Rhetoric of Irritation: Inappropriateness as Visual/Literate Practice." In *Defining Visual Rhetorics*, edited by Charles A. Hill and Marguerite Helmers, 243–258. New York: Routledge, 2012.

Ulmer, Gregory L. *Avatar Emergency*. Anderson, SC: Parlor Press, 2012.

———. *Electronic Monuments*. Minneapolis, MN: University of Minnesota Press, 2005.

———. *Teletheory*. New York: Atropos, 2004.

Index

For Product Safety Concerns and Information please contact our EU
representative GPSR@taylorandfrancis.com
Taylor & Francis Verlag GmbH, Kaufingerstraße 24, 80331 München, Germany

www.ingramcontent.com/pod-product-compliance
Lightning Source LLC
Chambersburg PA
CBHW071412050326
40689CB00010B/1840

*9 7 8 0 8 1 5 3 9 6 3 6 9 *